WITHDRAWN

Great American Lawyers

AN ENCYCLOPEDIA

Great American Lawyers

AN ENCYCLOPEDIA

VOLUME TWO J – Z

John R. Vile

A B C CLIO

Santa Barbara, California   Denver, Colorado   Oxford, England

Library of Congress Cataloging-in-Publication Data
Great American lawyers : an encyclopedia / [edited by] John R. Vile.
p.   cm.
Includes bibliographical references and index.
ISBN 1-57607-202-9 (acid-free paper) — ISBN 1-57607-205-8 (e-book)
1. Lawyers—United States—Biography.   I. Vile, John R.
KF353.G74   2001
340'.092'273—dc21
2001000980

06 05 04 03 02 01 10 9 8 7 6 5 4 3 2 1

This book is also available on the World Wide Web as an e-book.
Visit abc-clio.com for details.

ABC-CLIO, Inc.
130 Cremona Drive, P.O. Box 1911
Santa Barbara, California 93116-1911
This book is printed on acid-free paper.

Manufactured in the United States of America

DEDICATED TO
LAWYERS AND OTHER CITIZENS
WHO ARE COMMITTED TO
LIBERTY UNDER LAW

Contents

VOLUME TWO

Great American Lawyers

AN ENCYCLOPEDIA

JACKSON, ROBERT H.

(1892–1954)

ROBERT H. JACKSON

Robert H. Jackson at the Nuremberg Trials. (Bettmann/ Corbis)

AMERICANS FAMILIAR WITH the history of the Supreme Court readily recognize Robert H. Jackson as the name of one of the most distinguished justices to have served on the nation's highest tribunal. Many are also aware of his service as chief prosecutor during the Nuremberg war crimes trials that followed World War II. People are far less aware of Jackson's accomplishments as an attorney, which are impressive in their own right. Indeed, Jackson was successful in every aspect of legal practice: as general practitioner, litigator, government lawyer, prosecutor, and judge. Without question, he ranks among the most important and successful lawyers in American history.

Robert Houghwout Jackson was born to William Eldred Jackson and Angelina Houghwout Jackson on their family farm in Spring Creek, Pennsylvania, on February 13, 1892. Jackson's great-grandfather, Elijah Jackson, was a Scotsman who founded the first English-speaking settlement in Spring Creek. His mother was descended from early Dutch settlers. Jackson's parents were tough-minded, practical, hardworking individualists who preached self-reliance and self-discipline, values that they successfully imparted to their son.

When Robert was about five years old, his family moved to Frewsburg, New York, a village near Jamestown. Jackson attended public schools in Jamestown. Although he was an excellent student and a voracious reader, Jackson never attended college. Rather, on graduation from Jamestown

High School in 1910, Jackson began a three-year apprenticeship in the law office of Frank H. Mott. He attended Albany Law School for one year but did not complete the program. Indeed, Jackson did not receive a law degree until 1941, when Albany Law School bestowed an honorary degree on him.

In 1913, at age twenty-one, Jackson embarked on his legal career as a solo practitioner. Although he was a general practitioner, Jackson soon developed a reputation as a highly effective trial lawyer. His clients included the Jamestown Telephone Corporation, the Jamestown Street Railway Company, and the Bank of Jamestown, as well as farmers, labor unions, and small businesses.

On April 24, 1916, Robert Jackson married Irene Alice Gerhardt. Their union produced two children, Mary and William Eldred.

In 1918, Jackson was appointed corporation counsel for the City of Jamestown. Thus began his career as a government lawyer. Jackson's appointment was particularly noteworthy because Jamestown's mayor and city council were Republican. Jackson was a Democrat. Nevertheless, Jackson's legal acumen and tremendous skill as a litigator more than offset any concerns about his political party identification.

As corporation counsel was a part-time position, Jackson continued his successful private practice. He practiced alone until 1919, when he formed the firm of Dean, Edison & Jackson. In 1923, he formed a new partnership, Jackson, Manley & Herrick. In 1924, Jackson was elected president of the Jamestown Bar Association. From 1928 to 1930, he served as chairman of the Federation of Bar Associations of Western New York. In 1930, Jackson was appointed to serve on a state commission investigating the administration of justice in New York.

As a prominent Democrat in a predominantly Republican community, Jackson attracted the attention of New York's Democratic governor, Franklin D. Roosevelt. The two became friends, which led to Jackson being invited to Washington in 1934 to serve in the Roosevelt administration. At first, Jackson was reluctant. He actually rejected an offer to become general counsel to the Works Progress Administration (WPA). By this time, Jackson's law practice was thriving, and working for the WPA would have been less lucrative. Moreover, Jackson had philosophical reservations about the New Deal, especially the National Industrial Recovery Act (NIRA), with its emphasis on centralized bureaucratic control of the economy. Of course, the NIRA would be declared unconstitutional by the Supreme Court in A.L.A. *Schechter Corporation v. United States* (1935).

Later in 1934, Secretary of the Treasury Henry Morgenthau approached Jackson about serving as assistant general counsel of the Bureau of Internal Revenue. Jackson was hesitant to accept a full-time position, but Morgenthau assured Jackson that he could work part time in Washington and still attend to his private law practice. Jackson accepted, but he soon found that he was spending all of his time in Washington. His most notable achievement with the Bureau of Internal Revenue was successfully prosecuting former treasury secretary Andrew Mellon for income tax evasion. In 1935, Jackson was transferred to the Department of Justice as assistant attorney general in charge of the Tax Division.

In January 1937, Jackson was asked to head the Anti-Trust Division of the Justice Department. During the winter of 1937, Jackson became an effective advocate of President Roosevelt's judicial reorganization, or "court-packing," plan. Although Jackson did not participate in the drafting of the proposal, he made a number of public speeches and testified before the Senate on its behalf. During this time he also developed an even closer relationship with President Roosevelt as an advisor. Yet Jackson never regarded himself as a "New Dealer." He was not part of the New Deal "brain trust," nor was he one of Felix Frankfurter's "young turks." His rural origin, his relative lack of formal education, and his thoroughgoing individualism set him apart from the New Deal elite. Nevertheless, his skills as an advocate were widely recognized.

Jackson was appointed solicitor general in 1938, when Roosevelt appointed Stanley Reed to the Supreme Court. In that capacity Jackson took on his most important legal work, arguing on behalf of New Deal legislation that was continuing to face judicial review. Of course, that task was rendered easier by the Supreme Court's sudden turnaround in the spring of 1937 in *National Labor Relations Board v. Jones & Laughlin Steel Corporation*. There the Court upheld the Wagner Act, which recognized the right of employees to unionize and engage in collective bargaining. The Court's stunning action signaled the beginning of a new era in which the Court would accept government regulation of economic life. Nevertheless, Jackson's skills at appellate argumentation were quite evident, prompting Justice Louis Brandeis to remark that "Jackson should be Solicitor General for life." As solicitor general, Jackson's able advocacy facilitated the reoriented Court's decisions upholding important New Deal legislation such as the Agricultural Adjustment Act of 1938, which was sustained in *Mulford v. Smith* (1939). During Jackson's two-year tenure as solicitor general, he argued numerous cases before the Supreme Court and lost only one, *Perkins v. Elg* (1939), a deportation case of relatively minor importance.

In 1940, President Roosevelt appointed Jackson attorney general. By all accounts, Jackson did not relish his new position, which he compared to being "a maintaining clerk of a law office." Clearly, Jackson missed lawyering. Still, Jackson performed some very important work in this capacity, not least of which was working out the legal aspects of the "lend-lease" arrangement through which the United States supported Great Britain in the early days of World War II despite the official neutrality of the United States at the time.

Jackson did not remain attorney general for long, because he was tapped to fill a vacancy on the Supreme Court created by the retirement of Chief Justice CHARLES EVANS HUGHES in July 1941. Roosevelt considered nominating Jackson to be chief justice, but decided instead to elevate Associate Justice Harlan Fiske Stone.

Jackson was thus nominated to fill the position vacated by Stone's promotion. His nomination sailed through the Senate, and on October 6, 1941, Jackson was sworn in as associate justice of the Supreme Court. Jackson was not altogether happy with his new role, as he was more accustomed to advocacy than to judging. After the Japanese attack on Pearl Harbor, Jackson regarded much of the Court's work as dull and irrelevant. He was much more interested in the global struggle between democracy and authoritarianism. Jackson was also uncomfortable with the conflict that was taking place within the Court, much of which struck him as petty. Jackson had a particularly difficult time in his relationship with Justice Hugo Black, for whom he had little respect.

Jackson's tenure on the Court coincided with the newfound emphasis on civil rights and liberties. Jackson was anything but doctrinaire in his jurisprudence. Best described as a pragmatist, Jackson advocated judicial restraint and the careful weighing of facts. He recoiled from the absolutism of Hugo Black and the dramatics of William O. Douglas. But Jackson could be moved to eloquence. Perhaps the best example of this came in *West Virginia State Board of Education v. Barnette* (1943), in which the Court struck down a state law requiring all public school students to participate in a daily flag salute ritual. In what has become one of the most widely quoted First Amendment dicta, Jackson opined, "If there is any fixed star in our constitutional constellation, it is that no official, high or petty, can prescribe what shall be orthodox in politics, nationalism, religion, or other matters of opinion or force citizens to confess by word or act their faith therein." In an obvious reference to the nation's totalitarian enemies in World War II, Jackson observed that "those who begin coercive elimination of dissent soon find themselves exterminating dissenters. Compulsory unification of opinion achieves only the unanimity of the graveyard."

Justice Jackson's service on the Court was interrupted in 1945 when he agreed to serve as chief prosecutor in the Nazi war crimes trials in Nuremberg, Germany. This was the first time that individuals were held legally responsible for crimes against humanity committed during wartime. Unfortunately, there was no existing international law under which these crimes could be prosecuted, thus allowing the perpetrators to argue that they were victims of ex post facto laws. In the end, this legal barrier was overcome by moral outrage over the monstrous offenses committed by the Nazis. Without question, Jackson's conduct of the Nuremberg prosecution brought legitimacy to a legally dubious undertaking. Of particular importance in this regard was Jackson's careful effort to assemble documentary evidence rather than rely solely on oral testimony. To rely on testimony would have been more dramatic, but documents provided more reliable evidence of guilt. The fact that three defendants were acquitted and released further enhanced the legitimacy of the tribunal. As Jackson remarked, "You must put no man on trial under the forms of judicial proceedings if you are not willing to see him freed if not proven guilty." In the end the Nuremberg trials proved to be a landmark in the development of international law and human rights.

Jackson was criticized in some quarters for not resigning from the Supreme Court when he accepted the Nuremberg assignment. Certainly his one-year absence impeded the Court's work and increased the opinion-writing burden on Jackson's colleagues. Jackson's departure for Nuremberg particularly irritated Chief Justice Stone, who had not been consulted in the matter and who learned of Jackson's appointment through the newspaper. Stone's irritation was compounded by the fact that he did not respect the legality of the Nuremberg trials. Stone believed that they constituted little more than political retribution "with a false facade of legality." Jackson, on the other hand, regarded his work at Nuremberg as "the most satisfying and gratifying experience" of his career and "infinitely more important" than his service on the Supreme Court.

Jackson resumed his work on the Court in October 1946. Many scholars believe that the Nuremberg experience had a significant impact on Jackson's jurisprudence. More wary of extremist groups, Jackson became more conservative in his interpretations of the Bill of Rights. Certainly Jackson's concurring opinion in *Dennis v. United States* (1951) is consistent with this interpretation. There Jackson supported the Court's decision to uphold convictions of members of the Communist party under the Smith Act. Jackson's position was that the Communist party was a criminal conspiracy and, as such, could not invoke the protections of the First Amendment. Jackson wrote: "The Communist Party realistically is a state within a state, an authoritarian dictatorship within a republic. It demands these [First Amendment] freedoms, not for its members, but for the organized party. It denies to its own members at the same time the freedom to dissent, to debate, to deviate from the party line. . . ."

Justice Jackson suffered a heart attack in March 1954, but he managed to continue his service on the Court for several months. One of his final appearances on the bench was on May 17, 1954, the day the Court handed down its landmark decision in the "case of the century," *Brown v. Board of Education*. Although Jackson had reservations about the dramatic step the Court took on that day, he joined the unanimous bench in declaring racial segregation of public schools unconstitutional.

Robert Jackson died on the morning of October 9, 1954, while en route to the Court. His career is perhaps best summarized in the title of Eugene Gerhart's 1961 encomium: "Supreme Court Justice Jackson: Lawyer's Judge."

—John M. Scheb II

SOURCES AND SUGGESTIONS FOR FURTHER READING

Alton, Stephen R. "Loyal Lieutenant, Able Advocate: The Role of Robert H. Jackson in Franklin D. Roosevelt's Battle with the Supreme Court." *William & Mary Bill of Rights Journal* 5, no. 2 (1997): 527–530.

Desmond, Charles S., Paul A. Freund, Potter Stewart, and Lord Shawcross. *Mr. Justice Jackson: Four Lectures in His Honor.* New York: Columbia University Press, 1969.

Gardner, Warner W. "Robert H. Jackson: 1892–1954—Government Attorney." *Columbia Law Review* 55, no. 4 (April 1955): 438–444.

Gerhart, Eugene C. *Supreme Court Justice Jackson: Lawyer's Judge.* Albany: Q Corporation, 1961.

Hockett, Jeffrey D. "Justice Robert H. Jackson, the Supreme Court, and the Nuremberg Trial." In *The Supreme Court Review, 1990,* edited by Philip B. Kurland, Gerhard Casper, and Dennis J. Hutchison. Chicago: University of Chicago Press, 1991, 257–299.

Hockett, Jeffrey D. *New Deal Justice: The Constitutional Jurisprudence of Hugo L. Black, Felix Frankfurter and Robert H. Jackson.* Lanham, Md.: Rowman & Littlefield, 1996.

Hutchison, Dennis J. "The Black-Jackson Feud." In *The Supreme Court Review, 1988,* edited by Philip B. Kurland, Gerhard Casper, and Dennis J. Hutchison. Chicago: University of Chicago Press, 1989, 203–243.

Kurland, Philip B. "Robert H. Jackson." In *The Justices of the United States Supreme Court 1789–1969, Their Lives and Major Opinions,* edited by Leon Friedman and Fred L. Israel. Vol. IV(4). New York: Chelsea House, 1969, 2543–2571.

Magee, Nanneska Nall. "Playing It Dangerous: Justice Jackson's Passionate Style." *Scribes Journal of Legal Writing* (1991): 123–141.

Ransom, William L. "Associate Justice Robert H. Jackson." *American Bar Association Journal* 27 (August 1941): 478–482.

Rehnquist, Hon. William H. "Robert H. Jackson: A Perspective Twenty-Five Years Later." *Albany Law Review* 44, no. 3 (April 1980): 533–541.

Schwartz, Bernard. "Chief Justice Rehnquist, Justice Jackson, and the *Brown* Case." In *The Supreme Court Review, 1988,* edited by Philip B. Kurland, Gerhard Casper, and Dennis J. Hutchison. Chicago: University of Chicago Press, 1989, 245–267.

JAWORSKI, LEON

(1905–1982)

LEON JAWORSKI

Special Watergate prosecutor Leon Jaworski speaks with reporters outside U.S. district court in Washington, 16 May 1974. (AP Photo)

LEON JAWORSKI HAD ONE OF the most distinguished and politically important legal careers in U.S. history. His half-century of service touched on many of the most important public issues of the day and culminated in the forced resignation of a president of the United States.

Jaworski was a life-long Christian and could write with compelling simplicity and sincerity about the influence of his religious convictions on his professional conduct (Jaworski and Schneider 1981). Throughout his long career two themes emerged: first, the duty of the individual to resist a corrupt moral environment; and second, the importance of the rule of law. Jaworski's unclouded convictions often steeled him for action in the face of strong social pressure, and he consistently fought for a government of laws, not of men. Many of those embroiled in the controversies that he addressed had succumbed to social pressure or subverted the rule of law.

Leonidas Jaworski was born September 19, 1905, in Waco, Texas, to Joseph Jaworski, a minister, and Marie Mira. His parents had immigrated to the United States from Germany in 1903. His father originally was from Poland, and his mother was from Vienna. In his youth, Jaworski saw Waco come under the influence of a resurgent Ku Klux Klan until Klansmen held nearly every local political office. He was shocked to see prominent local citizens embracing bigotry and breaking the law, but he admired those few who opposed the Klan on grounds of conscience. He received his degree in law at Baylor University at nineteen, in 1925, and had to go to court to get permission to be admitted to the bar at his age. In 1926, he earned a master's degree in law from George Washington University and returned to Waco to practice.

Early in his career, Jaworski had to decide whether to act on his professional obligations in an unpopular cause. Jordan Scott, an African-American man, stood accused of the murder of a white farming couple. The court appointed Jaworski as defense counsel, along with another lawyer as assistant, both without pay. Local prejudice ran high, and a real danger arose that Scott might be lynched. Despite threats and abuse, Jaworski pursued the case with vigor, baffled and distressed that so many could lack respect for the right to counsel and to a fair trial, or to any trial at all. Scott had signed a confession (with an "X") and had led the police to the murder weapon, Scott's own gun, buried in a field. But he said the confession had been extracted by threats and that the crime was committed with his gun by an acquaintance, one Son "Rockbottom" Miller. Miller had returned the gun after the crime, and Scott had hidden it out of fear, he said.

Because of the danger of lynching, the judge set the trial date for just ten days after Jaworski's appointment as counsel. The jury convicted Scott, but the judge ordered a new trial because the prosecutor had referred to the defendant during closing argument as "This colored Negro, this brute, this assassin" (Jaworski and Herskowitz 1979, 34). With more time, Jaworski was able to do further investigation. He found that on the day before the murder, Rockbottom Miller had been released from jail in Waxahachie, Texas, and announced his intention to head for Waco, where the murders occurred. (Jaworski and Herskowitz 1979, 36.) This gave Jaworski new hope, but the drama was not to have a storybook ending. Miller turned out to have an ironclad alibi. When Jaworski confronted Scott with this fact, Scott confessed to Jaworski that he indeed had killed the two people. On retrial, a new jury convicted him again, and the state of Texas executed him.

In 1929, Jaworski moved to Houston, where he worked for a time with A. D. Dyess, and then moved to Fulbright, Crooker, Freeman & Bates. He remained with the latter firm for most of his life, taking leaves for other important work. In 1931, he married Jeannette Adam, and in the mid-1930s they had three children, Joan, Claire, and Joseph. Jaworski's law practice flourished along mostly conventional lines, with an emphasis on commercial litigation.

Jaworski was a resourceful and imaginative courtroom lawyer. In one case, his client, an oil-well wildcatter, was sued for allegedly polluting land adjoining one of his wells, making the land unusable. Jaworski managed to get a continuance of the case until springtime. Shortly before trial he visited the site with a motion-picture cameraman and found grass growing. Not content simply to film the grass, he had some nearby cows moved onto the land and had them filmed eating the grass. When the plaintiff testified at trial that the land was utterly lifeless and barren, Jaworski submitted the film into evidence. The use of motion-picture film in court was so novel that its introduction provoked strong objection and extended argument. But the court admitted the film, and the sight of cows grazing on the land destroyed the plaintiff's credibility. The jury returned a verdict favoring the defense.

On another occasion, Jaworski was trying to save his client from the death penalty. In his closing argument, he announced to the jury that if they wished the man killed, they should do it themselves. He then tried to hand one of the jurors a knife. The juror recoiled, and Jaworski's dramatization of the harshness of the proposed penalty convinced the jury to spare his client.

As his style matured and his reputation grew, Jaworski was known for his toughness, his integrity, and his ability to absorb and understand large amounts of complex evidence. He would need these traits during World War II, when he was in the Army as a colonel, prosecuting German prisoners of war accused of murder, and Nazi war criminals.

Typical of the prisoner-of-war cases was that of the murder of a young German soldier named Heller, a prisoner of war held at Camp Chaffee, Arkansas. Heller's sin, in the eyes of his more fanatical German comrades, had been to do work for the Americans, beyond what he could be required to do under the Geneva Convention, in order to send money back home to his wife. For this, some of his fellow soldiers lured him from his barracks and beat him to death with clubs. One of the main suspects was a minister in civilian life, and Jaworski was disgusted to read his diary and see evidence that this man of God condoned the worst sort of barbarism. Jaworski was not able to produce enough hard evidence to convict the minister. However, by an appeal to conscience, he was able to persuade a German sergeant named Abar to testify against one of his fellow German soldiers. On this basis, Jaworski secured one conviction. Such convictions helped to quell violence in the camps.

Immediately after the war, and before the Nuremberg prosecutions, Jaworski tried two war-crime cases of note. In the first, citizens of the small German town of Russelsheim had fallen upon and viciously beaten eight American pilots whom the Germans had captured. With the men piled atop one another dead or unconscious, a local Nazi had then fired several shots into their bodies. Miraculously, two of the men lived and were able to escape when an air raid drove their assailants to take cover. Jaworski secured convictions of ten of those involved; five were executed.

Another case left Jaworski appalled that seemingly normal human beings could perform the most barbaric acts because of ideology or simple social conformity. The Hadamar Institution in Hadamar, Germany, had been a mental hospital. The Nazis began putting the inmates of the institution to death. Then they began sending to Hadamar slave laborers who were too sick or starved to work, and finally simply those they wished to kill, sick or well. Members of the institution staff would lead the victim to a hospital bed, assure the victim of treatment, and then administer a lethal drug. The staff kept records, with falsified dates and causes of death—the records showed the victims in each group delivered to the institution as having died in alphabetical order, of natural causes. Jaworski secured seven convictions, of the chief administrator down to the gravedigger, with three death sentences. Watching one of the defendants in tears during her testimony, face-to-face with her own depravity, he reflected that "'there, but for the grace of God, go I' and other well-intentioned people if we let our moorings of morality slip" (Jaworski and Schneider 1981, 111).

After helping to gather evidence to be used in the prosecution of those involved in crimes against humanity at the Dachau concentration camp, Jaworski returned to private practice in Houston. He continued his involvement in important litigation. He successfully defended the right of Lyndon Johnson to appear on the ballot for senator in Texas in 1960, although he also was on the ballot as Democratic candidate for vice-president. After the election he successfully represented president-elect John F. Kennedy in a challenge to the vote count in Texas.

In 1962, Mississippi governor Ross Barnett defied court orders regarding the racial integration of the University of Mississippi. The Fifth Circuit Court of Appeals ordered the U.S. attorney general, Robert Kennedy, to pursue criminal contempt proceedings against Barnett. Jaworski took on the prosecution of the case at the request of Attorney General Kennedy. For this decision he faced criticism, much of it scathing, from friends and strangers alike. His secure belief in the importance of the rule of law gave him the strength to brave hostility even from those he knew and liked. Ultimately, the court in the Barnett case ruled that changed conditions, in particular the successful integration of the university, had "purged" the governor of his contempt.

In 1964, Jaworski was special counsel to the Warren Commission investigating the Kennedy assassination. Then and in later years, Jaworski fully supported the commission's conclusion that Lee Harvey Oswald acted alone in assassinating the president.

Elliot Richardson

In addition to special prosecutors ARCHIBALD COX and LEON JAWORSKI, who made their stand for the rule of law during the Watergate investigations, then–attorney general Elliot Richardson (1920–1999) also demonstrated a willingness to elevate principle over expediency and thus helped elevate the status of the legal profession at a time when leading White House practitioners (including the president and his chief advisors) were engaged in illegal behavior.

Born in 1920 to a doctor who taught at Harvard Medical School, Richardson earned both his undergraduate and law degrees at Harvard, interrupting his study in law school to serve in the army as a first lieutenant. He was part of the D-Day invasion of Normandy and earned two Purple Hearts and a Bronze Star for his service in Europe. After returning to Harvard, Richardson was editor and president of the *Harvard Law Review* and went on to clerk for Learned Hand and Felix Frankfurter.

After working for Ropes & Gray in Boston, Richardson subsequently served as an aide to Senator Leverett Saltonstall (1953), as lieutenant governor of Massachusetts (1965), as attorney general of Massachusetts (1967), as U.S. attorney in Boston, as undersecretary of state (1969), as head of the Department of Health, Education, and Welfare (1970), as secretary of defense (1973), as U.S. attorney general (1973), as ambassador to Great Britain (1975), as secretary of commerce (1976), and as ambassador at large (1977).

The only American ever to hold four cabinet posts, Richardson was best known for his short stint as attorney general. He and his assistant secretary, William Ruckelshaus, resigned rather than carry out President Richard Nixon's order to fire special prosecutor Archibald Cox (who was pursuing his investigation against the president) in the so-called Saturday Night Massacre. Pressuring Richardson to remain at his post, Nixon told Richardson he was sorry "that you insist on putting your personal commitments ahead of the public interests." Richardson responded, "Mr. President, I can only say that I believe my resignation is in the public interest" ("Legends in the Law," 5). The resulting firestorm led in large part to the appointment of special prosecutor Leon Jaworski with renewed authority and independence.

In 1984, Richardson, who was known for his reserved Boston Brahmin personality, was unsuccessful in obtaining the Republican nomination for governor of Massachusetts. In 1990, Richardson helped monitor the Nicaraguan elections, and in 1998 he received the Presidential Medal of Freedom. Richardson died in Massachusetts on December 31, 1999.

REFERENCES

"Legends in the Law: A Conversation with Elliot L. Richardson." <http://www.dcbar.org/about_bar/elliot.html>.

Lewis, Neal A. "Elliot Richardson Dies at 79; Stood Up to Nixon and Resigned in 'Saturday Night Massacre.'" *New York Times*, 1 January 2000.

The culmination of Jaworski's career was yet to come, during the Watergate scandal. The scandal arose from the burglary of the Democratic National Committee office in the Watergate complex on June 17, 1972, by employees of the Committee to Re-Elect the President. Throughout 1972, the administration managed to keep the burglars quiet, largely by cash payments. The Watergate matter received relatively little attention during the 1972 election campaign, and Nixon was reelected in a landslide. But the scandal gained greater prominence early in 1973, when some of the burglars alleged that John Dean, counsel to the president, and Attorney General John Mitchell had instructed them to commit perjury. When Dean began talking to prosecutors, the White House tried to portray him as untrustworthy. Ultimately this attempt failed, because Nixon had made tape recordings of numerous White House conversations that corroborated Dean's allegations. Access to these tapes became a central issue in the scandal.

By May 1973, Nixon had to accede to demands that a special prosecutor be appointed. Jaworski was approached for the job, but he turned it down because he did not believe the position offered sufficient independence of action. The post went instead to Archibald Cox, a professor at Harvard Law School. The "Saturday Night Massacre" of October 20, 1973, when President Nixon fired Cox for his insistence that Nixon produce some of the tapes, tended to confirm Jaworski's fears. But the firestorm of protest following the Cox firing made it politically almost impossible for the White House to move against any successor. When Alexander Haig, Nixon's chief of staff, approached Jaworski with assurances of adequate independence, he reluctantly accepted the post.

No one could accuse Jaworski of being a Nixon-hater. He had voted for Nixon in 1968 and again in 1972. And when he took over as special prosecutor he thought that only Nixon's subordinates, and not the president himself, were guilty of substantial wrongdoing. This optimism disappeared when he first heard some of the tapes Nixon had produced before his appointment. They showed Nixon discussing perjury and the payment of hush money to defendants in the Watergate burglary. "Nixon," Jaworski later wrote, "had sat in the chief executive's massive, carved mahogany desk, flanked by the American and District of Columbia flags and conspired with [John] Dean and [H. R.] Haldeman to evade the law like criminals in a dingy saloon" (Jaworski and Schneider 1981, 178). At that moment Jaworski foresaw with blood-freezing clarity the way the Watergate matter likely would end.

Jaworski was to obtain convictions of Attorney General John Mitchell, presidential aides John Ehrlichman and H. R. Haldeman, and convictions of or guilty pleas from a number of others. He chose not to indict Nixon himself, instead having him named an "unindicted co-conspirator." A turning point was the struggle between the special prosecutor and the White House over the production of additional tapes in the course of these prosecutions. Without them, the full extent of White House wrongdoing might never come to light. On April 16, 1974, Jaworski issued a subpoena for these tapes, and on May 20 Judge John Sirica ordered Nixon to produce them. But Nixon appealed, and Jaworski feared that a lengthy appeal process could effectively thwart the investigation. He asked the Supreme Court immediately to review the matter, bypassing the intermediate court of appeals. Because of the gravity of the issues presented, the Supreme Court granted the request. Jaworski argued before the Court on July 8, 1974, and the Court rendered its decision just over two weeks later, on July 24. The two central legal issues were justiciability and executive privilege. The president argued that the dispute over the tapes was not justiciable— did not present a "case or controversy" over which the Constitution granted the Court jurisdiction—because it was a dispute within the executive branch between the president and one of his subordinates, namely Jaworski himself, and that therefore the doctrine of separation of powers precluded intervention by the Court. Essentially this claim amounted to a repudiation of assurances made to Jaworski that as special prosecutor he would have the power to take the president to court. Still more central to the case was the president's argument that the tapes were protected by executive privilege, the presidential discretion to withhold information.

As a practical matter, the Supreme Court opinion in *United States v. Nixon*, 418 U.S. 683 (1974), was a total victory for the special prosecutor. The Court ruled unanimously that Nixon had to produce the tapes. Legally speaking, the holding was narrow, with the Court merely concluding that the case was justiciable and that in the particular circumstances the interest of law enforcement—ironically, a perennial Nixon campaign theme—took precedence over the claim of executive privilege. The political result was decisive, however. The tapes Nixon produced in response to the ruling contained the famous "smoking gun," the conversation of June 23, 1972, just six days after the Watergate burglary, in which Nixon and Haldeman discussed using the Central Intelligence Agency to thwart the Watergate investigation. The House of Representatives' Judiciary Committee had already approved three articles of impeachment in votes taken between July 27 and 30, after the Court's ruling but before production of the new tapes. The clear evidence of obstruction of justice contained in those tapes made Nixon's impeachment and removal from office virtually certain. On August 9, 1974, President Nixon resigned.

Jaworski's last major public efforts related to the so-called "Koreagate" scandal, in which persons acting for the government of South Korea allegedly tried to bribe U.S. congressmen. In the late 1970s, Jaworski investigated this matter on behalf of the House of Representatives. Though hobbled by the refusal of the South Koreans to produce a critical witness and by other difficulties, Jaworski was able to secure the conviction of one congressman and two private citizens. The House of Representatives reprimanded three of its other members.

In his last years, Jaworski gradually cut back his legal work. He died from a heart attack while cutting wood at the Circle J, his Texas ranch, on December 9, 1982. During his lifetime he had received numerous awards and honors, including the Legion of Merit and at least ten honorary degrees. Among other service to the profession, he was president of the State Bar of Texas (1962–1963) and of the American Bar Association (1971–1972).

In the end, Jaworski's career is testimony to the value of straightforward ethical principles steadfastly adhered to. When a more convoluted moral personality might have found reason to temporize, Jaworski followed his own uncluttered conscience.

—*Tim Hurley*

SOURCES AND SUGGESTIONS FOR FURTHER READING

Doyle, James. *Not Above the Law: The Battles of Watergate Prosecutors Cox and Jaworski*. New York: William Morrow, 1977.

Jaworski, Leon. *The Right and the Power: The Prosecution of Watergate*. New York: Reader's Digest Press, 1976.

Jaworski, Leon, with Mickey Herskowitz. *Confession and Avoidance: A Memoir*. Garden City, N.Y.: Anchor Press/Doubleday, 1979.

Jaworski, Leon, with Dick Schneider. *Crossroads*. Elgin, Ill.: David C. Cook, 1981.

Kutler, Stanley I. *The Wars of Watergate: The Last Crisis of Richard Nixon*. New York: Alfred A. Knopf, 1990.

United States v. Nixon, 418 U.S. 683 (1974).

JOHNSON, JOHN GARNER

(1841–1917)

JOHN GARNER JOHNSON
The Corcoran Gallery of Art

JOHN G. JOHNSON, NOTED corporate lawyer and art collector, was born in Chestnut Hill, Philadelphia, Pennsylvania, to John and Elizabeth Johnson. The son of a blacksmith and a milliner, he acquired his legal education from the law office of Benjamin and Murray Rush, graduating from the Law Department of the University of Pennsylvania in 1863. (He received an LL.D. from the University of Pennsylvania in 1915.) As part of his education, he participated in the Moot Courts of the Law Academy, becoming a member in 1862. This was also the year he joined the Union Army, a private in Battery A. He fought in the battle of Harrisburg and then returned to Chestnut Hill.

Starting as an office boy, he began by copying the legal papers of his employer, who, with his mother, encouraged him to study law. Murray Rush gave him odd jobs to be done for his relatives and friends. One of Rush's friends, Henry Williams, took Johnson under his wing. This was an important turning point in Johnson's career (Winkleman 1942, 21–23).

Williams was the counsel for the Pennsylvania Company, an insurance company that had turned to special corporation work. Williams employed William F. Judson, who would become Johnson's partner when Judson took over Henry Williams's affairs. This made two important contributions to

Johnson's career. First, it gave him an income while he was just starting out at a time when most beginning lawyers were struggling. Second, it lowered the class barriers that had prevented many able men from entering the profession (Winkleman 1942, 25, 27). Johnson was appointed general counsel of the Pennsylvania Company when Judson died in 1870.

Johnson chose to specialize in corporate law because he noticed that few people were selecting that specialty. It turned out to be a wise choice. He was widely recognized as "the King of the American Bar" (Twiss 1962, 208). So expert did he become that business leaders and corporate CEOs considered his advice the equivalent of a court opinion. For someone who wrote no judicial opinions nor published any books, Johnson had an enormous impact on American law. As counsel for the Pennsylvania Railroad Company, the New York Central Railroad Company, the U.S. Steel Corporation, the American Distilleries Company, and the National Hardware Association, he argued the corporations' position in a number of precedent-setting cases, including the *Oleomargarine Case* (1904), the *Northern Securities Case* (1904), and the *Standard Oil Cases* (1911).

The list of Johnson's cases is impressive. As the defender of the corporations' interests, he argued *U.S. v. E. C. Knight Co.* (1895), *U.S. v. Joint-Traffic Assn.* (1898), *Northern Securities Co. v. U.S.* (1904) and *Harriman v. Northern Securities Co.* (1905), *Standard Oil Co. of N.J. v. U.S.* (1911), *U.S. v. American Tobacco Co.* (1911), *U.S. v. Reading Co.* (1912), and *Wilson v. New* (1917). Two of these cases introduced key elements in the Social Darwinist interpretation of the Constitution during the "Robber Baron" era (1890–1929).

U.S. v. E. C. Knight Co., 156 U.S. 1 (1895), marks a turning point in constitutional interpretation of the commerce clause. Johnson's approach to that case is typical of his legal style. First, he chose a new point of law, which his opponent was not prepared to defend against. Second, he appealed not to principle or precedent, but to practical considerations of business. Finally, he tried to isolate in his briefs a single point that would command the attention of the justices, allowing them to do what they wanted to do (Twiss 1962, 210–211).

In *Knight*, Johnson developed the idea that manufacturing is not interstate commerce; only transportation is interstate commerce. While manufacturing may have an indirect affect on interstate commerce, Congress could only regulate when the objects of manufacture enter the stream of commerce. The Supreme Court turned to this argument as "an oasis in the shifting sands of contention" (Twiss 1962, 210).

Drawing on the belief that Congress had no authority to limit, under the commerce clause, a corporation's right to acquire, control, and dispose of its property in several states, he argued that it was immaterial that the property might become future subjects of commerce. Until they entered the stream of commerce, they were to be regulated by state law only. Manufacturing occurred before commerce began. Congress regulates "contracts to buy and sell or exchange goods to be transported, the actual transportation and instrumentalities of transportation," not manufacturing.

Johnson's argument was based on dual federalism. He astonished his opponent by conceding that there was a monopoly in the refining of sugar. States had the authority to regulate within their borders and the federal government did not. If manufacturing was not commerce, it fell within the states' prerogatives.

This case was a turning point for Johnson's career as well. From this point on, he was the person to whom corporations turned for advice. Even if he did not argue the case in court, his advice was frequently followed. Such was his reputation that Presidents James Garfield and Grover Cleveland both offered him a seat on the Supreme Court. He turned them both down.

Northern Securities Company v. U.S., 193 U.S. 197 (1904), involved the proposed merger of the Northern Pacific Railroad and the Great Northern through a holding company. Johnson argued that the combination, rather than being in restraint of trade, was to further trade because it was created to defend the two companies from takeover by the Union Pacific Company. In addition, owning stock in both companies was not illegal under the Sherman Act. Speaking to a packed Supreme Court courtroom, Johnson said the ownership of the stock did not necessarily lead to a conspiracy. "Few of us have a desire to commit murder," he said, "but many of us use a razor, which gives us the power to murder" (Winkleman 1942, 217). Unless a conspiracy exists, trade is not restrained.

The decision in that case was five to four in favor of the government, with Justice David Brewer writing a separate concurrence. It was also the occasion for one of Justice Oliver Wendell Holmes's great dissents. The narrowness of the government's victory confused the business world and left the impression that Johnson's was only a technical loss. A representative from the Northern Securities Company announced, "The properties of the Northern Securities Company are still there. They are as good as ever" (Winkleman 1942, 221). The spirit of the times prevailed, and Johnson's positions reflected that spirit.

The panic of 1907 was one of the reasons the Department of Justice brought suit against the Standard Oil Company, leading to a dissolution order. *Standard Oil Company of New Jersey v. U.S.*, 221 U.S. 1 (1911), was another technical victory for the government. When the Supreme Court announced the decision, it adopted Johnson's argument that only "unreasonable" restraints of trade were forbidden by the Sherman Act. "Bigness" itself was not necessarily bad.

These three cases reflect Johnson's basic contributions to U.S. constitutional law. They also raise the question of whether Johnson merely reflected his times or shaped them. Certainly he provided the legal rationale for the corporations' expansion, a rationale that protected them even when he lost the case. Johnson himself never lost faith in those principles.

Nonetheless, Chief Justice Edward White is reported to have said,

> When I first became a member of the court, Johnson was constantly before us, and we all thought of him as by far the most powerful advocate of his day. But when later Johnson argued the great anti-trust cases, which in fact gave him his national reputation, all the justices felt that he was not at his best because he had lived into an economic era which he could not understand. (Winkleman 1942, 244)

The same, of course, could be said for the court itself.

His courtroom style has been described as "forceful." He was not flamboyant, but his presentation was compelling as he hit his points "like railroad spikes into a tie" (Carson 1917; quoted in Twiss 1962, 206). His speeches were brief, concentrating on a few points, which he emphasized with authority. He overwhelmed his opponent with his expertise.

Winkleman's description of Johnson's style suggests he would not have succeeded as well in the television age. Yet he owed nothing to grace of manner or tricks of voice. He was bulky and awkward, and his voice was so high in pitch as to be sometimes shrill. In pouring out his words he was like a high-pressure fire hose. To hear him the first time was to suffer disappointment. His reputation for getting verdicts stirred visions of a CHOATE or a COCHRAN, a WEBSTER or a Brewster, a Culyer or a Sheppard. The actuality was simply force, overwhelming force: a huge man with an intense gaze, sweating at every pore, with both hands extended, one holding his eyeglasses, the other clutching his handkerchief, driving home a few points like railroad spikes into a tie. He jammed meaning into the words; his speeches were as rapid as they were brief. No one could tear the heart out of a situation with so swift and so powerful a hand, or spend so little time and effort on mere detail (Winkleman 1942, 200).

This did not mean that he would not use the intricacies of the law to win. A congressional investigation of the Sugar Trust is a case in point. The investigation concerned the contributions the officers of the American Sugar Refining Company had made to members of Congress in an attempt to influence the Wilson-Gorman Tariff of 1894. Indictments were issued, but the officers refused to give the information on the grounds that they had not been served a *subpoena duces tecum*, an excuse openly laughed at by journalists and members of the bar. On advice of counsel, they stated that their contributions to state and local elections were none of Congress' concern. Since both parties had benefited from the contributions, there was political pressure to quash the indictments, and that was eventually done, leaving the public outraged.

While everyone castigated Congress, the Sugar Trust, the political parties, and the Justice Department, Johnson himself was not criticized. The public accepted him as a hired advocate who had served his clients well. Indeed, he was even more admired by the companies he served as someone who could protect their interests (Winkleman 1942, 180).

Johnson's sense of humor tempered his forceful personality along with his ability to establish a rapport with the jury. When an opposing lawyer based his arguments on Gilbert Bacon's *Digest of English Law*, Johnson, relying solely on American precedents, turned to the court and said, "Surely, you are not going to prefer a little bit of English bacon to the whole American hog" ("John G. Johnson, Lawyer" 1917, 1358).

Known for his eccentric billing practices as much as for his courtroom ability, lawyers told stories about his low fees. The most famous example deals with his bill to the Sugar Trust of three thousand dollars. The other lawyers on the case asked him to reconsider because they were then embarrassed to present their own much larger bills. Johnson refused, saying that he had charged the exact amount that his services were worth ("John G. Johnson, Lawyer" 1917, 1354). Another time he returned a check for $25,000, charging, instead, $5,000. The board of directors of the coal company had been prepared to pay him $50,000 (Winkleman 1942, 297). This eccentricity made him available to those who were not millionaires or trust officials. His dedicated defense of these clients was as legendary as his billing practices.

The majority of his cases involved the usual business of lawyers: wills, divorces, property disputes. He prepared as extensively for these as he did for the cases he argued before the U.S. Supreme Court. One of the keys to his success at the trial level was his sensitivity to the politics of the times, including court politics. He knew which judge held what opinion and argued accordingly, delaying his case when the appropriate judge was not present (Winkleman 1942, 308). This knowledge of his audience, combined with a phenomenal memory, made him a master trial lawyer.

Johnson married Ida Powell Morrell, a widow with three children, on July 15, 1875. All indications suggest it was a happy marriage, and Johnson treated the three children like his own. His wife served as his hostess until her death in 1908.

Although his wife was socially active, Johnson was not. He preferred to keep a low profile, even refusing to put his name in *Who's Who*. He was a modest man. In fact, his will instructed that no monument was to be erected. Instead, "a plain low head and foot stone" with nothing but his name, date of birth and death were to be provided (Winkleman 1942, 286).

His will also provided that his house was to be turned into an art museum. He gave his extensive art collection to Philadelphia. As knowledgeable in art as he was in law, he served as a member of the Fairmont Park Commission, which built up the Wilstach Collection. His own impressive collection included works by Monet, Degas, Whistler, Sargent, and Homer. Today, he is remembered as much, if not more, for the art collection as he is for the great cases he argued.

—*Jane Elza*

Sources and Suggestions for Further Reading

Carson, H. L. "John G. Johnson, Esq." *Pennsylvania Bar Association Report* 23 (1917), 259.

"John G. Johnson, Lawyer." *Literary Digest*, 5 May 1917, 1352–1358.

Malone, Dumas, ed. *Dictionary of American Biography*. New York: Scribner, 1963.

The National Cyclopaedia of American Biography. Vol. 16. New York: J. T. White, 1893–1984.

Twiss, Benjamin R. *Lawyers and the Constitution: How Laissez Faire Came to the Supreme Court*. New York: Russell & Russell, 1962.

Winkleman, Barnie F. *John G. Johnson, Lawyer and Art Collector*. Philadelphia: University of Pennsylvania Press, 1942.

JOHNSON, REVERDY

(1796–1876)

REVERDY JOHNSON
Archive Photos

AFTER THE DEATH OF DANIEL WEBSTER in 1852, Reverdy Johnson was widely regarded for many years as the leader of the American bar. Also a prominent U.S. senator from 1845 to 1849 and again from 1863 to 1868, and briefly attorney general in the Zachary Taylor administration, he culminated his long career of public service as the U.S. minister to Great Britain in 1868 and 1869.

Born in Annapolis, Maryland, on May 21, 1796, to John Johnson—who served in both houses of the Maryland legislature, as state attorney general, as a judge of the court of appeals, and as chancellor—and Deborah Johnson, the daughter of Reverdy Ghieselen, Reverdy Johnson attended grammar schools and St. John's College in Annapolis until he was sixteen years old. He then began reading law, first with his father and later with a local judge. Serving briefly in the War of 1812 as a private in the Maryland militia, he was admitted to the bar in 1816 at age twenty (Steiner 1914, 1–2).

409

After one year in Upper Marlborough, Johnson moved his law practice to Baltimore, where it continued for almost sixty years. He soon won a reputation for thoroughness of preparation, skill in cross-examination, and deep-voiced, compelling argumentation. On November 16, 1819, Johnson married Mary Mackall Bowie, with whom he would have fifteen children. From December 1821 until March 1828, he was a senator in the state assembly, but he ultimately resigned because of the pressure of his professional responsibilities, which included coediting (with Thomas Harris) seven volumes of decisions of the Maryland Court of Appeals from 1800 to 1826 (Steiner 1914, 3–10).

By the 1830s, Johnson had an annual income of over ten thousand dollars from his law practice, mostly as an attorney for the Baltimore and Ohio Railroad, the Bank of Maryland, and other corporations. In 1842, however, he suffered a setback that might have ended the legal career of a less determined and resourceful attorney. While practicing shooting with a pistol, he received a ricochet that blinded his left eye, and the right eye soon became so severely strained that it also failed, which compelled Johnson thereafter to rely on others to do his reading for him and to rely on a tenacious memory. Rarely thenceforth did he cite specific authorities in his legal presentations, preferring instead to argue from fundamental principles (Steiner 1914, 11, 15–17).

Entering middle age, Johnson was described as sturdily built, of medium height, robust and strong featured, with a great shining dome of a head fringed with graying hair. He was an avid Whig, attending that party's national conventions in 1839 and 1844, and was selected by a Whig-dominated Maryland legislature to the U.S. Senate, beginning his service in that body on March 4, 1845. There he doggedly argued that Congress had no right to prohibit slavery in any of the western territories and persistently proposed that the issue be settled by the U.S. Supreme Court, then headed by Chief Justice Roger Taney, Johnson's close friend and fellow Marylander. On March 9, 1849, he resigned his Senate seat to accept appointment by President Zachary Taylor as U.S. attorney general, an office he held only until Taylor's death in July 1850, after which he resumed his private law practice in Baltimore. Perhaps his most significant act as attorney general was his refusal to allow the government of Prussia to fit out a warship in New York harbor in violation of U.S. neutrality laws (Steiner 1914, 18–21, 32–36).

While he was extremely busy trying patent and corporate law cases during the 1850s, Johnson also began to acquire a reputation as an authority on international law. In 1854, he was sent by the government to London to argue a claims case, and while there he became a popular figure among public men and prominent members of the English bar. Back home, his fees had grown to be among the largest of any American attorney; yet in 1856 he argued pro bono for the defense before the U.S. Supreme Court in the *Dred Scott* case. According to George T. Curtis, one of the opposing attorneys, Johnson's "forcible presentation of the southern view of the Constitution, in respect to . . . slavery in the territories . . . contributed more than anything else to bring about the decision that was made in this case." Chief Justice Taney, who wrote the most important portion of the *Dred Scott* decision, was known to be greatly influenced by Johnson (Steiner 1914, 37–38).

Meanwhile, Johnson had abandoned the Whig party and announced his affiliation with the Democrats, his former opponents. He campaigned for James Buchanan for president in 1856 and supported STEPHEN DOUGLAS for that office in 1860. He publicly spoke in favor of the so-called popular sovereignty solution to the slavery issue, of which Douglas was the principal proponent, and he urged the defeat of ABRAHAM LINCOLN, whom he accused of "reeking with the grossest heresies of political abolitionism." After Lincoln's election, however, he served as one of five Maryland delegates to the February 1861 Washington "Peace Congress," in which he was conspicuous for compromise and conciliation to stave off civil war. He deplored Southern secession but also opposed any effort of the federal government to force the seceding slave states back into the Union (Steiner 1914, 40–50).

Once the Civil War began at Fort Sumter, however, Johnson shifted sides and even publicly differed with his friend Taney in writing a defense of President Lincoln's constitutional authority to suspend the writ of habeas corpus in wartime, despite the chief justice's declaration to the contrary in *Ex parte Merryman* (1861). According to Johnson, the president had a constitutional duty to take care that the laws were faithfully executed, and that duty could frequently be performed in wartime or in cases of serious rebellion only by military means. Whereas the power to declare war was vested in Congress, the power to conduct that war, once declared, was exclusively bestowed by the Constitution on the president, who as commander in chief of the armed forces could therefore lawfully suspend the writ of habeas corpus and imprison people aiding or attempting to aid the Southern rebellion. This defense of presidential power foreshadowed the reasoning later used by Lincoln to justify his issuance in September 1862 of the Emancipation Proclamation, as well as to claim legitimacy for other controversial presidential acts during the Civil War (Steiner 1914, 51–52; Moore 1862, 2:185–193).

As the war progressed, Johnson denounced the "mad and wicked men" in Maryland who wanted that state to join the Confederate "armies of pestilence." Any person who favored secession was "in mind a fool, or in heart a traitor." Yet he also took fees from clients accused of disloyalty to win their freedom from federal confinement. Such efforts to stay in contact with both pro-Union and anti-Union elements in his state paid off politically, first in his election to the state legislature in November 1861, and then in his selection by that body to the U.S. Senate, in which he began his second period of service in December 1863 (Steiner 1914, 53–57).

Meanwhile, Johnson's continued friendliness toward individual secessionists, while publicly deploring their cause, influenced Secretary of State William H. Seward to appoint him as a special agent to investigate and report on complaints lodged by European consuls at New Orleans against General Benjamin F. Butler, who had offended them as he tightened the federal military occupation of that city. As a result of Johnson's inquiries, Butler was relieved of his command. Soon afterward, however, Johnson ended his support of the Republican administration, and in 1864 he zealously backed George McClellan, the Democratic "peace" candidate for president against Lincoln, whom he accused of seeking reelection by employing the "most unscrupulous and unexampled abuse of patronage and power." After Lincoln's assassination, Johnson defended Mary Surratt, one of the accused conspirators, without fee, but she was convicted by a military tribunal and hanged (Steiner 1914, 58–60, 115–116).

Although Johnson's biographer, Bernard Steiner, asserted that his subject "appeared before the Supreme Court in *Ex parte Milligan* and there won his case," which, if true, would have involved Johnson in one of the most important decisions of the wartime Court, it appears that he actually played no part in that particular proceeding of 1866. He did, however, represent a Catholic priest and an attorney, both Missourians, before the Supreme Court in contesting the constitutionality of a provision of the Missouri Constitution of 1865 that required a retrospective oath of loyalty to the United States before certain citizens of that state could practice their professions. In January 1867, the Court ruled in the companion decisions of *Cummings v. Missouri* and *Ex parte Garland* that such test oaths were unconstitutional (King 1960, 251–255; Niven 1998, 108–112, 146–147; Kutler 1977, 170–174; Randall and Donald 1969, 646; Niven 1995, 406–407).

Later in 1867, Johnson's longtime political opponent, Senator Charles Sumner, conceded his "eminence at the bar of the Supreme Court. He has no superior," said the Massachusetts abolitionist. But Secretary Seward voiced a common criticism of Johnson when he called him "untruthful." Perhaps the most apt contemporary characterization of Johnson, however, came from George H. Williams of Oregon, who served with him in the Senate and was later U.S. attorney general under Ulysses S. Grant. "Mr. Johnson," he said, "was an exceedingly amiable and accomplished gentleman. . . . He was a great lawyer and had a remarkable and accurate knowledge of the decisions of the Courts at his command. He was a frequent speaker in the Senate and a ready debater upon almost all of the questions that arose in that body. . . . He was not a man of very strong convictions and . . . could speak with equal readiness and facility upon one side of a question, as upon the other. . . . He was quite blind . . . and had to depend largely upon his memory, which was evidently a storehouse full of the learning of the law" (Steiner 1914, 118–119, 194).

During Andrew Johnson's 1868 impeachment trial, Reverdy Johnson, although by that time the oldest member of the Senate, was a dominant force among the minority of senators backing the president. At one point during the trial, he elicited important testimony from General William T. Sherman that greatly weakened the prosecution case. He also helped to arrange a private meeting in which President Johnson was induced to make certain pledges to several Republican senators that won him the votes needed for acquittal (Steiner 1914, 198–203; Trefousse 1989, 319–320, 323).

That same summer, the position of minister to Great Britain fell vacant and President Johnson offered it to Senator Johnson. Facing almost certain defeat for reelection because of having voted for key elements of the Republican Reconstruction program, Johnson gratefully accepted the appointment, which was unanimously confirmed by his Senate colleagues, who had long been impressed, as James G. Blaine put it, by Johnson's "talent for diplomacy and thorough knowledge of international law." Also, as Charles Sumner, the veteran chairman of the Foreign Relations Committee, declared, Johnson was "conservative and wise, . . . very amiable, and there was a general disposition to give him the compliment of the brief term of service which remained under the present administration" (Blaine 1884, 2:489; Pierce 1893, 383; Steiner 1914, 230–236).

Resigning his Senate seat on July 10, 1868, Johnson made his way to London carrying instructions from Secretary of State Seward to try to settle three Anglo-American controversies involving naturalized Irishmen, the location of the Canadian-American boundary line in Puget Sound, and the so-called *Alabama Claims* for damages allegedly incurred by citizens of both nations resulting from the American Civil War. Where hard bargaining was desirable, however, Johnson's legendary amiability and his hunger for popularity in England were liabilities. Although conventions that he negotiated with the British government covering all three of the above-mentioned issues were reluctantly approved by Seward and the president and submitted early in 1869 to Sumner's Foreign Relations Committee, they encountered almost immediate opposition from Republican Radicals reluctant to approve any measures submitted by the president they had recently impeached and his "evil genius," Secretary Seward. Anglophobic senators, of whom there were many, claimed to be furious about Reverdy Johnson's widely publicized "kowtowing" to the British aristocracy, and especially expressed indignation that he had been openly friendly to John A. Roebuck

Thomas Cooley: An Attorney as Scholar and Statesman

Although this book concentrates on lawyers who have distinguished themselves in trial or appellate advocacy, many others have distinguished themselves in other ways. Thomas Cooley (1824–1898) was acknowledged to be one of the greatest attorneys of the nineteenth century, and today the prestigious law school at the University of Michigan, where he once taught, is named after him.

Cooley's *Constitutional Limitations* (1883) was one of the most widely read American law books of the nineteenth century. In addition to writing this and other books and teaching at Michigan, Cooley served for many years on the Michigan State Supreme Court. He was also president of the American Bar Association.

Widely recognized for his fairness in assessing claims between rival parties, Cooley was appointed to, and was selected as chairman of, the Interstate Commerce Commission. This commission helped regulate railroads and was responsible for setting policies in regard to administrative law that were emulated by later federal agencies.

Cooley believed that "a public office is a public trust," and his example has served as an inspiration to many other attorneys who have followed in his footsteps. Professor Paul Carrington has described the work of Cooley and some of his outstanding successors in a recent book entitled *Stewards of Democracy* (1999).

REFERENCE

Carrington, Paul D. *Stewards of Democracy: Law as a Public Profession*. Boulder, Colo.: Westview Press, 1999.

and John Laird, two notorious partisans of the Southern Confederacy in the British Parliament. Some senators, like Sumner, were displeased that they had not been consulted during the progress of Johnson's negotiations, and some were genuinely concerned, as was Seward, that the third convention incorporated not only the *Alabama Claims* but also every other claim on both sides since the previous settlement of such disputes in 1853, a distinct advantage to Great Britain. Moreover, in justifying his course of action in two long dispatches sent to Seward, Johnson appeared to argue from the British perspective rather than from that of his own country (Cook 1975, 63–67; Willson 1928, 336–342; Steiner 1914, 237–250).

The Johnson-Clarendon Convention of 1868 was unanimously rejected by the Foreign Relations Committee and received only a single vote in the full Senate. Still, its provisions were not appreciably less favorable to the United States than the Treaty of Washington of 1871, which dealt substantially with the same issues in almost the same way and led to the momentous Geneva arbitration awards of 1872. In speeches, pamphlets, and interviews, Johnson defended what he had done in England, but, as Hamilton

Fish, secretary of state in the Grant administration, declared, the politics of the period had been against him. The jury—the American people—had been unimpressed (Steiner 1914, 251–258).

At age seventy-three, Johnson resumed his Baltimore law practice. "Universally respected" and "an antagonist to be dreaded to the end," he was a "colossal and familiar figure," recognized by his fellow lawyers as the "head of the bar of the Supreme Court." Displaying to the very end his "profound grasp of constitutional subjects" and his "wonderful power" of persuasion, he also retained a capacity for intense labor that was "almost miraculous. It despised the weight of years and the loss of sight" (Steiner 1914, 259–260; Cook 1975, 68–71).

On February 10, 1876, Johnson was a house guest at the governor's mansion in Annapolis, when, probably because of his blindness, he fell on a paved area outside the building and suffered head injuries that ended his life. The Maryland General Assembly eulogized him as having "the consummate ability and commanding intellect, which exalted him as the foremost jurist of America," and the U.S. attorney general praised him during a special ceremony in the Supreme Court as "one of the most eminent lawyers of this country and one of the very foremost counsellors of this court." Yet, amid the approbation for Johnson that accompanied him to the grave, his critics muttered certain guarded reservations, resembling those earlier expressed by Gideon Welles. Suggesting that Johnson had at least inferentially promised to vote against impeaching the president in return for having his son-in-law appointed U.S. district attorney in Maryland, Welles wrote that although the senator had "a good deal of legal ability, he is not overburdened with political principles" (Steiner 1914, 263–269; Beale 1960, 3:56).

—*Norman B. Ferris*

Sources and Suggestions for Further Reading

Beale, Howard K., ed. *Diary of Gideon Welles, Secretary of the Navy under Lincoln and Johnson.* 3 vols. New York: W. W. Norton, 1960.

Blaine, James G. *Twenty Years of Congress from Lincoln to Garfield.* 2 vols. Norwich, Conn.: Henry Bill, 1884.

Cook, Adrian. *The Alabama Claims: American Politics and Anglo-American Relations, 1865–1872.* Ithaca: Cornell University Press, 1975.

Kelly, Alfred H., and Winfred H. Harbison. *The American Constitution: Its Origins and Development.* 2 vols. New York: W. W. Norton, 1948.

King, Willard L. *Lincoln's Manager: David Davis.* Cambridge: Harvard University Press, 1960.

Kutler, Stanley I. *The Supreme Court and the Constitution.* 2d ed. New York: W. W. Norton, 1977.

Moore, Frank M., ed. *The Rebellion Record: A Diary of American Events*. New York: G. P. Putnam, 1862, 2:185–193.

Niven, John. *Salmon P. Chase, A Biography*. New York: Oxford University Press, 1995.

———, ed. *The Salmon P. Chase Papers*. Vol. 5. Kent, Ohio: Kent State University Press, 1998.

Pease, Theodore C., and James G. Randall, eds. *The Diary of Orville Hickman Browning*. 2 vols. Springfield: Illinois State Historical Library, 1925.

Pierce, Edward L. *Memoir and Letters of Charles Sumner*. Vol. 4. Boston: Roberts Brothers, 1893.

Randall, James G., and David H. Donald. *The Civil War and Reconstruction*. 2d ed. Lexington, Mass.: D. C. Heath, 1969.

Steiner, Bernard C. *Life of Reverdy Johnson*. Baltimore: Norman, Remington, 1914.

Trefousse, Hans L. *Andrew Johnson: A Biography*. New York: W. W. Norton, 1989.

Willson, Beckles. *America's Ambassadors to England (1785–1928): A Narrative of Anglo-American Diplomatic Relations*. London: John Murray, 1928.

JONES, WALTER

(1776–1861)

WALTER JONES
North Wind Picture Archives

WALTER JONES WAS AMONG THE most scholarly and influential lawyers in the new Republic, leaving an indelible mark on American constitutional law during its most formative years. He argued not only some of the most important cases of the period before the U.S. Supreme Court, but he also argued the greatest number of cases before the Court. His record of 317 cases is unparalleled, standing at more than twice the number of cases any attorney argued before the Court in the twentieth century (Sullivan 1998).

Jones was born in "Hayfield," which is listed as being in either Lancaster or Northumberland County, Virginia, on October 7, 1776. He was born to Alice Flood and Dr. Walter Jones, a prominent physician. Dr. Jones served as a delegate to the Virginia Constitutional Convention of 1788 and as a member of Congress representing Virginia from 1797 to 1799 and again from 1803 to 1811. Thomas Jefferson considered Dr. Jones to be a political ally and a personal friend, a relationship that would later yield benefits for the son of the doctor.

Jones was educated at home, receiving a classical education from Scottish tutor Thomas Ogilvie. He read law in Richmond, studying under Bushrod Washington, a man of "rare moral and judicial qualities" whom President JOHN ADAMS appointed an associate justice of the Supreme Court in 1799 (Warren 1926, 1:385). Jones proved to be an able student and was admitted to the Virginia bar in May 1796, before reaching the legal age of twenty-one.

He began his legal career practicing in Fairfax and Loudoun counties in Virginia. Jones quickly ascended the ranks of the Virginia legal establishment. Soon he relocated his practice to Washington, where the Supreme Court was moved from Philadelphia in 1801. In 1802, President Jefferson appointed Jones the U.S. attorney for the District of the Potomac; two years later Jefferson appointed him the U.S. attorney for the District of Columbia, an office Jones held until 1821. During his tenure in office Jones garnered considerable praise and built a solid reputation as a first-rate lawyer, one of a handful of attorneys that were considered the American equivalent of a British barrister.

In May 1808, Jones married Anne (or Ann) Lucinda Lee. Anne was the daughter of Charles Lee, the U.S. attorney general in the administrations of Presidents Washington and Adams, and the granddaughter of Richard Henry Lee, a signer of the Declaration of Independence. Anne bore fourteen children, eleven daughters and three sons. Twelve of the children lived to adulthood, but all three sons died unmarried and without progeny.

Jones possessed a deep and penetrating understanding of law, both in terms of legal theory and in practice. Though his contemporaries included such keen and nimble legal minds as DANIEL WEBSTER, WILLIAM PINKNEY, LUTHER MARTIN, CHARLES PINKNEY, HENRY CLAY, RUFUS CHOATE, WILLIAM WIRT, and numerous others, Jones easily stood among them. Jones was described as being "fully their equal in legal ability" (Warren 1926, 2:69). A correspondent for the New York Tribune referred to Jones as "the rival of Pinkney and Wirt and Webster and other leading counsel," noting that "as a common law counsellor he excelled them all in depth and variety of learning" (Warren 1926, 2:70n). Charles Sumner, in watching the arguments in Binney v. Chesapeake and Ohio Canal Company (1835), wrote that Jones was "a man of acknowledged powers in the law, unsurpassed, if not unequalled, by any lawyer in the country. . . ." (Warren 1926, 1:787).

Propelling Jones into the forefront of the legal profession was his towering intellect. He was said to be endowed with a photographic memory that not only enabled him to remember virtually everything he read, saw, or heard, but also imparted the ability to recall with precision where he had read, seen, or heard it. Jones was also gifted in his ability to employ analogies, allusions, and anecdotes to reify his complex, theoretical, and abstract arguments.

Jones was a man of small physical stature, but he possessed a powerful personal charisma. He was a modestly handsome man, with soulful eyes, which a fellow practitioner at the federal bar proclaimed "for piercing intelligence and shrewdness of expression I have never seen surpassed" (Warren 1926, 1:69). His appearance was made all the more intriguing by his eccentric dress. Regarding Jones's style of fashion, a correspondent to the *Boston Post* characterized him as being as "eccentric in his dress as John Randolph. The other day he appeared in Court in gray, and a stranger would sooner have taken him for a Georgia cracker than the eminently great lawyer" (Warren 1926, 1:70n).

He was not, however, a fiery, or even a rousing, orator as were some of his cohorts. Jones's general lack of an impassioned style and manner of speaking before the court adversely affected the public's perception of him. One reporter from the *New York Herald*, covering arguments in *Vidal v. Philadelphia* (1844), noted that the packed courtroom audience, eagerly awaiting Daniel Webster's presentation, grew somewhat restless awaiting the "transition from Gen. Jones soporifics" (Warren 1926, 1:127). The same *New York Tribune* correspondent who had lavished such praise on Jones's intellect and legal knowledge offered the following, much less flattering, narrative of Jones's courtroom performance:

> He speaks slowly and in a low tone, but with great purity of diction and clearness of thought. There is, however, a great want of force in his manner and few listen to him. Some years ago, a citizen of Ohio, after being in Court during an argument of General Jones, said to one of his acquaintances that he had witnessed that day the greatest curiosity which had ever met his observation; he had heard a man talk for two hours in his sleep! (Warren 1926, 1:70n).

Although the popular perceptions of Jones's presentations were anything but complimentary, Jones's fellow legal professionals praised his ability to communicate in the courtroom. His arguments before the court focused on the legal aspects of the case and were not made for the purpose of impressing a public audience or jury. His arguments were deft expositions on the law, making full use of the library of knowledge stored in his uniquely powerful memory, and thus frequently surpassed the ability of the average person, untrained in the law, to fully comprehend or appreciate. Hence, Jones was most effective in appellate tribunals arguing before judges who were educated at least to some degree in the law. Indeed, the difference in the perception of Jones's oral arguments between laypersons and members of the bar is striking. Rufus Choate marveled at Jones's "silver voice" (Wright 1933, 203). Another colleague at the bar, having witnessed the oral arguments in *Groves v. Slaughter* (1841) wrote of Jones:

> His voice was a thin, high pitched one, and he was without any pretension to grace of manner. Few men who occupied prominent places in the profession were ever listened to with more interest than Mr. Jones. His fluency was only equalled by the choiceness of his language. He was so deliberate, so quiet, that perhaps fluency does not accurately describe his oratory. He was one of the closest reasoners. He never spoke at random. His style was simplicity itself. (Warren 1926, 2:69–70)

Despite indications to the contrary, Jones apparently did possess the ability, even if he did not often employ it, to offer stirring orations for public consumption, as evidenced by an impromptu speech he made to an angry mob in the riots that gripped Baltimore in 1842. His words to the infuriated gathering apparently were effective in soothing their frustrations. Based on such conflicting views of his oration, it is quite reasonable to surmise that he possessed a range of forensic and speaking talents, but that he tailored his style to speak to his intended audience and in a manner appropriate to the forum.

Jones served as counsel in some of the most important cases before the U.S. Supreme Court, particularly those involving federal supremacy and states' rights questions. One such important case was *McCulloch v. Maryland* (1819), in which Jones joined Luther Martin and JOSEPH HOPKINSON (who both served as counsel in the successful defense of Justice Samuel Chase in his impeachment trial before the Senate), representing the state of Maryland in what would become a landmark decision. Daniel Webster, William Wirt, and William Pinkney represented the United States, arguing that the Constitution implicitly authorized Congress to charter corporations as federal agencies and that states may not interfere with them or with congressional control of them. Jones's argument, opposing Wirt, is little accounted, having been overshadowed by Pinkney's lengthy, passionate, and elegant argument before the Court. The famous opinion announced by Chief Justice MARSHALL for an unexpectedly unanimous Court upholding the constitutional existence of implied powers for the purpose of carrying out enumerated powers was a loss for Jones, but there is no indication that his reputation suffered from it; Jones was said to be as adept as Wirt at arguing either side of a case.

Another such case involving the authority of states vis-à-vis the federal government was *Ogden v. Saunders* (1827), in which Jones partnered with *McCulloch* adversary Wirt to argue for the validity of state bankruptcy laws against supersession by federal bankruptcy laws. Here Jones enjoyed some measure of success before the Court, arguing against Webster, counsel for the federal government. The Court upheld the New York bankruptcy laws but found them to be of no force, and superseded by federal statutes, in instances involving diversity of citizenship between debtor and creditor.

Jones argued in favor of the right of a state to exercise its police powers, even if it impinged on Congress's powers to regulate foreign commerce. In *Mayor of the City of New York v. Miln* (1837), Jones argued that a New York law requiring ships' masters to provide passenger lists as a means of protecting the state's fiscal resources against the influx of foreign paupers was a constitutional exercise of New York's police powers and did not interfere with Congress's authority to regulate foreign commerce. The Court agreed with Jones's argument, holding that a minor incursion on the power of Congress exercised pursuant to legitimate and constitutional powers did not infringe on Congress's power and was thus constitutional.

Jones's arguments before the Court were by no means confined to matters of competing power between the states and the national government; indeed, he argued many different questions and matters before the Court. He dealt in matters of criminal law, unsuccessfully prosecuting two of Aaron Burr's alleged co-conspirators in 1807. He was counsel in *Bank of the United States v. Deveaux* (1810), a diversity case that was decided in favor of the state courts, a decision that delayed development of a body of federal corporate law for some forty years. Jones also argued portions of the original argument in 1831 of *Charles River Bridge Company v. Warren Bridge Company*, which was not decided until 1837 after reargument before the Court. In *Vidal v. Philadelphia* (1844), Jones argued (with co-counsel Daniel Webster) against the faithful following of Stephen Girard's will. Girard, who, coincidentally, had been a director of the Maryland branch of the Bank of the United States made famous in *McCulloch v. Maryland*, willed several million dollars to the city of Philadelphia to establish a college for poor white orphans, subject to the exclusion of ministers and ecclesiastical officials from holding any position in the college, or even visiting the college. Despite Webster's fervent and intensely passionate presentation, which reportedly was much more of a fiery sermon than legal exposition, the Court unanimously upheld the terms of Girard's will.

Jones also waded into that thorniest of nineteenth-century legal issues, slavery, in *Groves v. Slaughter* (1841). The constitution of Mississippi prohibited the "introduction of slaves into [the state] as merchandise or for sale" after April 30, 1833 (Warren 1926, 2:68). The Court thus considered the question of whether this provision of the Mississippi Constitution was valid inasmuch as it conflicted with Congress's power to regulate commerce among the states. Jones joined Henry Clay and Daniel Webster as counsel for the United States. The volatile issue thus turned on whether the Court held that slaves were commodities or citizens. If the Court chose the former, it meant that the slave provision of the Mississippi Constitution violated the commerce clause of the federal Constitution. If the Court chose the latter proposition, that slaves were deemed to be persons, the Court would then be compelled to decide whether they were citizens of the United States. In short, *Groves* contained the elements of the *Dred Scott* case. Why that decision is memorable, and *Groves* is not, is that the Court handled the matter without reaching the constitutional question. The Court construed the provision in question as requiring a statutory enactment to set it into effect; since there was none, it indeed had not taken effect.

Despite Jones's close fraternity with many great political figures of the day, he never sought elected office. He, like his father, became a friend to Jefferson and was a strong supporter of the Jefferson Republicans. Though having no taste for political office, Jones nonetheless sought to influence policy in more subtle and behind-the-scenes ways. He frequently contributed editorials on issues of the day, most of which were published anonymously, to local papers and the *National Intelligencer*.

Jones was a founding member of the American Colonization Society, along with such notable persons as John Randolph, Bushrod Washington, and Henry Clay. He sat on the committee that drafted the constitution of the society, which was created "for the purpose of colonizing the free people of colour in the United States of America, in Africa, or elsewhere" (Wright 1933, 204). Jones was an ardent supporter of the Union, believing that supporters of secession committed treason against both the United States and Virginia.

Other than his positions as district attorney, the only other government offices that Jones held were military positions. In 1821, President James Monroe commissioned him a brigadier general in the militia. He later held the rank of major general in the militia of the District of Columbia. His military duties were mostly confined to leading forces in inaugural parades and other such displays of pageantry, as well as more somber ceremonies such as funerals. He oversaw the forcible quelling of riots in Washington in 1835. Jones's one wartime experience occurred in the War of 1812, in the 1814 battle of Bladensburg (Maryland). The militiamen were little match for the British forces, who fairly easily dispersed the American resistance and occupied Washington, burning the Capitol, White House, and other government buildings. For many years thereafter, Jones found himself, among several officers, on the defensive for his actions in the battle (Shepard 1999).

Financial problems ultimately caught up to Jones, who was a poor manager of money despite being a wise investor (Shepard 1999). He was gradually forced to sell his land holdings in Essex and Fairfax counties in Virginia, as well as his property in Washington and Alexandria, some of which had been received through his marriage, which also imparted numerous slaves to Jones. Walter and Anne, along with their unmarried daughters, eventually had to take residence in the home of their daughter Virginia, who was married to a physician. Jones remained there for nearly fifteen years, until the end of his life. He continued to practice law until he was beset by his final illness, which claimed his life after ten weeks in 1861.

—*Paul Lawrence*

Sources and Suggestions for Further Reading

Chroust, Anton-Hermann. *The Rise of the Legal Profession in America.* Vol. 2. Norman: University of Oklahoma Press, 1965.

Hammond, Bray. "The Bank Cases." In *Quarrels That Have Shaped the Constitution,* edited by John A. Garraty. New York: Harper & Row, 1987.

Shepard, E. Lee. "Walter Jones." In *American National Biography,* edited by John A. Garraty and Mark C. Carnes. Vol. 12. New York: Oxford University Press, 1999.

Sullivan, Brian. "Taking It to the Top: Modern-Day Court Record Set." *ABA Journal* 84 (February 1998): 14.

"Walter Jones." In *The National Cyclopædia of American Biography.* Vol. 1. New York: J. T. White, 1893–1984.

Warren, Charles. *The Supreme Court in United States History.* Vols. 1 and 2. Boston: Little, Brown, 1926.

Wright, Herbert F. "Walter Jones." In *Dictionary of American Biography,* edited by Dumas Malone. Vol. 10. New York: Scribner, 1933.

KAUFMAN, MARY METLAY

(1912–1995)

MARY METLAY KAUFMAN

Oliver Arsenault and Frank H. Fazekas flank their lawyer, Mary Kaufman, during the House Un-American Activities Committee hearing into Communist infiltration of Connecticut industry, 24 September 1956. (Bettmann/Corbis)

MARY METLAY KAUFMAN, LABOR AND CIVIL LIBERTIES ATTORNEY, was also a peace and human rights activist, an educator, an expert in international law, and a fierce advocate for the oppressed. Born November 9, 1912, in Atlanta, Georgia, Mary Metlay was the fourth of five children of Nathan and Etta (Kirschner) Metlay, who had emigrated from Russia three years earlier. The Metlays moved to Brooklyn, New York, when Mary was five. Her father was a sculptor, and both her parents supported the family through various occupations, including woodcarving and shopkeeping. Although poor, Mary grew up in an intellectual and socially conscious environment that instilled in her a strong sense of justice.

Kaufman attended James Madison High School and earned her bachelor's degree in political science from Brooklyn College in 1933. For the next four years she attended night classes at St. John's University Law School while working for the Remedial Reading Program of the Works Progress Administration (WPA). She was admitted to the New York bar in 1937. While continuing to work on WPA legal projects, she also took a job with labor lawyer Frank Scheiner, preparing cases to submit to the New York Labor Relations Board and the National Labor Relations Board on behalf of labor organizations and individuals fighting unfair labor practices. Kaufman was one of the original members of the progressive National Lawyers Guild, founded in 1937, although in those early years she devoted most of her organizing energy to the Lawyers' Security League, a union of WPA lawyers. Later, she would become quite active in the guild, serving on the national executive board as well as the New York City chapter for many years.

In 1940, Kaufman took a position with the National Labor Relations Board in Washington, D.C., as a review attorney, analyzing transcripts of hearings, reporting findings to the board, and writing decisions. In 1941, she married Frederick Kaufman and soon after left her job to return to New York, where she spent the next three years as a housewife and mother to their son Michael. In 1945, having separated from her husband, she returned with her son to Washington to work for the National War Labor Board, then as director of the Enforcement Appeals Program of the National Wage Stabilization Board. Mary and Frederick Kaufman were divorced in 1952.

When the Wage Stabilization Board closed in 1946, Kaufman was recruited to join the prosecution team of the U.S. Military War Crimes Tribunal in Nuremberg, Germany, in the case against the international chemical cartel, I. G. Farben (*United States v. Krauch*). A major financial backer of the Nazi regime, Farben also manufactured the gas used in the Nazi death camps, procured slave labor from the concentration camps, and pillaged the chemical industries of occupied Europe. Twenty-four members of the board of directors of Farben were charged with crimes against peace, war crimes, and crimes against humanity—the three categories of war crimes defined at Nuremberg. Kaufman arrived in Germany in February 1947. Her parents joined her to help care for her son. She went to Nuremberg assuming she would be a trial lawyer, but when she arrived the team had already been established and she found herself, as the only woman attorney on the team, in a battle against the sexist attitudes of her immediate superiors. However, with her characteristic persistence and excellent work, she soon won a position on the courtroom team.

Kaufman's primary responsibility was to collect and organize evidence and direct witness interrogations to establish proof of I. G. Farben's support of Nazi aggression. But as the Cold War progressed, the U.S. government began to view the Germans as potential allies against the growing threat of the Soviet Union, and the U.S. State Department often impeded the prosecution's attempts to implicate the Farben executives as war criminals. By 1948, Kaufman observed a renewed confidence in the (mostly Nazi) defense lawyers, who "were arrogantly projecting the Nazi ideology and reaffirming the pretext for the whole Nazi invasion, namely the need to defeat the Communists" (Ginger 1972, 190). In a letter to an unidentified recipient, about 1948, a disillusioned Mary Kaufman wrote, "The trial is . . . dominated by a total absence of censure of the fascist methods, techniques, and aims that existed in 1945. Today those methods, techniques, and aims are considered the natural and normal aims of any government or group of people . . . with a little more finesse perhaps so that the gas chambers and crematoriums make way for the atomic bombs" (Kaufman Papers). In the end, the defendants received only light sentences, ranging from four to eight years.

Kaufman returned to New York in the fall of 1948 to a domestic cold war, which, she later said, created "an atmosphere I hadn't watched develop and was appalled by" (James 1973, 91). Shortly after establishing her private practice in New York City, Kaufman joined the defense team for *United States v. Eugene Dennis* (orig. *United States v. Foster*). It was the first in a series of trials of members of the Communist party of the United States (CPUSA) indicted under the Smith Act, which, passed by Congress in 1940, made it a crime to teach or advocate the overthrow of the government by force or violence. The twelve defendants in the first trial were the top national leaders of the CPUSA. The trial began in March 1949 at the Foley Square courthouse, the Southern District Court of New York, under Judge Harold R. Medina. With little experience in a U.S. courtroom, Kaufman served as staff counsel, not as a trial lawyer. The other attorneys for the defense were Harry Sacher, Richard Gladstein, Louis McCabe, George Crockett, and Abraham Isserman.

At the end of the trial, the five courtroom defense attorneys were found guilty of contempt by Judge Medina, who Mary Kaufman described as "one of the most sophisticated baiters of lawyers one could find" (James 1973, 91). In addition to damaging the careers of the five attorneys, all of whom were given prison sentences, Medina's action contributed to the antagonistic political climate, and the defense found it increasingly difficult to find adequate counsel for the succeeding trials. For *United States v. Flynn*, two hundred of the attorneys approached refused to offer their services. Several of the twenty-one defendants had to represent themselves, and Kaufman was left to prepare the appeal brief on her own. Many of the Smith Act attorneys, including the five found in contempt, were members of the National Lawyers Guild, which the House Un-American Activities Committee (HUAC) had denounced as "the foremost legal Bulwark of the Communist Party" (Ginger and Tobin 1988, 115). They were paid little or no compensation, other than minimal travel and living expenses that could be raised by defense committees. This proved especially difficult for Kaufman, who was struggling to keep her private practice going and raise her son. In spite of the hardships, the Smith Act attorneys were extremely dedicated to defending the civil rights of their clients.

Kaufman represented mystery writer Dashiell Hammett, who was president of the New York State chapter of the Civil Rights Congress and a trustee of the Bail Fund of the Civil Rights Congress, which had posted bail for the Communists. The other three trustees were millionaire Frederick Vanderbilt Field, secretary of the Council on African Affairs W. Alphaeus Hunton, and Abner Green, executive secretary of the American Committee for the Protection of the Foreign Born. In July 1951, when the Supreme Court affirmed the *Dennis* conviction, four of the defendants fled New York, forfeiting $80,000 in bail. Anticipating the decision, the Communist party national leaders had selected the four to go underground to continue the work of the party. Judge Sylvester Ryan on the Second District Court called the Bail Fund trustees before him and demanded that they submit the names of the thousands of individuals who had donated bail money to the fund. When they refused, he charged them with contempt; Hammett and Hunton were each given a six-month prison sentence. Hammett was the first client Kaufman personally represented who was sentenced to prison. She fought to get her client out on bail, but when the donor of the $10,000 bail asked to remain anonymous, the district court refused to accept it. Kaufman also handled the contempt appeal of Robert Thompson, the New York Communist party chairman and one of the apprehended *Dennis* case fugitives, in 1952. Thompson, who had earned the Distinguished Service Cross from the army for heroism in the South Pacific, had his veteran's disability benefits revoked on the grounds of treason when he was convicted as a Communist. Kaufman assisted him in a series of appeals before the Veterans Administration board to retrieve his benefits.

After the *Dennis* case, Kaufman led the defense teams in four other Smith Act trials of second-tier and state-level CPUSA leaders across the country: *United States v. Elizabeth Gurley Flynn,* the second trial held at Foley Square, in 1952; *United States v. William Sentner,* in St. Louis, Missouri, from 1953 to 1954; *United States v. Bary* in Denver, 1955; and the third Foley Square trial, *United States v. Alexander Trachtenberg,* in 1956. The first Smith Act trial had been treated very much as a political stage by both the defense and the prosecution, who were more intent on attacking or defending the political stance of the Communist party than on focusing on the individuals on trial. The Communists took advantage of the public forum to give speeches in support of their cause, while the Smith Act Victims Defense Committee, chaired by Elizabeth Gurley Flynn, and the Civil Rights Congress of New York led a massive publicity campaign to rally public support for the defendants and organized regular demonstrations outside the courthouse. The following trials were less circus-like, in part due to Mary Kaufman's leadership. She focused the defense on the civil liberties and First Amendment rights of the individuals rather than on defending the ideology of the party (Belknap 1977). "Generally speaking," she said, "it is not productive to use the courtroom as a political forum. You can be much more effective organizing outside the courtroom" (Ginger 1972, 214–215).

Although they were less dramatic, the later Smith Act trials were no less political. In his opening statement for *Flynn*, defense attorney Frank Serri told the jury, "We are at grips here with fundamental matters that go to the roots of government and democracy and freedom, and in your hands is one of the great cases of our time" (CEDC 1952). All the trials followed the same general pattern as the *Dennis* case. The indictments were the same, as were many of the witnesses, the evidence, and attorneys. The prosecution read the same lengthy quotations from the classic Communist texts, dating back to 1919 and usually taken out of context. They also produced numerous informers (former Communist party members with dubious motives) to testify to the Communist party's intent to promote violent revolution. Kaufman noted, "The government's theory was that the defendants were responsible for anything said by anybody who had ever been a member of the Communist Party because it claimed the party was the conspiracy" (Ginger 1972, 205). The outcome was also always the same—the Communists were convicted and sent to prison. Cold War propaganda and the fear it generated were very effective. "It was a period," said Kaufman, "in which no juror in the country . . . would have dared acquit" (Ginger 1972, 208).

In reflecting on her work on the Smith Act trials, Kaufman said she learned to be a "political lawyer," educating "the jurors, your co-counsel, and people outside the courtroom" (Ginger 1972, 212). The prosecution of Communist party members slowed after the Supreme Court decided in *United States v. Yates* (1957) that the Smith Act did not apply to the teaching of abstract ideas, only to action incitements. From the mid-1950s through the early 1960s, Kaufman represented individuals and organizations brought before HUAC and the Subversive Activities Control Board (SACB) and handled immigration cases of Smith Act defendants and others threatened with deportation or who had difficulties obtaining passports because of their Communist affiliations.

Nineteen sixty-six was a turning point in Kaufman's career, when she took stock of her life: "I was terribly troubled by the racism in our society and the war in Vietnam. I spent a long time researching and reviewing the Nuremberg war crimes trials. I was overwhelmed by the similarity of the patterns of the Nazis with our own. I knew we were as guilty of genocide at home and in Indochina as were the Nazis" (James 1973, 93). She began participating in antiwar activities and applying the Nuremberg Principles to the war in Vietnam. In 1966, she organized a conference of the New York City chapter of the National Lawyers Guild commemorating the twentieth anniversary of the Nuremberg Tribunal, and published "Judgment at Nuremberg—An Appraisal of Its Significance on Its Twentieth Anniversary" in the *National Lawyers Guild Practitioner*. During this time, Kaufman developed her strategy of interpreting international law and the Nuremberg Principles to defend those arrested in political actions against war crimes. One such principle, that of individual responsibility, stated that individuals have international duties that transcend the national obligations of obedience imposed by individual states. She traveled extensively through Europe from 1966 to 1967, visiting the Soviet Union, Czechoslovakia, and the German Democratic Republic to lecture and to study their legal systems and represented the National Lawyers Guild at the International War Crimes Tribunal in Paris sponsored by the Bertrand Russell Peace Foundation in 1967 to investigate U.S. war crimes in Vietnam. In 1970, she joined an international group of speakers who toured the Federal Republic of Germany in "Solidarity with Indochina."

In December 1967, hundreds of war protesters were arrested in New York City during "Stop the Draft Week," and the National Lawyers Guild set up the Mass Defense Committee, chaired by Kaufman, to defend them. It was the first time the organization undertook direct representation of people arrested in political actions. In April 1968, when more than a thousand people were arrested during the Columbia University strike, parents of students arrested helped to raise enough money to set up the Mass Defense Office (MDO). Mary Kaufman took on the job of director with a legal staff that included attorneys Elliot Wilk, Mitchell Horn, and Richard Greenberg. From 1968 to 1971, she supervised more than two hundred volunteer lawyers, law students, activists, and legal workers and directed the defense of thousands arrested in political protests. Their defendants included Black Panther party members, draft resisters and deserters, demonstrators against welfare cuts and for school desegregation, members of the Young Lords party (a Puerto Rican youth group organizing the barrios of East Harlem and the South Bronx), and prisoners in New York City jails and Attica prison, among others. By 1970, the MDO had an active docket of more than nine hundred cases, and in their first three years they had won over 78 percent of their cases ("The Mass Defense Office" 1970). The office in New York became a model for others, and Kaufman traveled around the country speaking at lawyers' conferences and running workshops on civil disobedience and mass defense tactics. Kaufman encouraged the legal staff to work in a collective manner and take direction from clients in planning legal strategies. One "graduate" claimed that "the Mass Defense Office changed forever the traditional dynamic between lawyer and client" (Reichbach 1996, 6). Kaufman served as a dynamic mentor for young radical lawyers wanting to fight societal and political oppression and to change the elitism of the legal profession.

In 1971, Kaufman stepped down as director of the MDO, and, for a time, she returned to her roots, representing rank-and-file union members in various cases. In the fall of 1972, she accepted a position as visiting professor of law and director of the undergraduate legal studies program at Antioch College, an alternative liberal arts school in Ohio. She also taught at Hampshire College in Amherst, Massachusetts, from 1975 to 1976. Described by one former student as a "white-haired fireball" (Sobel 1995, 36), Professor Kaufman was especially admired for her conviction and passion. At Hampshire College, the student body overwhelmingly chose her to give the 1976 commencement address. Inspiring young activists and future lawyers was one of Mary Kaufman's greatest contributions to her profession and to the movements she embraced.

While teaching, Kaufman did some legal consulting and continued her political activism. In 1972, she served as legal advisor in *United States v. James Vincent Albertini, James Wilson Douglass, and Charles A. Giuli* of anti–Vietnam War protesters known as the Hickam Three. They were arrested for breaking into the Hickam Air Force Base in Honolulu and pouring blood on military documents in protest of the air war over Indochina. Kaufman testified on their behalf as an expert on international law and the Nuremberg defense. In the end, the government reduced the charges from felony to misdemeanor to avoid presenting the sensitive files that would have established the defense's claim that the military was committing war crimes (Jones 1972, 1, 6).

From the late 1970s into the 1980s, Kaufman spent most of her time traveling and lecturing on international law, attending conferences, and organizing for the antinuclear movement. In 1977, she went to Japan as a member of an international team of experts invited to investigate the full implications of the use of the atomic bomb over Hiroshima and Nagasaki. She consulted in a series of civil disobedience trials in support of activists arrested for protesting the Trident nuclear submarine at the U.S. naval base in Bangor, Washington, and testified as an expert witness in the 1979 and 1983 trials. Still active well into her seventies, Kaufman sat on an international tribunal in Brussels to investigate the Reagan administration's foreign policy sponsored by the International Progress Organization in 1984.

She barely slowed during the last decade of her life. When not traveling, she resided with her second husband, Paul Albert, on New York's Upper West Side, where she worked on organizing her papers in order to write her memoirs. She died on September 7, 1995.

Mary Kaufman's life spanned the major social movements and political events of the twentieth century, which greatly influenced and shaped her career as a political lawyer and activist, as well as providing a certain continuity. As she put it, "I went from one case to the next as a logical step in the struggles of the people of our country" (Ginger 1972, 203). In a 1971 interview, she explained her perseverance: "I'm naturally an optimistic person or else I wouldn't be participating in the struggle. I'm the sort of person who thinks each day you are alive and fighting is that much to the good. But that doesn't mean I am a Pollyanna. I have optimism that we can in time change the system, but I know it can't be done without hard and persistent organization" (James 1973, 96).

—*Margaret Jessup*

Sources and Suggestions for Further Reading

Belknap, Michal R. *Cold War Political Justice: The Smith Act, the Communist Party, and American Civil Liberties*. Westport, Conn.: Greenwood Press, 1977.

Citizens Emergency Defense Conference (CEDC). *Smith Act Trial Report*, no. 4, 1 May 1952. Mary Kaufman Papers. Sophia Smith Collection, Smith College, Northampton, Mass.

Ginger, Ann Fagan, ed. "War Crimes and Cold War Conspiracies." In *The Relevant Lawyers: Conversations out of Court on Their Clients, Their Practice, Their Politics, Their Life Style*. New York: Simon & Schuster, 1972.

Ginger, Ann Fagan, and Eugine M. Tobin, eds. *The National Lawyers Guild: From Roosevelt through Reagan*. Philadelphia: Temple University Press, 1988.

James, Marlise. *The People's Lawyers*. New York: Holt, Rinehart & Winston, 1973.

Jones, Larry, ed. "Unique Defense in Hickam Trial." *Another Voice*, 29 Aug. 1972. Mary Kaufman Papers. Sophia Smith Collection, Smith College, Northampton, Mass.

Kaufman, Mary Metlay. "The Individual's Duty under the Law of Nuremberg: The Effect of Knowledge on Justiciability." *National Lawyers Guild Practitioner* (1968): 27.

_____. "Judgement at Nuremberg—An Appraisal of Its Significance on Its Twentieth Anniversary." *National Lawyers Guild Practitioner* (1966): 66. Reprint, *National Lawyers Guild Practitioner* (1983).

_____. "Never Again." *Jewish Affairs* 11, no. 2 (March/April 1981): 3–5.

_____. "Statements, Declarations and Agreements Leading to the War-Crimes Trials at Nuremberg, Germany and Relevant Documents." *National Lawyers Guild Practitioner* (1966): 88.

_____. "Vietnam and Nuremberg." *New Times*, 29 Mar 1967, 29

Mary Metlay Kaufman Papers (1917–1994). Sophia Smith Collection, Smith College, Northampton, Mass.

"The Mass Defense Office," 1970. Mary Kaufman Papers. Sophia Smith Collection, Smith College, Northampton, Mass.

Obituary. *New York Times*, 11 September 1995

Obituary. *Washington Post*, 12 September 1995.

Reichbach, Gustin. "The Best Offense is a Mass Defense." In *Annual Dinner of the National Lawyers Guild/NYC Chapter* (program), March 8, 1996, including tributes to Mary Kaufman by Bruce Bentley, Tim Coulter, Dan Myers, Gustin Reichbach, Ollie Rosengart, and Elliott Wilk.

Sobel, Robert. "A Woman of Conviction and Compassion." *Guild Notes* 14, no. 2 (Fall 1995): 36–37.

Such, Rod. "Radical Lawyers: 'Turn the Accused into the Accuser.'" *Guardian*, 26 May 1971, 4.

KING, CAROL WEISS

(1895–1952)

CAROL WEISS KING
UPI/Corbis-Bettmann

"CAROL KING REALLY BELIEVED the things so many of us only talk about. She really believed a democracy must be bold, dynamic, and advancing" (Ginger 1993, 544). These words, from the eulogy presented by friend and Yale law professor Tom Emerson at the funeral of human rights lawyer Carol Weiss King, accurately express the philosophy of the woman who placed advocacy for social change on a pedestal. King was at the center of the legal struggle over the defense of constitutional rights throughout her career. She began defending clients during the era of the Palmer raids brought by the U.S. attorney general against alleged subversives in the 1920s and continued until her death in 1952, when the United States was in the throes of McCarthyism. She made countless contributions to the legal profession and participated in several landmark cases of her era: defending the Scottsboro Boys against racially motivated rape charges and defending men accused of being Communists. She cultivated pro bono cases and developed expertise in cases relating to the foreign born, thereby deploying her skills in defense of civil liberties.

Although the majority of her cases involved working-class and immigrant defendants, King came from a completely different background: an upper-middle-class, intellectual New York Jewish family. Her father was a corporate lawyer who represented companies such as Standard Oil, and her brother would follow suit. Considering her family background and the liberal views of her parents, it was obvious from an early age that Weiss would not follow the traditional path considered acceptable for women. In 1912, she entered Barnard College, where she excelled in athletics; she later claimed that her athletic ability helped her to be the first in line to file for cases (Berry 1996, 118–119). Immediately after graduating from Barnard, Weiss met Gordon King, a children's book author, at a party, and they were married several months later. Considering that Weiss rarely followed the traditionalist stance, it is surprising that she married so young, but she never allowed her married status to interfere with her work. She and Gordon were confidantes, and his death at age thirty-five from pneumonia would leave a void in her life, one that she attempted to fill with countless cases in support of the "underdog." Yet, her early marriage is just one of the contradictions of her enigmatic personality. She would often retain a male lawyer to argue a brief that she herself had written because she doubted her ability to argue effectively before the court. In addition, she would be a target of the Federal Bureau of Investigation (FBI), which kept a file on her presumed Communist activities (Ginger 1983, 257). Although she was undoubtedly leftist in her political leanings and established quite a reputation for defending accused members of the Communist party, she and her friends would vehemently deny any affiliation with the party.

Shortly after her marriage, King took the first steps on the path that would allow her to defend the underprivileged. She entered New York University Law School in 1917, and she proceeded as a student with relative ease, despite her frustration with the dearth of courses on civil rights or labor law (Berry 1996, 122). She joined the practice of Hales, Nelles & Shorr in 1920, yet she would continue to feel the tension between gender and professional identity that often intruded into the private life of female lawyers. King, however, represented a departure from the "typical" female American lawyer. She was part of the changing face of the law; where once the women who entered the legal profession had been primarily upper- or middle-class white Protestants, King was a Jew, and she was inordinately proud of her cultural background (Drachman 1998, 4–7).

King began her career in the midst of the Palmer raids against union members as well as both aliens and citizens, and this early experience provided her with a model that would allow her to challenge existing constitutional laws. She began to make frequent trips to Ellis Island to represent immigrants who had been detained and threatened with deportation. The combination of her shrewd intelligence and friendly demeanor allowed her to quickly obtain hearings for her clients despite the maze of bureaucracy. After her first jury case, she began to doubt her efficacy as a trial lawyer, and she began to devote much of her time to nonlitigation work, primarily in constitutional cases. With the assistance of prominent lawyer Walter Pollack, she broke new ground by arguing that the portion of the Fourteenth Amendment that stipulated that no state should deprive any person of life, liberty, or property without due process of the law was intended to protect citizens from violation of their rights by individual states. She and Pollack lost this case in argument before the U.S. Supreme Court, but they had raised a valid point.

King's point regarding issues of constitutionality led to numerous victories in small civil cases. After the death of Gordon King in 1929, Carol King and other lawyers began the International Juridicial Association (IJA), which dealt specifically with human rights issues. As editor of the *IJA Bulletin*, she helped to compile the first systematic records of court decisions affecting constitutional rights. In 1931, she took her interest in human rights a step further with her involvement in the *Scottsboro Boys* case, in which a group of young African-American men in Alabama had been unjustly charged with rape. The case would drag on until 1933, when the Supreme Court reversed the convictions, finally ruling that African-Americans could not be excluded from juries or denied the right to due process and equal protection of the law (Berry 1996, 122–125).

King continually had numerous cases on which she was working, and, in addition to working on human rights violations, she devoted time to defending labor. In a plea to her clients, she wrote, "The government seldom has much information about a worker when a deportation proceeding starts, but usually obtains enough information when the worker talks freely with an inspector. In many instances the alien worker has lost his case by loose talking before his hearing" (Ginger 1983, 273). Yet, King did not work with only alien workers, as she proved by accepting the case of well-known labor leader Henry Bridges. This was the era of the New Deal legislation, in which big business attacked each of the measures to help the "little man." This case would mark a new era in her own litigation, as well as in the area of free speech law. The prevailing law in the 1930s denoted that any person suspected of affiliation with or membership in the Communist party could be deported. In the case of Bridges, the Immigration and Naturalization Service (INS) had arrested him on charges of a connection with the Communist party in his past. King would state at the time that the "principle [in the *Bridges* case] has been badly developed," particularly as the first round of administrative hearings for the *Bridges* case continued for weeks. Although King and her colleagues won this first round, gaining a cancellation of the warrant for Bridges's deportation, their victory was short-lived when Bridges was arrested again on new charges of affiliation with the Communists (Berry 1996, 125; Ginger 1993, 362).

Concurrent with the national attention garnered by the *Bridges* case, King accepted the case of an unknown, William Schneiderman. Schneiderman represented her typical pro bono case, for which King had become well known, but again, she attracted national attention by recruiting the services of former Republican presidential candidate Wendell Willkie. King had first heard about the *Schneiderman* case in 1939, and she was intrigued by the tale of the man who grew up poor in Los Angeles, after his family had immigrated to the United States from Russia in 1905 when he was three. He had applied for naturalization and became a U.S. citizen in 1927. In 1930, he became a member of the Communist party, in which he held several posts. His path even crossed with Bridges after 1930 when both had participated in demonstrations against unemployment, or other political rallies and strikes. In 1939, an attorney for the INS had filed for revocation of the citizenship granted to Schneiderman in 1927 on the grounds that it had been "fraudulently and illegally procured." The INS believed it had a strong case, since the law stated that no alien could be naturalized unless the person had been of "good moral character" for the five years preceding the naturalization, and Schneiderman had been a member of the Worker's party at the time of his naturalization. (The Worker's party joined with the Communist party in 1930.) The defense, however, argued that Schneiderman had not been asked at the time of his naturalization if he were a member of the Worker's party (Ginger 1993, 365).

Schneiderman testified in his own behalf, stating that he had been and was a Communist, but that he had never advocated overthrow of the government. After the district judge ruled against Schneiderman in 1941 and revoked his citizenship on the grounds that it had been "illegally obtained," Schneiderman retained the services of King. King raised numerous due process points, arguing that

> the oath may be held false because views were expressed of political beliefs which some displeased official has later concluded are inconsistent with a pledge to support the Constitution. Or, what is infinitely worse, . . . falsity may be attributed from association with a party and a selection of interpretations of party doctrines that do not represent the views of the affiant. (Ginger 1993, 367)

To increase Schneiderman's chances of victory, King needed the assistance of a lawyer with an inordinate commitment to the democratic process, and Wendell Willkie, the 1940 Republican presidential candidate, agreed to defend Schneiderman. In the publication of the proceedings of the *Schneiderman* case by the American Committee for the Protection of the Foreign Born in 1943, King praised Willkie. "Great credit is due Wendell L. Willkie for his fearless and brilliant defense in the Supreme Court not only of the citizenship and political rights of William Schneiderman, but of the citizenship and political rights of all the American people" (Ginger 1993, 369–370; King 1943, 6). After the Supreme Court had reached a decision, King wrote that

> the decision . . . is a landmark in the development of American constitutional history. The issues at stake in this case transcend the status of any one political party or the rights of any one individual. . . . The rights upheld by this decision are not the rights of the Communists alone, but of all Americans of whatever political faith. . . . The opinion of the Supreme Court in the Schneiderman case helps to assure all Americans, naturalized no less than native born, "a political status as citizens in a free world." (King 1943, 5–6)

At the time of the *Bridges* and *Schneiderman* cases, the FBI had begun to compile a file on King. On October 28, 1941, J. Edgar Hoover, director of the FBI, recommended that "this individual be considered for custodial detention in the event of national emergency." In March 1942, FBI agents broke into King's office and photocopied various items, including the names of other legal contacts in King's address book (Ginger 1993, 368–371; FBI File).

Shortly after the announcement of the *Schneiderman* decision, King returned to the *Bridges* case, arguing it before the Supreme Court in 1945. She was victorious, and Bridges became a naturalized citizen in late 1945. She soon retained another client, Benjamin Saltzman, with a similar case. He had been born in Lithuania in 1895 and came to the United States in 1913. He did not apply for naturalization until 1942, but, during the application process, he admitted to a one-year membership in the Communist party in 1936. The INS summoned him in 1944 for a hearing, and he retained King as his lawyer. The case took four years to reach the courts, and this only occurred after INS officials had arrested Saltzman for deportation. Saltzman was not deported, but his case was typical of the cases King took on during the last years of her life (Ginger 1993, 475–479).

In 1951, she argued a similar case, that of John Zydoc, before the Supreme Court, her first opportunity to present her own oral arguments before the Supreme Court in thirty years of practice. At the time of her arguments, however, King was seriously ill with cancer. She would lose the *Zydoc* case in a 5–4 decision, but the dissents provided the basis for later civil rights cases. The Court ruled that the attorney general could arrest John Zydoc for deportation and hold him infinitely without bail (Berry 1996, 126–127; Ginger 1993, 537). *Zydoc* was her last case, but her memory would live on in other cases. She and her colleagues had thwarted the work of the INS and the FBI, as well as the Department of Justice. They had prevented a Supreme Court decision that could have labeled the Communist party as illegal. Not only did King acquire a reputation for her pro bono and low-fee cases, but she also made a name for herself by defending such high-profile Communists as Harry Bridges. She risked the possibility of deportation by the FBI, since Hoover and other members of the FBI kept close tabs on her activities in 1,665 pages of files (Ginger 1993, 547).

The woman who frequently referred to herself as the "he-woman with a heart" had become a role model for activist attorneys devoted to civil rights. She and her colleagues had proved that the combination of well-known and lesser-known clients could equally set precedents. King chided the legal system for its imperfections, but she used each of her cases to point out the flaws in the system. Although she knew the impact of her gender, as her biographer Ann Fagan Ginger has pointed out, she did not fight openly for the rights of women. Rather, "she assumed and exercised them. Her victories commanded respect—sometimes open, often grudging—and frequent efforts of emulation"(Ginger 1993, 543). Her greatness, therefore, is not based on the number of clients she had, or on the fact that she made great waves, but essentially on the fact that she made the lives of many foreign-born Americans better simply for her tenacity in arguing cases such as *Schneiderman v. United States* and *Bridges v. California* before the Supreme Court. Both of these cases have become legal landmarks and represent the commitment of one woman to the judicial process.

—*Jennifer Harrison*

Sources and Suggestions for Further Reading

Berry, Dawn Bradley. *The 50 Most Influential Women in American Law*. Los Angeles: RGA Publishing Group, 1996, 119–127.

Drachman, Virginia G. *Sisters in Law: Women Lawyers in Modern American History*. Cambridge: Harvard University Press, 1998.

Files on Carol Weiss King. 1,665 pages. Federal Bureau of Investigation.

Ginger, Ann Fagan. *Carol Weiss King: Human Rights Lawyer, 1895–1952*. Niwot: University Press of Colorado, 1993.

_____. "Worker's Self-Defense in the Courts." *Science and Society* 47 (Fall 1983): 257–284.

King, Carol. "Introduction to the Schneiderman Case: United States Supreme Court Opinion." New York: American Committee for Protection of Foreign Born, 1943.

KUNSTLER, WILLIAM M.

(1919–1995)

WILLIAM M. KUNSTLER
CNP/Archive Photos

WILLIAM M. KUNSTLER—WITH his deep bass voice, his rumpled clothing, his glasses perched on top of his forehead, and his constant barrage of criticisms of government and racism—by the 1970s had become the personification of the "radical lawyer." He led the legal battles in most of the major court struggles of the 1960s and 1970s that pitted activist forces against the law-and-order establishment, as in the defense of H. Rap Brown and the Black Power advocates, the *Chicago Seven* trial, the Attica prison uprising, and the *Wounded Knee Leadership* trial.

A central paradox of Kunstler's personal life is that he craved admiration, love, and a sense of belonging. Yet he made such provocative public statements—for example, that President John Kennedy had deserved to die—that he must have known would result in extreme public disapprobation. Kunstler was a man who craved love and harvested hatred. Actually, he cared little for public opinion as such, but if he found himself in a room with conservatives Kunstler would earnestly attempt to persuade them to his progressive positions. On a personal level, almost all who met the man thought he was both self-centered and also extremely charming.

Fighting anti–African-American racism was the cutting edge of Kunstler's practice, but over time he extended his fight to include racism directed at other minorities—American Indians, Chicanos, and ultimately Arab-Americans. He developed great skill in publicizing the human side of his clients, and, from their perspective, the viciousness of the government oppression of them and their causes.

Kunstler was born on July 7, 1919, in Manhattan, of middle-class Jewish parents. Raised on the Upper West Side, he attended public schools and developed a strong sense of the injustice with which African-Americans were treated. He attended Yale University, where he majored in French literature and developed a strong self-centeredness. He spent the war years as a decorated army officer, and, paradoxically in light of his subsequent anti-government career, he enjoyed his army experience. In 1943, he married Lotte Rosenberger, a childhood acquaintance, with whom he would have two daughters.

After the war, Kunstler attended Columbia University Law School, becoming a lawyer in 1948. For more than a dozen years he and his brother had a rather mundane legal practice in New York City. The 1950s practice was not sufficient to contain Kunstler's restless intellect, and he simultaneously taught law at New York Law School and served as the host of numerous law-related radio interview and dramatization shows. At the same time, he also wrote extensively: book reviews for dozens of periodicals and newspapers, and full-length books on famous lawyers and legal cases. One of these books, *The Minister and the Choir Singer: The Hall-Mills Murder Case*, published in 1964, became a bestseller.

Kunstler held a local reputation in the New York suburb where he lived for being "radical" even in the 1950s, but his break into the public limelight came with the civil rights struggle of the early 1960s. Asked by the American Civil Liberties Union in 1961 to serve as an observer to the trials of the Mississippi Freedom Riders, he became a participant. Kunstler threw himself into the civil rights litigation, defending Freedom Riders, sit-in protesters, and all variants of civil rights protesters. He was one of the National Lawyers Guild attorneys active in the struggle, always taking a more militant stance than the lawyers from the Legal Defense and Educational Fund (commonly referred to as the "Inc. Fund") of the National Association for the Advancement of Colored People. Martin Luther King Jr. retained Kunstler on occasion to defend militants whom his official lawyers, the Inc. Fund conservatives, refused to defend.

Kunstler gained publicity and a small notoriety from his work, but his public persona became even more visible in the later 1960s when he ably defended the East Coast Black Panthers and especially black power advocate H. Rap Brown. Kunstler catapulted into fame with his representation of the Chicago Seven, Vietnam War protesters charged with attempting to disrupt the 1968 Democratic National Convention in Chicago. The Richard Nixon administration put these defendants on trial in 1969, and virtually put protest itself on trial by selecting representative defendants from every stripe of the war protest movement.

Kunstler and the defendants were fortunate in the assignment of Julius Hoffman, an unintelligent martinet, as their trial judge. Through wit and zany behavior, Kunstler and his clients were able to provoke Hoffman into excessive reactions followed by courtroom disruptions that made most young Americans sympathetic to their cause. The nadir of the trial came when Hoffman ordered Bobby Seale, the token black defendant, gagged and tied to his chair for daring to represent himself. The *Chicago Seven* trial lasted many months and was widely followed by the American public. It pushed Kunstler into celebrity, and a favorable celebrity for young people and liberals. The trial itself has been the subject of several books; radio, television, and staged dramas; and an HBO movie. Leonard Weinglass, more subdued and perhaps more technically skilled, assisted Kunstler in the trial.

By the time of the Chicago trial, Kunstler had perfected his style of radical lawyering, using, however, techniques that were common currency to radical lawyers of the period. Those included deferring to the political aims of political activists by rejecting technical legal defenses in favor of defenses that would allow radical clients to use a trial as a forum for expressing political views. It meant putting the government itself on trial by making counterallegations of government wrongdoing and bringing affirmative lawsuits, a sort of legal counteroffensive against the very government agencies bringing the charges. Other key elements of radical lawyering involved the use of a trial as a means of educating the masses about the underlying oppressive nature of the government or economic system that truly was responsible for the particular prosecution. That meant using a prosecution as an opportunity for organizing defense committees and garnering publicity, in part to pay for defense costs but equally to utilize the prosecution's educational possibilities. Radical lawyers would actively participate in these activities and not adopt the position of a cool, removed professional.

Implicit in these views is a rejection of a criminal trial as a method of determining "truth." Rather, it is seen as a political struggle that should be utilized for advancing the defendants' political views. Law is likewise seen as merely a tool to be manipulated for these purposes. In turn, this meant that the radical lawyer must politically justify the representation of criminal defendants. This became hard to do in the 1980s when Kunstler occasionally represented mobsters, but he gamely insisted he was merely protecting their First Amendment rights and attacking the prejudice suffered by those of Italian extraction.

Sam Ervin, Country Lawyer

Few more unlikely heroes emerged from the Watergate crisis than North Carolina senator Sam Ervin (1896–1985), who was then in his seventies. Born in the horse-and-buggy era, Ervin—who had attended the University of North Carolina and (after service in World War I) Harvard Law School—had returned to his hometown of Morganton to practice law with his father. Ervin served for three terms in the state legislature and was later appointed to fill out the term of his brother, who had committed suicide while serving in the U.S. House of Representatives. In 1937, Sam Ervin was appointed to serve as a superior court judge. He resigned after seven years but was later appointed to the North Carolina Supreme Court. In 1954, Ervin was appointed by the state governor to fill out a term in the U.S. Senate; he served there until 1975.

Like most southerners of his day, Ervin strongly opposed the Supreme Court's decision in *Brown v. Board of Education*

(1954) calling for school desegregation. Ervin was a strong force in opposing most civil rights legislation of his day. He would also strongly oppose the Supreme Court's *Miranda* decision and the proposed Equal Rights Amendment (which he thought ignored inescapable physiological differences between the sexes).

Ervin was, however, strongly committed to the freedoms embodied in the Bill of Rights. He fought for the rights of mental patients and Native Americans, strongly opposed governmental invasions of personal privacy, and opposed preventive detention of suspects not accused of capital offenses. Ervin also strongly opposed what he considered to be executive invasions of legislative powers.

Ervin gained his greatest fame as chair of the Senate committee responsible for investigating the scandals tied to the break-in at Democratic National Head-

(continues)

Again, these attitudes and techniques of radical lawyering are not unique to Kunstler. Kunstler perfected the methods of politicizing criminal defenses and of gaining wide publicity for his criminal clients and their claims of injustice. Beyond his theatricality, however, Kunstler won most of his trials by the old-fashioned lawyerly skills of cross-examination, close reading of documents, eloquent jury arguments, and knowledge of the rules of evidence. In most trials, he was the model of civility; the image of courtroom disruption, taken from the Chicago trial, is misleading.

Kunstler's most significant cases of the 1970s were his representation of the Attica inmates during their 1971 uprising and takeover of Attica prison and his defense of several militant American Indians. The 1971 Attica uprising, which ended in the tragic deaths of inmates and hostages alike at the hands of the New York State Police, spawned several books, the best of which is Tom Wicker's *A Time to Die* (1975). In 1973, the American Indian Movement seized the South Dakota hamlet of Wounded Knee to protest

(*continued*)

quarters at the Watergate and its subsequent cover-up. To television viewers of the hearings that ultimately uncovered the evidence that forced President Richard Nixon to resign, Ervin became known for his ability to make a point by citing Shakespeare, the Bible, and other works of literature as well as through his ability to tell stories from his own experiences practicing law in North Carolina. Accused on one occasion of harassing a witness, Ervin retorted that, "I'm an old country lawyer and I don't know the finer ways to do it. I just have to do it my way" (Clancy 1974, 273).

On another occasion when Ervin was holding hearings on presidential impoundments of legislative funds, Ervin acknowledged that the president had the right to advise Congress on the budget, but he could not resist telling one of his many stories:

> But I submit, the Congress should have the same power as the old lady who came to see me in my law office many, many years ago and asked my advice on a point of law. I took down the law book to enlighten myself as to what her legal rights were, and what she ought to do. She got up and started out of my office and I said, "Wait a minute, you owe me five dollars." She said, "What for?" I said, "For my advice." She said, "Well, I ain't going to take it." (Clancy 1974, 257–258)

Beneath Ervin's apparent rustic simplicity and southern prejudices was a firm commitment to principles of basic decency, respect for the U.S. Constitution, and commitment to the rule of law that did much to restore the faith of many Americans who had observed the unethical and illegal behavior of many other attorneys, from the president and the attorney general on down, who had betrayed their trust.

REFERENCE

Clancy, Paul R. *Just a Country Lawyer: A Biography of Senator Sam Ervin*. Bloomington: Indiana University Press, 1974.

---

the federal government's treatment of the Lakota Indians. After a seventy-one-day siege, the leaders of the movement went on trial in St. Paul. In an eight-month trial, Kunstler, assisted by Ken Tilsen, represented defendant Russell Means. Mark Lane, of Kennedy conspiracy theory fame, represented defendant Dennis Banks. Kunstler was tireless in bringing out prosecutorial misconduct during the course of the trial, and ultimately the federal trial judge, Fred Nichol, dismissed the case on basis of misconduct by the prosecutor and the Federal Bureau of Investigation (FBI). This trial also resulted in a book, John William Sayer's excellent *Ghost Dancing the Law: The Wounded Knee Trials* (1997).

In a separate 1975 incident, two FBI agents were shot and killed on the Lakota Pine Ridge Reservation. Three Native Americans were tried for murder: Darrelle Butler and Robert Robideau in one trial, and Leonard Peltier in another. Kunstler obtained an acquittal for Butler and Robideau but could not represent Peltier at trial because of a conflict in dates. After

Peltier's conviction, Kunstler handled the appeal for many years. The Peltier case has gone on to become a cause célèbre on the American left.

Kunstler's marriage foundered in the early 1970s, at least in part because of Kunstler's own flagrant, large-scale, and very public womanizing. He began living with a new inamorata, Margie Ratner, and within a few years he divorced his first wife and married Ratner. This union, which remained intact until Kunstler's death, resulted in two more daughters.

Kunstler had many radical clients in the 1980s, but they were much further from the national public eye than those in the 1960s and the 1970s. Although he still had some out-of-town trials, the focus of his practice shifted to New York City. One of his masterly defenses was that of Larry Davis, a young African-American man who shot his way out of a gun battle with more than a dozen New York police officers, escaping unscathed but leaving several officers wounded. Davis was ultimately arrested and brought to trial for attempted murder. In his defense, Kunstler took the audacious position that the police had cornered Davis, not to arrest him, but to kill him, and that Davis was simply acting in self-defense. With extreme skill, and with plausible but not overwhelming evidence, Kunstler fashioned the theory that Davis had been employed by corrupt police officers to sell narcotics for them. When Davis reneged on the arrangement, owing the crooked officers a great deal of money, the police threatened his life and then sought to kill him. Before trial, Kunstler beat the publicity drums masterfully, seizing on some very real evidence of mistreatment in jail. He and his colleagues spoke before numerous defense rallies and church groups in the Bronx, trying to radicalize people and also to influence the potential jury pool. Kunstler dramatized the story as an example of an African-American man fighting back against the "killer cops," as he called them. He ultimately sold the story to a Bronx jury that had years of experience with New York policemen killing young African-American men. He argued that the case was about "how the police treat young third-world people in the depressed communities of our city" (Langum 1999, 305), and Larry Davis was acquitted.

The Larry Davis case is a good example of the trial tactics that conservative lawyers criticized. A close examination of Kunstler's own statements on the case suggests strongly that the defense story was changed slightly over time and therefore was probably contrived. Kunstler made dramatic efforts to publicize the case before trial and turn the public perception against the police. Once in trial, Kunstler made overt racial appeals in favor of the African-American defendant before a jury that consisted of nine African-Americans and three Hispanics. Kunstler would say "so what?" to these sorts of charges. A trial is merely a political struggle of the oppressing class against the oppressed, not a search for truth. If he could manage events, manipulate facts, so that the oppressed could win a trial, all to the good.

Most of Kunstler's 1980s practice was less dramatic. In addition to a few mobsters and the countless number of nonpolitical defenses through which he made his living, a sampling of his clients in that decade includes "a state senator caught in an FBI sting involving money laundering; customers of Citibank who had their account erroneously credited with ninety-seven thousand dollars and then were accused of theft; a prostitute and a man who claimed he could not have normal sexual relations in a suit to declare the New York prostitution statute unconstitutional; a group of Syracuse cabdrivers in a beef with their city over access to the airport; a Bronx elementary school principal charged with crack possession; a man charged in a plot to illegally sell arms to Iran; a female entertainer who attacked a passport clerk; a fiery black Baptist minister jailed in contempt for refusing to give up the membership list to church dissidents; a homeless black man who murdered a Rockette; a black marine who became a Muslim and refused to go to Lebanon because he feared the wrath of Allah; and two graffiti artists who alleged that New York City had failed in its duty to provide a space for public art" (Langum 1999, 270–271). These cases provided a colorful practice. However, it was a far more diversified practice, and on the whole less seriously political, than Kunstler had enjoyed in the earlier two decades.

In 1982, a young man named Ronald Kuby began working for Kunstler, at first as a part-time student law clerk, and thereafter as an associate. For years Kunstler had managed many of his cases in collegial relationships with younger attorneys. The younger colleagues would do most of the routine legal work—the research, investigations, and depositions—and Kunstler would be the master strategist and lead attorney at trial. After Kuby's association in the firm, Kunstler had less need to bring in outside lawyers as colleagues, although he still did on occasion. Kuby became not only an associate and confidant, but also, as Kunstler described him, a partner and alter ego.

In the 1990s, Kunstler became once again much more in the national public's notice. In 1990, an Arab named El Sayyid Nosair was charged with the murder of the notorious radical rabbi Meir Kahane. Notwithstanding the constant picketing in front of his Greenwich Village home by the Jewish Defense Organization and death threats, Kunstler, a Jew, represented Nosair, an Arab and alleged rabbi-killer, and obtained an acquittal. This case more than any other single case resulted in Kunstler becoming a pariah in New York City. Kunstler came to see Arabs as the new racial outcasts of the United States. He represented several of the Arab defendants in the World Trade Center bombing, including Sheik Omar Abdel-Rahman, until federal prosecutors and judges forced him off the case through hypertechnical accusations of conflicts of interest.

Also in the 1990s, Kunstler successfully represented flag burners before the U.S. Supreme Court, establishing flag burning as symbolic speech protected by the First Amendment. He briefly represented a Jamaican immigrant named Colin Ferguson who killed six and wounded nineteen passengers on the Long Island Railroad. Ferguson's victims were mostly white, and there seemed little question that he acted out of racial motivation. Kunstler proposed a controversial "black rage" defense, in which an already insane person could be driven over the edge by racial discrimination encountered in the United States. Ferguson was so insane that he did not realize he was well represented, and he fired Kunstler just before trial. Kunstler's last important case was his defense of Qubilah Shabazz—daughter of militant Nation of Islam leader Malcolm X—who was charged with hiring someone to murder rival activist Louis Farrakhan. Kunstler negotiated a very favorable plea bargain after conducting a well-organized publicity campaign to discredit the government's chief witness. These cases once again brought Kunstler national attention.

Over the years, Kunstler faced great criticism from the conservative bar for his style of lawyering. He received fines for frivolous lawsuits, threats of disbarment for courtroom disruption arising from the *Chicago Seven* trial, and several threats or actual contempt-of-court citations. He referred to his censure by the New York Appellate Division in 1993 as a "badge of honor" (Langum 1999, 315).

Although Kunstler was a workaholic, he did have personal pleasures. In addition to his children, he enjoyed opera, poetry, Mets baseball games, and, above all, spirited conversation. He enjoyed writing poetry in perfect sonnet form. The poetry itself was lackluster, although his books on legal cases and famous lawyers written in the 1950s and early 1960s are first rate. Kunstler's motivation was ideological, and he accumulated very little wealth over the course of his years. Nonetheless, he lived a very happy life. All who knew him personally agree that he was utterly charming and utterly pleased with his life's work, which was, as he saw it, the defense of society's outcasts and oppressed. William M. Kunstler died of heart failure on September 4, 1995.

—*David J. Langum*

Sources and Suggestions for Further Reading

Kunstler, William M. *Deep in My Heart*. New York: William Morrow, 1966.
Kunstler, William M., with Sheila Isenberg. *My Life as a Radical Lawyer*. New York: Birch Lane Press, 1994.
Langum, David J. *William M. Kunstler: The Most Hated Lawyer in America*. New York: New York University Press, 1999.

LANGSTON, JOHN MERCER

(1829–1897)

JOHN MERCER LANGSTON
Perry-Castaneda Library

JOHN MERCER LANGSTON, AN African-American educated at Oberlin College, was the first African-American elected to public office in the United States in the nineteenth century. In Langston's long, distinguished career, he practiced law in Ohio, served as inspector general of the Freedmen's Bureau, and was the first dean of the law school at Howard University in the 1870s. He also served as the attorney for the Board of Health for the District of Columbia and later was appointed U.S. minister and consul general to Haiti and chargé d'affaires to Santo Domingo. He was the first African-American elected to the U.S. House of Representatives from the Commonwealth of Virginia in 1888.

John Mercer Langston was born free in Louisa County, Virginia, on December 14, 1829, the son of Lucy Jane Langston, a part–Native American, African-American slave emancipated in 1806, and Ralph Quarles, a Revolutionary War captain and wealthy planter. Upon the death of Quarles in 1834, Langston received a portion of his father's estate and moved with Gideon and Charles, his two older brothers, to Chillicothe, Ohio, to live with William D. Gooch, a family friend. In 1845, at age fourteen, he enrolled in Oberlin College. Noted for its egalitarianism, the college recognized both racial and gender diversity. The faculty encouraged Langston to excel in rhetoric, and he graduated with honors in 1849 (Garraty 1999, 165). His failure to gain admission to law schools and offices stifled his early efforts to study law. He returned to Oberlin to study theology in 1852 and was one of its first African-American graduates. Langston, however, disappointed with the failure of churches to oppose slavery, refused to enter the ministry. Throughout his life, Langston remained skeptical of organized religion. A year later, Judge Philemon Bliss, a Republican antislavery activist in Elyria, Ohio, accepted Langston as a law student. He was admitted to the Ohio bar on September 13, 1854, when a "judicial panel reluctantly ruled that Langston's light skin entitled him to the rights of a white man" and he became the first African-American to be admitted to the bar in the United States (Cheek and Cheek 1988, 110).

After his 1854 marriage to Caroline Matilda Wall, the daughter of a slave woman and a wealthy white North Carolina planter, the couple settled in Brownhelm, Ohio, an all-white area near Oberlin, and Langston established his first law practice. He involved himself in local politics and the Free Democratic (Free Soil) party and was elected town clerk in 1855, thus becoming the first African-American elected to public office in the United States. Langston also accepted and won his first law case in Brownhelm. A year later he returned to Oberlin and established a new law practice in the community known as a "biracial town." White bootleggers and livestock thieves provided the bulk of his clients early in his practice, but he gradually attracted clients with civil cases.

In 1862, he accepted one of his most important cases in the Oberlin area. The case involved Mary Edmonia Lewis, an Oberlin student accused of poisoning two of her classmates, who later recovered. Although Langston won an acquittal for Lewis, she left the college. She later became the first noted African-American sculptor. The significance of this case is not the acquittal but what it demonstrated about Langston—the person and the lawyer. First, it demonstrated his oratorical skills and his legal preparations. Second, and most important to Langston, it demonstrated that African-Americans "were capable of discharging society's obligations with efficiency and with profit to the community" (Cheek and Cheek 1989, 306). His biographers, William and Aimee Lee Cheek, noted that despite Langston's reputation as an "adroit attorney," he failed to attract many African-American clients, "a failure he attributed mainly to their fears of the prejudicial effects of his race in a hostile legal system" (Cheek and Cheek 1988, 110). Over time, African-Americans in and around Oberlin would seek out his services. Langston's private practice was enhanced by his public service. He was elected town clerk, served as secretary of the school board (1856), and was a member of the Oberlin city council (1857–1860).

Throughout Langston's career, he was an outspoken advocate for the rights of African-Americans and was a well-known figure and speaker at

Ohio's and other northern states' Negro Conventions during the 1850s. He organized the Ohio State Anti-Slavery Society to protest the Fugitive Slave Act (1858). The law allowed slave owners to recover runaway slaves and denied alleged fugitives the basic rights to protect themselves. The law also provided for U.S. commissioners to conduct hearings and to authorize the return of runaways, which in effect increased the enforcement of the law. For Langston and other free African-Americans living in the North, the new law threatened their safety because they could be legally kidnapped. Langston called on delegates to fight the unjust law with the law. The Fugitive Slave Act, he said, was a "hideous deformity in the garb of law. It kills alike, the true spirit of the Declaration of Independence, the Constitution, and the palladium of our liberties" (Nieman 1991, 31). Langston's well-tempered militancy caused him even to support John Brown's insurrection at Harpers Ferry when legal means seemed at an impasse (Cheek and Cheek 1989, 349–372).

During the Civil War, Langston recruited African-American soldiers for the Massachusetts Fifty-fourth and Fifty-fifth Regiments and for Ohio's Fifth Regiment. A long-time advocate for African-American suffrage, Langston traveled the South as a Republican party organizer for African-American voters and as school inspector general of the Freedmen's Bureau after the war.

After fifteen years of practicing law in Oberlin and the surrounding communities, Langston moved his family to Washington, D.C., in 1868 at the request of Colonel Oliver Otis Howard, director of the Freedmen's Bureau, to organize the law department at the recently established Howard University (1867), which offered the LL.B. degree following two years of training. Designed along the Oberlin model, Howard was envisioned by Langston as an egalitarian institution with high academic standards open to both races and sexes. The curriculum "emphasized classical as well as professional training, moral and social concerns, and a thorough grounding in oratory" (Cheek and Cheek 1988, 118). Langston opened the department with six students. Within a year, this number increased to twenty-two. The department graduated its first ten students on February 3, 1871. Of this group, eight were admitted to the bar in Washington, D.C., on the next day. Appointed dean in 1870, Langston stressed practical experience and used his influence to gain his students appointments in the offices of the Ulysses S. Grant administration.

In 1872, Charlotte E. Ray graduated as Howard's first African-American woman to earn a law degree. Although Ray is also recognized as the first woman to be admitted to practice law before the Supreme Court, she left the profession and became a schoolteacher in Brooklyn, New York, because of the discrimination she encountered as a woman. (Drachman 1998,

45–46). Also graduating with Ray was James C. Napier, who became registrar of the U.S. Treasury (1911–1913) and a member of Howard's board of trustees (1911–1940).

During Langston's six and a half years at Howard, he served as professor, dean, vice-president, and acting president. Troubled by his non-accommodationist racial progressive views, his strong advocacy for an expanded law school, as well as his well-known views on organized religion, the trustees rejected his bid for the presidency in 1875. In protest, the entire law department resigned their positions. Between 1877 and 1884, Langston served as minister and consul general to Haiti and chargé d'affaires to Santo Domingo. He assumed the presidency of Virginia Normal and Collegiate Institute in 1885 and served there for three years. After Virginia's Democrats forced Langston to resign his presidency at the institute, he ran as an independent for the U.S. House of Representatives in the primarily African-American Fourth District, of which Petersburg was the urban center. His opponents included a white Democrat and a white Republican (William Mahone). At the end of a long ten-month campaign, the Democratic candidate was declared the winner. Langston immediately challenged the election results. Congress voted in September 1890 to seat Langston, almost two years after the election. Langston served as a congressman for only three months (the first African-American elected to the U.S. House of Representatives from the Commonwealth of Virginia) before his official term ended. Nevertheless, Langston argued in Congress for popular suffrage and college and professional higher education for African-Americans. He lost his bid in the next election to retain his congressional seat from the Fourth District and returned to the practice of law. Langston retired in 1894 and published his autobiography, *From the Virginia Plantation to the National Capital*. He died in Washington, D.C., on November 15, 1897.

—Thaddeus M. Smith

Sources and Suggestions for Further Reading

Cheek, William, and Aimee Lee Cheek. "John Mercer Langston." In *Black Leaders of the Nineteenth Century*, edited by Leon Litwack and August Meier. Urbana: University of Illinois Press, 1988, 103–126.

———. *John Mercer Langston and the Fight for Black Freedom*. Urbana: University of Illinois Press, 1989.

Drachman, Virginia G. *Sisters in Law: Women Lawyers in Modern American History*. Cambridge: Harvard University Press, 1998.

Garraty, John A., and Mark C. Carnes, eds. *American National Biography*. New York: Garland, 1972.

Harding, Vincent. *There Is a River: The Black Struggle for Freedom in America*. New York: Vintage Books, 1983.

Langston, John Mercer. *Freedom and Citizenship*. Washington: Rufus H. Darby, 1883. Reprint, Miami: Mnemosyne, 1969.

———. *From the Virginia Plantation to the National Capital*. Hartford, Conn.: American, 1894. Reprint, New York: Bergman, 1969.

Litwack, Leon F. *Been in the Strong So Long: The Aftermath of Slavery*. New York: Vintage Books, 1980.

Malone, Dumas, ed. *Dictionary of American Biography*. New York: Scribner, 1977.

Nieman, Donald G. *Promises to Keep: African-Americans and the Constitutional Order, 1776 to the Present*. New York: Oxford University Press, 1991.

Quarles, Benjamin. *Black Abolitionists*. New York: Oxford University Press, 1969.

LEE, REX E.

(1935–1996)

REX EDWIN LEE WAS A CON-
servative constitutional lawyer,
law school founder, and university president who served as President Ronald Reagan's first solicitor general. Lee was born on
February 27, 1935, in Los Angeles, the son of Rex and Mabel
Lee. His father was killed in an
accident before Lee was born; his
mother then married Wilford
Shumway. The Shumways moved
to St. Johns, Arizona, where Lee
was reared and graduated from
high school. He attended Brigham Young University, graduating as valedictorian in 1960. Lee
married Janet Griffin in 1959;
they had seven children.

Lee attended the University of
Chicago Law School from 1960
until 1963. After graduating first
in his law school class, he moved
to Washington, D.C., to clerk for
Supreme Court Justice Byron R.
White. In 1964, Lee returned to
Arizona and joined the Phoenix
law firm of Jennings, Strouss,
Salmon & Trask. He was made a
partner three years later. Lee was
appointed the founding dean of
the J. Reuben Clark Law School
at Brigham Young University

REX E. LEE
AP Photo/Deseret News, Stuart Johnson

452

(BYU) in 1972. U.S. Attorney General Edward H. Levi (dean of the University of Chicago Law School when Lee was a student) hired Lee in 1975 to serve as assistant attorney general in charge of the Civil Division of the Department of Justice. He remained in Washington, D.C., until the end of the Gerald Ford administration in January 1977.

Returning to the BYU law school, Lee continued as dean until 1981, when President Ronald Reagan nominated him to be solicitor general of the United States. Although he was astonished at being picked for the position, he recognized its importance. He called it "the creamiest lawyering job in the country" (Salokar 1992, 33). Since the solicitor general must be confirmed by the Senate, Lee appeared before the Senate Judiciary Committee on June 19, 1981. The Republican party was in the majority in the Senate after the 1980 election, and Republicans were in the majority on the panel. Despite this fact, Lee faced critical questioning from Democratic senator Edward Kennedy of Massachusetts, the leading liberal on the committee. Feminists also criticized the nominee. National Organization for Women president Eleanor Smeal testified that Lee was unacceptable for the position because of his membership on the board of litigation of the Mountain States Legal Foundation. The conservative foundation was known for its opposition to affirmative action and its conservative legal philosophy of limited government (Salokar 1992, 50). Smeal also pointed out the nominee's published opposition to the Equal Rights Amendment. Lee had written a book, *A Lawyer Looks at the Equal Rights Amendment* (Lee 1980), in which he questioned the propriety of amending the U.S. Constitution to provide sexual equality. In his testimony before the committee, he indicated his support of women's rights through statute. His book, while presenting a conservative ideology, was a review of U.S. case law regarding equal rights and was written to inform the lay reader. It hardly suggested Lee's future course of action as solicitor general.

Lee's second book, *A Lawyer Looks at the Constitution* (Lee 1981), had not yet been published at the time of the hearing, but it still briefly attracted the attention of Senator Kennedy. Critics attacked both books as having been written at the request of Mormon church leaders, a charge Lee refuted even though the books were published by Brigham Young University Press.

Lee's Mormon beliefs also were questioned at the confirmation hearing. Several opponents, including the group Mormons for the Equal Rights Amendment, were concerned about the role religious beliefs would have on the nominee's decisions as solicitor general. Their concerns centered on Lee's position on the role of women as stated in his books and in Mormon tradition. Despite the unusually strong opposition, the full Senate confirmed Lee in July 1981.

William Bentley Ball

Like LEO PFEFFER and WILLIAM MULLEN, William Bentley Ball, born in 1916, specialized in cases involving religious freedom. Arguing nine cases before the U.S. Supreme Court and assisting in twenty-five others, Ball was also active in state and in lower federal courts. A devoted Roman Catholic, Ball earned degrees from Western Reserve University and the University of Notre Dame. He taught for a time at Villanova University and founded the Harrisburg firm of Ball, Skelly, Murren & Connell, with which he remained associated until his death.

Ball was a member of the Christian Legal Society and the Catholic League for Civil and Religious Rights; he was also vice chair of the National Committee for Amish Religious Freedom. It was for this last group that Ball argued what may have been his most important case in *Wisconsin v. Yoder* (1972). In that case, Ball helped persuade the Supreme Court that the parents of Amish children should not be forced against their beliefs to send their children to public school beyond the eighth grade.

Ball died in January 1999 at age eighty-two.

REFERENCE

Saxon, Wolfgang. "William Ball Is Dead at 82; Defended Religious Rights." *New York Times*, 18 January 1999.

As solicitor general, Rex Lee labored in two roles. He was responsible for protecting the legal interests of the executive branch in the Supreme Court. He also advised the justices and served as a "gatekeeper" controlling the litigation brought to the Court, working as the so-called tenth justice (Caplan 1987). According to Lee (1991, 59), the solicitor general is "an officer of the Court and an advocate for a client." Although he identified a congruence in the roles, they did conflict from time to time. He often found himself pressured by colleagues in the Department of Justice when he refused to file amicus briefs in "agenda cases." According to Lee (1991), some members of the Reagan administration, particularly Assistant Attorney General for Civil Rights William Bradford Reynolds, wanted him to bring cases before the Court to enact the administration's conservative social agenda. Lee refused to file when he felt that taking action would endanger the solicitor general's credibility with the Court (Lee 1986). By not filing in these cases, Lee came in conflict with conservatives within and outside the Reagan administration.

Solicitor General Lee participated in a number of important cases during his four-year tenure. The government was on the winning side in about seventy-seven percent of the cases Lee brought before the Court either as a party or as an amicus. Critics point out that Lee won often because he refused to file cases presenting truly difficult questions. In *Immigration and*

Naturalization Service v. Chadha, 462 U.S. 919 (1983), the administration was on the winning side when the Court found the "legislative veto" to be an unconstitutional exercise of power by the Congress.

The government lost on abortion in cases such as *City of Akron v. Akron Center for Reproductive Health*, 462 U.S. 16 (1983). In this case, Lee felt that he had pushed too far too fast on abortion and that the Court had punished him for bringing the case. Social conservatives disagreed. The Court did side with the solicitor general on issues related to First Amendment exercises of religion. For example, the Court ruled in *Lynch v. Donnelly*, 465 U.S. 668 (1984), that the city of Pawtucket, Rhode Island, could include a crèche in a Christmas display that also included a number of nonreligious Christmas figures. The ruling was not a clear victory for President Reagan's social agenda, however.

An important case in which Lee did not participate, raising the ire of social conservatives, was *Bob Jones University v. United States*, 461 U.S. 574 (1983). In 1970, the Internal Revenue Service (IRS) prohibited granting tax-exempt status to private schools that practiced racial discrimination. Although Bob Jones University did not discriminate in admissions, the school did not allow interracial dating among its students. The Reagan administration argued that the IRS did not have the authority to deny tax-exempt status; however, the government's brief was written by one of Lee's deputies, a holdover from the Jimmy Carter administration. The deputy, in his position as acting solicitor general, indicated that he did not believe in the government's position. The Supreme Court ruled in favor of the IRS.

The *crèche* and *Bob Jones* cases were important to the implementation of President Reagan's agenda (Caplan 1987, 96). The cases were part of a series of appeals known as the *Religion Cases* that became a key indicator of the strained relationship between the solicitor general and other officials in the Justice Department. Assistant Attorney General Reynolds regularly asked Lee to push harder to get the Court to change its interpretation of the First Amendment free exercise clause from strict separation to one involving the "accommodation of religion." The Reagan administration wanted government to be able to promote religion without endorsing a specific sect. James McClellan, founder of the conservative Center for Judicial Studies and its journal *Benchmark,* amplified the administration's arguments on the issue of church and state. He criticized Solicitor General Lee for having written a "weak" brief in the *crèche* case. McClellan argued that Lee should have raised questions about the Court's previous interpretations of the establishment clause and forced the justices to change or defend their position (McClellan 1984). McClellan called for Lee's removal from office because the solicitor general was not aggressively promoting the Reagan agenda.

Lee resigned as solicitor general in June 1985. His public explanation was that he could not continue to support his large family on the solicitor general's salary. He alluded to a second reason for resigning: he was tired of the pressure from conservatives (Caplan 1987, 106–107). In short, the man who some felt was too conservative to be solicitor general in 1981 was, by 1985, not conservative enough. Although Lincoln Caplan (1987) exaggerates the conflict between conservatives and Lee, one legacy of this internecine battle is Lee's clear statements of the proper role of the solicitor general in the U.S. legal system (e.g., Lee 1986; 1991). Harvard law professor Charles Fried succeeded Lee.

Lee joined the law firm of Sidley & Austin as partner focusing on appellate cases on July 1, 1985. He reached an arrangement with that firm and BYU that allowed him to split his time between teaching and private practice. In 1986, after spending a year establishing a relationship with Sidley & Austin in the firm's Washington office, the Lees moved back to Provo, Utah, where Lee became the George Sutherland Professor of Law in the Clark law school. Lee continued to split time with the firm even after being named president of BYU in 1989. He continued to argue cases before the Supreme Court until his death in 1996. In fact, he was preparing a case when he died.

Lee argued sixty cases before the U.S. Supreme Court during his relatively short career. In most of the cases, he appeared in his role as solicitor general. At Sidley & Austin, he was sought after as a "Supreme Court specialist." Lee faced other former solicitors general in a number of cases. In *R. J. Reynolds Tobacco v. Durham County*, 479 U.S. 130 (1986), Erwin Griswold represented R. J. Reynolds, while Lee was successful in representing Durham County, North Carolina. He represented Escondido, California, in *Yee v. City of Escondido*, 503 U.S. 519 (1991), a case involving the constitutionality of the city's rent control policies. Former federal judge and solicitor general Robert Bork represented the Yees.

One of the first cases Lee argued before the Supreme Court in private practice was particularly important to him. The case, *Corporation of the Presiding Bishop of the Church of Jesus Christ of Latter Day Saints v. Amos*, 483 U.S. 327 (1987), involved a custodian at a Mormon church–owned gymnasium who was fired after being unable to prove that he was a Mormon church member and eligible to enter its temples. The custodian sued the church alleging religious discrimination, although religious organizations are exempt from Title VII of the Civil Rights Act and allowed to discriminate based on religion. The federal district court in Utah found that the religious exemption to Title VII was an unconstitutional establishment of religion. The Supreme Court did not agree and upheld the constitutionality of the exemption. In another famous case from the October 1986 term of the Supreme Court, Lee successfully argued the National Collegiate Athletic Association's case in its fight with University of Nevada at Las Vegas basketball coach Jerry Tarkanian, *NCAA v. Tarkanian*, 488 U.S. 179 (1987).

Lee's most significant fight was outside the courtroom. In 1987, he was diagnosed with lymphoma, a type of fast-spreading cancer. He underwent an experimental treatment at the National Institutes of Health in Bethesda, Maryland, and the cancer went into remission. While undergoing treatment, Lee briefly left the hospital to present oral arguments in *Karcher v. May*, 484 U.S. 72 (1987), the New Jersey moment-of-silence case. Wearing a wig to conceal baldness caused by the radical chemotherapy, he presented Karcher's case to the Court. He argued that the moment-of-silence law should be upheld as enacted by the New Jersey legislature in 1982. Lee lost the case on standing. Karcher had been the speaker of New Jersey's general assembly when that body approved the law. By the time the legal challenge reached the Supreme Court, Karcher was no longer speaker and the present legislature opposed any defense of the law. The Court ruled that Karcher did not have standing to bring the case, affirming the lower court's ruling of unconstitutionality.

In 1989, apparently cancer-free, Lee accepted an offer to serve as the president of BYU. He continued to practice law, dedicating one-sixth of his time to his practice. He was BYU's president until December 1995, when he resigned because of health problems. During his seven years as president, he still argued nine cases before the U.S. Supreme Court. In 1991, he represented natural gas producers in *Mobil Oil Exploration v. United Distribution Cos.*, 498 U.S. 211 (1991). According to Carter Phillips (1996, 6), this was the only argument of Lee's in which the justices asked no questions. The justices listened intently to Lee's defense of his clients' position. The Court ruled in favor of the natural gas producers. Another important case argued by Lee while he was BYU president was *Freeman v. Pitts*, 503 U.S. 467 (1992), a case involving the termination of a school desegregation decree in DeKalb County, Georgia. The school system, his client, was successful in the case.

The fight against cancer returned to Lee's life in 1990 when he was diagnosed with an incurable, but controllable, form of lymphoma. While his health slowly deteriorated, he continued practicing law and presiding over BYU. On December 31, 1995, Lee resigned as BYU president. He lost his fight with cancer on March 11, 1996, dying of respiratory failure at a hospital in Provo, Utah. The final case Lee argued before the Supreme Court was *O'Melveny & Myers v. FDIC*, 512 U.S. 79 (1994). Lee represented a law firm that had been sued by the government corporation for negligence in the advice the firm had given a failed savings and loan association. In his presentation, he argued that if the Court ruled in favor of the Federal Deposit Insurance Corporation (FDIC), the Court would be creating law to supplement federal statute (Phillips 1996, 6). The justices agreed. Writing for the Court, Justice Antonin Scalia stated that if state law protects lawyers from being sued by a failed savings and loan, then the FDIC, acting as receiver of the savings and loan, is also prohibited from suing the lawyers. When he died, Lee was preparing for oral arguments scheduled for March 18, 1996, in the case of *Arizona v. Reno*, a case involving the application of amendments to the Voting Rights Act. Lee had represented the state of Arizona at every step in the process from the original complaint in the district court. Before the Court heard arguments, the federal government settled.

In a legal career that spanned thirty-three years before being ended by illness, Rex Lee made significant contributions to the U.S. legal system. These contributions include the building of a law school from scratch as well as other aspects of legal education. Working with Chief Justice Warren Burger, Lee created the American Inns of Court in 1980; these associations of judges, lawyers, and law students are designed to raise professional and ethical standards. He protected the solicitor general's office from being politicized by the Reagan administration and its supporters. Acting counter to the fears of his liberal detractors, he did not use his office to force a Mormon worldview on the jurisprudence of the United States. His entire legal career, in government service and in private practice, reflected his dedication to the words of the Constitution. He followed an ideology of judicial restraint, even when he angered his colleagues in the "Reagan Revolution."

—*John David Rausch Jr.*

Sources and Suggestions for Further Reading

Caplan, Lincoln. *The Tenth Justice: The Solicitor General and the Rule of Law*. New York: Alfred A. Knopf, 1987.

Craig, Barbara Hinkson. *Chadha: The Story of an Epic Constitutional Struggle*. New York: Oxford University Press, 1988.

Lee, Rex E. *A Lawyer Looks at the Constitution*. Provo, Utah: Brigham Young University Press, 1981.

———. *A Lawyer Looks at the Equal Rights Amendment*. Provo, Utah: Brigham Young University Press, 1980.

———. "Lawyering for the Government: Politics, Polemics and Principle." *Ohio State Law Journal* 47 (1986): 595–601.

———. "The Office of Solicitor General: Political Appointee, Advocate, and Officer of the Court." In *An Essential Safeguard: Essays on the United States Supreme Court and Its Justices*, edited by D. Grier Stephenson Jr. New York: Greenwood Press, 1991.

McClellan, James. "Editor's Brief: A Lawyer Looks at Rex Lee." *Benchmark* 1 (March/April 1984): 1–16.

Phillips, Carter G. "Remembering Rex Lee." *The Recorder*, 27 March 1996, 6.

Reece, Mark, and Sharon Haddock. "Pneumonia Claims Former Y. President Rex Lee." *Salt Lake City Deseret News*, 12 March 1996, 1.

Salokar, Rebecca Mae. *The Solicitor General: The Politics of Law*. Philadelphia: Temple University Press, 1992.

LEIBOWITZ, SAMUEL SIMON

(1893–1978)

SAMUEL S. LEIBOWITZ, a leading criminal defense attorney of the 1920s and 1930s, was born in Iasi (Jassy), Romania, on August 13, 1893, the only son of Isaac and Bina Lebeau. The Lebeaus were orthodox Jews who immigrated to the United States in 1897 to escape second-class citizenship. Before moving to Brooklyn, they lived in Manhattan and took the advice of a friend—another recent immigrant—to "Americanize" the family name. In school, Leibowitz enjoyed theater and public speaking. In 1911, Leibowitz entered Cornell University and, deferring to his father's wish that he prepare to become a lawyer, excelled academically and in sports, debate, and drama. Torn between his father's wishes and

SAMUEL SIMON LEIBOWITZ
(*middle*) *Library of Congress*

his desire to pursue professional acting, Leibowitz spent much of his last college summer observing criminal trials. He imagined himself in various roles and found a solution for his dilemma: As a defense lawyer, he would dramatize real-life situations persuading flesh-and-blood audiences for high stakes on behalf of his clients.

Graduating in 1915, Leibowitz passed the bar examinations at the top of his group and endured four years of low-profile legal apprenticeship in Brooklyn at several civil practice firms before volunteering for appointment to his first criminal defendant. Harry Patterson, a derelict lush, was in a

460

drunken stupor when police arrested him and charged him with breaking into a saloon to steal seven dollars and a bottle of whiskey. The police obtained Patterson's confession and a key Patterson took from his pocket saying he used it to enter the saloon. Patterson told Leibowitz he was innocent and confessed only because the police beat him. In the two weeks before defending Patterson, Leibowitz thought about nothing else. He constructed the prosecutor's case, then looked for a reasonable doubt, fastening on the key from Patterson's pocket as the key to the case. At trial, after the prosecution's case, Leibowitz called Patterson—limping—to the stand to testify that he confessed only because the police beat him. Then, Leibowitz demanded proof the key from Patterson's pocket would open the saloon door. Caught by surprise, the prosecution sniffed that the issue was irrelevant, and rested. The jury deliberated only four minutes before returning with a verdict of "not guilty." Afterward, Leibowitz asked the prosecution to try the key in a courthouse hall door. It opened them all.

Leibowitz immediately went into practice by himself. A defense lawyer who did not socialize with criminals, Leibowitz acquired clients as the press and jailhouse grapevine spread word of his successes. Leibowitz protested later that his success was due to preparation rather than courtroom legerdemain, but he would not present a defense he could not believe, and he knew exactly how to perform. He investigated the facts and the evidence—including the scene where relevant events had taken place—for himself. He constructed the case as if he were the prosecutor, identifying the elements of the case and the strengths and weaknesses of each. Only then did Leibowitz begin working on a defense. He learned everything available of the life history, personality, habits, and character of his client, potential witnesses, prosecuting attorney, presiding jurist, and potential jurors. Since high-profile criminal cases were usually tried in the newspapers first, he mastered handling the press. At trial, Leibowitz preferred "showing"—pictures, models, reenacting—to "telling" with mere verbal testimony. With witnesses he could be gentle or bruising, flamboyant or subtle, cool or emotive. His recall was immediate and accurate. He made expert witnesses understandable, and he engaged juries in thinking problems through to the solutions he wanted. Leibowitz had an exceptional ability to "read" the personality and character of others and to relate as an equal. Dramatics were carefully calculated and tailored to fit the needs of the case.

In only a decade—by 1929—Leibowitz was New York City's preeminent criminal defense attorney. He attained national recognition by his defense of Harry Hoffman. Hoffman was a Staten Island movie projectionist who had already been convicted of second-degree murder in the shooting of a young woman last seen entering a Model T sedan driven by a man with brown hair wearing a brown hat, brown overcoat, and glasses. The evidence against Hoffman was entirely circumstantial. As the description of the probable murderer was publicized, Hoffman realized his car, pistol, clothing, and appearance matched. Worse, he could not account for his whereabouts. Hoffman cut his hair, arranged to repaint his car, mailed the pistol to his brother, burned the holster, and asked his brother and friends to lie to create alibis. In the original trial, two eyewitnesses placed Hoffman near the place and time of the murder, a ballistics expert identified Hoffman's gun as the murder weapon, and the history of Hoffman's attempted alibi fabrications was told. The jury convicted Hoffman of second-degree murder, which was, however, inconsistent with the indictment. When a new trial was ordered, Hoffman wrote to Leibowitz. Becoming convinced of Hoffman's innocence, Leibowitz believed he had to show that (1) the eyewitness identifications were unreliable, (2) Hoffman's pistol was not the murder weapon, and (3) Hoffman's reason for asking others to lie for him was innocent. Leibowitz asked each potential juror about possible connections with Horatio J. Sharrett—brother of Staten Island's political boss—and got as many jurors as possible with technical or mechanical knowledge. In his opening statement, Leibowitz boldly promised to show that the murderer was someone other than Hoffman. Never fingering anyone as guilty, Leibowitz named Sharrett as someone near the murder scene whose description matched that of the Model T's driver but who was not adequately investigated. Leibowitz got one of the prosecution's eyewitnesses to admit that she remembered little about anything except identifying Hoffman as the driver and not being able to do that until he was shown to her several times. Another prosecution eyewitness—a Staten Island policeman—claimed he saw Hoffman driving the Model T nearby at the time but admitted he spoke up only at the direction of the district attorney a month later when the reward money exceeded eight thousand dollars. Leibowitz also extracted a concession that the angle of the sun and its reflection off the windshield obscured the officer's vision of the driver. Leibowitz obtained testimony from the medical examiner that the bullets traveled from the left front to the right rear of the victim's body, making it likely the killer was right-handed. When the prosecution felt forced to put Sharrett on the stand, Leibowitz gently obtained testimony about Sharrett's twenty-year friendship with the district attorney, and that he was driving his Model T sedan nearby only minutes after the murder. The prosecution's ballistics expert asserted that Hoffman's pistol fired the killing bullet but would not reveal his "trade secrets" for determining that fact. Not only did Leibowitz's expert deny Hoffman's pistol fired the killing bullets, but Leibowitz set up a comparison microscope so the jurors, one by one, could compare for themselves a killing bullet and one from Hoffman's pistol. Leibowitz introduced testimony about ornaments and equipment making Hoffman's Model T readily distinguishable from the killer's. To deal with Hoffman's attempts to change his appearance and create cover stories, Leibowitz had Hoffman testify of friends' jokes about his resemblance, his vain attempts to find someone who remembered seeing him elsewhere at the time of the murder, a friend's tale of being beaten by the police as a suspect, and his own exaggerated fears from watching movies about victims of mistaken identity. Leibowitz also introduced evidence—not previously mentioned—of Hoffman's left-handedness and inability to use his own right-handed revolver. In his summation, Leibowitz carefully analyzed the evidentiary defects of the case against Hoffman and made a frankly emotional appeal: If it did not acquit, the jury should give Hoffman the death penalty rather than send him back to jail. After three hours, the jury returned with a verdict of not guilty.

Leibowitz participated in events of lasting national importance when he defended the Scottsboro Boys—nine African-American youths sentenced to death (one to life imprisonment) for allegedly gang-raping two white prostitutes in broad daylight on a loaded freight train gondola between Chattanooga, Tennessee, and Huntsville, Alabama. Taken up initially by Communists, the case became a symbolic battlefield in which evidence was secondary to class warfare, organizational rivalries, sectionalism, and white supremacy. Finding that the defendants had been deprived of their constitutional right to counsel in a capital case, the Supreme Court overturned the original convictions (see *Powell v. Alabama*, 287 U.S. 45 [1932]). Now Leibowitz was retained. At his own expense, and with considerable personal bravery, Leibowitz shredded the prosecution's case and created the record for appeal—conviction by a jury regardless of the evidence being assured by the accusation. After the first jury voted to convict, the trial judge set aside the verdict. The conviction in the next retrial was appealed eventually to the Supreme Court, where Leibowitz successfully argued that the systematic exclusion of qualified African-Americans from lists of potential jurors denied the defendants the "due process" guaranteed by the Fourteenth Amendment (see *Norris v. Alabama*, 294 U.S. 587 [1935]). Thereafter, Leibowitz took a less prominent role as the cases ground down to conclusions unsatisfying to all.

Leibowitz was the impresario supreme in *People v. Vera Stretz*. Around 2 A.M. on November 25, 1935, police were called to help search the upper floors of the Beekman Towers apartments in Manhattan after tenants reported hearing gunshots. A woman (Stretz) encountered on the nineteenth floor said that a man in the apartment of a Dr. Fritz Gebhardt two floors up might need help. An assistant manager using a passkey found Gebhardt's lifeless body with four bullets in it. Meanwhile, a patrolman found a distraught Stretz—now on the stairs below the third floor—weeping and clutching a large handbag. It contained a revolver still warm from being fired, two spent shell casings, a passport and stock certificates in Gebhardt's name, and a silk nightgown wet with blood stains. Asked if she shot the man upstairs, Stretz said, "Yes, I did. But please don't ask me why I did it." Stretz refused to explain and was charged with first-degree murder. The newspapers portrayed Stretz as an ice-cold femme fatale who murdered Gebhardt because he wanted to end their affair. Stretz's father retained Leibowitz. Stretz talked freely about her affair but not about the events of the fatal night. Finally, Leibowitz remarked he thought Stretz was unable to talk about it because she felt ashamed—and not because she felt guilty. Now Stretz poured out her story. Leibowitz promptly told the newspapers he would show in court that Gebhardt got what he deserved, but said no more. During jury selection, Leibowitz asked each venireman if he knew anything of Nietzsche's philosophy, and if deadly self-defense was justified for a woman to avoid being the victim of a felony. Leibowitz waived making an opening statement, leaving both prosecution and jury with only hints as to Stretz's defense. During the prosecution's case, Leibowitz obtained testimony that Stretz pointed the searchers to Gebhardt's apartment and disconsolately admitted shooting him, and that the physical evidence from Gebhardt's room could be interpreted in a manner different from that asserted by the prosecution. During the questioning of the prosecution's twenty-three witnesses, Stretz cried often and lost her composure entirely several times. By the time Leibowitz put her on the stand, Stretz had become a sympathetic figure. Leibowitz led Stretz through a calm recitation of why she had a handgun, and how she met Gebhardt. Then, Leibowitz asked, "By the way, you shot Dr. Gebhardt, didn't you?" Stretz closed her eyes and said softly, "Yes." Reminded of why they were there, those whose attention had begun to wander resumed listening again. Now Leibowitz had Stretz tell of her eleven-month fascination and affair with the brilliant and cultured older Gebhardt; his story of a wife back home in Germany to whom he was married in name only; Stretz's hopes for a life together; her adoring and passionate letters; Gebhardt's visit to Germany and letter apparently promising marriage; her disappointment when Gebhardt (who was well connected in high Nazi circles, and believed—in the Nazi way of appropriating Nietzsche—he was exempt from ordinary morality and that women should be used but not loved) returned and wanted them to go on as before; Stretz's decision to make a clean break; and Gebhardt's persistence in wooing her back. At last Leibowitz came to the shooting. Stretz testified calmly and in detail—at Leibowitz's increasing tempo—of Gebhardt's nocturnal telephone call asking her to bring a heating pad to ease his abdominal pains, her visit, and his rape of her. Getting Stretz to testify now became more difficult as she either sobbed or spoke into her handkerchief and chewed at it. Stretz writhed under Leibowitz's questions forcing her to recall Gebhardt's words—"If you want to make it the last night, you will have to make it a good one"—as Gebhardt attempted to make her serve his pleasure further. Stretz told of Gebhardt's threat to kill her, his curses, their struggle, and her shots. But still Stretz had not said what Gebhardt wanted her to do. Finally, Leibowitz dragged from Stretz's lips Gebhardt's awful words ordering her to engage in sodomy (a felony in New York) and his attempt to force her. The judge ordered Stretz to repeat her testimony. Stretz repeated herself and collapsed. When she recovered, Stretz told of leaving Gebhardt's apartment, cleaning up and dressing in her own room, and encountering investigators who arrested her. The prosecution's four-hour cross-examination did not shake Stretz's story. In his summation, Leibowitz emphasized Gebhardt's campaign to dazzle and flatter, tracing the emotional trajectory of Stretz's infatuation, hopes for—and exaltation at the promise of—domestic bliss, crushing disappointment, and final humiliation by Gebhardt. Leibowitz concluded by emphasizing Stretz's right under state law to defend herself if she believed a felony was about to be committed against her. The prosecution said Stretz was acting. When the jury returned a verdict of not guilty, it was the 116th of 139 consecutive verdicts Leibowitz won to clear clients facing the death penalty.

In 1941, Leibowitz left the rigors of his practice to be a judge on the Kings County Court in Brooklyn. Judge Leibowitz was known for stiff sentences, his support of capital punishment, and leading a lengthy grand jury investigation into organized crime influence in the New York City Police Department. In 1953, Leibowitz ran for mayor but withdrew. In 1969, when no more extensions beyond retirement age could be granted, Leibowitz retired from the bench to teach, lecture, and practice law until his death in Brooklyn, on January 11, 1978.

—*James A. Keim*

Sources and Suggestions for Further Reading

Johnson, Alva. "Let Freedom Ring." *New Yorker*, 4 and 11 June 1932.

Leibowitz, Robert. *The Defender: The Life and Career of Samuel S. Leibowitz, 1893–1933*. Englewood Cliffs, N.J.: Prentice-Hall, 1981.

Obituary. *New York Times*, 12 January 1978.

Papers and audiotapes of Samuel Simon Leibowitz and publications about him. Department of Manuscripts and University Archives, Cornell University Libraries, New York.

Pasley, Fred D. *Not Guilty! The Story of Samuel S. Leibowitz*. New York: G. P. Putnam, 1933.

Reynolds, Quentin. *Courtroom: The Story of Samuel S. Leibowitz*. New York: Farrar, Straus, 1950.

LINCOLN, ABRAHAM

(1809–1865)

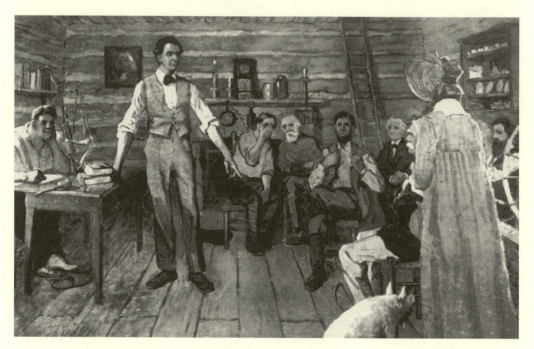

ABRAHAM LINCOLN

A painting of Abraham Lincoln in the courtroom, created for the Chicago & Illinois Midland Calendar Series, by Fletcher Granson. (The Frank and Virginia Williams Collection of Lincolniana)

HISTORIANS HAVE CONSISTENTLY RANKED ABRAHAM LINCOLN, along with George Washington and Franklin Roosevelt, as one of the three greatest presidents of the United States. Unlike Washington and Roosevelt, Lincoln was also a highly respected lawyer who, during his career at the bar, helped to craft landmark decisions during more than two decades of an extensive law practice.

Almost entirely self-educated, this product of the Kentucky backwoods and Midwestern pioneer settlements nevertheless dealt effectively during the Civil War years with the most formidable aggregation of unprecedented legal and constitutional issues ever faced by an American president.

466

Lincoln was born in Hardin (later Larue) County, Kentucky, on February 12, 1809. His father, Thomas Lincoln, was an uneducated farmer and carpenter; his mother, Nancy Hanks Lincoln, was reputedly "intellectual," but she could not write her own name. From Knob Creek farm in Kentucky, where he lived as a small child, Lincoln and his sister Sarah were taken by their parents in 1816 to a small settlement near Pigeon Creek in Perry (later Spencer) County, Indiana, where they lost their mother to brucellosis when Abraham was only ten. A year later, Thomas Lincoln married Sarah Bush Johnston, a widow from Elizabethtown, Kentucky, and she and her three young children joined Abraham and his father and sister to make up a crowded but apparently happy household (Donald 1995, 1–228).

Once he learned to read, Lincoln was insatiable in his thirst for knowledge. As early as 1827, a warrant sworn out against him by two Kentucky ferrymen caused the youngster to borrow and study a copy of the *Revised Laws of Indiana*. In 1831, he left home and eventually settled in the village of New Salem on the Sangamon River in Illinois. There he was a farm laborer, boatman, surveyor, and store manager. He began to study English grammar and arithmetic and to read Shakespeare and the poetry of Robert Burns, and he joined a literary and debating club that met weekly at a local tavern. One day, at age twenty-three, he came into possession of a discarded copy of William Blackstone's *Commentaries*, from which he learned many of the basic principles of early-nineteenth-century jurisprudence. His early practical experience with the law came as an untaught litigant: he was sued at least four times during his New Salem years and, beginning in 1834, acted as a pettifogger, drawing up deeds, wills, mortgages, and other legal documents and pleading the cases of his neighbors in the permissive surroundings of the local justice of the peace court (Woldman 1994, 9–22).

Less than a year after his arrival in New Salem, Lincoln served in the militia in the so-called Black Hawk campaign but saw no combat. On his return from military service he ran for the legislature in the election of August 1832 but was badly beaten, the only time he ever lost an election by popular vote. Two years later, having in the meantime received appointments as village postmaster and assistant county surveyor, he easily won a legislative seat and followed with three additional successive terms.

On March 1, 1837, without undergoing any formal examination, Lincoln was granted a license to practice law in all the courts of Illinois. A month later, he left New Salem and moved to the new state capital at Springfield, where he became the law partner of John T. Stuart, with whom he had become friendly during the Black Hawk campaign. His principal duties were to conduct office business, including the preparation of pleadings and briefs in longhand, and to appear in trials involving rudimentary issues, while

Stuart ran for Congress against Stephen A. Douglas and then served two terms in Washington.

Fortunately for Lincoln, Illinois was still a young state, and there were few precedents or formidable authorities to research and cite. He was able to try most of his cases, such as his first one, *Hawthorne v. Wooldridge* (1837) (typically settled out of court), on principle rather than on precedent. Polishing his debating and public speaking skills by participating in a young men's lyceum, he began traveling the Eighth Judicial Circuit, joining a cavalcade of lawyers and Judge Samuel H. Treat, who rode in rickety buggies or on horseback over muddy trails, fording swollen streams, to hold court for several days in each of fourteen county seats, spread across an area comprising virtually one-fifth of the entire state of Illinois (Woldman 1994, 26–37, 85–86).

Although the practice of Stuart and Lincoln was more extensive than that of any other Springfield firm, it was not lucrative for its junior member. In 1841, the thirty-two-year-old Lincoln changed law partners, affiliating with former Judge Stephen T. Logan, who insisted that his junior associate be more thorough, methodical, and precise in the preparation of his cases. The firm of Logan & Lincoln, from April 1841 until it dissolved in the autumn of 1844, dominated the dockets of the state supreme court, participating in several landmark decisions, such as *Grable v. Margrave*, 4 Ill. 372 (1842), which became a standard for the assessment of damages in cases of sexual seduction (Woldman 1994, 38–42).

In December 1844, the firm of Lincoln & Herndon was formed. William Henry Herndon, nine years Lincoln's junior, came from New Salem and had been a law student in the office of Lincoln & Logan. Although Herndon was an impulsive radical abolitionist who did most of the menial work for the firm, and Lincoln was a cautious conservative Whig who tried practically all of its most important cases, the two split all of their income, mostly in the form of five- and ten-dollar fees, equally (Woldman 1994, 49–51, 56).

In 1842 (the year he married Mary Todd of Kentucky), and again in 1844, Lincoln had tried but failed to obtain the Whig nomination for Congress from the central Illinois district. In 1846, however, he was successful, and in August he won the election over his Democratic opponent, Peter Cartwright. Taking his seat in the House of Representatives in December 1847 as the only Whig member from Illinois, he immediately spoke out against the continuation of the Mexican-American War, which he viewed as an attempt to add more slave territory to the United States. He was also admitted to practice before the U.S. Supreme Court and argued his first case there in March 1849, just before returning home to Springfield to try to rebuild a disintegrated law practice, after accusations of lack of patriotism had caused him not to be a candidate for reelection to Congress (Donald 1995, 94, 111–115, 119–125).

At age forty, Lincoln energetically set to work riding circuit with newly elected judge David Davis, being away from home for six months of the year, sleeping two to a bed in rustic inns or farmhouses with other lawyers, with no room in his saddle bags for law books, and relying largely on his wits and anecdotal abilities to win his cases with unsophisticated juries. Before the appearance in Illinois of railroads, telegraph lines, or daily newspapers, itinerant lawyers were the principal sources of news, political opinion, and witty repartee, at which Lincoln was the acknowledged master, and court days were local holidays for people, including members of juries, seeking both entertainment and enlightenment. Under these circumstances there was little incentive for the drawing up of elaborate briefs, even if there had been an opportunity to do so; hence, arguments comprised original reasoning based on broad constitutional principles, rather than per judicial precedents. It was during the years Lincoln traveled the Eighth Illinois Circuit that he developed the legal and political attitudes that characterized his peculiar presidency.

Although he was one of the most popular circuit-riding attorneys of his day, Lincoln's income from that portion of his practice was negligible. His clients tended to be poor and his travel expenses considerable. He was compelled to split fees with local lawyers who supplied clients, temporary office space, and local knowledge. But his gypsy-like meandering from one county courthouse to another during the 1840s and 1850s was invaluable to him politically, both because it enabled him to become closely acquainted with a coterie of fellow attorneys scattered across the region who became his avid supporters and organizers when he began once more to seek political office, and because it put him in touch with the opinions, aspirations, and mental processes of so many ordinary Americans, contributing immensely to the development of his famous "common touch" (Woldman 1994, 87–98).

For many years, Lincoln's cases were typical of a law practice in a region less than a generation removed from pioneering days. Civil litigation—involving quarrels between neighbors over land titles and boundaries or stray animals, and the enforcement of contracts, tried in local justice of the peace courts or on circuit—predominated. Less than one-tenth of his practice involved criminal cases. During the middle 1850s, however, Lincoln began to undertake much more complicated causes, involving vast property holdings and considerable technical knowledge. Banks, railroads, gas and insurance companies, and manufacturing concerns were examples of the large businesses that, along with municipal corporations, were increasingly among his clients. He began to participate in litigation dealing with patent rights and infringements. Still confronting new and frequently unforeseen situations, he continued to argue fundamental constitutional principles, rather than search for precedents in the evolving law of his region. Indeed, some of the decisions resulting from his arguments became landmarks of Illinois jurisprudence affecting railroad construction, such as *Barrett v. Alton & Sangamon Railroad*, 13 Ill. 504 (1852); *Klein v. Alton & Sangamon Railroad*, 13 Ill. 514 (1852); *Alton & Sangamon Railroad v. Carpenter*, 14 Ill. 190 (1853); *Alton & Sangamon Railroad v. Baugh*, 14 Ill. 211 (1853); and *Chicago, Burlington & Quincy Railroad v. Wilson*, 17 Ill. 123 (1856) (Woldman 1994, 133–148, 171–174; Guelzo 1999, 167–170).

Perhaps the most important case that Lincoln won in the Illinois Supreme Court was that of the *St. Louis, Alton & Chicago Railroad v. Dalby*, 19 Ill. 353 (1857), in which the tribunal, by holding the railroad corporation responsible for the acts of its authorized agents, established the rule of law that was to govern all such questions thereafter. But Lincoln's most famous case, involving a contest for supremacy over the nation's transportation system between railroad and steamship corporations, was that of *Hurd v. Railroad Bridge Co.* (1857), which was ultimately settled by the U.S. Supreme Court in his client's favor (Basler 1953, 2:415–422; Woldman 1994, 175–176, 182–185; Guelzo 1999, 167–170).

From the time when he was able to command retainers of only two or three dollars to the time when he could successfully obtain a fee of five thousand dollars, Lincoln tried mostly common law and chancery cases, with criminal causes constituting less than 10 percent of his practice. Adapting himself to every imaginable kind of litigation, client, and court, he appeared as an appellate attorney in at least 290 cases in the Illinois Supreme Court and represented clients in state and federal courts in over 4,500 additional cases. One authority has estimated that he won favorable verdicts in approximately 70 percent of his cases (Long 1993, i–ii; Woldman 1994, 126–127, 148n).

Lincoln was universally thought by the most eminent jurists of his region to be a superb lawyer. David Davis, before whom most of his later circuit court practice took place, and who later served on the U.S. Supreme Court, testified that as an attorney Lincoln had few equals. Sidney Breese, the chief justice of the Illinois Supreme Court in Lincoln's day regarded him as "the finest lawyer I ever knew," and Judge Thomas Drummond, who presided over the U.S. District Court at Chicago during the same era, declared that Lincoln was "one of the ablest lawyers I have ever known." According to Representative Isaac N. Arnold, who traveled the eighth circuit with Lincoln for many years, his Springfield colleague was "the strongest jury lawyer we ever had in Illinois." No one objected when Lincoln substituted on the bench for Davis, as he did frequently when the judge was absent because of illness or personal business. The judicial temperament that Lincoln later exhibited as president in countless cases of military justice and in dealing with clashes within his cabinet was already evident in his calm, commonsense rulings as an irregular state "judge" (Woldman 1994, 149–160).

Lincoln's main weakness as an attorney was his lack of legal learning. His longtime partner declared that he had never observed Lincoln do more than glance at law books to find specific references, and that he knew little of the rules of evidence or of pleading and seemed to care little about them. He might cram for a specific case but otherwise read little law (Woldman 1994, 242–244).

Another weakness was a sometimes inconvenient fastidiousness that impeded his effectiveness whenever he became convinced that his cause was unjust. A contemporary recalled that "it was morally impossible for Lincoln to argue dishonestly. Lacking the willingness to employ subterfuges, sophistries, and appeals to prejudice, he was a poor advocate for a client who came into court with unclean hands" (Whitney 1940, 261).

But when he believed in the justness of his cause, he was unmatched in his ability to make the most intricate matters understandable to the farmers, laborers, and tradespeople who composed the juries in the courts of Illinois. His faculty for reducing issues to questions of basic principles, elucidated in plain language and illustrated with telling anecdotes, not only won him local fame and a host of clients in Illinois, but also suited him well for explaining to a distracted nation the essence of the complicated constitutional controversies that precipitated and arose during the American Civil War (Woldman 1994, 193–200).

In 1858, Lincoln was the nominee of the Illinois Republican party to unseat Senator STEPHEN A. DOUGLAS. In a series of seven regional debates, the two lawyers argued the issues of the day, including the legitimacy of the recent *Dred Scott* decision, the validity of Douglas's doctrine of popular sovereignty, and the relationship of the Constitution to the question of the extension of slavery. Although more votes were cast for Republican candidates for the Illinois legislature in the ensuing election than for Democrats, the existing apportionment of legislative seats enabled the Democratic party to maintain control in Springfield and to reelect Douglas over Lincoln to the Senate. Lincoln, nevertheless, had become a national figure through the publicity given to his losing campaign; moreover, by forcing Douglas to take positions on slavery unpopular in the deep South, he had helped to create a division in the national Democratic party between a Northern Douglas faction and an extreme proslavery group that refused to accept the Illinois senator as their presidential candidate (Donald 1995, 211–224).

Famous Law Partners

Although their trial work is not as well known as that of their colleagues, the partners of at least two of the lawyers covered in this book—ABRAHAM LINCOLN and CLARENCE DARROW—have carved their own niche in history.

William H. Herndon, Lincoln's long-time partner, is perhaps best known for his portrait of Lincoln published in 1889. Edgar Lee Masters, author of the famed *Spoon River Anthology*, included a portrait of his neighbor Herndon contemplating in his declining years the life of a man [Lincoln] who had arisen "from the soil like a fabled giant/And thrown himself over a deathless destiny" (Masters 1992, 291).

Masters's own one-time partner was none other than Clarence Darrow. In *Songs and Satires* (1916), Masters penned a poem described as "the harshest assessment of the moral character of Clarence Darrow" (Uelmen 2000, 640). This assessment is in precarious balance with a much more favorable poem about Darrow that Masters later printed in *The New Republic* (also reprinted in Uelmen 2000, 641).

REFERENCES

Herndon, William H. *Herndon's Lincoln: The True Story of a Great Life*. Edited by David F. Hawke. Indianapolis: Bobbs-Merrill, 1970.

Masters, Edgar Lee. *Spoon River Anthology*. Edited by John E. Hallwas. Urbana: University of Illinois Press, 1992.

Uelmen, Gerald F. "Who Is the Lawyer of the Century?" *Loyola of Los Angeles Law Review* 33 (January 2000): 613–653.

In 1860, as a result of a lawyerlike indictment of slavery in a speech at Cooper Institute in New York City, and strenuous efforts on his behalf at the May Republican National Convention in Chicago, Lincoln became his party's candidate for president. When the Democratic party split and nominated two competing candidates, Lincoln was easily elected, thus ending his professional career as a practicing lawyer. When he left Springfield for Washington in February 1860, he told his law partner, Herndon, to let their shingle hang undisturbed, for if he lived he would return to resume practicing law "as if nothing had happened" (Weik 1922, 298).

The great questions that divided the United States and plunged it into four years of civil war that extended through most of Lincoln's presidency involved intricate issues of constitutionality, of legality, and of justice. The times demanded a national leader whose experience, intellect, disposition, and temperament permitted him to confront those issues forcefully and effectively. Was the secession of Southern slave states constitutional? Was the resulting conflict a war or an insurrection? Did the president have the right to order large-scale military movements without the approval of Congress? Did he have the right to suspend the writ of habeas corpus at his discretion, even where civilian courts were functioning, and to order the arrest and jailing of people without judicial warrants first being issued? Did he have the right to increase the size of the nation's armed forces beyond previously authorized levels without prior congressional consent? Was it legal for him to levy taxes and spend money from the treasury without the previous approval of Congress? And could he confiscate the property of persons whom he had declared were engaged in rebellion against the United States, including, especially, their slaves?

Had Lincoln not been vastly experienced in the law, and particularly had he not been oriented to broad principles of constitutionality and justice rather than to hair-splitting technicalities, he would have lacked the tools adequately to meet the unprecedented legal and constitutional challenges with which he was continually confronted from his first day in office until the day he died. In his first inaugural address, a lawyerlike appeal for the maintenance of law and order and a plea to people in the North and the South to refrain from quarreling and stay "friends," Lincoln upheld the integrity of the Union as a solemn contract and refused to recognize the independence of the insurrectionary states in any way. Soon he established military courts, suspended the writ of habeas corpus, increased the armed forces, declared a naval blockade of the Southern coastline, and eventually issued proclamations emancipating the slaves of rebels because of "military necessity."

Lincoln's position in his notorious constitutional confrontation with Chief Justice Roger Taney in the *Ex parte Merryman* (1861) case, involving a Marylander's imprisonment by military authorities for alleged sedition when the civil tribunals were functioning, was upheld by Congress and by the Supreme Court in the so-called *Vallandigham* case, although it was partly overturned in a split decision by a postwar Supreme Court in the case of *Ex parte Milligan* (1866). Otherwise, both Congress and the courts generally endorsed Lincoln's position that his duty to preserve the Union and see that the laws were faithfully executed justified his acting in anticipation of congressional approval of certain military and financial decisions, and his temporary suspension of a single constitutional protection, namely habeas corpus, in order to protect the integrity of the Constitution as a whole (Neely 1991, 3–14, 51–74, 90–92, 164–184, 218–221; Silver 1998, 119–155, 217–232).

During slightly more than four years as president, Lincoln made five appointments to the U.S. Supreme Court. These men—Associate Justices Noah H. Swayne, Samuel F. Miller, David Davis, and Stephen J. Field, and Chief Justice Salmon P. Chase—ensured that the Court, for another generation, would tend to uphold national authority over states' rights, refuse to sanction any form of male social slavery, and validate the traditional Republican emphasis on the power of corporate wealth over governmental interference (Silver 1998).

But Lincoln's legal legacy most of all was that of incorporating the ideals of the Declaration of Independence into the U.S. Constitution. While working to preserve the Union, he temporarily assumed the role of a military dictator, but one whose veneration for legality and constitutionality permeated his every act. His state papers, models of legal argument, are a lawyer's briefs against disunion and state sovereignty. They illustrate his three greatest contributions to U.S. jurisprudence: (1) the annihilation of the previously popular doctrine of state supremacy over national authority, (2) the rededication of the nation to the idea of equal rights and equal justice for all, and (3) the enunciation of a national mission to provide for all humankind a model government "of the people, by the people, for the people."

—*Norman B. Ferris*

Sources and Suggestions for Further Reading

Basler, Roy P., ed. *The Collected Works of Abraham Lincoln*. 9 vols. New Brunswick, N.J.: Rutgers University Press, 1953.

Donald, David H. *Lincoln*. New York: Simon & Schuster, 1995.

Duff, John J. *A Lincoln: Prairie Lawyer*. New York: Rinehart, 1960.

Frank, John P. *Lincoln as a Lawyer*. Urbana: University of Illinois Press, 1961.

Guelzo, Allen C. *Abraham Lincoln: Redeemer President*. Grand Rapids, Mich.: Eerdmans, 1999.

Long, John. *The Law of Illinois*. Vol. 1, *Lincoln's Cases before the Illinois Supreme Court from His Entry into the Practice of Law until His Entry into Congress*. Shiloh, Ill.: Illinois Company, 1993.

Matthews, Elizabeth W. *Lincoln as a Lawyer: An Annotated Bibliography*. Carbondale: Southern Illinois University Press, 1991.

Neely, Mark E., Jr. *The Fate of Liberty: Abraham Lincoln and Civil Liberties*. New York: Oxford University Press, 1991.

Randall, James G. *Constitutional Problems under Lincoln*. Urbana: University of Illinois Press, 1951.

Silver, David M. *Lincoln's Supreme Court*. Urbana: University of Illinois Press, 1998.

Weik, Jesse W. *The Real Lincoln: A Portrait*. Boston: Houghton Mifflin, 1922.

Whitney, Henry C. *Life on the Circuit with Lincoln*. Caldwell, Idaho: Caxton Printers, 1940.

Woldman, Albert A. *Lawyer Lincoln*. New York: Carroll & Graf, 1994.

LOCKWOOD, BELVA

(1830–1917)

BELVA LOCKWOOD
Library of Congress

"WE PLEDGE OURSELVES, IF elected, with power so far as in us lies, to do justice to every class of citizens without distinction of color, sex, or nationality" (Fox 1975, 135). These words, from Belva Lockwood's acceptance speech as a candidate for the 1884 presidential election, exemplify her fight for equality during the nineteenth century. Belva Ann McNall Lockwood was the first female attorney to practice before the Supreme Court. Her active involvement in attempts to redress injustice against various underrepresented groups, such as Native Americans and women, made her a woman both reviled and respected. She was a "latecomer" to the field of law, but she was the first woman to graduate from a national law school, and she soon cemented her reputation by successfully representing the Eastern Cherokee Indians in an eight-million-dollar lawsuit before the Supreme Court. Not only did she test the waters of equality in the courtroom as the first woman to practice in federal courts, as well as before the Supreme Court, but

475

she was the first woman actually to run for president, not once, but twice, during the 1884 and 1888 presidential elections.

Born in upstate New York in 1830, Lockwood always had her own ideas about gender relations and equality. She would consistently argue with her father about things girls were not supposed to do, and early on, she recognized that there were very few things that women could not accomplish as well as men if they were given the chance (Fox 1975, 19). As a child, Belva was the top student in her class, and after graduation from her county school at age fourteen, she taught for one summer before heading to the Girls' Academy in Royalton, New York. Soon afterward, she married the son of her former headmaster, Uriah McNall, and moved with him to the milltown of Gasport, New York. Their daughter, Lura, was born a year later. After the loss of her husband in 1853 to poor health, she attempted to get a teaching job but turned down the offer after discovering that the salary was less than half what a male teacher would make. Disillusioned only for a short time, she sent Lura to live with her parents, who had since moved to Illinois, and moved to Lima, New York, to study at Genesee Wesleyan Seminary, known today as Syracuse University.

Genesee Wesleyan Seminary had just opened its doors in 1854, and the choice to pursue higher education was still an extraordinary one for a woman, particularly for a widow with a young child (Babcock 1997). Already a victim of prejudice, Lockwood found that she could easily express herself publicly on the issue of equal rights. After attending a lecture given by Susan B. Anthony, she gained an increased interest in changing the existing laws regarding property and voting rights for women. Soon after her arrival at Genesee Wesleyan Seminary, she had convinced the administration of Genesee College to admit her as a student, and she finished college in three years instead of the traditional four. Just before graduation in June 1857, the president of the college, Dr. Joseph Cummings, offered her the position of preceptress of the Lockport Union School District, in which she would be responsible for the education of approximately six hundred boys and girls between the ages of fourteen and eighteen (Dunnahoo 1974, 30–32).

Lockwood quickly distinguished herself by encouraging public speaking for both girls and boys, and every Saturday afternoon, each of the girls in her classes gave a short speech to an audience of parents and curious onlookers. There were many protests against her activities, but she refused to vacillate from her stance that boys and girls should receive the same education. As the Civil War began, Lockwood combined her efforts as president of a Ladies' Aid Society with teaching, soon opening her own female seminary, the McNall Seminary in Oswego, New York. After the end of the war in 1865, she decided that all the action was happening in Washington,

D.C., and after resigning her position as head of the McNall Female Seminary, headed to Washington with Lura. She wrote to a friend that she went to Washington, "this great political centre,—this seething pot,—to learn something of the practical workings of the machinery of government, and to see what the great men and women of the country felt and thought" (Winner 1958, 221).

Lockwood immediately became involved in the women's suffrage movement. She and Lura lived in the residence halls of the Union League Hall and opened their own private coeducational school, leasing the schoolrooms to religious, temperance, and political organizations in the evenings. She soon met Dr. Ezekial Lockwood, who became a staunch supporter. Their relationship quickly turned to romance, and on March 11, 1868, they were married. Considerably older than Belva, Dr. Lockwood was well established in Washington, but he closed his existing dentistry practice and opened a new office just down the hall from Belva in the Union League Hall. In January 1869, Belva gave birth to a daughter, whom the couple named Jessie Belva Lockwood (Fox 1975, 80–92).

Soon after the birth of Jessie, Lockwood accepted a position as vice-president of the newly formed Universal Franchise Association (also known as the Equal Rights Association), and it was not long before she had begun to petition Congress on suffrage matters. Her interest in law increased, and she applied for admission to Columbian Law School on October 23, 1869. Rejected, she received a letter from the president, George W. Sampson, which read, "Madam, The Faculty of Columbian College have considered your request to be admitted to the Law Department of this institution, and after due consultation, have considered that such admission would not be expedient, as it would be likely to distract the attention of the young men" (Dunnahoo 1974, 66). She was also refused by Georgetown University on the grounds that women had never been admitted, but her third attempt was a partial success. She applied in 1869 to the new National University Law School, whose vice-chancellor, William Wedgewood, had often spoken in favor of women's rights. The university refused her admission, but Wedgewood offered to teach private classes for her and other interested women. However, he made it clear that this would not entitle her to a diploma (Kerr 1947, 76–77).

As a law student, Lockwood continued her interest in the disadvantaged. In 1869, she took on a new project, fighting for equal pay for female Civil Service employees (Fox 1975, 100). She enlisted the support of Horace Greeley and proposed the Civil Service bill that reached Congress in 1870. The bill passed, and it read, "Hereafter all clerks and employees in Civil Service of the United States shall be paid irrespective of sex with reference to the character and amount of services performed by them" (Kerr 1947,

81). This was both a personal and a public victory, but this victory was dampened by the death of her daughter, Jessie. By May 1873, she had finished her course of study at the National University Law School, but she did not receive a diploma. Lockwood was unrelenting, however, in pursuit of the diploma she had rightfully earned, and she wrote to the current president of the United States, Ulysses S. Grant, also titular head of the National University Law School by virtue of his office. In her letter, she wrote, "Sir, You are, or you are not, President of the National University Law School. If you are its President, I desire to say to you that I have passed through the curriculum of study in this school, and am entitled to, and *demand*, my diploma" (Winner 1958, 224). Therefore, at age forty-three, Belva Lockwood prepared to embark on a new career as the first woman lawyer in the history of the United States. (Fox 1975, 107; Kerr 1947, 97).

Admitted to the bar of the Supreme Court of the District of Columbia on September 24, 1873, Lockwood quickly began arguing cases before the court. On behalf of her first client, Mary Ann Folker, she petitioned the court to grant a divorce in light of the ten years of cruel treatment Mrs. Folker had suffered at the hands of her husband. Lockwood won the case, obtaining the divorce for Mrs. Folker and a court judgment that Mr. Folker would pay for his ex-wife's expenses until she found means to support herself. When she was told that Mr. Folker would never pay, she reopened the case, and Frederick Folker went to prison until he promised to support his wife and children (Fox 1975, 105–108). Although this was her first case, it was a later case that brought her increased notoriety. Her defense of an accused murderer, a woman who was clearly guilty of shooting a constable, invoked the importance of common law. She argued,

> The laws must be enforced. My client is guilty. She has committed the double offense of resisting an officer of the law, then shooting the man. But gentlemen, the District of Columbia is under the common law. That law says a woman must obey her husband. She must obey him without question. Her husband told my client to load a gun and shoot the first man who tried to force his way into the house. As a good wife, she obeyed him. . . . Surely, gentlemen, you would not have a woman resist her husband. (Dunnahoo 1974, 114)

The jury returned a verdict of not guilty, and this strengthened her claim for seeking admission to the U.S. Court of Claims. Her appeal was denied, but for the first time, women had a sympathetic champion in the courtroom. She took on another case that a male lawyer would have refused to touch, that of the widow Charlotte VonCort, who had sued the U.S. government for the infringement of a patent for a torpedo boat invented by her late husband. The case, won in a lower court, needed to go before the U.S. Court of Claims. Since Lockwood's claim to practice in this court of claims was denied, she herself appealed to the court. Her attorney, A. A. Hosmer, pleaded for her admittance, but Chief Justice Drake denied the plea, with the refusal, "Mistress Lockwood, you are a woman." Lockwood appealed, and the second verdict was even more harsh: "Mistress Lockwood, you are a *married* woman." This reasoning included the possible danger that a married female attorney would invite corruption, misapply funds, or commit fraud for which her husband would be liable under common law (*In re Mrs. Belva Lockwood, ex parte v. United States*, 9 Cl. Ct. 350–353 [1983]).

If Lockwood were to advance, she needed to supersede this barrier, so her immediate response was a petition to Congress, seeking a declaratory act or ;joint resolution that stated, "No woman otherwise qualified, shall be debarred from practice before any United States Court on account of sex." In 1876, Lockwood applied for admission to the U.S. Supreme Court bar, but her claim was denied since "none but men are admitted to practice before [the court] as attorneys and counselors . . . and the court does not feel called upon to make a change, until such change is required by statute, or a more extended practice in the highest courts of the States" (Babcock 1997, 6). Her dismay was heightened by the death of Ezekial Lockwood in the spring of 1877, but she forged ahead, and in the fall of 1877, H.R. 1077 was introduced by Representative John M. Glover. Although this bill had been presented before the House on numerous previous occasions, this time Senator Aaron Sargent spoke of Lockwood's acceptance by members of the legal profession. Many states, he argued, were admitting women to the bar, including his own state of California. "There is no reason why women should not be admitted to this profession or any other provided they have the learning to enable them to be successful in those professions. . . . Where is the propriety in opening our colleges . . . to shut them out?" (Dunnahoo 1974, 153). Despite Sargent's efforts, the bill's proponents were unable to obtain a vote of the full Senate. The bill was finally submitted to a vote on February 7, 1879, and Senator Sargent again made an impassioned plea. "No man has a right to put a limit to the exertions or the sphere of woman. . . . The enjoyment of liberty, the pursuit of happiness in her own way, is as much the birthright of woman as of man." The bill passed by a vote of 39 to 20, with 17 abstaining, on February 7, 1879, and was signed by the president on February 15. The story received full coverage in the national newspapers, and on March 3, 1879, Lockwood became the first woman admitted under the new law to practice before the Supreme Court. Three days later, she was admitted to the bar of the U.S. Court of Claims (Kerr 1947, 130). The claim cases became her favorite, and she broke another traditional prejudice when, on February 20, 1880, she approached the

U.S. Supreme Court with a motion to admit Samuel Lowry, an African-American lawyer, to the court. With her assistance, Lowry was admitted to the bar (Dunnahoo 1974, 164–165).

Her interest in the underrepresented made her a logical choice to represent the women of Washington at the Republican National Conventions in 1880 and 1884. Both times, she called for a sixteenth amendment to give women the right to vote. Disgusted at the lack of action, she sent a letter to Marietta Stow, the editor of the *Woman's Herald of Industry*, suggesting that suffrage might be obtained with the election of female candidates. She wrote,

> Why not nominate women for important places? Is not Victoria Empress of India? Is not history full of precedents of women rulers? The Republican party, claiming to be the party of progress, has little else but insult for women. . . . It is quite time we had our own party, our own platform, and our own nominees.

The result was the endorsement of Lockwood as a candidate for the presidency of the United States. Belva Lockwood became a much reviled character in the press, but she garnered more than four thousand of the popular votes, and when she ran again in 1888 on the same ticket of the Equal Rights party, the results were fairly similar.

These efforts were a direct result of her stance on equal rights issues and led to her advocacy of equal citizenship rights for Native Americans. A Cherokee, Jim Taylor, for whom Lockwood had already worked, enlisted her assistance in helping his people with their long-standing claim against the government. She represented the Eastern and Emigrant Cherokees in *Cherokee Nation v. United States*, a suit brought to the court of claims in 1903 and then appealed to the Supreme Court. This lawsuit addressed the claims of Cherokees who had been forced off their land in North Carolina, Georgia, and Tennessee by federal marshals. Her work on this case extended into the early twentieth century, and although the court of claims agreed the government owed her clients more money, Belva Lockwood was not satisfied and she took the case to the Supreme Court, where she won five million dollars for her clients (Dunnahoo 1974, 184–185). Not only was this a triumph for the law, but it set a precedent for female lawyers to fight against all injustice (Babcock 1997, 15). The Supreme Court justices who listened to Lockwood's arguments later said that she had made "the most eloquent argument of any of the attorneys before the Court" (Emert 1996, 78).

Lockwood lived to age eighty-six, and she worked actively on the claims cases that were so dear to her until three weeks before her death on May 19, 1917. She was a highly visible woman, and as an effective speaker, she tirelessly worked to pass legislation to fight injustice. Her record of litigation reflects her devotion to equal justice and civil rights.

—*Jennifer Harrison*

Sources and Suggestions for Further Reading

Babcock, Barbara. "Belva Ann Lockwood: For Peace, Justice, and President." 1997. <http://www.stanford.edu/group/WLHP/papers/lockwood.htm>.

Dunnahoo, Terry. *Before the Supreme Court: The Story of Belva Ann Lockwood.* Boston: Houghton Mifflin, 1974.

Emert, Phyllis Raybin. *Top Lawyers & Their Famous Cases.* Minneapolis: Oliver Press, 1996.

Fox, Mary Virginia. *Lady for the Defense: A Biography of Belva Lockwood.* New York: Harcourt Brace Jovanovich, 1975.

Kerr, Laura. *The Girl Who Ran for President.* New York: Thomas Nelson, 1947.

Winner, Julia Hull. "Belva A. Lockwood: That Extraordinary Woman." *New York History* 39 (1958): 321.

MARSHALL, JOHN

(1755–1835)

ALTHOUGH JOHN MARSHALL is best known as the fourth chief justice of the United States—from February 1801 until his death on July 6, 1835—he was also one of Virginia's finest litigators. Marshall's clientele ranged from the very rich and influential to the very poor and disenfranchised: his clients ranged from aristocratic British loyalists, to Revolutionary War veterans trying to recover back pay, to manumitted slaves forced into court to prove their freedom.

Early Years

John Marshall was born September 2, 1755, in Prince William (later Fauquier) County, Virginia, near Germantown. John was the eldest of fourteen children born to Thomas and Mary Marshall. His father, Thomas Marshall, a Welsh immigrant, was a self-educated and self-made man, who got his start, like his friend George Washington, as a surveyor. His profession gave him knowledge of land, which in turn led to the land investments with which Thomas Marshall accumu-

JOHN MARSHALL
Library of Congress

482

lated wealth and prominence. At his death, in 1802, Thomas owned over 200,000 acres in Virginia and Kentucky (Smith 1996, 31). Thomas Marshall was known as a tolerant and intelligent man who helped found a non-denominational church in Fauquier County. He was also a clever inventor, responsible for creating the Marshall's Meridian Devise, a tool used to calculate true north based on magnetic north (Smith 1996, 32).

Thomas Marshall's wife, the former Mary Randolph, was descended from the most prominent family in all of Virginia. Through the Randolphs, John Marshall was related to both Richard Henry "Light Horse Harry" Lee, the father of Robert E. Lee, and to Thomas Jefferson. Some have speculated that Marshall's great respect for and devotion to women stemmed from his admiration for Mary Marshall. Growing up in the backwoods of Virginia, young John and his siblings were instilled by their parents with the virtues of education, duty, and hard work.

Soldier, Suitor, Student

Marshall was eighteen when the Revolutionary War began, and he served in the Continental Army from July 30, 1776, until resigning his commission as captain of light infantry in General Washington's army in February 1781. Marshall fought in engagements at Brandywine, Germantown, and Monmouth; he suffered the cold at Valley Forge; and he participated in the capture of Stony Point.

In 1779, Marshall joined his father, brothers, and cousins at Yorktown, where Thomas Marshall was commander of the Yorktown artillery. John's brother, Thomas Markham Marshall, and his cousin Humphrey served as officers under Thomas's command. The fortunes of war caused Thomas Marshall to be a welcomed and frequent guest in the home of Jacquelin and Rebecca Burwell Ambler. The senior Marshall had shared his son John's letters from the front with the Amblers and with one of their daughters, Mary Willis Ambler, known to all as Polly. When Marshall joined his family, the Amblers held a ball in honor of the heroic Captain John Marshall. There, John became infatuated with Polly and began courting his future wife; they were eventually married on January 3, 1783.

During Marshall's stay in Yorktown, a deadlock in the Virginia legislature made it impossible to muster troops for the war effort. While young Marshall awaited troops or orders, he entertained and educated Polly and her sister, Eliza Ambler. At the urging of his family and the Amblers, John began the study of law at the nearby College of William & Mary. Marshall later confessed, "From my infancy I was destined for the bar" (Smith 1996, 75). Thomas Marshall certainly did not discourage his son's choice of profession; in fact, he had been a charter subscriber to the first edition of

Blackstone's *Commentaries on the Laws of England* available in the colonies, when it was offered for purchase in 1772. Thereafter, father and son had studied the influential treatise together.

Marshall attended lectures on the common law at William & Mary, given by the then-preeminent American legal scholar, GEORGE WYTHE. Among Marshall's classmates were Bushrod Washington, future associate justice of the Supreme Court and nephew of George Washington; and Spencer Roane, who would ultimately sit on the Virginia Court of Appeals—Virginia's highest court—and become Chief Justice Marshall's Virginia nemesis. Although Marshall was a diligent student, his law notebook shows evidence that his fancy occasionally turned to thoughts of the lovely Polly Ambler: Marshall frequently scribbled Polly's name on various pages of his notebook (Smith 1996, 80). Despite Marshall's brief course of study at William & Mary, he was called to the bar on August 28, 1780, in Fauquier County, Virginia.

On resigning his commission in 1781, Marshall was elected to serve in the Virginia Assembly. Marshall's experiences in the military and in the state assembly shaped his later nationalistic outlook. Years later, Marshall said that

> I partook largely of the sufferings and feelings of the army and brought with me into civil life an ardent devotion to its interests. My immediate entrance into the state legislature opened to my view the causes which had been chiefly instrumental in augmenting those sufferings, and the general tendency of state politics convinced me that no safe and permanent remedy could be found but in more efficient and better organized central government. (White 1988, 369)

Lawyer and Legislator

Initially, Marshall's somewhat careless appearance hampered his practice. Eventually, however, his brilliant legal ability shone through and his practice prospered, as an often-repeated story illustrates. A man came to Richmond to seek the services of a "city lawyer." When he asked an innkeeper who was the ablest lawyer in Richmond, the innkeeper informed the country gentleman that John Marshall was the finest lawyer in town. The gentleman sought out Marshall, but Marshall's appearance caused him second thoughts, and he retained a lawyer who wore a powdered wig. The gentleman then went to court and saw Marshall in action. Realizing that he had made a mistake, he asked Marshall to take his case, sheepishly explaining that he came to Richmond with $100, and that the first attorney had taken $95 as the fee. Nevertheless, Marshall agreed without hesitation to accept the case for $5 (Baker 1974, 77).

At first, like many young lawyers of the time, Marshall struggled financially. But his growing reputation, as well as his family connections, served him well in his political and legal career. Marshall was recognized as a rising star and attracted the kind of help given to promising young men. Marshall's seat in the Virginia Assembly provided him with a small salary. In 1782, Marshall was also selected for a position on the Virginia Council of State, largely due to the influence of his wealthy father-in-law, Jacquelin Ambler. Marshall's cousin, EDMUND RANDOLPH—the first U.S. attorney general and governor of Virginia—allowed Marshall to use his office until Marshall's practice picked up. It was through this gesture that Marshall indirectly inherited the law practice of his cousin and future political antagonist, Thomas Jefferson (Smith 1996, 90–91). In 1774, when Jefferson became governor of Virginia, he turned his practice over to Edmund Randolph; in 1786 when Randolph was elected governor, the entire practice then devolved to Marshall. John Amber, Polly's cousin, and by then patriarch of the Amber family, also retained Marshall in 1784 to serve as counsel for the family. With the richest man in Virginia as a client and friend, Marshall attracted even more new clients (Smith 1996, 101). James Monroe, himself a rising star in the Virginia political firmament, and a longtime friend of Marshall's, retained Marshall to handle his financial affairs on Monroe's election to the Continental Congress.

Marshall's military service also generated legal business. Revolutionary War veterans enlisted Marshall's services in getting their back pay and obtaining their pensions. Records indicate that Marshall's military service enabled him to secure many a soldier's pension (Baker 1974, 79).

But Marshall's community standing did not prevent him from following the dictates of his conscience. A free black woman named Angelica Barnet was sentenced to death for the killing of a white intruder. She was subsequently raped and impregnated by the jailer while awaiting execution. First Polly, then later John, signed a petition for Barnet's pardon, which was eventually granted (Baker 1974, 101).

The Fairfax Estate

By far the longest-running litigation in which Marshall was involved concerned the disposition of the estate of Lord Fairfax. When Lord Fairfax died in 1781, he owned some five million acres encompassing the equivalent of seven Virginia counties and six counties in what would become West Virginia. Thomas Marshall had surveyed much of the land and was the superintendent of Leeds Manor; both Marshall and George Washington counted Lord Fairfax among their friends. After Fairfax's death, the disposition of his land generated decades of litigation and had a tremendous impact on

John Marshall's reputation and practice. One contemporary lawyer stated that the Fairfax litigation ensured Marshall's position "at the head of the practice" (Smith 1996, 107). Not until Marshall was well into his tenure as chief justice would the matter of Lord Fairfax's estate finally be settled.

Marshall's initial involvement with the Fairfax lands came in the 1786 case of *Hite v. Fairfax*. It was Marshall's first major case and his first appearance before the Virginia Court of Appeals (Smith 1996, 105). At issue was who held title to the land in Virginia originally granted to Lord Fairfax. Marshall represented the Fairfax descendants as co-counsel, and was opposed by the considerable legal talents of Edmund Randolph and John Taylor of Caroline. The Court ruled in favor of the *Hite* claim, but in doing so it reaffirmed Fairfax's ability to convey title to the vast tract. Therefore, in effect it was a major step in quieting title of all those who had taken from Lord Fairfax or his descendants.

Marshall himself had a great desire to invest in the Fairfax property. Lord Fairfax's heir, Denny Martin Fairfax, lived in England and was anxious to sell the property before it escheated to Virginia. (During and after the Revolution, many states passed laws confiscating the estates of Loyalists and of British subjects residing abroad.) In 1794, the state had sold a 788-acre tract of the Fairfax land to David Hunter. In April 1795, Marshall represented Martin by filing suit to stop the sale to Hunter, claiming that Virginia did not have title to the land it was attempting to convey. The state court ruled in favor of Martin and Marshall—Judge St. George Tucker held that Hunter must initiate proceedings to clear title before the sale could be effected. Marshall, confident of his ability to defend the suit, immediately dispatched his brother James to England to negotiate a sale of 215,000 acres of the land. In doing so, Marshall thus created a direct conflict of interest, which by modern professional ethics standards would have rendered him unable to continue representing Martin, but such practices were not uncommon in Marshall's day.

Several county courts held that the state could proceed with the sale. To make matters worse, the Eleventh Amendment—which prohibited citizens of states and foreign countries from suing one of the United States in federal court—was pending. Quickly, Marshall filed suit against Hunter in federal court in April 1795; in June, a federal circuit court ruled in favor of Denny Martin Fairfax. Hunter appealed, and in 1816 the Marshall Supreme Court (minus the chief justice, who recused himself) finally settled the matter in *Martin v. Hunter's Lessee*. In the meantime, Marshall returned to the Virginia House of Delegates in 1796 and was able to effect a settlement in which Marshall and his brother received 50,000 acres of the estate (Smith 1996, 166–168).

Statesman and Lawyer

As soon as his position among the leaders of the Virginia state bar seemed all but assured, events compelled Marshall to resume a measure of public service. Daniel Shay's 1786 rebellion alerted Marshall to the immediate need for constitutional reforms to ensure a central government adequate to preserving the Union. Marshall wrote of the revolt, "[It] cast a deep shade over that bright prospect which the Revolution in America and the establishment of our free governments had opened to the votaries of liberty throughout the world" (Corwin 1933, 318). Though not a delegate to the Philadelphia Convention in 1787, Marshall was a member of the Virginia ratifying convention. His speeches defending the new federal court system are testament to Marshall's capable legal mind, as well as his skill as a persuasive advocate. Once Virginia ratified the Constitution, Marshall retired from the state legislature and returned to the full-time practice of law; he even rejected an appointment as U.S. attorney for Virginia in 1789.

That same year, Marshall's account book indicated that he served more than three hundred clients, most of whom he represented in some sort of litigation (Smith 1996, 145). Marshall was joined by PATRICK HENRY on two cases, thus constituting a veritable eighteenth-century "Dream Team": a case of infanticide and a case regarding the collection of debts owed the British. The first involved a flurry of rumor, innuendo, and insinuation that shocked Virginia society. Richard Randolph was called before a grand jury to answer for his alleged involvement with his sister-in-law Nancy Randolph and murder of the infant allegedly produced by their taboo affair. Henry's examination of the witnesses coupled with Marshall's ordered closing arguments resulted in no charges being brought against Richard Randolph (Smith 1996, 153). Some years later, in 1815, Nancy revealed that the baby, who had died shortly after being born, was that of her fiancé, Theordoric Randolph, who died shortly after conceiving the child with Nancy.

Henry and Marshall's other dual appearance concerned the disposition of Virginians' debts owed to British creditors. At the end of the American Revolution, American debtors owed some five million pounds sterling to British creditors—almost half of it owed by Virginians. These debts caused considerable friction in relations between the two countries after the war. Although the 1783 Treaty of Paris provided for the recovery of such debts, Virginia initially allowed debtors to pay sums to the state treasury. When the currency depreciated, many shrewd Virginians—including Washington and Jefferson, the Randolphs, and a number of other monied citizens—seized on this loophole. In addition, Virginia passed a law totally barring recovery by the British in Virginia state courts. Marshall served as counsel for nearly all of the defendants, who ended up being sued in federal courts. Marshall and Henry served as counsel all the way to the Supreme Court, but they lost the case of *Ware v. Hylton*, which held that the terms of the Treaty of Paris were controlling and Virginia's debt sequestration statute was null and void (Smith 1996, 158). Marshall's skill in prosecuting the litigation, however, overshadowed the fact that he lost the case. One observer stated that "the discussion was one of the most brilliant exhibitions ever witnessed at the Bar of Virginia." Another stated that "Marshall . . . excelled himself in sound sense and argument, which you know is saying an immensity" (Smith 1996, 157).

Prolegomenon to Greatness

After refusing several federal posts, Marshall finally accepted a post in 1797 as minister to France, where he became enmeshed in the notorious XYZ Affair. In 1800, he agreed to be John Adams's secretary of state, and eventually, in 1801, chief justice of the United States, a post he held until his death. Although Marshall's reputation was secured on the national stage, his legal skill and forensic powers were very much in evidence as he began his career in Virginia.

—*Christian Biswell and Brannon P. Denning*

SOURCES AND SUGGESTIONS FOR FURTHER READING

Baker, Leonard. *John Marshall: A Life in the Law*. New York: Macmillan, 1974.

Corwin, Edward S. "John Marshall." In *Dictionary of American Biography*, edited by Dumas Malone. New York: Scribner, 1933, 315

Smith, Jean Edward. *John Marshall: Definer of a Nation*. New York: Henry Holt, 1996.

White, G. Edward. *The Marshall Court and Cultural Change, 1815–1835*. New York: Macmillan, 1988.

MARSHALL, THURGOOD

(1908–1993)

THURGOOD MARSHALL

Attorneys who argued the case against segregation stand together smiling in front of the U.S. Supreme Court building after the high tribunal ruled that segregation in public schools is unconstitutional. Left to right are: George E. C. Hayes, Washington, D.C.; Thurgood Marshall, special counsel for the NAACP; and James Nabrit Jr., professor and attorney at law at Howard University in Washington, 17 May 1954. (Bettmann/Corbis)

THURGOOD MARSHALL MAY WELL BE THE SINGLE MOST IMPORTANT lawyer of the twentieth century. During his years as legal counsel of the National Association for the Advancement of Colored People (NAACP), Marshall argued thirty-two cases before the Supreme Court and participated in eleven others. His life's work literally defined the movement of race relations in the United States throughout the twentieth century:

It was Marshall who ended legal segregation in the United States. He won Supreme Court victories breaking the color line in housing, transportation, and voting, all of which overturned the "separate but equal" apartheid of American life in the first half of the [twentieth] century. It was Marshall who won the most important legal case of the century, *Brown v. Board of Education*, ending the legal separation of black and white children in public schools. The success of the *Brown* case sparked the 1960s civil rights movement, led to the increased number of black high school and college graduates and the incredible rise of the black middle class in both numbers and political power in the second half of the century. (Williams 1998, xv–xvi)

Thoroughgood Marshall was born in Baltimore, Maryland, on July 2, 1908, the second son of William Canfield Marshall, a sleeping car porter, and Norma Williams Marshall, a teacher. Thurgood (his name was changed officially in 1914) was raised in an activist African-American community in racially divided Baltimore. He received his diploma from the segregated Frederick Douglass High School in 1925. Five years later, he obtained the A.B. degree, graduating with honors from the all-male, all-black Lincoln University in Oxford, Pennsylvania. Statutorily barred from admittance to the University of Maryland law school because of the state's segregation policy, Marshall matriculated at the all-black Howard University School of Law in Washington, D.C., in 1930. There Marshall studied under CHARLES HAMILTON HOUSTON, the first African-American person to win a case before the Supreme Court. Houston consistently encouraged his students to use the law as a medium to eliminate the racist segregation system of Jim Crow. As Marshall later put it, Houston was "hell bent on establishing a cadre of Negro lawyers, dedicated to fighting for equal rights" (Tushnet 1994, 6). After three years, Marshall earned the LL.B. degree, finishing first in his class. That same year he was admitted to the Maryland bar and opened a private practice in Baltimore.

Marshall's practice developed slowly, in part due to his involvement with the NAACP. Marshall was recruited to assist the organization by his former law school professor, and head of the NAACP's legal office, Charles Hamilton Houston. To introduce Marshall to the enormity of the civil rights battle—and to bring him face to face with bitter segregationists—Houston took Marshall on a trip through the South. Houston wanted his protégé to understand that the lawyers' "toolbox" included more than the rules of the courts; "it also included an appreciation of the social setting in which the law operated. Lawyers therefore had to be able to explain to lawmakers how rules actually operated in society, and to do that they had to draw on the information that sociologists, historians, and other students of social life made available" (Tushnet 1994, 6). In 1934, inspired by Houston's commitment and methodology, Marshall relinquished his private practice and became chief counsel for the Baltimore branch of the NAACP.

The following year, Marshall won his first major civil rights case, *Murray v. Pearson* (1935), in which a state court ordered that a qualified African-American man—who had applied to the University of Maryland law school and been rejected on account of his race—be admitted. (Marshall later said that he wanted to "get even" with Maryland for not letting him go to its law school.) Supervised closely by Houston, *Murray* was Marshall's "real introduction to the careful practice of law." For the next two years, Marshall and Houston—teacher and student—worked side by side. To give credit to Marshall as a great lawyer is to recognize Houston as a great teacher. From Houston, Marshall "learned that the events in the courtroom were only a small part of the trial lawyer's work. Far more important, he had to develop the facts through intensive investigation. Once the facts were in hand, Marshall learned, the trial lawyer had to be sure that they were admitted into evidence. Even if the trial judge ruled against him, as would frequently happen in civil rights cases, Marshall had to be sure that he developed a record that would allow an appellate court to reverse the trial judge. There was nothing flashy about this part of the job . . ." (Tushnet 1994, 11). This methodology served Marshall the lawyer well for the next three decades.

In 1936, Marshall joined the national staff of the NAACP, where he served in a number of positions: assistant special counsel (1936–1938), chief legal counsel (1938–1940), chief legal counsel, Legal Defense and Educational Fund, Inc. (1940–1950), and director–chief legal counsel, Legal Defense and Educational Fund, Inc. (1950–1961). During this twenty-five-year period, Marshall traveled throughout the country protecting the rights of African-Americans. He represented African-Americans who had been the victims of discrimination in employment, housing, and transportation. He spoke up for African-Americans accused of murder, theft, and rape. He counseled African-Americans in tenant-landlord disputes, labor disputes, and courts-martial. And he fought against coerced confessions, jury exclusion, and witness tampering. When clear racial overtones prejudiced a case, Marshall and the NAACP were prepared to provide assistance.

Marshall's courtroom style was persuasive but not forceful. One associate noted that Marshall did not "purport to be a legal scholar, but [was] an effective lawyer because he [had] common sense and a good instinct for facts." Marshall knew full well that the success of any case was more dependent on preparation than on courtroom theatrics. Accordingly, Marshall spent many hours conducting research, evaluating precedents, consulting with witnesses, and writing and rewriting briefs (Bland 1973, 8). At trial, the fruits of his labor, masterful in content, were delivered in his hallmark style: straightforward and plainspoken. "Marshall's trial work was rarely the thrust-and-parry dramatized in film; much more often it was the patient compiling of facts to present to hostile juries and judges. His oral advocacy was commonsense and down to earth, capturing the heart of the moral cause for transforming civil rights law" (Tushnet 1994, vii). Marshall preferred the power of the argument to the power of the delivery.

Beginning in 1938, Marshall participated either by direct argument or by assisting in the preparation of the legal brief in forty-three cases brought before the U.S. Supreme Court by the NAACP. In thirty-two cases he participated by direct argument; he was victorious in twenty-nine. In eleven other cases Marshall assisted in the preparation of the legal brief. These cases constitute much of the significant civil rights litigation of the twentieth century. During Marshall's tenure at the NAACP, the Supreme Court decided a host of cases with great constitutional and societal significance. Perhaps the most important were those in which the Court struck down "whites only" primaries, restrictive property covenants, and segregated public educational facilities: *Smith v. Allwright* (1944), *Shelley v. Kramer* (1948), and *Brown v. Board of Education* (1954). In each, Marshall was the mastermind behind the litigation strategy.

In Texas (and many other southern states) the Democratic party prohibited African-Americans from voting in primary elections. (The Supreme Court had upheld this practice in 1935.) This exclusion was critical, for in the one-party South the victor in the Democratic primary was, with rare exception, the victor in the general election. In 1941, however, in a case unrelated to race, the Court ruled that primaries were "an integral part" of the political process. Marshall saw an opening: "[If] state law . . . made the primary an integral part of the procedure of choice [then] . . . in fact the primary effectively control[led] the choice of Senators and Representatives. . . . The legal consequence of this . . . [was] that the right to vote in Texas primary elections [was] secured by the [Fifteenth Amendment]." When a "whites only" primary was once again challenged before the Supreme Court, the justices accepted Marshall's argument. Thus, *Smith v. Allwright* (1944) overthrew the South's "white primary," permitting greater participation for African-Americans in the political process. WILLIAM H. HASTIE (who later became the first African-American judge on the U.S. Court of Appeals), Carter Wesley, and George M. Johnson assisted Marshall in this case.

A restrictive property covenant prohibited a certain class of persons from owning or occupying land. (In 1926, the Supreme Court had sustained the use of such covenants.) These covenants, often racially motivated, limited the supply of housing available to African-Americans. As such, Marshall committed the NAACP to a crusade against these agreements. Marshall opted to use sociological and economic material as the principal point of at-

Litigators as Judges

This book includes a number of lawyers who served as justices on the U.S. Supreme Court. They include JOHN MARSHALL (who, although he was a leading member of the Richmond bar prior to his appointment to the U.S. Supreme Court, is partly included in this volume because of his dramatic impact on American law as chief justice of the Court), LOUIS BRANDEIS, ROBERT JACKSON, JOHN MARSHALL HARLAN II, THURGOOD MARSHALL, and RUTH BADER GINSBURG. A number of other justices—for example, Roger Taney, Hugo Black, and Lewis Powell—were also known as outstanding trial attorneys and might very well have been included had someone else drawn up the list or were it somewhat longer. Indeed, at the Constitutional Convention, Benjamin Franklin had suggested that judges should be selected, as in Scotland, by fellow lawyers "who always selected the ablest of the profession in order to get rid of him, and share his practice [among themselves]" (Farrand 1937, 1:120).

Although the U.S. Constitution outlines minimal qualifications for members of Congress and the president, it specifies no formal requirements for federal judges and justices other than appointment by the president and confirmation by the U.S. Senate (Vile and Perez-Reilly 1991, 198). In this century, a law degree has become an understood prerequisite (earlier, justices were sometimes self-educated, often "reading law" under another experienced attorney rather than attending law school). Although some appointees to the U.S. Supreme Court have distinguished themselves in trial work, others have engaged in other kinds of legal practice.

The central debate among scholars regarding appointments to the U.S. Supreme Court has centered not on the trial experience of appointees but rather on their prior judicial experience. One of the most famous articles on the subject was written by Supreme Court justice Felix Frankfurter, who had made his reputation before his appointment to the Court primarily as an advisor to President Franklin D. Roosevelt and as a Harvard law professor.

Frankfurter noted that many of the most outstanding justices—including John Marshall, Bushrod Washington, JOSEPH STORY, Roger Taney, Louis Brandeis, and CHARLES EVANS HUGHES—had come to the Court without prior judicial experience. He concluded that "greatness in the law is not a standardized quality" and that "judicial experience is not a prerequisite for that Court" (Murphy and Pritchett 1986, 163).

Despite Frankfurter's judgment, presidents have increasingly looked to the bench in making their appointments to the U.S. Supreme Court.

REFERENCES

Farrand, Max. *The Records of the Federal Convention of 1787*. 4 vols. New Haven: Yale University Press, 1937.

Frankfurter, Felix. "The Supreme Court in the Mirror of Justices." *University of Pennsylvania Law Review* 105 (1957): 781.

Murphy, Walter F., and C. Herman Pritchett. *Courts, Judges, and Politics: An Introduction to the Judicial Process*. 4th ed. New York: Random House, 1986.

Vile, John R., and Mario Perez-Reilly. "The U.S. Constitution and Judicial Qualifications: A Curious Omission." *Judicature* 74 (December-January 1991): 198–202.

tack. When the case was argued before the Supreme Court, thirty-eight pages of data showing the disastrous sociological and economic effects of racially segregated housing were submitted to the justices (Bland 1973, 51). But Marshall did not rely solely on sociological data. He also focused on "state action": The equal protection clause of the Fourteenth Amendment prohibited a state from denying the right to own and occupy property to any person solely because of race. This civil right was protected from invasion by a state legislative body, of course, but should be protected from invasion by a judicial body, for "the acts of state courts are those of the state itself within the meaning of the limitations of the Fourteenth Amendment." Then, using an instrument from Houston's "toolbox," Marshall noted the wreckage caused by judicial enforcement of restrictive covenants: "[It] has created a uniform pattern of unprecedented overcrowding and congestion in the housing of Negroes and an appalling deterioration of their dwelling conditions. The extension and aggravation of slum conditions have in turn resulted in a serious rise in disease, crime, vice, racial tension, and mob violence." Although the Court ignored most of the social data, Marshall's "state action" argument was persuasive. Although the covenants themselves constituted private behavior—activity beyond the scope of the Constitution—judicial enforcement of those covenants violated the equal protection clause. Thus, *Shelley v. Kraemer* (1948) struck down racially restrictive covenants, increasing the supply of housing available to African-Americans.

Marshall's most lasting contribution, however, came in the area of desegregating public education. Beginning in the 1930s, the NAACP brought suits in state and federal courts challenging, as violative of the equal protection clause, state-imposed racial segregation in public education. The NAACP strategy was twofold. First, seek to ensure that states in fact provided *equal* educational facilities. Marshall thus instructed local chapters of the NAACP "to conduct research, collect, collate, acquire, compile and publish facts, information, and statistics concerning education facilities and educational opportunities and the inequality in the educational facilities and educational opportunities provided for Negroes out of public funds" (Brand 1973, 73). Second, persuade the justices that "separate but equal" educational facilities were inherently unequal. Accordingly, Marshall gathered extensive sociological and psychological materials evidencing the damaging effects of segregated public schools on children of all races.

Brown v. Board of Education of Topeka, Kansas (1954) was the magnum opus of Marshall's litigation career. The NAACP's finest legal talent—JACK GREENBERG, Louis L. Redding, James Nabrit Jr., George E. C. Hayes, Robert Carter, and SPOTTSWOOD ROBINSON—assisted him. Before the Supreme Court, and opposed by JOHN W. DAVIS, former solicitor general of the United States, Marshall forcefully advanced both constitutional and sociological arguments. First, segregated public schools denied to blacks the equality of educational opportunity required by the equal protection clause. Second, segregation of African-Americans imposed on them "a badge of inferiority." To support the second assertion, Marshall introduced an array of sociological data—supported by such leading sociologists as Gunnar Myrdal, E. Franklin Frazier, and Kenneth Clark—discussing the negative effects of segregation. An appendix to Marshall's brief—a position paper entitled "The Effects of Segregation and the Consequences of Desegregation: A Social Science Statement" and supported by thirty-two leading sociologists—attested to the psychological and social damage incurred as a result of segregation. Obviously Marshall had not forgotten the important extralegal strategies taught him by Charles Hamilton Houston.

The Court's opinion read like Marshall's brief: "Education . . . is a right which must be made available to all on equal terms." Relying heavily on the sociological evidence introduced, the Court noted, "To separate [Negro children] from others . . . solely because of their race generates a feeling of inferiority as to their status in the community that may affect their hearts and minds in a way unlikely ever to be undone." The Court then concluded, in perhaps its most famous edict, "In the field of public education the doctrine of 'separate but equal' has no place. Separate educational facilities are inherently unequal."

Marshall's reliance on sociological data was later subjected to severe criticism. Nevertheless, it had been persuasive to the justices. And *Brown v. Board of Education* remains both Marshall's and the NAACP's greatest legal victory; moreover, it is perhaps the most important Supreme Court decision of the twentieth century. In 1975, Richard Kluger authored *Simple Justice,* a superb study of the desegregation efforts of Marshall and the NAACP. The book was later made into a movie.

Seven years after *Brown,* Marshall left the NAACP. In 1961, President John F. Kennedy nominated Marshall for a seat on the U.S. Court of Appeals for the Second Circuit. When a group of hostile conservative southern senators impeded his confirmation, Marshall served for a brief period under a recess appointment. The Senate eventually confirmed him on September 11, 1962, by a vote of 54 to 16. While serving on the court of appeals, Marshall authored 112 opinions, none of which was overturned.

Marshall resigned his judgeship in 1965, accepting the position of solicitor general of the United States. During his stint in the Department of Justice, Marshall argued nineteen cases for the government before the U.S. Supreme Court. In fourteen of those cases, the government prevailed, including *Harper v. Virginia Board of Education* (1966), in which the Court held that state taxes or fees that limit the right to vote were unconstitutional.

On June 13, 1967, President Lyndon B. Johnson nominated Marshall to succeed Associate Justice Tom Clark on the U.S. Supreme Court. In announcing his selection, Johnson said, "It is the right thing to do, the right time to do it, the right man and the right place." On August 30, 1967, by a vote of 69 to 11, the Senate confirmed Marshall. He thus became the first African-American to sit on the highest bench in the land. While there, Justice Marshall continued to seek remedies for the damage remaining from the nation's history of slavery and racial bias. "Justice Marshall gave a clear signal that while legal discrimination had ended, there was more to be done to advance educational opportunity for blacks and to bridge the wide canyon of economic inequity between blacks and whites" (Williams 1998, xvi). Marshall retired on June 27, 1991, at age eighty-two, having served on the high court for twenty-four years.

Marshall received numerous awards and honors, including the NAACP's highest honor—the Springarn Medal—in 1946; the Robert S. Abbott Memorial Award, for fighting to "secure basic human rights guaranteed every citizen," from the *Chicago Defender* in 1953; the Philadelphia Liberty Medal in 1992; and the American Bar Association's highest award—now appropriately named the Thurgood Marshall Award—also in 1992. He also received a number of honorary degrees from various universities.

During his lengthy civil rights career, Marshall wrote a number of articles that appeared in various publications, including *The Crisis*, the *Journal of Negro Education*, and the *Harvard Law Review*. A fair number of his speeches have also been published.

On January 24, 1993, Thurgood Marshall, at age eighty-four, died of heart failure in Bethesda, Maryland.

—*Richard A. Glenn*

Sources and Suggestions for Further Reading

Bland, Randall R. *Private Pressure on Public Law: The Legal Career of Justice Thurgood Marshall*. Port Washington, N.Y.: Kennikat Press, 1973.

Davis, Michael D., and Hunter R. Clark. *Thurgood Marshall: Warrior at the Bar, Rebel at the Bench*. New York: Birch Lane Press, 1992.

Greenberg, Jack. *Crusaders in the Courts*. New York: Basic Books, 1994.

Kluger, Richard. *Simple Justice*. New York: Alfred A. Knopf, 1975.

Marshall, Thurgood. "Equal Justice under the Law." *The Crisis* 46 (July 1939): 199–201.

———. "Reflections of the Bicentennial of the United States Constitution." *Harvard Law Review* 101 (November 1987): 1–5.

———. "The Rise and Collapse of the 'White Democratic Primary.'" *Journal of Negro Education* 26 (Summer 1957): 249–254.

———. "Summary Justice—The Negro G. I. in Korea." *The Crisis* 58 (May 1951): 297–304, 350–355.

Rowan, Carl T. *Dream Makers, Dream Breakers: The World of Justice Thurgood Marshall*. Boston: Little, Brown, 1993.

Tushnet, Mark. *Making Civil Rights Law: Thurgood Marshall and the Supreme Court, 1936–1961*. New York: Oxford University Press, 1994.

_____. *The NAACP's Legal Strategy against Segregated Education, 1925–1950*. Chapel Hill: University of North Carolina Press, 1988.

Williams, Juan. *Eyes on the Prize*. New York: Penguin Books, 1987.

_____. "Marshall's Law." *Washington Post Magazine*, 7 January 1990.

_____. *Thurgood Marshall: American Revolutionary*. New York: Random House, 1998.

MARTIN, LUTHER

(1744–1826)

LUTHER MARTIN'S DISTIN-guished legal career began in 1772, shortly before the beginning of the American Revolution, and extended to 1819 when, shortly after arguing *McCulloch v. Maryland*, Martin suffered a debilitating stroke at age seventy-one. Martin was a member of the Continental Congress and a member of the Federal Convention, and he served thirty years as Maryland's first attorney general. Luther Martin is best known for defending Aaron Burr in his famous treason trial and Supreme Court associate justice Samuel Chase in an 1805 impeachment trial. His legal acumen, vast memory, loquacity, and penchant for high-profile, difficult cases distinguish the redoubtable Martin as one of the finest lawyers in American history.

Beginnings

Little is known about Luther Martin's youth, except that he was the third of nine children and was born near New Brunswick, New Jersey, in 1744. For his education, Martin was enrolled at the College of New Jersey (later Princeton

LUTHER MARTIN
Kean Collection/Archive Photos

University). At the College of New Jersey—aptly described by Andrew Burnaby, a contemporary English traveler, as "a handsome school for the education of dissenters" (Clarkson and Jett 1970, 14)—Martin met future chief justice of the United States Oliver Ellsworth, before whom Martin would later argue many cases. Martin graduated from the College of New Jersey in 1766 and became a schoolmaster at Queen Anne's Country Free School in Queenstown, Maryland. In 1770, Luther embarked on the study of law as an apprentice, while maintaining a teaching position at an Accomack County, Virginia, grammar school, and was called to the bar in 1772.

Lawyer, Revolutionary, Framer, and Anti-Federalist

Aided by his good reputation and sound judgment, Martin's practice flourished. In recognition of his growing prominence, in 1774, Martin was elected to the Somerset County Committee of Observation and was later appointed as a delegate to the Annapolis Convention. Martin was among the first revolutionaries in predominantly Tory Somerset County, Virginia. An outspoken critic of the British government, he acquired and circulated Thomas Paine's essay *Common Sense* (Clarkson and Jett 1970, 35). Martin and British general Sir William Howe exchanged salvos in a propaganda battle waged in the *Maryland Gazette* and the *Maryland Journal*. To gain support for the revolution, Martin undertook a personal effort to distribute these exchanges in the isolated Eastern Shore counties (Clarkson and Jett 1970, 37). It was during this period that Martin formed a close relationship with another future Supreme Court associate justice, Samuel Chase. Chase, a leader of the Sons of Liberty and signer of the Declaration of Independence, recommended Martin for the position of first attorney general of Maryland. Years later, Martin would defend Chase in a politically motivated impeachment undertaken by the party of Thomas Jefferson to chasten the Federalist-controlled judiciary.

During his tenure as Maryland attorney general, Martin was a delegate to the 1787 Constitutional Convention (White 1988, 230). There, Martin earned the reputation as an "excessively voluble orator"—in one instance delivering a speech to the convention that lasted the whole of two days—and, as a consequence, he also earned the enmity of some of his fellow delegates. A persistent advocate for the small states and an opponent of a powerful central government, Martin played a part in rallying support for equal representation of small states in the Senate and argued for a single-term executive. Ironically, Martin, the opponent of a powerful central government, played a major role in drafting the supremacy clause, which makes the Constitution, laws, and treaties supreme over conflicting state laws. At the convention, Martin also exhibited a passion for human rights and civil liberties. He was vehemently opposed, on moral and philosophical grounds, to the continuation of the slave trade (Clarkson and Jett 1970, 127–128). He also advocated a federal bill of rights guaranteeing specific individual liberties. Unable to convince his fellow delegates to adopt his suggestions, Martin, along with John Francis Mercer, took leave from Philadelphia without signing the document. Subsequently, Martin publicly opposed Maryland's ratification of the new constitution, enumerating his objections in a report to the Maryland legislature printed as *The Genuine Information* (1788). Again, there is an irony in Martin's activities on behalf of the anti-Federalist cause—years later, Jefferson excoriated Martin, who had become a critic of the president, as a "federal bulldog."

Attorney General of Maryland

Martin served as Maryland's first attorney general from 1778 until 1805, gaining prominence and notoriety for his diligent efforts during his long tenure. During the war years, Martin's duties took him from county to county—libeling vessels, prosecuting loyalists for arson and treason, and prosecuting criminals. Martin resigned his post in 1805, but he served again briefly from 1818 to 1819, until he was debilitated by a stroke. In between, Martin served as chief judge of a Baltimore city court from 1813 until 1816, when that court was abolished.

It was during his last, brief tenure as attorney general that Martin delivered a two-and-a-half-day closing argument before the Supreme Court in *McCulloch v. Maryland*. Martin, then seventy-one, was one of the few members of the Philadelphia Convention still living. During his argument, Martin shrewdly used his own historical import to garner prestige for Maryland's cause and to remind the other justices of their close association with the framers' generation (White 1988, 238). Despite Martin's efforts, Maryland did not prevail. The Supreme Court held that the Constitution's necessary and proper clause empowered Congress to charter a national bank and that a state could not subsequently tax a federal bank. Albert Beveridge considered Martin's arguments in *McCulloch* to be "the last worthy of remark which that great lawyer ever made" (White 1988, 240).

Practice and Personal Life

The nascent federal judiciary created by the Constitution that Martin opposed furthered Martin's reputation as a skilled practitioner. In time, Martin would also become one of a small number of lawyers who regularly made appearances before the U.S. Supreme Court—second only, some said, to DANIEL WEBSTER. In addition to his duties as attorney general, Martin acquired a growing federal practice, which frequently took him to Boston, New York, and Philadelphia; and he remained his home state's most sought-after appellate attorney.

One span of less than ten months in 1801 and 1802 attests to Martin's reputation as a tireless litigator. During that time, Martin argued before the U.S. Supreme Court, the federal circuit court, two state general courts, the Maryland Court of Appeals, and Baltimore criminal court. Court reports indicate that between January 1 and February 5, 1802, alone, Martin argued daily in the general court, the court of appeals, and the chancery court (Clarkson and Jett 1970, 194).

Between 1808 and 1813, Martin argued more than two dozen cases before the U.S. Supreme Court (White 1988, 235). Most of these cases involved maritime law of prize, admiralty, and insurance; others touched on issues of evidence, sales, wills, property, and constitutional law (White 1988, 235). The seminal case of *Fletcher v. Peck* (1810) was among the latter (Clarkson and Jett 1970, 283). Members of the Georgia legislature had transferred millions of acres of Georgia's western lands, which include what are now Alabama and Mississippi, to several land companies. Outraged at this large-scale corruption, known as the Yazoo land scandal, voters turned out nearly the entire legislature at the polls. The new legislature repealed the sale and even publicly burned the original offending act. In the meantime, however, the land companies had sold parcels of the land to innocent third parties. Despite the self-dealing that accompanied the original sale, in which all but one legislator was said to have profited, the Supreme Court protected the contracts between the subsequent purchasers and the land companies.

Although he was an unqualified professional success, Martin's family life was tragic, a fact that might explain the alcoholism to which Martin's contemporaries made frequent reference. His wife, Maria Cresap, died young. Two of his daughters married young and against their father's will. One daughter, Maria, eventually separated from her husband, went insane, and died young. The other, Eleonora, eloped with one Richard R. Keene, precipitating a public feud between Martin and Keene, in which the father and his son-in-law traded barbs in pamphlets.

Martin's indulgences, and his penchant for unpopular causes, made him the target of jealous rivals and political opponents. One such rival, Benjamin Galloway—smarting over being bested in the courtroom by Martin, who had also disparaged Galloway's character in court—petitioned the Maryland General Assembly for the attorney general's impeachment based on Martin's many drunken court appearances (Clarkson and Jett 1970, 204). Despite the fact that the allegation was no doubt true, the house of delegates' treatment of the proposal, memorialized by the following entry in its journal, best expresses that body's esteem and affection for Martin: "On motion, the question was put, that the said letter [from Galloway] be ordered to lie on the table? Determined in the negative. Ordered, that the said letter be thrown under the table" (Clarkson and Jett 1970, 205).

Another client, a Quaker, once extracted from Martin a promise to abstain from drink during the course of the representation. At trial, Martin apparently struggled during the court's morning session, torn between keeping his word and giving his client effective assistance of counsel. As the story goes, Martin soaked a loaf of bread in brandy and then proceeded to eat the potent loaf with a fork and knife. He then proceeded to win the case that afternoon (Clarkson and Jett 1970, 281).

Chief Justice Roger Taney observed that Martin "seemed to take pleasure in showing his utter disregard of good taste and refinement in his dress and language and his mode of argument" (White 1988, 237). Joseph Story described Martin as "a singular compound of strange qualities. With a professional income of ten thousand dollars a year, he is poor and needy; generous and humane, but negligent and profuse. . . . He never seems satisfied with a single grasp of a subject; but urges himself to successive efforts, until he models and fashions it to his purpose" (White 1988, 236). Yet, despite his excesses, Martin retained the respect and esteem of his contemporaries. The redoubtable Martin's legal shrewdness, vast memory, loquacity, and penchant for controversial cases distinguished him as one of the finest lawyers in American history. Martin was also loyal to friends, as shown by his willingness to represent, without charge, Aaron Burr and Samuel Chase in two of the most politically charged trials of the early nineteenth century—both of which set important precedents that today remain part of our constitutional fabric.

The Chase Impeachment Trial

In 1804, Luther Martin went to the aid of his longtime friend and political ally, Samuel Chase. Jeffersonians schemed to use the machinery of impeachment to remove Federalist judges appointed by JOHN ADAMS and replace them with jurists more sympathetic to the Republicans. Chase, a rock-ribbed Federalist, was accused of partisan bias in the handling of several cases and was impeached.

Historians agree that Martin's arguments during Chase's Senate trial are among the finest ever delivered. (White 1988, 231; Clarkson and Jett 1970, 206). Henry Adams wrote of Martin's eloquence, "Nothing can be finer in its way than Martin's [argument]," noting "its rugged and sustained force; its strong humor, audacity, and dexterity; its even flow and simple choice of language; free from rhetoric and affections; its close and compulsive grasp of the law; [and] its good natured contempt for the obstacles put in its way"

(White 1988, 231). Martin's persuasiveness carried the day despite the determination of the prosecutors; Chase was acquitted. In a stroke, Martin deflated Republican efforts to bring the judiciary to heel, and he may have saved the independent judiciary, now regarded as an essential element of our constitutional order. The Chase trial also helped establish the principle that the machinery of impeachment should not be cranked up for purely partisan purposes. Disgusted at the failure to impeach the intemperate Chase, Jefferson later dismissed impeachment as a mere "scarecrow."

The Trial of Aaron Burr

Former vice-president Aaron Burr's treason trial, which lasted through the fall of 1807, stemmed from allegations that Burr intended to launch an attack on territory belonging to Spain, a nation with which the United States was at peace. Evidence implicating Burr came in a letter, which found its way into the hands of President Jefferson.

Martin's involvement with the Aaron Burr conspiracy began as co-counsel in the appeal of the denial of a habeas corpus motion of two of Burr's alleged coconspirators, Dr. Justus Bollman and Samuel Swartwout. Martin, with co-counsel Robert Goodloe Harper, persuaded the appellate court to discharge the two men because treason, defined in the Constitution as levying war on the United States, had not been committed in the District of Columbia.

At his trial, Burr's defense team consisted of John Wickham, EDMUND RANDOLPH, Benjamin Botts, Jack Baker, and Luther Martin. Martin, the consummate friend, provided his services free of charge and, along with four others, even gave surety for Burr's bond. Martin's trial work instilled fear in the prosecutor, George Hay, and earned Martin the everlasting enmity of President Jefferson. Martin argued the issue of whether Burr should be entitled to documents in the possession of Jefferson relating to the charge of treason. Hay so feared the unleashing of Martin's considerable talents that he wrote to Jefferson urging the immediate production of the documents (Smith 1996, 362). Hay's fears ripened when Martin forcefully argued that Jefferson must produce the documents. Chief Justice JOHN MARSHALL, who presided at Burr's trial in his capacity as a circuit judge, agreed. Martin was successful in persuading Marshall to rule that Burr was entitled to the evidence prior to the grand jury indictment and that a subpoena may be issued to any party with material evidence, including the president. Martin's arguments, which contained remarks critical of Jefferson, and Marshall's subsequent decision enraged Jefferson. Jefferson, in a letter to Hay, referred to Martin as an "unprincipled and impudent federal bulldog" and suggested that Martin too be charged with treason (Smith 1996, 363).

Martin, though drinking heavily, delivered a fourteen-hour closing argument over the course of three days with tremendous vigor. The jury quickly returned a verdict of not guilty. However, the victory came at a price to the great litigator. Martin's association with Aaron Burr cost him his reputation and his personal finances. The defense of Burr was a contributing factor to his defeat in an 1811 Maryland House of Delegates bid; shortly after the trial, a Baltimore mob burned effigies of Martin, Marshall, Burr, and an alleged coconspirator (White 1988, 234). Baltimore police had to protect the former attorney general's residence from being looted. Adding private injury to public insult, Burr—a conspiracy charge still pending against him in Ohio—fled for Europe, leaving his friend Luther Martin personally responsible for approximately twenty thousand dollars of Burr's bail (White 1988, 235).

Last Years

Later in life, when most legal careers are winding down, Martin remained a tireless and vociferous advocate at the bar. Martin's age and alcoholism apparently did not diminish his activity. One volume of *Harris Johnson's Reports*, published around the time that the seventy-one-year-old Martin argued *McCulloch*, indicated that Martin had argued 27 of the 107 cases reported in the volume, winning 15 (Clarkson and Jett 1970, 294).

Martin was a colorful character in an intolerant and critical age. Throughout his life, Martin was known as a good friend, a chronic alcoholic, and a horrible manager of his personal finances. Although he courted public approbation with his defense of Chase and Burr, he eventually regained the affections of his fellow statesmen, and he never lost the admiration of members of the bar for his legal genius. After his stroke in 1819, Martin was insolvent; in 1822, the Maryland legislature passed a resolution assessing members of the state bar five dollars to the benefit of Luther Martin. Martin even reconciled with Aaron Burr. In his final days, Martin was invited to live out his days at the New York home of Aaron Burr, where he remained until his death in 1826.

—*Christian Biswell and Brannon P. Denning*

SOURCES AND SUGGESTIONS FOR FURTHER READING

Clarkson, Paul S., and R. Samuel Jett. *Luther Martin of Maryland*. Baltimore: Johns Hopkins University Press, 1970.

Smith, Jean Edward. *John Marshall: Definer of a Nation*. New York: Henry Holt, 1996.

White, G. Edward. *The Marshall Court and Cultural Change, 1815–1835*. New York: Macmillan, 1988.

MASON, JEREMIAH

(1768–1848)

JEREMIAH MASON
Archive Photos

ALTHOUGH HE IS NOT NEARLY as well known, Jeremiah Mason was a contemporary of DANIEL WEBSTER, who counted him as one of the greatest lawyers of his day. Descended from Captain John Mason, who had led a successful campaign against the Pequot Indians in 1637, Jeremiah was born in Lebanon, Connecticut, the sixth of nine children of Jeremiah Mason, a farmer who acted as a local magistrate and a Revolutionary War militiaman, and Elizabeth Fitch. Jeremiah received little formal education, but at age fourteen he began two years of study under Master Tisdale in a public school in Lebanon about six miles away before going to Yale in 1784.

After completing his degree in four years and distinguishing himself in forensics (Mason argued against capital punishment as part of the forensic exercises connected with graduation), Mason headed for New York but was later persuaded by his father to remain in Connecticut. Mason read law with Simeon Baldwin of New Haven, who was married to a daughter of Roger Sherman,

505

and with Stephen Rowe Bradley of Westminster, Vermont, who allowed him to argue many of his cases in court even before his training was complete. Although noting that such practice detracted from his studies, Mason also observed that "it put me early in the habit of relying on my own resources, and I am inclined to think that it was on the whole advantageous to me" (Mason 1917, 20). Mason found the bar of New Hampshire to be more challenging and lucrative than that of Vermont, and he moved to Portsmouth in Rockingham County. There he married Mary Means, with whom he would have eight children. Mason spent most of his life in Portsmouth but moved to Boston in 1832.

Shortly after moving to New Hampshire, Mason served for three years as the state's attorney general. He resigned, apparently for financial reasons, and possibly because he had a preference for defense work. An ardent Federalist who appears to have enjoyed the practice of law more than holding political offices, Mason served in the U.S. Senate from 1813 to 1817 and argued against drafting state militia into federal service. He was also elected to a number of terms in the state legislature. Mason also served for a time as president of the Portsmouth branch of the U.S. National Bank. Mason turned down a number of judicial appointments, including the job of New Hampshire chief justice, apparently for financial reasons.

Although Mason represented many clients, most of the records of his arguments have been lost, and he never argued before the U.S. Supreme Court (Stites 1999, 653). In an early case involving an action of trover for two pigs, which brought him public notice, Mason made a solid argument for the unconstitutionality of a legislative action taken against his client (Gray 1907, 11).

The most famous case in which Mason was involved was the landmark *Dartmouth College Case* (1819), in which the heirs of the original trustees of the college questioned the state's attempt to alter the way the college was governed. Although Daniel Webster argued the college's case before the U.S. Supreme Court, Mason had been among those who had prepared the way in arguments before the Superior Court of New Hampshire. Mason helped advance the argument, which Webster developed further, that Dartmouth College was a private eleemosynary institution whose charter, or contract, New Hampshire had no right to alter (Stites 1972).

Another more factually dramatic case involving Mason was a Rhode Island case, *State v. Avery* (1833). Avery, a preacher who could not give an adequate account of his whereabouts at the time, had been accused of killing a young woman named Sarah Maria Cornell, who was found hanged near the town of Fall River in December of 1832 with a note in her box at the mill where she worked directing inquiries to Avery. Although circumstantial evidence pointed to Avery, it was also possible that Cornell, who was pregnant, had hanged herself and pointed to Avery in revenge for the fact that he had excommunicated her. In a seven-hour address to the jury, Mason questioned the adequacy of the evidence and won a victory on Avery's behalf. Apparently, Mason used the intense personal feelings of the community against Avery to suggest that this prejudice had unduly swayed the testimony against his client (Gray 1907, 23). During the trial, one of Avery's adherents reputedly ran into Mason's office to tell him that "An angel from Heaven appeared to me last night and declared that brother Avery is innocent!" Mason reputedly responded, "Have the angel summoned into court to testify" (Bell 1894, 504).

In another case, Mason appears to have played the part of a modern-day Johnnie Cochran in defending a will against allegations that its testator was mentally incompetent through repetitive use of a phrase that would stick in the jurors' minds. Mason repeatedly told the jury that whatever mental incapacities the testator might have had, "he had mind enough to know who he loved." The observer reported that Mason brought everything back to this point and won a verdict on behalf of his client (Gray 1907, 26).

Physically, Mason was an imposing man of considerable girth whose height was six feet six or seven inches tall and who was once likened to "the Ajax or Agamemnon" of the Rockingham bar (Plumer 1969, 179). Daniel Webster, fourteen years Mason's junior, is quoted as saying, "If you asked me who is the greatest lawyer I have known, I should say 'Chief-Justice MAR-SHALL,' but if you took me by the throat and pushed me to the wall, I should say, 'Jeremiah Mason'" (Gray 1907, 3). Similarly, another friend, Joseph Story, referred to Mason's status "in the first rank of the profession, and supported by an ability and depth and variety of learning, which have few equals, and to which no one can bear a more prompt and willing testimony than myself" (Gray 1907, 30).

A juryman who watched both Webster and Mason in action reported, "Oh, Mr. Webster is the greatest, yet Mr. Mason's clients won all the verdicts." His explanation, which might well cast light on Mason's persuasive powers was, "Oh, that was because Mr. Mason always happened to be on the right side" (Gray 1907, 25).

Most of the encomiums that Mason garnered centered on a number of characteristics. These included thorough preparation and mastery of the common law (Remini 1997, 90–91), solid reasoning, hard work, an ability to use simple unadorned speech, his powers of cross-examination, and his powers of sarcasm. Webster, who was known for his own florid rhetoric, apparently learned much from Mason's own less ornamental style. Webster seems to confirm another biographer, who noted that "he addressed the jury in the plainest language and in conversational tones, sometimes standing with one foot on the floor and the other in a chair before him" (Bell 1894, 507). Webster reported that Mason

> had a habit of standing quite near to the jury, so near that he might have laid his finger on the foreman's nose; and then he talked to them in a plain conversational way, in short sentences, and using no word that was not level to the comprehension of the least educated man on the panel. (Remini 1997, 90)

Webster also observed that

> if there be in the country a stronger intellect; if there be a mind of more native resources; if there be a vision that sees quicker, or sees deeper into whatever is intricate, or whatsoever is profound, I must confess I have not known it. (Gray 1907, 29)

John F. Lord, one of Mason's students, referred to the court as "the field of his glory." He continued,

> He had great power with the Court; for he was respectful, lucid, and always panoplied with a well prepared legal argument. When he addressed the jury on trials, he was felicitous in presenting the strong points of his case, as it were, in a nut-shell, and in hiding out of sight, as much as possible, the strong points of his opponent's case, and commenting with severity upon his weak points. No matter what the case was, he was ready for trial, with his witnesses, his brief, and his authorities at hand. He seemed to have an intuitive knowledge of character, especially jurors, and when he addressed them, adapted his speech to their comprehension, their judgment, and their consciences. He aimed to be brief, clear, and argumentative, and not prosy, florid, and declamatory. (Mason 1917, 45)

Known for his powers of cross-examination, Mason could sniff out a witness falsely dressed in borrowed clothes to look like a Puritan or fondling a paper on which an attorney had written out testimony (Gray 1907, 28). After recounting the story in which Mason had successfully cross-examined and exposed an untruthful witness, a biographer notes that Mason apparently proceeded on the "theory that no story could be fabricated so ingeniously that when pursued into remote and unlooked-for details it would not disclose inconsistencies" (Bell 1894, 505).

Mason's power of sarcasm was legendary. After commenting on the lucidity of his arguments, one author noted that the only passion, indeed, which he ever seemed to feel, was that of contempt; contempt for his opponent, his client, and his witnesses; contempt, even, for the court and the jury which he was addressing; a feeling which those who were its objects in vain strove to resist, and which was, in fact, one of the strong agencies by which he wrought them to his purpose. Speaking of the terrible power of his sarcasm, Mr. Webster said it was "not frothy or petulant, but cool and vitriolic." (Plumer 1969, 213)

As another biographer has noted, Mason's "conversation was seasoned with salt and sometimes with pepper, for he could be sarcastic outside of the court as well as before a jury" (Gray 1907, 33). Once, listening to negative comments about a judge he despised, Mason noted,

> You should not be too hard on ———. He has twice as much to do as any other Judge. Other Judges have to consider "What ought I to do." But ——— has also to consider, "Shall I do it." (Gray 1907, 3)

Mason was known for working long hours. He appears to have served as counsel in two-thirds of the cases before the New Hampshire courts during his tenure there (Gray 1907, 16). Similarly, John F. Lord, who served as a student in Mason's office, noted in a letter that "the number of original entries he made at every session of court was usually more than of all the other attorneys of Portsmouth and more than three times as many as any other lawyer in the county; and he was employed in the defence of every important suit." Referring in this same letter to Mason as "a peace-maker," Lord, however, also noted that "Mr. Mason magnified his position by exerting all his influence to prevent litigation, or the commencement of suits upon mere quibbles, or for the purpose of procrastination, or to gratify personal vindictiveness, or retaliation" (Gray 1907, 28).

Mason died in Boston in 1848 of a stroke, approximately ten years after retiring from active practice. His wife, to whom he had been deeply devoted, lived until 1858.

—*John R. Vile*

Sources and Suggestions for Further Reading

Bell, Charles. *The Bench and Bar of New Hampshire*. Boston: Houghton Mifflin, 1894.

Gray, John Chipman. "Jeremiah Mason." In *Great American Lawyers*, edited by William D. Lewis. Philadelphia: John C. Winston, 1907, 3:3–36.

Mason, Jeremiah. *Memoir, Autobiography and Correspondence of Jeremiah Mason*. Kansas City, Mo.: Lawyer's International, 1917.

Plumer, William, Jr. *Life of William Plumer.* New York: Da Capo Press, 1969.

Remini, Robert. *Daniel Webster: The Man and His Time.* New York: W. W. Norton, 1997.

Stites, Francis N. "Mason, Jeremiah." In *American National Biography,* edited by John A. Garraty and Mark C. Carnes. Vol. 14. New York: Oxford University Press, 1999, x:652–653.

————. *Private Interest & Public Gain: The Dartmouth College Case, 1819.* Amherst: University of Massachusetts Press, 1972.

MOTLEY, CONSTANCE BAKER

(1921–)

CONSTANCE BAKER MOTLEY
Library of Congress

CONSTANCE BAKER MOTLEY, the United States' first African-American female federal judge, was born in New Haven, Connecticut, on September 14, 1921. Her parents, Willoughby Alva Baker and Rachel Huggins Baker, had recently immigrated to the United States from the island of Nevis in the West Indies, and her father became a chef for a Yale University fraternity. She married real estate and insurance broker Joel Wilson Motley Jr. in 1946, and they had one child, Joel Wilson Motley III.

Motley attended New Haven public schools as a child, but despite academic success, her parents lacked the money to send her to college. Thus, she began working for the National Youth Administration, and soon she became president of the New Haven Negro Youth Council. It was at this time that one of her public speeches was observed by a wealthy local businessman and contractor, Clarence Blakeslee. Blakeslee was so impressed that he subsequently paid for her higher education.

Beginning her undergraduate studies at Fisk University in Nashville, Motley ultimately received her bachelor's degree in economics from New York University in 1943. She then studied law at Columbia University Law School. Graduating near the top of her class, she received her law degree in 1946. Yet, it was while she was a student at Columbia that she began her work for the National Association for the Advancement of Colored People's (NAACP's) Legal Defense and Educational Fund. On graduation, she declined an attractive offer from a Wall Street law firm and was hired instead as a full-time law clerk by THURGOOD MARSHALL. This would prove to be the beginning of a career at the Legal Defense Fund that would span two very full and momentous decades, beginning in 1945. Stately in appearance, as well as brilliant and forceful in presentation, Constance Motley was the consummate litigator. And this consummate litigator had now found her niche.

Barely out of law school, she headed for Mississippi to begin her fight for civil rights. In Mississippi, she traveled much of the time with co-counsel Robert Carter. As the two litigated across the state, they were subjected to their full share of racial segregation. Unlike Connecticut, and more like her years at Fisk University in Tennessee, Motley came face-to-face with the degradation of Jim Crow restrictions on such decisions as where she could eat and where she could room.

Motley's very first civil rights trial involved assisting lead counsel Robert Carter in a locally unpopular 1949 challenge to racially unequal teacher and administrator pay in the nation's poorest state, Mississippi. Not choosing to challenge the Jim Crow education system per se at this point, the NAACP instead sued to make separate more equal. Using the Fourteenth Amendment's equal protection clause, they filed suit in Jackson federal court, arguing that African-American teachers and administrators teaching at all-black schools should be guaranteed the same pay as their white counterparts.

The case was filed as a class-action suit on behalf of all the state's African-American teachers and funded largely by the Negro Teachers Association. Their first challenge, however, was to locate individuals willing to be the named plaintiffs. No sooner had Jess Brown agreed, than he was fired from his teaching position. The trial itself took place beneath a large mural depicting life in the antebellum South. White women were dressed in frilly blouses and silk bonnets, while their white male counterparts wore high silk hats and cutaway coats. Meanwhile, black men and women stood next to bales of cotton, with the black men in farm work clothes and the black women dressed like Aunt Jemima. The case was ultimately thrown out on the basis of a jurisdictional technicality, and the U.S. Supreme Court refused to review the decision.

Before she was finished, however, Motley would participate in virtually every significant civil rights case from 1954 through 1965. Armed primarily with the equal rights and due process clauses of the Fourteenth Amendment, she and her fellow attorneys at the Legal Defense Fund challenged segregating Jim Crow laws and policies across the South. They defended arrested Freedom Riders, for example, as well as many of those arrested in various sit-in demonstrations. In addition, she and Fund attorneys represented Martin Luther King Jr. and other civil rights leaders actively involved in the nonviolent struggle for equal rights. They also mounted a defense in federal court for hundreds of Birmingham students suspended from school for participating in local civil rights protests.

In the realm of school desegregation, Motley helped write the Legal Defense Fund's briefs in the two *Brown v. Board of Education* (1954) cases. It was the *Brown* decision that finally laid to rest the principle that "separate but equal" public facilities could actually be legally equal, although its enforcement was to be painstakingly slow. She then proceeded to help the NAACP press for what circuit court judge Harvey Johnsen referred to as totally "disestablishing" segregated school systems, as opposed to merely opening the doors of white schools to a few African-American students.

Motley's legal efforts also helped integrate the University of Texas Law School through her work in the *Sweatt v. Painter* case (1950); she was equally as successful in *Hawkins v. Board of Control,* integrating the law school at the University of Florida. In addition, she helped write the Legal Defense Fund's brief in *McLaurin v. Oklahoma* (1950), which ultimately barred intraschool segregation. Other school desegregation efforts included the often physically perilous attempts to enter Autherine Lucy and Polly Ann Hudson into the University of Alabama (*Lucy v. Adams* [1955]), James Meredith into the University of Mississippi (*Meredith v. Fair*), Harvey Gantt into Clemson College (*Clemson Agricultural School of South Carolina v. Gantt*), and both Charlayne Hunter Gault and Hamilton Holmes into the University of Georgia (*Holmes v. Danner* [1961]).

When Thurgood Marshall left the Legal Defense Fund in 1961, this opened the door for Motley to present arguments before the U.S. Supreme Court. Among her crowning achievements was winning nine of the ten cases she argued before the nation's highest judicial body.

In *Hamilton v. Alabama* (1961), an African-American man named Charles Clarence Hamilton was accused of breaking and entering at night with the intent to ravish, at that time a possible capital offense. Nevertheless, despite the high stakes, his right to counsel was denied at arraignment, a critical juncture in any trial, as that is the opportunity to make key motions, for example, to challenge the racial makeup of the grand jury that brought the indictment.

Justice William O. Douglas wrote for the Court's majority, overturning the conviction due to this denial of counsel. In his opinion, Douglas emphasized the Court's previous decision in *Powell v. Alabama* (1932), in which the court stated unequivocally in a unanimous decision that a defendant in a capital case "required the guiding hand of counsel at every step in

Clara Shortridge Foltz

Among the remarkable speeches collected in a recent book highlighting notable closing arguments is a speech by Clara Shortridge Foltz delivered in 1889 or 1890 in defense of an unknown Italian defendant accused of arson. Foltz, a mother of five whose husband had abandoned her, had studied under an attorney, drafted and successfully lobbied for a bill permitting women to practice law in California, and had in 1878, at age twenty-nine, passed an examination to become California's first woman attorney. She had subsequently become influential in the movement for public defenders.

Colonel Thetas Stonehill, a Confederate veteran, was serving as prosecutor of the Italian immigrant, but he apparently focused less on the defendant than on her attorney. During his closing, he said,

> SHE IS A WOMAN. She cannot be expected to reason; God Almighty decreed her limitations, but you can reason, and you must use your reasoning faculties against this young woman. (Lief, Caldwell, and Bycel 1998, 216)

Responding in kind, Foltz ridiculed the prosecutor's appeal to prejudice and responded proudly to the accusation by pointing to the fact that she had raised five children and by appealing to the jury "in the name of the mothers who nursed you, and of the wives and maidens who look love into your eyes." Noting that the prosecutor had called her a "lady lawyer," she noted,

> I am sorry I cannot return the compliment, but I cannot. I never heard anybody call him any kind of a lawyer at all. (Lief, Caldwell, and Bycel 1998, 220)

Asking that she be judged as a lawyer and not as a woman, Foltz said,

> I am neither to be bullied out or worn out. I ask no special privileges and expect no favors, but I think it only fair that those who have had better opportunities than I, who have had fewer obstacles to surmount and fewer difficulties to contend with should meet me on even ground, upon the merits of law and fact without this everlasting and incessant reference to sex—reference that in its very nature is uncalled for and which is as unprofessional as it is unmanly. (Lief, Caldwell, and Bycel 1998, 220)

Reference

Lief, Michael S., H. Mitchell Caldwell, and Ben Bycel. *Ladies and Gentlemen of the Jury: Greatest Closing Arguments in Modern Law.* New York: Scribner, 1998.

---

the proceeding against him. Without it, though he be not guilty, he faces the danger of conviction because he does not know how to establish his innocence."

In *Turner v. Memphis* (1962), Motley and the Legal Defense Fund challenged Tennessee's segregation law when Carl Rowan, then U.S. ambassador to Finland, was refused service at an airport restaurant on his way through Memphis. Jessie Turner, a local NAACP official, filed the suit. The

Supreme Court found that the law blatantly violated the Fourteenth Amendment's equal protection clause, and they ordered the district court to enjoin enforcement in this case.

Motley also appealed on behalf of five different individuals arrested for lunch counter sit-ins, and she succeeded in getting all five convictions overturned (*Gober v. Birmingham* [1963], *Shuttlesworth v. Birmingham* [1969], *Bouie v. Columbia* [1964], *Barr v. Columbia* [1964], and *Lupper v. Arkansas* [1965]). The *Lupper* case commenced just before passage of the hotly contested 1964 Civil Rights Act, and Motley referred to it as "the most difficult case I argued."

Lastly, she successfully argued *Watson v. Memphis* (1963), wherein the city of Memphis was ordered to accelerate the desegregation process for its city parks. Then, she was comparably successful in *Calhoun v. Latimer* (1963), this time succeeding in having Atlanta's school desegregation efforts sent back to the district court to be reviewed in light of the two *Brown* decisions, after the school district tried to get by through merely amending its student assignment policy to allow for free transfers.

The only case Motley lost before the nation's top court was *Swain v. Alabama* (1965). In its decision, the Court upheld the principle of preemptory challenges, whereby litigators can strike a set number of potential jurists without having to show cause. In this particular case, a prosecutor used his preemptory challenges to eliminate all African-Americans from the jury of an African-American man accused of raping a white woman. Such a use of preemptory challenges and the subsequent all-white juries for African-American defendants was a practice that had been going on for years in that particular county. Nevertheless, the Court ruled that there was still not enough evidence of discriminatory intent to warrant throwing out the subsequent conviction, let alone the practice of preemptory challenges itself, even though such challenges are fraught with the danger of being used for thinly veiled racist purposes. Twenty years later, however, in its *Batson v. Kentucky* (1986) decision, the Supreme Court vindicated Motley by significantly moderating its earlier ruling in *Swain*.

In a 1980 interview, U.S. Supreme Court justice William O. Douglas classified Constance Motley as one of the top ten appellate attorneys he heard argue in his long tenure on the federal bench. After U.S. attorney general Ramsey Clark heard her present one of her cases before the Supreme Court, he promptly recommended that President Lyndon Johnson appoint her to the federal bench. She was initially nominated for a position on the second circuit of the U.S. Court of Appeals, but the president was forced to withdraw the nomination when considerable opposition arose, apparently at least in part because she was a woman, and an African-American woman at that. Among other things, however, Senator James Eastland of Mississippi branded her a Communist, based on individuals she had associated with in her student days.

Such discrimination plagued Motley for much of her legal career. For example, judges and opposing attorneys often refused to address her as "Mrs. Motley," instead referring to her as "Constance" or "Connie" if they called her anything at all. In addition, some federal judges actually refused to face her when she argued cases in their appellate courts. Even when she sat on the bench herself, she was still openly insulted by some of the other federal jurists.

In 1964, she left the Legal Defense Fund and won a seat in the New York Senate, the first African-American woman to sit in that body. A year later she was elected borough president in Manhattan, where she was the first woman borough president and the first woman to sit on the New York Board of Estimates, a governing body composed of the city's five borough presidents.

President Johnson finally made her the nation's first African-American female federal judge in 1966, successfully appointing her to the U.S. District Court in southern New York. She became the district's chief judge in 1982 and then a senior judge in 1986.

Constance Motley received numerous honorary recognitions in the course of her life. Among these were Hobart and William Smith College's Elizabeth Blackwell Award, the New York Women's Bar Association's Florence E. Allen Award, and her induction into the National Women's Hall of Fame. She also served on the board of trustees for New York University and received honorary doctorates from more than twenty colleges and universities, including Yale, Brown, Smith, Fordham, Howard, Spelman, and Morehouse.

—*Marcus Pohlmann*

Sources and Suggestions for Further Reading

Bass, Jack. *Unlikely Heroes*. New York: Simon & Schuster, 1981.

Lowery, Charles, and John Marszalek, eds. *Encyclopedia of African-American Civil Rights: From Emancipation to the Present*. New York: Greenwood Press, 1992.

Motley, Constance Baker. *Equal Justice under Law*. New York: Farrar, Straus & Giroux, 1998.

_____. "My Personal Debt to Thurgood Marshall." *Yale Law Journal* (November 1991).

MULLEN, ARTHUR

(1873–1938)

ARTHUR MULLEN
Nebraska State Historical Society

ALTHOUGH HE ARGUED ONLY two cases before the Supreme Court, Arthur Mullen joins the ranks of the great litigators because of the lasting influence of his actions. Mullen gained recognition during his lifetime for his participation with the Democratic National Committee, his arguments before the U.S. Supreme Court in *Shallenberger v. First State Bank of Holstein* (1911) and *Meyer v. Nebraska* (1923), and for the continuing influence of the Court's decision in *Meyer*.

Born in Kingston, Ontario, Canada, in May 1873, Mullen was educated in Nebraska public schools before reading for the law at the University of Michigan. He served as the county attorney of Holt County, Nebraska, from 1901 to 1907, and as attorney general of Nebraska from 1910 to 1911 and considered himself a product of the American West. He also served as secretary of the Nebraska Tornado Committee in 1913. He became active in statewide politics in 1908 when he served as manager of the Nebraska campaign for William Jennings Bryan, the Democratic presidential candidate (he later changed his views of Bryan, whom he believed had deserted the progressive movement) (Garraty and Carnes 1999, 72). Mullen served as a member of the Democratic National Committee from 1916 to 1920 and from 1924 to 1935 (Marquis 1938, 1823). From 1932 to 1934, he served as vice chairman of the National Democratic Campaign Committee, and he acted as the floor leader of the Roosevelt contingent of the committee's 1932 convention in Chicago. Mullen was a prominent Roman Catholic layman (Ross 1994, 4), whose most forceful advocacy was made on behalf of the rights of parents to send their children to parochial schools. In 1938, Loyola University of Chicago awarded Mullen an honorary doctor of laws degree, specifically mentioning his victory in *Meyer v. Nebraska* (Mullen 1940, vii).

As Roosevelt's floor manager, Mullen was charged with polling delegates to gauge support for Roosevelt among the convention participants and for the other strong candidates for the nomination, Speaker of the House John Nance Garner and Alfred E. Smith. After the first and second roll calls, the committee was deadlocked, unable to choose a nominee. A third roll call also resulted in a deadlock, after which Mullen held a press conference, stating:

> We have taken a new poll of our rockbound strength, and it convinces us that 650 of our delegates will stay here until Roosevelt is nominated or hell freezes over. If the emissaries of corrupt interests continue to halt the nomination of the man who is clearly the choice of the majority of the party, we shall speak out. We will denounce the damnable hypocrisy of the people who misrule New York City, Jersey City, and Chicago, coming here to stand behind Mr. Smith in an effort to seize the power in the nation or else throw the party on the rocks. (Arlahan 1971, 112)

Mullen's strategy at the convention was to arrange for one of the stronger candidates, John Nance Garner, to join with Roosevelt as the vice-presidential candidate, bringing with him the Texas delegates and winning the nomination. Mullen went on to serve as vice chairman of Roosevelt's campaign committee, helping to draw the votes of midwestern progressives. Mullen later became critical of Roosevelt's expansion of the presidential power, fearing, as did many progressives, that a stronger federal government threatened individual freedom (Garraty and Carnes 1999, 73).

Aside from his political involvement, Mullen was also an active litigator throughout the various stages of his career. He took particular satisfaction in a case involving Roy Youngblood and four other U.S. servicemen who had been given life sentences in a court-martial for the murder of an English citizen in Germany. Effectively establishing that Youngblood and his friends were the victims of mistaken identification and a faulty system of military justice, Mullen was able to secure a pardon for them by President Warren G. Harding (Mullen 1940, 200). In another case, Mullen defended a potato seller against charges that he had bribed army officers to accept inferior products. In his speech to the jury, Mullen compared his client to Saint Peter and the army "spies" to Judas Iscariot; his client was exonerated (Mullen 1940, 240).

While serving as attorney general of Nebraska, Mullen argued *Shallenberger v. First State Bank of Holstein*, 219 U.S. 114 (1911), before the U.S. Supreme Court. The Court's decision in this case upheld a Nebraska act that forbade banking except by a corporation formed under the act and that provided for the public guaranty of bank deposits. However, it is Mullen's second case before the Supreme Court, decided in 1923, which is responsible for his lasting influence in U.S. jurisprudence.

In the wake of World War I, paranoia and fear of foreigners and foreign cultures gripped the United States, and Mullen's home state of Nebraska was no exception. In 1919, the Nebraska legislature passed three measures to stop the spreading influence of foreign languages in the state. The first, Senate File No. 15, ended a previous requirement that county board proceedings and land sales be published in German-, Swedish-, and Bohemian-language newspapers statewide (Tatolovich 1995, 34). Senate File No. 237 stated that all public meetings must be conducted in English. The third measure, Senate File No. 24, sponsored in part by Senator H. E. Siman, stated that

> no person, individually or as a teacher, shall, in any private, denominational, parochial or public school, teach any subject to any person in any language than the English language. Languages other than the English language, may be taught as languages only after a pupil shall have attained and successfully passed the eighth grade as evidenced by a certificate of graduation issued by the county superintendent of the county in which the child resides. (Tatolovich 1995, 34–35)

Violation of this restrictive legislation, which became known as the Siman Language Law, was a misdemeanor charge carrying the possibility of a fine of twenty-five to one hundred dollars or confinement in county jail not to exceed thirty days (Tatolovich 1995, 35).

The Siman Language Law was first challenged in *Nebraska District of Evangelical Lutheran Synod of Missouri v. McKelvie*, 187 N.W. 927 (1919). The Nebraska Supreme Court upheld the law as constitutional, taking judicial notice of several pieces of information regarding foreign-born Nebraskans:

The operation of the selective draft law disclosed a condition in the body politic which theretofore had been appreciated to some extent, but the evil consequences of which had not been fully comprehended. It is a matter of general public information, of which the court is entitled to take judicial knowledge, that it was disclosed that thousands of men born in this country of foreign language speaking parents and educated in schools taught in a foreign language were unable to read, write or speak the language of their country, or understand words of command given in English. It was also demonstrated that there were local foci of alien enemy sentiment, and that, where such instances occurred, the education given by private or parochial schools in that community was usually found to be that which had been given mainly in a foreign language.

The court found that remedying this "very apparent need" was precisely the purpose of the Siman Law. Furthermore, the court discussed the right and duty of the state to educate its people to an end of building an "intelligent American citizenship, familiar with the principles and ideals upon which this government was founded." Finally, the court upheld the law on the basis that it fell within the power of the state to exercise its police powers to safeguard the public by insisting that the "fundamental basis of the education of its citizens shall be a knowledge of the language, history and nature of the government of the United States, and to prohibit anything which may interfere with such education."

This was the social environment prevailing when, in 1922, the Nebraska Supreme Court went even further to uphold criminal penalties against a schoolteacher in a Lutheran school charged with teaching the German language to a student who had not yet passed the eighth grade. In *Meyer v. State*, 187 N.W. 100 (1922), Robert T. Meyer, having been found guilty of violating the Siman Law, appealed to the Nebraska Supreme Court, claiming that because he had taught the child from a book of biblical stories written in German, the teaching constituted religious instruction with which the state should not interfere. The court ruled that the biblical nature of the material could not act as a shield to the defendant, who clearly violated the Siman Law by teaching the German language. The Court further ruled that the statute did not interfere with the right of religious freedom, stating that

the legislature had seen the baneful effects of permitting foreigners, who had taken residence in this country, to rear and educate their children in the language of their native land. The result of that condition was to be inimical to our own safety. To allow the children of foreigners, who had emigrated here, to be taught from early childhood the language of the country of their parents was to rear them with that language as their mother tongue. It was to educate them so that they must always think in that language, and, as a consequence, naturally inculcate in them the ideas and sentiments foreign to the best interests of this country.

In addition, the court ruled that, although the instruction in the German language took place during a time of day when school attendance was not compulsory, this measure was taken solely to evade the law. It was recommended that the previous decision in *McKelvie* should be modified to remove the stipulation that the action must take place "during school hours" in order to be illegal (Tatolovich 1995, 59). The Siman Language Law was once again upheld in its entirety, causing Meyer, represented by Arthur Mullen and two of his associates, to appeal to the U.S. Supreme Court.

On February 23, 1923, Mullen, who had been influential in persuading Roman Catholic leaders to join in the challenge to this law (Ross 1994, 97), argued before the Supreme Court in *Meyer v. Nebraska*, 262 U. S. 390 (1923), that the liberty protected by the Fourteenth Amendment to the Constitution may not be interfered with by legislative action that is "arbitrary or without reasonable relation to some purpose within the competency of the state to effect"; that the Siman Language Law deprived teachers and parents of liberty without due process of law and without such "reasonable relation"; that the law could not be taken as an appropriate use of state police power as it could not be shown to legitimately protect the health of children by limiting mental activities; and that the police powers deemed appropriate by the state legislature are not conclusive, but are subject to supervision by the courts. The opinion of the Court, authored by Justice James McReynolds, concluded that the statute in question did in fact unreasonably infringe on the liberty guaranteed to the plaintiff by the Fourteenth Amendment. McReynolds stated that the term "liberty," as it is used in the Fourteenth Amendment, is not specifically defined but has been partially defined by case precedent to include freedom from bodily restraint, the right of the individual to contract, acquire useful knowledge, marry, establish a home, raise children, worship according to the dictates of conscience, and "generally to enjoy those privileges long recognized at common law as essential to the orderly pursuit of happiness by free men." The Court ruled that the state may compel attendance at a school, and it may require that instruction be given in English, but there was not sufficient reasonable relation to a state interest to allow for the prohibition set forth in the Nebraska law.

The *Meyer* decision in itself is sufficient to assure Arthur Mullen a place in history, especially as it came at such a time as to stem the tide of rising nativism after World War I. However, the influence of that decision as cited in later cases is also quite remarkable. In the 1977 case *Maher v. Roe*, 423 U.S. 464 (1977), the Court ruled that the decision of *Roe v. Wade*, 410 U.S. 113 (1973), did not necessitate the funding of abortions by the state. In the majority opinion, Justice Lewis Powell compared the issue at hand to the decision in *Meyer v. Nebraska*, remarking that although *Meyer* required the state to cease prohibiting instruction in foreign languages, it could in no way be construed to require that the state fund public education in foreign languages. Such, argued Powell, was the case in *Maher v. Roe*. Although the state could not forbid a woman to undergo an abortion, it was not required to pay for the procedure. As the state of Nebraska was within its rights to prefer and to fund only instruction given in the English language, the state of Connecticut was within its rights to prefer and to fund only childbirth.

The *Meyer* decision is also cited in cases where the Court must point out the rights and roles of parents as the primary authority in decisions as to how their children will be raised, whether it be in reference to education, religious instruction, or medical decisions. The case of *H. L. v. Matheson*, 450 U.S. 398 (1981), is one such case in which the Court referenced *Meyer* in its decision to uphold a statute requiring doctors to notify the parents of minor women before performing an abortion.

Thus, Arthur Mullen's argument of *Meyer v. Nebraska* is one that continues to be significant to judicial deliberations today and one that still influences modern education and cultural relations, assuring Mullen a seat at the table of the great American litigators.

—*Brandi Snow Bozarth*

SOURCES AND SUGGESTIONS FOR FURTHER READING

Arlahan, Richard. *The Man Who . . . The Story of the 1932 Democratic National Convention*. New York: Dial Press, 1971.

Garraty, John A., and Mark C. Carnes, eds. *American National Biography*. Vol. 16. New York: Oxford University Press, 1999.

Marquis, Albert Nelson, ed. *Who's Who in America: A Biographical Dictionary of Notable Living Men and Women of the United States*. Vol. 20. Chicago: A. N. Marquis, 1938.

Mullen, Arthur F. *Western Democrat*. New York: Wilfred Funk, 1940.

Ross, William G. *Forging New Freedoms: Nativism, Education, and the Constitution, 1917–1927*. Lincoln: University of Nebraska Press, 1994.

Tatolovich, Raymond. *Nativism Reborn?: The Official English Language Movement and the American States*. Lexington: University Press of Kentucky, 1995.

NEAL, JAMES F.

(1929–)

JAMES NEAL
AP Photo/Mark Humphrey, File

JAMES F. NEAL WAS A FEDERAL prosecutor in many important cases of the 1960s and 1970s. Neal was born in rural Oak Grove in Sumner County, Tennessee, just north of Nashville, to Robert Gus and Emma Clendenning Neal. His parents had a hundred-acre farm where they raised strawberries, tobacco, and dairy cows and where James worked before and after school. Neal traces his own interest in law to his father, who often lingered around the county courthouse to listen to cases, which he shared with his family. After graduating from a public high school, the five-foot eight-inch Neal won a football scholarship to the University of Wyoming, where he played running back and was part of a team that had an undefeated season and beat Washington & Lee in the Gator Bowl in 1950.

Neal served in the U.S. Marine Corps from 1952 to 1954 and reached the rank of captain; he was a defense counsel in courts-martial and then regimental legal officer. He subsequently returned to Tennessee and attended Vanderbilt Law School, where he became a Founders Medalist by graduating first in his class. Shortly thereafter, he earned a master of law degree in taxation from Georgetown University, during which time he was associated with the Washington, D.C., firm Turney & Turney.

523

When President John F. Kennedy was elected in 1960, he appointed his brother Robert as attorney general. Robert Kennedy recruited Neal to serve as a special assistant to deal with labor corruption issues. The result was an early high-profile case in which Neal directed the prosecution of Teamster leader Jimmy Hoffa on charges that he had accepted kickbacks. Although this case ended in a mistrial, Neal subsequently succeeded in winning the first prosecution victory against the formidable Hoffa on charges of jury tampering. The trial made headlines, not only for Neal's victory but also for the time when a deranged man came in the courtroom and shot Hoffa with what turned out to be a relatively harmless gas pellet gun. Neal claims Hoffa's description of him—"The most vicious prosecutor who ever lived"—as a badge of honor (Gallese 1985, 109).

Neal continued his work as a prosecutor by serving as a U.S. district attorney for the Middle District of Tennessee from 1964 to 1966. One of the tasks that he successfully conducted during this time was to close down illegal gambling establishments in Nashville and the surrounding area. He subsequently became a partner in the firm of Cornelius, Collins, Neal & Higgins, from 1966 to 1970, and then joined a colleague to form Neal & Harwell in 1971.

Neal, who began lecturing at the Vanderbilt School of Law during this time, was called by Special Prosecutor ARCHIBALD Cox to be the chief trial counsel of the Watergate special prosecution force. He succeeded in getting convictions against such high-profile presidential counselors as H. R. Haldeman, Bob Ehrlichman, and Attorney General John Mitchell. When the defendants claimed that their contributions to the Watergate burglars had been for charitable purposes, Neal pointedly asked why they wore gloves when they passed the money along (Curriden 1990, 67). Neal would utilize similar skills when successfully pursuing the Senate Abscam investigations in the early 1980s.

After his service in the Watergate cover-up case, Neal returned to Nashville, where he continued his association with Aubrey B. Harwell Jr. Another Vanderbilt graduate, Harwell, who—like others in the firm—has a formidable trial reputation in his own right, is the firm's managing partner who facilitates Neal's strengths as a trial attorney through his efficient administration. As their firm has matured, it has increasingly taken on the defense of white-collar crimes and has specialized in corporate, bankruptcy, contract, and entertainment law.

The cases that Neal has taken as a defense attorney are as well known as the cases that he prosecuted. These have included the defense of Elvis Presley's doctor, George Nichopoulos, against charges that he illegally prescribed drugs to the rock singer; movie director John Landis, who was charged with criminal negligence in the deaths of actor Vic Morrow and

Barry Scheck and the Innocence Project

Stories of innocent people being wrongly convicted are among the most dramatic tales that the law has to offer. Recent advances in DNA testing on bodily fluids, first developed by Dr. Alec Jeffries in England, have allowed some individuals, especially those accused of sex crimes, to show that they were not guilty. As of August 1999, sixty-seven individuals, including many on death row, have been exonerated by this technique (Scheck et al. 2000, xiv).

Attorneys Barry Scheck and Peter Neufeld have created the Innocence Project at the Benjamin N. Cardozo School of Law at Yeshiva University, where they teach. This project seeks to use DNA evidence to exonerate individuals who have been wrongly convicted.

Scheck, a graduate of Yale (where he developed a reputation for radicalism) and the University of California at Los Angeles, started out in legal aid in the Bronx and subsequently went into private practice. In addition to working with the Innocence Project, Scheck has served in a number of high-profile cases. He was employed by the "Dream Team" defense as a DNA expert in the O. J. Simpson criminal defense case, in which he helped call laboratory procedures into question. Also recognized as an expert on spousal abuse,

Scheck defended Hedda Nussbaum from prosecution after her husband killed their six-year-old daughter. Although Scheck lost his defense of Louise Woodward, a British au pair charged with murdering an eight-month-old in her care, the judge reduced her sentence to involuntary manslaughter (Bumiller 1998).

In a book devoted to their Innocence Project, Scheck and Neufeld, along with journalist Jim Dwyer, describe cases of innocent individuals who were convicted and seek to identify the factors that led to such convictions. These include mistaken identity, faulty laboratory work, police or prosecutorial misconduct, bad lawyering, testimony by false witnesses and jailhouse snitches, and false confessions (Scheck et al. 2000, 263). These findings reveal that, even in a system devoted to justice, mistakes can occur. They further highlight the need for the presumption of innocence and vigorous defense in criminal cases.

REFERENCES

Bumiller, Elisabeth. "Public Lives; That Dress, Those Gloves and This Lawyer." *New York Times*, 12 August 1998, B-2, col. 4.

Scheck, Barry, Peter Neufeld, and Jim Dwyer. *Actual Innocence: Five Days to Execution and Other Dispatches from the Wrongly Convicted*. New York: Doubleday, 2000.

two Vietnamese child actors who were killed during a helicopter crash in the filming of *Twilight Zone: The Movie;* the Ford Motor Company against homicide charges in connection with the explosion of gas tanks on the Ford Pinto that had resulted in fatalities; the Exxon Corporation against felony charges in connection with the grounding and subsequent massive oil spill in Alaskan waters by the oil tanker *Exxon Valdez;* the first individual charged with air piracy; and Louisiana governor Edwin Edwards against racketeering charges.

Neal's defense of Nichopoulos grew out of charges that the doctor's over-prescription of drugs had led to Presley's early demise. In the face of evidence that Nichopoulos had prescribed numerous medications to Presley over a long period, Neal succeeded in defending Nichopoulos by portraying him as a modern-day "Good Samaritan" who, rather than rejecting a patient who was already abusing drugs, accepted him and attempted to wean him from his habit by prescribing placebo pills and saline injections and squirting much of the contents of needles on the floor while Presley was not looking. Although pretrial surveys that Neal's firm commissioned showed that the citizens of Shelby County, where the case was being tried, had great affection for Presley, they also showed that most people held Presley himself responsible for his own addiction (Couric 1988, 202–203). When the jury returned its verdict, many hugged the doctor, believing that his actions had extended, rather than shortened, the life of the great singer.

In defending movie director John Landis, Neal acknowledged that Landis had illegally hired child actors but kept the focus of the trial on whether the helicopter crash was an act of homicide or simply a tragic accident. After demonstrating through testimony that Landis was exposed on the set to dangers similar to those of his actors, Neal succeeded in persuading the jury that the deaths of the actors were not the result of criminal negligence but simply a tragedy.

Neal pursued a similar strategy in the *Ford Pinto* case, in which three girls had been incinerated on their way to church after their car's gas tank exploded after being rear-ended by another car. Arguing that no car was completely safe, Neal showed that there was a necessary tradeoff in the building of any vehicle between safety and costs. He also produced a surprise, but credible, witness who indicated that the vehicle was stationary when it was hit at about 50 miles per hour, twice the speed that had been alleged. Under similar circumstances, Neal showed that gas tanks in other cars would also have exploded (Lusky 1991, 20). Neal, who says he fought a two-front war in this case, "in the courtroom and in the press," is also credited for holding daily meetings with the press in which he presented reporters with background material favorable to his side (Gallese 1985, 110).

Neal is a strong believer in attempting to derail prosecutions before charges are ever filed. Indeed, he has said that avoiding such indictments "is the most critical thing a white-collar criminal defense attorney can do" (Couric 1988, 195), and where possible he has someone from his firm interview individuals who testify for the prosecution as they leave the grand jury room. As a former prosecutor, Neal not only has contacts, but he has the advantage of being able to think like a district attorney. He also recognizes that there are times when it is better to negotiate a plea than to take a case to court. In defending Jake Butcher, a Knoxville banker accused of making illegal loans that caused his bank to fail and faced with more than five hundred years in penalties, Neal reluctantly settled for a twenty-year sentence. Likewise, in the *Exxon Valdez* case, Neal agreed to settle for criminal fines of $100 million (the company had already paid $900 million in civil fees) rather than the $750 million for which the government had asked (Lusky 1991, 18).

Sometimes likened to a "bantam rooster," who struts as he fights (Lusky 1991, 24), Neal has not lost his southern accent or small-town charm. The prosecutor in the *Landis* case, Lea D'Agostino, has described Neal as "very cunning," and charged that "he plays the country boy who's just simple folk, when we all know he's anything but that" (Curriden 1990, 68). For his part, the cigar-puffing Neal has stayed close to his roots and has said that "people often underestimate the power of simply being yourself" (Lusky 1991, 22). Moreover, Neal has been described both as being able "to blur the lines between himself and the defendant" and to portray himself "as a champion of the truth, even when defending cases that run strongly against the tide of public opinion" (Lusky 1991, 20).

There are several keys to Neal's success. One is meticulous preparation. In the *Ford Pinto* case, Neal is reported to have spent six months on pretrial motions and depositions and another five months learning how to assemble an automobile (Curriden 1990, 67). Neal believes that a good attorney should never promise more in an opening statement than the attorney can deliver and believes that a good attorney should be able to describe 90 percent or more of his closing argument before cross-examining the first witness (Couric 1988, 208).

Neal likes to stipulate commonly accepted facts rather than chasing dead ends or running down tangents; he believes that a casual admission can often take the sting out of facts that would otherwise be worrisome. He thinks that, especially on the defense, an attorney needs to look for openings created when the other side makes a mistake. Neal's resolution "not to beat himself" has been described as his overriding motto, and he has cited the maxim that he learned in football that "the team that makes the fewest mistakes wins" (Couric 1988, 190). Drawing on the same football experience, Neal adds, "Unless you know everything about a case, you can't recognize a fumble when it occurs" (Curriden 1990, 68).

Neal can be relentless on a witness who so falters. In the Nichopoulos trial, Neal (who had checked on the witness's credentials beforehand) was able to expose the fact that a doctor called by the prosecution as an expert witness and who claimed to have numerous publications could not name a single one, even after an hour's recess (Couric 1988, 212). Neal believes in meticulously preparing his own witnesses and requiring that they become familiar with all key papers in a case, even if that requires that he treat the witness brutally in pretrial mock trials that he conducts in his offices. Neal says,

> The defendant is the number one pivotal witness. There is nobody else who comes close in importance. A defendant who is a good witness can carry the day, even if most everything else has gone against you. (Couric 1988, 217)

Although he values charisma and can turn on the charm, Neal thinks that thorough preparation is more important. He also emphasizes explaining things clearly. Neal has noted that

> jurors will really understand 50 percent of what they hear—and remember 50 percent of what they understand. That gives you about 25 percent of everything that goes on. What you've got to do is make sure that the jury understands—and remembers—that 25 percent that you want them to understand and remember. (Couric 1988, 191)

Neal, who wishes he could have served as attorney general of the United States, has never held an elected public office. As one who has very much enjoyed his law practice, in 1978 Neal decided not to allow his name to be submitted as a possible director of the Federal Bureau of Investigation after he was told that the president was looking for a ten-year commitment. In 1982, he further decided against running for governor of Tennessee. When approached, after Watergate, about becoming commissioner of the National Basketball Association (NBA), Neal said he would not consider the position unless the NBA moved to Nashville (Curriden 1990, 67).

Neal, who has two children, acknowledges that trial work can be hard on families. He is now married to attorney Dianne Ferrell Neal, who served as former Tennessee governor Ned McWherter's legal counsel. A longtime Democrat, Neal serves as a personal attorney for former vice-president Al Gore. He also serves as a member of the Tennessee Racing Commission, of which he was chairman for two years.

—*John R. Vile*

Sources and Suggestions for Further Reading

Battle, Bob. "Renowned Lawyer Makes Case for Working Hard to Reach Goal." *Nashville Banner*, 16 August 1990, B3.

Couric, Emily. *The Trial Lawyers: The Nation's Top Litigators Tell How They Win.* New York: St. Martin's Press, 1988.

Curriden, Mark. "From Elvis to Exxon." *American Bar Association Journal* (November 1990), 65–68.

Gallese, Liz Roman. "Lawyers for Companies in Deep Trouble." *Fortune*, 14 October 1985, 106–114.

Lusky, Karen. "Where There's Smoke, There's James Neal." *Nashville Business & Lifestyles*, April 1991, 18–26.

NIZER, LOUIS

(1902–1994)

BEGINNING WITH HIS INTRO-
duction as a young attorney to the
world of prominent people in
1928, Louis Nizer attracted a
clientele that became what might
constitute the quintessential "Blue
Book" of glitterati. The list of
clients he represented in trial and
appellate courts all over the country from California to the U.S.
Supreme Court in Washington,
D.C., includes film, stage, and television performers Charles Chap-
lin, Mae West, Johnny Carson,
and Elizabeth Taylor; artist Sal-
vador Dalí; athletes Julius Erving,
Muhammad Ali, and Joe Namath;
writer Jacqueline Susann; astro-
nauts Alan Shepard and Neil
Armstrong; columnists Igor Cas-
sini and Quentin Reynolds; and
captains of industry Roy Fruehauf
and Armand Hammer. He helped
establish and successfully defend
the Motion Picture Code and Rating Program, sued Captain Marvel
on behalf of Superman, and prosecuted the song "Rum and Coca-
Cola" representing its progenitor,
"L'Année Passée." He wrote several bestselling books that portrayed his variegated legal career.
Furthermore, enactments of his

LOUIS NIZER
Archive Photos

trial experiences have been performed on stage, screen, and television, with some notable actors—Van Heflin, George C. Scott, and Edward Asner—portraying him.

Although much has been written about Nizer's life in court—for the most part by Nizer himself—very little has been written about his personal life. In fact, the main source of information about Nizer outside his court-room memoirs comes from his *Reflections without Mirrors: An Autobiography of the Mind* (1978), and very little of this book concerns his personal life. Indeed, *Reflections* barely contains a mention of his parents and does not even hint at his mother's name. Be that as it may, Louis Nizer was born February 6, 1902, at Whitechapel Road in London, England, to Joseph and Bella Bialestock Nizer. The elder Nizer immigrated to the United States in 1904, followed the year afterward by his wife and son. The Nizer family settled in over the family's dry-cleaning business on Sumner Avenue in the Williamsburg section of north Brooklyn, where Nizer spent most of his childhood.

Joseph Nizer's long hours at the cleaning establishment and Bella Nizer's night work at a nearby textile factory enabled their family to prosper. The young Nizer's graduation from Boy's High in Brooklyn, noted for other illustrious alumni, including the author Norman Mailer and the composer Aaron Copland, was followed by four years at Columbia University and the Columbia University Law School, one of New York's best and most expensive schools. Nizer sharpened his oratorical skills while at Columbia with his participation in forensic competition, twice winning one of Columbia's highest awards, the George William Curtis Prize, given for excellence in the public delivery of English orations. Governor Al Smith and Charles Evans Hughes, who was between his tenures as associate justice and chief justice of the U.S. Supreme Court, were present in the audience on the first occasion. The public-speaking skills that were to serve Nizer so well during a career spanning seven decades were actually manifested at a much younger age. When he was barely in high school, Nizer could be found standing on public podiums extolling the virtues of socialism alongside such notables as Morris Hillquit, himself an accomplished attorney who represented many socialists charged with espionage during World War I. A still youthful Nizer (age fifteen) also took to the rostrum at local cinemas and legitimate theaters on Broadway during World War I promoting Liberty Loans, for which he received a certificate of merit from the national government.

A position in his chosen profession initially eluded Nizer after he was graduated from law school in 1924 and had successfully completed the New York State bar examination. Yet, he was not to be denied. His first litigation opportunity, which turned out to be a major break, arrived while he was serving dispossess summonses for seven dollars a week on defaulting tenants in buildings owned by a lawyer named Emily Janoer. The case was notable for several reasons, not the least of which were that he actually "beat city hall," and not only that, New York's highest court sustained his victory, with the already famous Benjamin N. Cardozo presiding. The case involved a dispute between some Ellery Street merchants who complained of the commissioner of market's decision denying them the privilege of having push carts loaded with merchandise parked on the sidewalk, a privilege that the commissioner had granted their across-the-street competitors. Apparently Nizer was the merchants' last hope, a long line of attorneys having turned down a seemingly hopeless case (among them Emmanuel Celler, who later served with distinction in the U.S. House of Representatives).

Undaunted, the plucky Nizer, "calling on my vast fund of political inexperience and naïveté," as he put it years later, told the merchants, "Certainly, you can fight City Hall." Nizer's clients prevailed largely due to his thorough preparation of facts that showed many gross inconsistencies in the commissioner's actions. Nizer gave the *Pushcart* case credit for instilling in him the truth that "preparation equates with proficiency." The law in the *Pushcart* case was straightforward and simple: The commissioner has discretionary leeway. Consequently, and obviously, he had nothing to rely on but factual application of that discretion. To be sure, as Nizer acknowledged, the fact that the trial judge was not a protégé of Tammany Hall—unlike the vicarious defendants on the other side of Ellery Street—and the ill-preparedness of the city counsel who exclusively relied on the law of administrative discretion, bolstered his clients' legal position (Nizer 1978, 82–93).

Nizer's break came when his success in the *Pushcart* case was reported in the newspapers, leading in turn to an employment offer from Louis Phillips, who had known Nizer's parents in London. More important to Nizer's budding career, Phillips was the executive secretary and general counsel to the New York Film Board of Trade, an association that would ultimately lead to Nizer's affiliation with the upper crust, not only of filmdom, but of politics, business, and society as well. Within two years, Nizer's performance produced an invitation from Phillips to become his full partner. This association was to last for a quarter of a century as the two built a law firm specializing in contract, copyright, libel, divorce, plagiarism, and antitrust litigation that continues to bear their names: Phillips, Nizer, Benjamin, Krim & Ballon. Nizer served as executive secretary and counsel of the New York Film Board of Trade and also represented the Motion Picture Association of America (MPAA), including most of its members' companies, most notably United Artists.

His association with the motion picture industry not only introduced him to elites. It led him to very select cases as well. For example, a major case came his way in the early 1960s when the vice-president elect of the American Federation of Television and Radio Artists, John Henry Faulk, took a stand against the McCarthyite practice of blacklisting entertainers accused of having ties to the Communist party, or even considered to have seditious tendencies. Faulk quickly found himself on the blacklist. After being fired from his popular CBS radio show because of alleged subversive activities, Faulk retained Nizer to sue AWARE Inc., a group of self-appointed vigilantes paid by television networks to report on entertainers with purported Communist leanings. In 1962, Nizer won a record $3.5 million libel judgment against AWARE and two of its chief officers. Although Faulk's award was reduced on appeal to $550,000, it was still a record recovery. While Faulk experienced years of unfortunate decline and received only a portion of the award, his cause was credited with ending blacklisting in the broadcast industry, and no doubt enhanced an already flowering reputation for Nizer.

Not long after the *Faulk* case, Nizer was appointed general counsel for the MPAA. He immediately set to work, along with the also newly appointed association president, Jack Valenti, to protect the industry from censorship by an increasingly concerned public. In general terms, the impetus for this concern was the explosion of films containing material that was sexually explicit both in subject matter and photographic display, and specifically, the opportunity provided by Supreme Court decisions indicating that local jurisdictions could constitutionally enact legislation protecting minors from pornography. One decision was *Interstate Circuit, Inc. v. Dallas* (1968), in which Nizer had argued on behalf of United Artists, one of the parties. *Dallas* held that the city ordinance regulating the exhibition of "sexual promiscuity" to minors was unconstitutional because of vagueness, but the decision, considered with another case decided about the same time, *Ginsberg v. New York* (1968), suggested that a properly drawn ordinance might be found constitutional. The result of this effort by Nizer and Valenti was the Motion Picture Code and Rating Program adopted by MPAA later in the year. Although the ratings did not attempt to judge the aesthetic quality of a film, only its suitability for children, Tropic Film Corporation sued the association for restraint of trade because its film *Tropic of Cancer*, based on Henry Miller's novel, received an "X" rating. The district court refused to grant any relief, finding that the rating program did not eliminate competition but merely advised motion picture exhibitors and the public of the content of films. Subsequently, the case was voluntarily withdrawn.

With the Motion Picture Code and Rating Program, Nizer and Valenti had taken a leading role to protect freedom of expression by self-regulation in the private realm. Nizer was also a significant participant in the public realm. An instance of this was one of his many arguments before the U.S. Supreme Court, in *Jenkins v. Georgia* (1974). *Jenkins* followed the famous *Miller v. California* (1973) decision in which the Court set forth what the justices touted as the definitive definition of obscenity. Among other things, the *Miller* opinion had indicated that the "prurient interest" and the "patently offensiveness" aspects of the obscenity test could be determined by local juries based on local standards. *Jenkins* was the first post-*Miller* case to reach the Supreme Court regarding this national-local dichotomy. A local superior court jury in Albany, Georgia, had determined the film *Carnal Knowledge* to be obscene and in violation of the Georgia anti-obscenity statute, and had therefore convicted a local theater manager, Billy Jenkins, of a crime. The Georgia Supreme Court upheld the jury verdict, relying on *Miller*'s apparent green light for local juries to apply local standards.

The MPAA arranged for Nizer to represent Jenkins in an appeal to the U.S. Supreme Court. Overcoming the insistence of many associates and amicus curiae colleagues to attack the *Miller* holding straight from the shoulder, much in the way that dissenting Justice William O. Douglas and others had done in *Miller*, and the Georgia dissenters had done in *Jenkins*, he opted—sticking to his standard practice—to leave existing law within the court's purview, emphasizing factual aspects instead. In short, Nizer argued for the distinction between ordinary and constitutional facts, granting jurors the last word in the former but subjecting the latter to judicial scrutiny. As Nizer stated during his argument, "When we are dealing with the precious rights of the First Amendment and a constitutional question is involved, this Court should not hesitate to express its parental care of the constitution that is exclusively vested in it." The opinion, written by Justice William Rehnquist, did just that, substituting its standard in place of the Georgia jury.

Not all of Nizer's Supreme Court appearances were as successful as *Jenkins*. One such case was *Fortnightly Corporation v. United Artists Television* (1968). This case involved the practice by which cable television systems captured transmission of copyrighted programs produced by movie producers and distributors and retransmitted them without paying the originators' royalty fees. Although the originators claimed copyright infringement, the cable operators compared their behavior with customers building taller antennae. United Artists Television, one of Nizer's clients, sued Fortnightly, a cable system in West Virginia. United Artists sought damages and injunctive relief. Despite having prevailed in the district and circuit courts without dissent, United Artists did not fare so well in the Supreme Court. Obviously, there could be any number of reasons that the Court ruled in a 5–1 decision that the copyright statute did not prohibit the cable operator's actions, but one commentator suggests that Nizer had become a bit too comfortable with the Court, if not overly vain. According to this source, when Nizer appeared before the Court to argue on behalf of the producers, he "adopted an attitude of disdain for the cable operators. His demeanor appeared to some of those in the courtroom to be a snub of the justices themselves who had agreed to hear the case, in which the outcome, Nizer implied, should have been obvious. He gave the impression to some who heard his arguments that the court was wasting his and everybody else's time by even hearing a case that was so clear cut" (Southwich 1998, 3).

Nizer's litigation forte—at trial, and on appeal—was to combine the discovery of all relevant facts with a thorough preparation of them for presentation. In fact, he conceptualized this custom in formulaic terms as ($IQ + WQ^2 = S$), which stands for "Intelligence Quotient plus Work Quotient squared equals Success"; or, as he put it more prosaically, "[Preparation] is the be-all of good trial work. Everything else—felicity of expression, improvisational brilliance—is a satellite around the sun. Thorough preparation is that sun" (Simpson, 1988). He also coined a little aphorism that captures this fetishism that goes like this: "Yes, there's such a thing as luck in trial law but it only comes at three o'clock in the morning. You'll still find me in the library looking for luck at three o'clock in the morning" (Simpson, 1988).

Louis Nizer was not only a consummate trial attorney; he was also something of a Renaissance man. He produced some prizewinning paintings that were exhibited at New York's Hammer Gallery, the Boston Museum, and the Galerie Heritage in Toronto. Composing musical pieces was another of his hobbies. Several of his songs were published, including two about places he visited, "Hawaii" and "Jamaica," along with several that he composed for his grandchildren, which were published by RCA under the title *Songs for You*. Nizer actually held a membership in the American Society of Composers, Authors, and Publishers. Nevertheless, when he represented the motion picture companies in a class-action lawsuit filed by seventy-one of his "fellow" musical composers, neither his clients nor the plaintiffs considered him to have a conflict of interest. Even so, he was nominated for a Grammy award for a song in which he analyzed several decisions written by Justice Oliver Wendell Holmes Jr. Nizer was at different times offered presidential appointments to be a federal judge and attorney general, to which he would respond "I enjoy the ardor, and also the freedom of a law office practice" ("Louis Nizer" 1994).

Nizer obviously had an indefatigable personality. In the midst of his kinetic law practice, he somehow managed to write ten books, alongside many articles and essays. He was for a time the chair of the Algonquin Hotel Round Table, which was a daily luncheon engagement for many of the city's literati. His books, spanning more than half a century, began with a legalistic work entitled *New Courts of Industry: Self-regulation under the Motion Picture Code, Including an Analysis of the Code* (1935) and ended with the 1992 publication of the story of Murray Gold, a man who withstood four trials for the double murder of a Connecticut attorney and his wife. In

Catspaw: The Famed Trial Attorney's Heroic Defense of a Man Unjustly Accused, Nizer recounts the four trials, two of which ended in mistrials, two in convictions. Nizer did not represent Gold at trial, but he did represent him in a successful appeal after the first conviction and in a successful habeas corpus petition after the second.

One of Nizer's best-known books is *My Life in Court* (1961), a didactic account of some of his more notable trials. It rose to the top of the *New York Times*'s bestseller list and remained there for a year and a half. One trial described in the book was the notorious libel suit Nizer filed for writer Quentin Reynolds against the Hearst newspaper columnist Westbrook Pegler. The *Reynolds-Pegler* trial became a popular drama, forming the foundation for playwright Henry Denker's stage play *A Case of Libel*. It was performed on Broadway and was later adapted for television in 1969 and for film in 1983. *My Life in Court*, like most of Nizer's books—particularly *The Jury Returns* (1967), and perhaps excepting parts of *Between You and Me* (1963), which covers many aspects of jury trials of interest to a would-be trial attorney—are popularized accounts of his courtroom experiences noted perhaps more for who the participants are than for any significant professional insight. Even so, they have surely added to the public's appreciation for the judicial process and its institutions.

Nizer's combination of hard experience and abundant wit not only equipped him to write so prodigiously. It made him a favored speaker and master of ceremonies. One of his books, *Thinking on Your Feet* (1940)—a Book-of-the-Month Club selection—is a compilation of many of his toastmaster speeches and introductions. Thus, it is not surprising that he is frequently quoted. Some of his quotations, especially as far as they render some insight into his approach to trying lawsuits, are worth repeating: "A speaker who does not strike oil in ten minutes should stop boring"; "I know of no higher fortitude than stubbornness in the face of overwhelming odds"; "Mud thrown is ground lost"; "The man who committed the crime is not the one you see now"; and "A fine artist is one who makes familiar things new and new things familiar." Such a man was he. His life and achievements could not be better summed than by the fact that two universities, Pepperdine University and Iowa Wesleyan College, bestowed on him honorary doctor of law degrees, and another, Tel Aviv School of Law, dedicated a new library wing bearing his name; except perhaps for the comments made by his friend and colleague, Jack Valenti, on the occasion of the first Louis Nizer Lecture on Public Policy at the Carnegie Council on Ethics and International Affairs:

Louis Nizer is the only person I know or knew who could come close to matching Francis Bacon. Lawyer, courtroom genius, public speaker, bestselling author, painter, composer, lyricist, historian, counselor to presidents and public officials: he was all these things and more. And in each he performed with exceeding intellect and ascending success.

—*Clyde Willis*

Sources and Suggestions for Further Reading

Current Biography Yearbook. New York: H. W. Wilson, 1955, 449–450.

"Louis Nizer, Attorney, Best-Selling Author Dies." *Los Angeles Times*, 11 November 1994, A35.

Nizer, Louis. *Between You and Me*. New York: Beechhurst Press, 1948. Reprint, New York: T. Yoseloff , 1963

_____. *Catspaw: The Famed Trial Attorney's Heroic Defense of a Man Unjustly Accused*. New York: D. I. Fine, 1992.

_____. *The Implosion Conspiracy*. New York: Doubleday, 1973.

_____. "Introduction, Analysis and Commentary." In *Report of the President's Commission on the Assassination of the President, John F. Kennedy*. Garden City, N.Y.: Doubleday, 1964.

_____. *The Jury Returns*. Garden City, N.Y.: Doubleday, 1967.

_____. *My Life in Court*. Garden City, N.Y.: Doubleday, 1961.

_____. *New Courts of Industry: Self-regulation under the Motion Picture Code, including an Analysis of the Code*. New York: Longacre Press, 1935. Reprint, New York: J. S. Ozer, 1971.

_____. *Reflections without Mirrors: An Autobiography of the Mind*. New York: Doubleday, 1978.

_____. *Songs For You*. New York: Bourne, 1956.

_____. *Thinking on Your Feet*. New York: Liveright, 1940.

_____. *What to Do with Germany*. Chicago: Ziff-Davis, 1944.

Simpson, James B. *Simpson's Contemporary Quotations*, 1988. http://www.bartleby.com/63.

Southwich, Thomas P. "Cable Television: The First 50 Years." Chapter 4, "The Dark Ages." *Cable World*, 1998. Available at <http://www.cableworld.com/articles/50th/199804pg1.htm>.

OTIS, JAMES, JR.

(1725–1783)

As one of the best-known colonial-era lawyers, James Otis was not only an imposing precursor of several aspects of constitutional jurisprudence—including judicial review, search and seizure law, and full equality for African-Americans and women—he represents the finest tradition among common law lawyers, namely, community building based on reason and common sense rather than blindly following statutory and judicial precedent. Otis was a revolutionary, not because he resisted English rule, for he clearly did not, but because he revolted against blind adherence to English legal tradition, and he was an activist, not by taking up arms against the English, which he refused, but because he sought to uphold his revolutionary ideas in each and every lawsuit he undertook, from simple crimes to the famous 1761 *Writs of Assistance* case.

In 1635, Otis's grandfather four times removed, John Otis I (1581–1657), moved from Hingham in Norfolk, England, to become one of the initial residents of Hingham, Massachusetts, on the bay some fifteen miles southeast of

James Otis Jr.
Library of Congress

538

Boston. His grandson, John Otis III (1657–1727), moved to Barnstable, fifty-fives miles farther south, where he was judge of the common pleas and probates courts, as was his son James Otis Sr. (1702–1778), commonly called Colonel Otis, who was the father of James Otis Jr., who was destined to become a leading revolutionary-era patriot.

James Otis Jr. was born February 5, 1725, at the family home at Great Marshes, in what is now called West Barnstable, Massachusetts. It was his "upwardly mobile family" (Waters 1968, viii), endowed with opportunistic roots, that permitted the family of John Otis III to blossom during the Glorious Revolution in 1688 when William and Mary ascended to the British throne. The elder James Otis continued his family's achievements in the legal, commercial, and political community of Barnstable, a small provincial town on Cape Cod, steeped in Whig and Congregationalist conservatism, that was the last township in the colony to move for independence from England. Although Otis was infused with Whig conservatism, he did not formally affiliate with the church nor conduct family prayer (Waters 1968, 136). In fact, he appeared to be unaffected by such movements as the Great Awakening.

Otis entered Harvard College in June 1739 and took an A.B. degree in 1743, and the A.M. three years later. He forged a core natural law position while studying the classics that later informed his legal-political argument about the legitimacy of legislative enactments that violated fundamental natural laws. In fact, he used this argument early on in a rather brash defense of a Harvard Fellow who had been dismissed by the overseers. Otis claimed that the overseers had exceeded their authority, thereby constituting a "miserable, Despicable and arbitrary Government" (Waters 1968, 112). After graduating from Harvard, in addition to caring for family business matters, Otis engaged in an apprenticeship at law drawing up writs and reading "black letter" law under Jeremiah Gridley, a friend of the Otis family and one of Massachusetts's leading lawyers.

In 1748, yielding to his father's wishes, Otis established a law practice in Plymouth. With the Colonel's law practice including the same circuit, it was inevitable that father and son would meet as legal adversaries. They met early (September 1748), with Otis Jr. prevailing in a case in the court of common pleas that involved a disputed thirty-two-shilling debt. Otis Sr. unsuccessfully appealed the case to superior court. That same year they met once more in the case of *Veazie v. Duxbury*, a notable case in which Otis Jr., representing Duxbury, found himself again on the prevailing side. Duxbury, a small township some eight miles north of Plymouth abrogated the contract of its pastor, the Rev. Samuel Veazie, who retained the services of Otis Sr. to sue the town for nonsupport in violation of the contract. Otis Jr. used excerpts of Veazie's sermons to convince the jury that Veazie had not complied with the contract by failing to be the "faithful, pious, and learned minister" he contracted to be, thereby releasing the town from its obligation. Although Otis Jr. won the battle, he lost the war, so to speak, for the result hardly impressed the church people in his district, who held Otis Jr. responsible (Waters 1968, 114–115). Whatever the reasons, Otis's law practice failed to prosper. For example, during May 1749, Otis obtained only one new case, while the average among leading practitioners was fifteen, and his father alone obtained more than thirty. Faced with this state of affairs, Otis Jr. left Plymouth for Boston in 1750.

In Boston, Otis achieved much success not only practicing law representing the city's leading commercial interests, but serving his family's business interest as well. He also became known outside Boston. One early case that gave him widespread notice was his successful defense of three men who were on trial for piracy in Halifax. His law practice—typical of lawyers throughout history—included liaison efforts between commercial interests and government officials, which inevitably led him to take a leading role in legal-political battles. Otis joined a faction of lawyers and merchants in opposing what they deemed to be excessive taxation. He also served as the spokesperson for commercial interests in their affairs with the colonial governor, Thomas Pownall, who sought Otis's association to bolster his opposition to the lieutenant governor, Thomas Hutchinson. Pownall appointed Otis to the prestigious post of deputy advocate general of the vice admiralty court.

After five years of success in Boston, Otis married Ruth Cunningham, daughter of a wealthy businessman. They had three children—two daughters and one son, James, who became a midshipman and died in 1777 as a British prisoner of war. The older daughter, Elizabeth, married an English officer from Lincolnshire and after the war lived in England, only returning for a short visit in 1792; the youngest, Mary, married a distinguished military officer who, being a distinguished Massachusetts lawyer after the war, died prematurely, as did Mary in 1806. Otis's sister, Mercy Otis Warren (1728–1814), was a notable American writer famous for her satirical plays, *The Adulateur* (1773) and *The Group* (1775), directed against the Tories. She married the well-known revolutionary James Warren of Plymouth.

Among the important and highly influential works of Otis that have survived are *The Rights of British Colonies Asserted and Proved* (1764) and *A Vindication of the British Colonies* (1765). Otis's writing contains some of the most radical egalitarianism of that period, far greater than is found in most Quaker works and those of Thomas Jefferson as well. For example, in *Rights of the British Colonies*, he insists on total equality for women, posing the rhetorical question, "Are women not born as free as men?" which he answers in the affirmative. He was equally adamant concerning the equality of black slaves, asserting that "colonists are by the law of nature freeborn, as indeed all men are, white or black" (Bailyn 1965, 420, 439). At age thirty-five Otis published a work that typifies the broad liberal arts education of lawyers in that period and before—a characteristic that is becoming ever more rare among members of the modern bar. This was a linguistic analysis of style in Latin poetry and prose entitled *The Rudiments of Latin Prosody: A Dissertation on Letters and the Principles of Harmony in Poetic and Prosaic Composition* (1760). He wrote a companion book to illustrate the principles of Greek prosody (the study of the metrical structure of verse). JOHN ADAMS, quite the classical scholar himself, praised Otis's linguistic publications as works of "profound learning and great labor" (Adams 1969, 10:263, 275).

James Otis was best known to his contemporaries—and to history alike, for that matter—as the lawyer who resigned as counsel to the admiralty court and argued against the Crown in the 1761 *Writs of Assistance* case. In fact, his appearance in this case led the loyalist governor, Francis Bernard, to say of him, "Troubles in this Country take their rise from, and owe their Continuance to one Man, [James Otis]." The patriot John Adams, then a young lawyer whose notes at the trial account for most of our knowledge of the trial, stated that the trial was "the first scene of the first act of opposition to the arbitrary claims of Great Britain. Then and there, the child of Independence was born" (Adams 1969, 2:124).

The appointment of Francis Bernard as governor and the deaths of Chief Justice Samuel Sewall and King George II as 1760 was drawing to a close laid the foundation for the *Writs of Assistance* case that is perhaps, along with the 1735 trial of John Peter Zenger in New York, one of the most well known and influential trials in colonial America. Near the successful conclusion of the French and Indian War, the Crown no longer had a need to curry favor with Boston's commercial interest, and thus it began to enforce taxes more stringently. Thomas Pownall had recently been replaced as governor by Bernard, who was much more inclined to enforce the tax and enjoy his one-third share of the revenue than Pownall had been (one-third of the tax revenue was supposed to go to the province, one-third to the governor, and another third to the Crown). Moreover, Bernard appointed Lieutenant Governor Thomas Hutchinson to replace the late Chief Justice Sewall, who had been quite reluctant to issue the writs of assistance. Finally, with the death of King George II, reissuance of the writs became mandatory because they expired six months after the death of a reigning monarch.

The 1733 Molasses Act levied a six-pence-per-gallon tax on molasses, which was used to make the rum that was so economically dear to many New England merchants. So much so that smuggling was almost a way of life for the affected commercial interests. Writs of assistance were an effective tool in ferreting out smuggled goods, which made them detestable to many local merchants. These writs, issued by superior courts—unlike ordinary search warrants that were based on sworn affidavits manifesting legitimate suspicion and limited to specific places and goods—permitted customs officers not only repeatedly to search any place at will, but to enlist assistance from anyone. Moreover, the authority granted by the writs did not expire until six months after the death of the reigning monarch. Writs of assistance were so named because they were orders ("writ" being Middle English for a written order issued by a court, commanding the party to whom it is addressed to perform or cease performing a specified act) that required others to assist officers in case of necessity while pursuing their duties, in this situation collecting taxes.

In November 1760, James Cockle, a deputy customs official at Salem, petitioned the superior court for a writ of assistance seeking authority to "break open ships, shops, cellars, houses, &c., to search for prohibited goods and merchandise, on which duties had not been paid" (Adams 1969, 2:124). Merchants of Salem and Boston filed a petition resisting the issuance of the writ and retained Oxenbridge Thacher and James Otis, who had recently resigned his admiralty position rather than advocate on behalf of the application for the writ. The customs officials retained Otis's former mentor, Jeremiah Gridley.

Actually, Otis had already become involved in the writs of assistance matter by petitioning the general court on December 17, 1760, claiming that Bernard's new trade policy was illegally administered by using the commonwealth's share of the forfeiture to pay for informers rather than for legitimate provincial matters. The petition called for the province to sue the customs collector, Charles Paxton, for £475, which it did successfully in the common law court of common pleas, only to have the decision overturned by the superior court with Thomas Hutchinson now sitting as chief justice. The reversal was based on an obscure jurisdictional dispute between actions in common law courts and prerogative courts that deprived the common law court of jursidiction.

By the time the *Writs of Assistance* trial began on February 24, 1761, public opinion, especially among the commercial interests, was running quite decidedly against Governor Bernard's general trade policy and these writs in particular. Gridley opened the trial with a review of the legal authority, pointing out that Parliament had authorized the writ by statute in the fourteenth year of Charles II, which by statutes 7th and 8th of William III's reign were later applied to the colonies. Furthermore, he argued that reasons of state demanded that individual liberties must stand aside in this case, claiming that while "it is true the common privileges of Englishmen are taken away in this Case . . . 'Tis the necessity of the Case and the benefit of the Revenue that justifies the Writ . . . without which the Nation could neither be preserved from the Invasion of her foes, not the Tumults of her own Subjects" (Knappman 1994, 33).

On behalf of the commercial interests, Oxenbridge Thacher responded first by asserting that even if the (prerogative) Court of Exchequer in England had the authority to issue such writs, no similar authority resided with a colonial (common law) superior court. Otis then followed with his four-hour tour de force by first reciting his reasons for refusing to represent the admiralty court's application. He then requested "patience and attention to the whole range of an argument that may perhaps appear uncommon in many things, as well as to the points of learning that are more remote and unusual, that the whole tendency of my design may the more easily be perceived, the conclusions better descend, and the force of them be better felt." The latter point—seeing law suits as an integral means of constituting community—is a most exemplary component of legal advocacy, and Otis's legal practice takes a backseat to no one in this regard. Otis made a specific attack on Gridley's reliance on parliamentary enactments. Otis claimed that they authorized only those "special writs directed to special offices, to search certain houses etc. especially set forth in the writ," not the perpetual, open-ended, and general writs of assistance. However, his principal contention—the one requiring patience and attention—granted for the sake of argument that Parliament had authorized the writs. Otis opined, "An act against the Constitution is void; and if an act of Parliament should be made, in the very words of this petition, it would be void. The executive Courts must pass such acts into disuse" (Adams 1969, 2:524).

Otis readily conceded the propriety of one type of search warrant—as we would call it today—"that is special writs, directed to special officers, and to search certain houses, &c. specially set forth in the writ, granted by the Court of Exchequer at home, upon oath before the Lord Treasurer by the person who asks for it, that he suspects such goods to be concealed in those very places he desires to search." He also conceded that one can find general writs issued by justices of the peace in times past, but, anticipating Fourth Amendment jurisprudence, he went on to say that "in more modern books you will find only special warrants to search such and such houses specially named, in which the complainant has before sworn that he suspects that goods are concealed; and you will find that special warrants only are legal" (Adams 1969, 2:522–524).

Otis fortified this position with a four-point attack against the application. First, the "writ is universal, being directed to 'all and singular Justices, Sheriffs, Constables, and all other officers and subjects'"; second, it is "perpetual, there is no return [date]"; third, the holder of this writ "may enter any and all houses, shops &c. at will, and command all to assist him"; and fourth, "by this writ not only deputies, &c., but even their menial servants are allowed to lord over us." Most important, however, Otis reiterated that these violations could not be sanctioned even by parliamentary action, since such would violate "one of the most essential branches of English liberty [namely] the freedom of one's house." As Otis employed what has become a habitual proverb in our culture, "A man's house is his castle," Gridley responded, yes, but "Everybody knows that the subject has the privilege of house only against his fellow subjects, not versus the King either in matters of crime or fine," citing acts of Parliament and the provincial law in Massachusetts (Adams 1969, 2:523).

Otis responded by invoking Lord Coke's dictum in *Bonhan Case* (1610), declaring, "when an act of Parliament is against common right or reason, or repugnant, or impossible to be performed the common law [judges] will control it, and adjudge such act to be void." Many scholars have rightly pointed out that Otis misstated English constitutional history, failing perhaps to comprehend that the Glorious Revolution left Parliament supreme, meaning that whatever it enacted was, and is, unlike U.S. congressional enactments, not subject to constitutional attack (Bailyn 1965, 100–104, 412). Some scholars, like Bernard Bailyn, have even suggested that Otis misread Lord Coke as well. Even so, if Otis's position regarding judicial review does not comport with English constitutional history nor Lord Coke's position a half century earlier, it was most certainly a precursor of the U.S. doctrine of constitutional scrutiny and Chief Justice John Marshall's position a half century later in *Marbury v. Madison*.

Otis was not content to rely entirely on abstract principles of natural law. He recited several specific cases of abuse, such as the situation when a Mr. Pew who had one of these writs passed it over to his successor, Mr. Ware, who was totally unknown to the issuing magistrate. He cited another case in which a holder of the writ blatantly used it to harass his political enemies. Otis's vision did not prevail in this case. The court did not grant the application, but neither did it decide unfavorably, forwarding the matter to the colonial agent in England for clarification on the jurisdiction of superior courts. They ultimately upheld the legality of the writs and the superior court's jurisdiction, which issued the writs, although they were never enforced by local customs officials.

Otis's continuing legacy is not that he dwelled in some world of abstraction—for he clearly did not. Nor is it that he misrepresented the historical tradition of English law—which he may have done. Rather, it is that his aspiration elevated mundane and daily concerns to what have become some of our most cherished constitutional traditions in the areas of judicial

Lawyers as Scoundrels: William F. Howe and Abraham H. Hummel

Every profession has individuals who are professionally able but morally weak. Few lawyers have better fit this description than William F. Howe and Abraham H. Hummel (Howe & Hummel), who practiced law in New York City from 1869 to 1907. Their office featured a sign thirty to forty feet long and three to four feet wide, reading "Howe and Hummel's Law Offices."

Senior partner Howe is believed to have defended more than 650 individuals, most successfully, on murder and manslaughter charges (Rovere 1947, 5). Howe was especially adept at finding legal loopholes and on several occasions almost emptied the New York City jails. The firm also defended brothel owners, brokers, bankers, petty thieves, and various practitioners of organized crime, as well as major theatre performers and other entertainers of the day.

Howe was a large man who loved to wear ostentatious diamond jewelry to court; the more somber Hummel usually dressed in black and was often likened to a toothpick. Howe's background was obscure; he may or may not have been born and/or raised in England and/or previously practiced medicine. Best known for his criminal work, he handled some of the most notorious cases of his day. Howe was especially known for his emotional appeals to the jury, where he would often supply not only professional witnesses but also supportive wives and children for defendants. Howe could apparently command tears at will and once made an extended jury appeal on his knees. He also argued a number of insanity defenses, including some in which he directed his clients to enter court with their heads wrapped in bandages.

American-born Abraham Hummel, about twenty years Howe's junior, started as Howe's clerk and concentrated more on civil matters. Hummel was especially adept as a divorce lawyer and as a successful blackmailer of rich and famous men who had seduced young women who were willing to make charges and split fees with Hummel. Hummel was very interested in the theatre and developed this aspect of the firm's work.

In a book, *In Danger, or Life in New York. A True History of a Great City's Wiles and Temptations*, Howe and Hummel practically advertised New York City as a haven for criminals smart enough to seek the services of their law firm.

Howe tried his last case in 1897 and died in 1902. Hummel went to jail in 1907 when a plan to secure a divorce backfired after a witness he had bribed was finally located after months of dissipation (financed by Hummel) in faraway cities. The firm was shut down, and Hummel left the country, dying in London in 1926.

Although Howe and Hummel contributed to the great store of lawyer anecdotes that have added interest to the profession, they also left a legacy of lawyers as shysters that has done much to taint the reputations of more ethical practitioners.

Reference

Rovere, Richard H. *Howe & Hummel: Their True and Scandalous History*. New York: Farrar, Straus & Giroux, 1947.

review, search and seizure law, and equality for African-Americans and women. In fact, Otis, in the best tradition of the bar—thinking globally and acting locally, as a contemporary bumper sticker puts it—continued to champion his vision of society even in the most run-of-the-mill cases. A case in point is his participation, not long before his death, as a self-appointed amicus curiae in a lawsuit begun by a Boston widower seeking to recover land. Defense counsel, having produced a deed executed by the plaintiff, duly acknowledged and recorded, the plaintiff offered evidence that he was insane at the time. Whereupon the defendant's counsel produced legal authorities that people are not permitted to "stultify" themselves (alleging or seeking to prove insanity so as not to be legally responsible). At this point, Otis, a spectator in the courtroom, stepped forward and offered his opinion that since we had become a new nation, we might base judicial decisions on "the dictates of reason and common sense," rather than on the books, however long and complete they may appear. Two of the judges voted to permit the evidence, and the jury found in favor of the plaintiff.

Otis had been afflicted with mental instability for some time when a blow to his head by a British officer almost rendered him completely disabled in 1769. From that time on, he eased in and out of periods of sanity—completely withdrawing in 1771 from his profession and public service. Between his lucid periods he could perform such acts as spending two entire days destroying most of his correspondence and other writings. James Otis died in 1783 after being struck by lightning in his home at Andover, where he resided the last two years of his life on the farm of an acquaintance, a Mr. Osgood.

—*Clyde Willis*

Sources and Suggestions for Further Reading

Adams, John. *The Works of John Adams, Second President of the United States*. Edited by Charles Francis Adams. Vols. 2 and 10. Freeport, N.Y.: Books for Libraries Press, 1969.

Bailyn, Bernard, ed. *Pamphlets of the American Revolution*. Vol. 1, *1750–1776*. Cambridge: Belknap Press of Harvard University Press, 1965.

Breen, T. H. "Subjecthood and Citizenship: The Context of James Otis's Radical Critique of John Locke." *New England Quarterly* 71, no. 3 (September 1998): 378–403.

Galvin, John R. *Three Men of Boston*. New York: Thomas Y. Crowell, 1976.

Knappman, Edward W., ed. *Great American Trials: From Salem Witchcraft to Rodney King*. Detroit: Gale Research, 1994.

Markham, Edwin, ed. *The Real America in Romance*. Vol. 9. Chicago: Lakeside Press, 1911.

"Otis, James." In *Encyclopædia Britannica*. Available at <http://www.britannica.com/bcom/eb/article/1/0,5716,59091+1+57651,00.html?query=james%20otis>.

Schumacher, Paul. "Conkling Could Have Been Chief Justice." *Stamps* 251, no. 12 (17 June 1995).

Tudor, William. *The Life of James Otis of Massachusetts*. 1823. Reprint, New York: Da Capo Press, 1970.

Waters, John J., Jr. *The Otis Family: In Provincial and Revolutionary Massachusetts*. Chapel Hill: University of North Carolina Press, 1968.

PENDLETON, EDMUND

(1721–1803)

EDMUND PENDLETON, NOTABLE early Virginia attorney and judge, was born in 1721, the seventh child of Mary Taylor Pendleton and Henry Pendleton, a farmer who had died four months previously. In 1723, Mary Pendleton was remarried to Edward Watkins. Edmund's schooling was fairly sparse, and he is believed to have had only two years of schooling before age fourteen, when he was apprenticed to Benjamin Robinson, the Caroline County, Virginia, court clerk. This very practical experience, along with three months of study in a Latin school, constituted Pendleton's legal education, but Pendleton had already served as a clerk to the vestry of St. Mary's Parish before being admitted to the bar in 1741 at age nineteen. That same year, he married Elizabeth "Betty" Roy, but seven months after she died in childbirth, he married Sarah Pol-

EDMUND PENDLETON
Library of Congress

lard. Although the couple had no children, they took in a three-year-old orphaned nephew (John Taylor of Caroline), who subsequently studied in Pendleton's law office and went on to achieve notoriety as a theorist of Republican principles. A number of other lawyers, including John Penn, who signed the Declaration of Independence as a delegate to the Continental Congress from North Carolina, also studied with Pendleton at his home.

By 1744, Pendleton had been appointed a prosecutor, or "deputy attorney," and in 1751 he was made a justice of Caroline County. The next year

548

he was elected to represent his county in the state general assembly, and by his career's end, he had at one time or another headed each of the three branches of state government (Mays 1952, 1:22). In contrast to many other Virginia leaders of his day, Pendleton was not from a prominent family and had no great inheritance. As his main biographer notes, "Pendleton was entirely a self-made man. He had inherited nothing and he had been compelled to create Edmundsbury [his Caroline County home] from the proceeds of his profession" (Mays 1952, 1:107). Pendleton did succeed in amassing considerable lands in Caroline County, in North Carolina (later Tennessee), and elsewhere in Virginia. Like other planters of his day, Pendleton was a slaveholder, and many of the cases he handled as a judge dealt with punishing slaves who had violated the law, often quite severely.

Pendleton began to emerge as a colonial leader during the successive crises brought about by British attempts to tax colonial goods. Through most of this period, Pendleton was regarded as a moderate who strove for reconciliation. Pendleton disfavored closing the courts at the outset of the American Revolution, and, in a position very similar to the modern idea of judicial review, he declared that the Stamp Act was unconstitutional and therefore void (Mays 1952, 1:171).

When John Robinson—who had served both as the speaker of the House of Burgesses and as Virginia's treasurer—died, Pendleton was asked to handle his estate. Few tasks could have been more complicated, because Robinson had generously loaned not only his own money but also that of the state and was owed more than £130,000, most of which had been taken from the state treasury. Pendleton spent more than fifteen years on the tedious job of settling Robinson's estate, but the fact that he was entrusted with the job was undoubtedly a sign of the high esteem in which he was generally held.

Although he was both a justice in Caroline County and a Caroline County representative to the House of Burgesses, Pendleton continued his law practice. He was especially active in the court in Williamsburg, where he established himself as being among the best of a very able group of attorneys. Pendleton's talents have been most frequently compared to those of GEORGE WYTHE, with whom he was often at loggerheads, although they sometimes took cases together. Pendleton was no match for Wythe's wide classical learning, but he was his equal, if not his superior, in the courtroom. With Pendleton's wide knowledge of people and public affairs, he was especially good at answering logical arguments that Wythe thought to be irrefutable. HENRY CLAY, who worked for a time transcribing for Wythe, has noted that

> Mr. Wythe's forte, as I have understood, lay in the opening of the argument of
> a case, in which for thorough preparation, clearness and force, no one could

excel him. He was not so fortunate in reply. Mr. Pendleton, on the contrary, was always ready both in opening and concluding an argument, and was prompt to meet all the exigencies which would arise in the conduct of a cause in court. The consequence was that Mr. Pendleton was oftener successful than Mr. Wythe in their struggles at the bar. (Mays 1952, 1:229)

As an illustration of his generalizations, Clay went on to tell a story:

On one occasion, when Mr. Wythe, being opposed to Mr. Pendleton, lost the cause, in a moment of vexation he declared, in the presence of a friend, that he would quit the bar, go home, take orders, and enter the pulpit. You had better not do that replied his friend; for if you do, Mr. Pendleton will go home, take orders, and enter the pulpit too, and beat you there. (Mays 1952, 1:229)

Clay further noted that "Mr. Pendleton was far less learned than Mr. Wythe, but he possessed more versatile talents, was an accomplished gentleman, and better adapted to success in general society and in the busy world" (Mays 1952, 1:229).

In analyzing Pendleton's skill as a legislative leader, Thomas Jefferson undoubtedly provided insight into Pendleton's skills in the courtroom as well. Jefferson noted,

Taken in all, [Pendleton] was the ablest man in debate I have ever met with. He had not indeed the poetical fancy of Mr. [Patrick] Henry, his sublime imagination, his lofty and over-whelming diction; but he was cool, smooth and persuasive; his language flowing, chaste & embellished, his conceptions quick, acute and full of resource; never vanquished; for if he lost in the main battle, he returned upon you, and regained so much of it as to make it a drawn one, by dexterous maneuvers, skirmishes in detail, and the recovery of small advantages which little singly, were important altogether. You never knew when you were clear of him, but were harassed by his perseverance until the patience was worn down of all who had less of it than himself. (Mays 1952, 2:130)

Pendleton apparently attracted clients from throughout Virginia. On the eve of a battle, George Washington turned to Pendleton to write a will for him (Mays 1952, 2:234). Pendleton's biographer observed that "Pendleton attracted clients because he was what every client has always wanted—a winner" (Mays 1952, 1:234).

Pendleton was chosen as a member of the Virginia Committee of Correspondence and as a Virginia delegate to both continental congresses. In the second, he was one who helped draft yet another petition asking King George III for redress. When the hope of avoiding war was not realized,

Pendleton was selected as president of both of Virginia's revolutionary conventions in 1775 where, as president of the Committee of Safety, he was the de facto state executive (Konig 1999, 276). Pendleton's decision to deny chief military command of the Virginia forces to fellow attorney Patrick Henry (who had advocated independence long before the more conservative Pendleton) resulted in continuing ill will between the two lawyers that lasted through the rest of their lives.

Elected again to preside over the Virginia Convention of 1776, Pendleton was now ready for independence, and Virginia urged its representatives in Congress to make such a declaration. Pendleton was elected as speaker of the Virginia House of Delegates for a time but naturally gravitated toward the judiciary, which he hoped would be an anchor of stability. With Thomas Jefferson and George Wythe, Pendleton helped adjust the law to independence by revising the laws of Virginia.

In 1777, Pendleton injured his hip in a riding accident that left him in frequent pain and that forced a man once regarded as "one of the handsomest men in Virginia" (Mays 1952, 2:144) to use a crutch or a cane through most of the rest of his life.

Pendleton spent most of this time at the bench, gaining a reputation, after a distinguished English jurist, as "Virginia's Mansfield" (Konig 1999, 276). Pendleton was chief justice of Virginia's high court of chancery, created in 1777, where he served with George Wythe and Robert Carter Nicholas; he also presided over a new court of appeals, established in 1778 (Konig 1999, 276). When this was replaced by yet another court of appeals, Pendleton became chief justice, a position that (much to Wythe's chagrin) allowed him to review—and in many cases to reverse—decisions of George Wythe, who was now the lone chancellor of Virginia. Pendleton and his court are said to have reversed or modified a majority of the more than 150 cases that were appealed to them from Wythe's court (Mays 1952, 2:290).

When faced in *Commonwealth v. Caton* (1782) with the legitimacy of a pardon issued by the state legislature, Pendleton worked to avoid a direct confrontation by squaring the law with the state constitution, but he and other justices helped establish the groundwork for judicial review of unconstitutional legislation. Although he did not attend the Constitutional Convention in Philadelphia, Pendleton was chosen as chair of the Virginia Ratifying Convention. Despite their rivalry on other issues, Pendleton worked successfully with other Federalists, including George Wythe, who was selected to preside over the Committee of the Whole, thus enabling Pendleton to play a key role with James Madison and EDMUND RANDOLPH in debates, where PATRICK HENRY and George Mason led the fight against ratification. Pendleton was one of the main defenders of Article III of the new constitution providing for an independent judiciary, and he and other

Federalists successfully beat back proposals that would have made ratification of the new constitution contingent on the prior adoption of a series of proposed amendments, some of which were later incorporated into the Bill of Rights.

When George Washington became president, he offered Pendleton a position on a U.S. district court, but Pendleton declined in order to continue serving in Virginia. Although he gravitated toward the Democratic-Republican party and toward the philosophy of states' rights espoused by Thomas Jefferson and James Madison, Pendleton remained friends with Washington. After Jefferson's successful election as president in 1800, which Pendleton had supported, Pendleton authored a pamphlet entitled *The Danger Not Over* in which he proposed a series of amendments designed to curb what he regarded as encroachments by the national government.

As a jurist, Pendleton was known for his extreme practicality that appeared to mirror his approach as a lawyer. His chief biographer notes that "Again and again he would cut through involved arguments over the meaning of words used by men in their wills or contracts. What would a plain man take the words to mean? That was the test he applied" (Mays 1952, 2:281). Such an unadorned approach to law was undoubtedly one of the factors that led Wythe to bring his own conflict with Pendleton to the public attention, but Wythe's critiques were so complex that they had little impact on the reading public, and Pendleton decided not to reply in kind.

A longtime supporter of the once-established Anglican Church in Virginia, Pendleton was prepared to overturn a state law adopted in 1801–1802 allowing for the sale of church lands for the support of the poor. The case had been appealed from Wythe's court, which had upheld the law. Although Pendleton had written his decision, he died before he was able to give it, and the equally divided court on which he sat thus had the effect of affirming Wythe's judgment.

Pendleton's death was greeted with mourning both in the state and in national counsels. As a self-made lawyer and jurist, Pendleton epitomized many of the values that made the new nation such a great one.

—*John R. Vile*

SOURCES AND SUGGESTIONS FOR FURTHER READING

Konig, David Thomas. "Pendleton, Edmund." In *American National Biography*, edited by John A. Garraty and Mark C. Carnes. New York: Oxford University Press, 1999, 17:275–277.

Mays, David John. *Edmund Pendleton, 1721–1803: A Biography*. 2 vols. Richmond: Virginia State Library, 1952.

PETIGRU, JAMES LOUIS

(1789–1863)

JAMES LOUIS PETIGRU
Library of Congress

JAMES LOUIS PETIGRU—LAWYER, antebellum South Carolina Whig, and Unionist politician and civic activist—never held a judicial office, yet is deemed "a great jurist"; never occupied high public office, yet is revered as a "statesman"; never established charitable institutions, yet is honored as a "great-hearted philanthropist"; never authored books or treatises, yet is regarded as a scholar of the law, a "lawyer's lawyer." Petigru's life is one of contradictions. His was at once a life of professional triumphs over a half century at the bar, high social status in a patrician society, personal tragedies, dramatic financial oscillations, and political marginality.

Petigru was born on May 10, 1789, near Abbeville in the Palmetto State's northwestern Ninety-Sixth District. He was the eldest child born to a struggling upcountry farmer, William Pettigrew, and Louise Guy Gibert, whose Huguenot ancestry and associated Calvinistic values led the upwardly mobile son to Huguenotize the spelling of his last name. Educated in a log academy, where he was taught by Moses Waddell, a graduate of Presbyterian divine John Witherspoon's College of New Jersey (later Princeton University), and at South Carolina College, from which he graduated in 1809, he subsequently read law with Beaufort attorney William Robertson. His legal career began, following admission to the bar in 1812, in Coosawhatchie, the rural court town of coastal Beaufort District. There he became district solicitor under the sponsorship of the politically powerful and nationalist local planter Daniel E. Huger. The daughter of another planter became Petigru's wife in 1816. Jane Amelia Postell, who bore him four children, suffered frequent illnesses that were symptomatically treated with addicting morphine.

A move to Charleston in 1819 brought him into partnership with future congressman and governor James Hamilton Jr. Petigru took over the practice in 1822, the same year that the legislature named him attorney general of South Carolina. He held that post until late 1830, when he won elective office on the Unionist ticket. The nullification storm that engulfed South Carolina in the wake of the 1828 protective tariff ("Tariff of Abominations") doomed Petigru's Whiggish political career in the state legislature, which had included advocating public financing of the state's economic infrastructure. Thereafter, only appointed offices lay open. The death of Charlestonian and U.S. Supreme Court associate justice William Johnson in 1834 found Petigru in the running as his successor. The aspirant doubted his chances, an insight verified by President Andrew Jackson's appointment of his loyal political ally Georgian James Moore Wayne. Even more abortive was the lofting of an aged Petigru's candidacy in 1862 to fill the Supreme Court seat vacated by JOHN ARCHIBALD CAMPBELL, who resigned on the secession of his native Alabama. Even the position of attorney general of the United States lay beyond his grasp. President Millard Fillmore, a fellow Whig, considered his nomination, but the solid opposition of the South Carolina delegation thwarted it. Instead, Fillmore named Petigru as U.S. attorney for the District of South Carolina. In the midst of a furor over the Compromise of 1850 supported only by the tiny Whig/Unionist constituency in South Carolina, the post was so unattractive that only Petigru would reluctantly accept the appointment. He held it from 1850 to 1853.

To the end of his life, Petigru remained a political maverick who embraced conservative principles in an order-shattering Jacksonian age that fostered a sea change in the political culture of South Carolina. He, however, glorified the founders' handiwork and praised the Constitution and the frame of government it created as bulwarks of liberty, unity, and progress. In Petigru's view, the Constitution rested not on a national compact among sovereign states, as John Calhoun argued, but rather on the sovereign people, as Chief Justice JOHN MARSHALL maintained. At the great chief justice's death in 1835, Petigru authored the Charleston bar's memorial resolutions incorporated in the published proceedings of the U.S. Supreme Court. In it he alluded to Marshall's conception of the Constitution, the protection it accorded to vested property rights, and to judicial independence. For South Carolinians, however, dwelling in a state roiled by the nullificationist response to the tariff and surging toward secession, as Petigru perceived in 1833, Madisonian democracy and Marshallian constitutionalism faded as anchoring forces.

Notwithstanding pervasive tensions between fidelity to Federalist-Whig principles and loyalty to hearth and home, the political never became personal. Petigru's cheery temper, warm, hearty, and courtly manners rendered him a veritable "punctilio of etiquette" and enabled him to win and retain friendships with even his fiercest political opponents. Fate did not spare him the premature deaths of children, afflictions of siblings, a disabled and extravagant wife, or the collapse of his quest for the acknowledged cachet of social status—a landed estate. His six-hundred-acre Savannah River rice plantation became a casualty in the 1837 panic of risky speculative investments with ex-partner Hamilton. Financial recovery by the mid-1850s reflected the fruits of a flourishing law practice. Whether as state's attorney or as private counsel, Petigru's practice carried him from his Charleston home to every judicial district in South Carolina, to trial and appellate courts in that state, and often into neighboring states. His was an unpredictable, peripatetic life, made so by the relatively few state judges who, having completed the docket in one district, immediately moved on and opened the next court. Petigru's modern biographer has calculated that, although he eschewed criminal business in the 1840s, his firm appeared in 20 to 25 percent of all civil cases heard in Charleston's equity court. And during the 1840s and 1850s, his successful practice averaged ten reported appeals court cases per year.

From 1830 to the early 1850s, hardly a term of the U.S. Sixth Circuit Court—held alternately in Charleston and Columbia—passed without civil cases involving Petigru's clients on that court's usually uncrowded trial docket. Petigru and senior partner Hamilton appeared before circuit-riding Supreme Court justice William Johnson and district judge Thomas Lee in 1821, two years after Petigru's arrival in Charleston. Court cases carried to judgment by Petigru and partner Lewis Cruger occasionally appeared on that court's docket during the 1820s and early 1830s. They increased in number in the late 1830s and the 1840s, when ex–U.S. attorney Robert Budd Gilchrist replaced Lee and Georgian Wayne succeeded Johnson as the sixth circuit justice. By then, Petigru, in his fifties, was in partnership with a young Henry Lesesne, who resigned in 1850, succeeded by Henry King.

In an era of legendary courtroom combat, Petigru pursued mediation and legislative strategies on his clients' behalf. The former aimed to achieve court-approved compromise solutions. The latter sought monetary settlement unavailable through the judicial process. His citation of arbitration awards and his compromise offers in marine salvage cases met rebuff in published decisions handed down by the federal district court in Charleston. Yet his renown as an arbitrator took him to New York to settle a dispute involving telegraph inventor Samuel F. B. Morse. Lobbying the Georgia legislature nearly fifty-five years after the Supreme Court's nationalistic decision in *Chisholm v. Georgia* (1793), Petigru won for his claimants-clients authorization of a bond issue to pay the principal owed for supplies purchased by Georgia during the Revolutionary War.

Petigru's courtroom demeanor differed substantially from the nineteenth-century oratorical model. A contemporary described him as a person of "elastic step and erect carriage" that suggested a height greater than his five feet ten inches (Pope, 1908, 58). His "great muscular power" made him seem larger than he was. A "rather low but broad brow, . . . strong massive chin, . . . magnificent dark gray eyes, gave dignity, character and intellectual vivacity" to an otherwise plain face that hid a V-shaped vein, "which in moments of high physical or intellectual excitement flamed out like a veritable scarlet letter" (Pope, 1908, 58). Noteworthy too were his hands as elements in his courtroom theatrics. They grasped a professional green bag and the gold head of his walking stick. During arguments they brushed back from his forehead his long, never-graying hair, toyed with spectacles and pinched the sneeze-inducing contents of his gold snuff box. Thus did he punctuate what another contemporary described as a "quaint, original, magnetic eloquence" (Pope, 1908, 35). His oral presentations were founded on careful preparation, a parsimonious style that made for logical and lucid induction from his premises that, as a contemporary recalled, "*turnpiked* the legal pathway out of the most complicated labyrinth of law and fact" (Henry A. DeSaussure in *Memorial* 1866, 11). Precision rather than more common redundancy of language marked his courtroom performances. Oratorical pauses signaled his search for "the right word in the right place" (Pope, 1908, 57). Mood changes, wit, flashes of humor, sarcasm, and the unleashing of "wondrous powers of ridicule" trapped witnesses and won over juries (Isaac W. Hayne in *Memorial* 1866, 13). His professional reputation brought students to his office. His biographer estimates that 10 percent of all lawyers admitted to practice before the South Carolina Court of Appeals between 1825 and 1860 read law under Petigru's mentorship. Attesting to his national eminence was his election by Harvard law students in 1852 as president of their association named after Marshall's close Supreme Court associate, JOSEPH STORY.

Petigru's law practice reflected the legal business spawned by an agricultural slave state; it was largely devoid of issues that influenced enduring changes in the law's development. Only glacial legal change affected probate, trust, and real property law, which constituted much of Petgru's practice, in cases brought by planter clients. Unusual for the region were his other clients: banks, railroads, and corporations. These carried Petigru close to the cutting edge of legal change. Whether as a private attorney or as a public prosecutor, even run-of-the-mill cases pitted him against the dominant culture and its norms. As a courageous prosecutor, he contested appeals by slave owners who had murdered their slaves and he sided with ejected tenant farmers who were about to harvest their crops. Illegitimate children, battered women, and imprisoned debtors all found in him a stout courtroom defender. So too did clients discriminatorily branded as products of miscegenation. Although he was a slave owner who, as a devout Episcopalian, doubted the morality of slavery, Petigru worked, not always successfully, in a hostile legislative climate, to make manumission a reality for slaves on the brink of freedom.

Such "against-the-tide" cases made little societal impact other than on his clients. Some, however, raised important public policy issues involving federalism, civil liberties, corporations, and private property rights. As attorney general of South Carolina, in the early 1820s he had eluded participation in the state's enforcement of the infamous Negro Seamen's Act and the associated Denmark Vesey slave insurrection conspiracy. Years later, while simultaneously serving as attorney for the British consul in Charleston and as U.S. attorney, he invoked in *Roberts v. Yates* (1853) Supreme Court justice William Johnson's circuit court decision in *Elkison v. Deleisseline* (1823) to assert the supremacy of a British-American treaty over South Carolina's internal security measures aimed at quarantining the example and messages carried by free black mariners. And, in the midst of the nullification crisis, he successfully challenged in Judge Gilchrist's district court a test of the constitutionality of the federal tariff act brought by the Nullifiers, among whose leaders was former law partner Hamilton.

The relationship between the Constitution and corporate citizenship figured in a landmark Taney Court case, *Louisville, Cincinnati, and Charleston R.R. v. Letson* (1844), one of two reported Supreme Court cases in which Petigru served as counsel. He represented Yankee contractor Letson, who sought damages against a railroad originally promoted by ardent states' righters to compete with northern roads linking the Midwest to eastern markets, but which failed in the wake of the 1837 panic. With stockholders residing in the contractor's home state, the railroad invoked hoary Marshallian jurisprudence relating to corporations to assert the absence of diverse citizenship, hence its unsuability in the federal forum. Justice Wayne, before whom Petigru successfully argued Letson's case in the U.S. circuit court, affirmed that decision and praised "the really distinguished ability of the arguments of counsel." Wayne, however, did not embrace Petigru's central argument that corporations were "a state in miniature" and that the residency of corporate officers, not just of stockholders, fixed corporate citizenship. Instead, he followed the argument proffered by Petigru's fellow South Carolina Whig and President Tyler's attorney general, Hugh S. Legaré, to hold that the place of incorporation and place of doing business determined corporate citizenship in a developing national market economy.

Curbing overreaching by government, whether power excesses arose from rampant majoritarianism or from elite manipulation, was a hallmark of Petigru's legal practice. Repeal of South Carolina's Nullification Ordinance was followed by a Nullifier stratagem of imposing on all state officers a test oath of allegiance to the state. The oath, aimed squarely at dissident Unionists, was challenged by Petigru, who argued before the state appeals court in *McCready v. Hunt* (1834) that the oath evoked memories of religious and political oppression in Europe and conflicted with state and federal constitutions. The duty of the court was plain, he stated. "The free and generous principles of the law which the court is sworn to administer favor liberty." The oath deprived "the humblest citizen of his liberty." Therefore, the judges, he continued, "must take the law as they find it, and if it does not conform to the Constitution declare it null and void." Success capped his effort. Successful as well was his invocation in federal district court of the fair trial and due process rights of Yankee woodcutter and fraternizer with slaves Reuben Smalle, whose nonconformist ways had been subjected to harsh public and private suppression. Later, in the Confederate district court, before ex–U.S. district judge Andrew Gordon Magrath, then robed in gray, to whom he had taught law, Petigru fearlessly came to the defense of private property owned by enemy aliens residing in the North that the Confederate Congress sought to confiscate and sequester. Petigru argued fervently against the writ of garnishment and attached interrogatories respecting such property held by him as trustee while decrying the government's demand that he betray his clients. Privately doubting the very legitimacy of the Confederate Constitution, he assailed in Magrath's courtroom the power of the Confederate Congress to interfere with the moral obligations of debtors to creditors and, as a government of limited constitutional powers, to usurp the sequestration powers implicitly reserved to the states. Soaring rhetoric marked his conclusion. Should, he asked, such legislative powers be inferred from a constitutional text that restricted laws to effect only powers expressly granted? "Forbid it, Heaven!" he declaimed, "for if it is, mankind have been deluded by a vain hope, and paper Constitutions are no more than a cheat practiced on the credulity of poor suffering human nature."

Suffering defeat in Magrath's courtroom, failing health, war-induced evaporation of his law practice, destruction by fire of his Charleston home, and loss of kin in war, Petigru nevertheless labored on in his twilight years as a law reformer. Legal reform had occupied his attention since the 1820s, when he sought reform in the state's equity system to promote, in the Federalist-Whig tradition, enterprise and commerce. The legislature in 1859 named Petigru to codify, unify, and harmonize the common and statutory laws of South Carolina by producing a modern civil code. Posthumously rejected by the legislature that had commissioned it, his efforts provided a foundation for the Reconstruction legislature's codification of the state's laws in 1872.

An anomaly in life, Petigru had stood with an old and conservative political order against fire-eating revolutionary forces of Southern glorification and nationalism. The vanguard of these forces assembled in Columbia in December 1860. Petigru then allegedly directed an inquiring stranger seeking the "Lunatic Asylum" to the secession convention filled, at that moment, he said, with "one hundred and sixty-four maniacs." Three years later, federal troops hovered at Charleston's doorstep. On March 9, 1863, the pillar of the South Carolina bar, persevering defender of the Constitution, advocate for rich as well as disadvantaged clients, untiring law reformer, promoter of civic causes, and courageous political iconoclast died. He died in virtual political exile among those who ironically eulogized their noble native son as one who stood "at the head of the profession . . . in this State; and . . . both in the old Union and in the new Southern Confederacy" (Richard Yeadon, in *Memorial* 1866, 15). And chiseled into the marble monument marking his grave in Charleston's St. Michael's churchyard was an epitaph reminding visitors that

In the great Civil War/He withstood his People for his Country/But his People did homage to the Man/Who held his conscience higher than their praise/And his Country/Heaped her honors on the grave of the Patriot,/To whom living,/His own righteous self-respect sufficed/Alike for Motive and Reward.

—*Peter G. Fish*

Sources and Suggestions for Further Reading

Carson, James Petigru. *Life, Letters and Speeches of James Louis Petigru: Union Man of South Carolina.* Washington, D.C.: W. H. Loudermilk & Co., 1920.
Ford, Lacy. "James Louis Petigru: The Last South Carolina Federalist." In *Intellectual Life in Antebellum Charleston,* edited by Michael O'Brien and David Molthe-Hansen. Knoxville: University of Tennessee Press, 1986, 152–185.

Memorial of the Late James Louis Petigru: Proceedings of the Bar of Charleston, S.C., 25 March 1863. New York: Richardson & Company, 1866.

Minutes, Circuit and District Courts, District of South Carolina, 1789–1849 and Index to Judgments, Circuit and District Courts, 1792–1874, M11181, microfilm roll 2. Washington, D.C.: National Archives and Records Service.

Pease, William H., and Jane H. Pease. *James Louis Petigru: Carolina Lawyer, Southern Unionist, American Conservative.* Athens: University of Georgia Press, 1995.

Pope, Joseph Daniel. "James Louis Petigru, 1789–1863." In *Great American Lawyers: The Lives and Influence of Judges and Lawyers Who Have Acquired Permanent National Reputations, and Have Developed the Jurisprudence of the United States,* edited by William Draper Lewis. Philadelphia: John C. Winston Company, 1908, 4:29–73.

"Tribute to the Memory of Chief Justice Marshall" (July 17, 1835). In *Obituary,* 35 U.S. (10 Peters) v–vi (1836).

PFEFFER, LEO

(1909–1993)

LEO PFEFFER
American Jewish Congress

LEO PFEFFER, EMINENT LAWYER, scholar, author, and advocate for religious and civil liberties, was perhaps best known as an ardent defender of the separation of church and state. His frequent and compelling oral arguments before the U.S. Supreme Court significantly shaped American church-state law under the U.S. Constitution. Pfeffer, whether as lead attorney, filer of amicus curiae brief, or litigation consultant, was personally involved in more than 50 percent of establishment clause cases that were heard by the Supreme Court during his career. Samuel Krislov, a noted scholar of the U.S. judicial system, described Pfeffer in this way: "Leo Pfeffer is probably sui generis. . . . No one comes to mind . . . to rival Pfeffer's intellectual dominance over so vital an area of constitutional law for so extensive a period" (Wood, 1985, 421). In a tribute to Pfeffer, James E. Wood Jr., former director of the J. M. Dawson Institute of Church-State Studies at Baylor University, said, "In Leo Pfeffer were combined the scholar and the jurist, the thinker and the participant, the theoretician and the practitioner. . . . Deeply involved in his concern for a broad range of human rights and civil liberties, he was a passionate advocate of religious liberty and an eloquent defender of the institutional separation of church and state which he always saw as a corollary to the constitutional guarantee of the free exercise of religion" (Wood, 1985, preface).

Leo Pfeffer entered the arena of church-state litigation in the post–World War II era, just as the Supreme Court, by making the establishment and free exercise clauses binding on the states, opened the doors to an increasing docket of church-state cases. Two basic interpretations of the religion clauses emerged in this period. The first held that the constitutional framers intended to separate church and state, creating a secular state that was to be neutral with regard to religious matters. The second interpretation held that the framers never intended to create a secular state. Rather, government could assist religion provided it was done in an evenhanded, nonpreferential manner. It was the first position, the separationist framework, which found in Leo Pfeffer its most articulate legal advocate. He therefore argued that "complete separation of church and state is best for the church, and best for the state, and secures freedom for both" (Pfeffer 1967).

Background

Leo Pfeffer, the youngest of five children, was born in 1909 to Hungarian Orthodox Jewish parents. His father was a rabbi. Two years after his birth, his family immigrated to the United States and settled in the Lower East Side of New York City. When Leo was six, his parents enrolled him in a nearby public school, but when the school considered introducing released-time religious instruction into the school his parents withdrew him and enrolled him in a yeshiva school. He subsequently attended the Rabbi Isaac Elchonon Talmudical Academy for his secondary education, which later became Yeshiva University. Pfeffer received his college education at the City College of New York and, at age twenty-three, his law degree from New York University in 1933. In 1937, he married his lifetime mate, Freda Plotkin. They had two children, Alan and Susan.

Among the events that formed the context for Pfeffer's career was his religious upbringing. As the son of an Orthodox rabbi, he grew up with a sense of respect for his religious tradition and for the traditions of others. His Talmudic education in Jewish philosophy and his love for the prophetic tradition informed his argument and concern for social justice. Moreover, the Holocaust and the anti-Semitic resurgence in the United States during and after World War II made him critical of majoritarianism and aroused his concern for the rights of minorities. Often excoriated as an atheist due to his commitment to church-state separation, his genuine devotion to his Jewish faith was never questioned by those who knew him.

Leo Pfeffer joined the staff of the Commission on Law and Social Action of the American Jewish Congress (AJC) in 1945. As counsel, special counsel, and director, he served the commission for much of the remainder of his career, becoming a church-state expert in the process. During his career, he also served as counsel for the New York Committee for Public Education and Religious Liberty (PEARL), and the National Coalition for PEARL. In addition, he held several academic positions: lecturer, New School of Social Research, 1954–1960, and Mt. Holyoke College, 1958–1960; David W. Petergorsky professor of constitutional law, Yeshiva University, 1962–1963; and professor and chair of political science, Long Island University, 1964–1979. He died on June 4, 1993.

Pfeffer received many awards, including an honorary doctor of laws degree from Hebrew Union College; the Trustee Award for Scholarly Achievement from Long Island University; the Thomas Jefferson Religious Freedom Award from the Unitarian Universalist Church; the Rabbi Maurice N. Eisendrath Memorial Award from the Union of American Hebrew Congregations; the Citation for Contribution to Public Education from the Horace Mann League; the distinguished American Jewish Council Award; and the Certificate of Merit from the Council of Jewish Federation. In 1985, the J. M. Dawson Institute of Church-State Studies, Baylor University, in recognition of Pfeffer's twenty-four years of service as a member of the editorial council of the institute's *Journal of Church and State*, published a 596-page festschrift in his honor.

Leo Pfeffer's scholarly writings reflect his devotion to religious liberty and church-state separation. They include *Church, State and Freedom* (1953), described by one authority as "the most authoritative constitutional history of America's experience with the double faceted principle of religious liberty and separation of government and religion"; *The Liberties of an American: The Supreme Court Speaks* (1956); *Creeds in Competition: A Creative Force in American Culture* (1958); *Church and State in the United States* (1964); *This Honorable Court: A History of the United States Supreme Court* (1965); *God, Caesar, and the Constitution: The Court as Referee of Church-State Confrontation* (1974); *Religious Freedom* (1976); and *Religion, State, and the Burger Court* (1985). He published many pamphlets, and his more than 240 articles and numerous book reviews appeared in diverse religious and secular publications. He left many unpublished materials, most of which are part of an extensive collection of Pfeffer's papers maintained at Baylor's Dawson Institute. Syracuse University also houses an extensive collection of Pfeffer materials.

Litigation Activities

Pfeffer's first legal assignment with the AJC was to prepare a memorandum on the merits of "released time" for religious instruction. Released time is a

Ellis Rubin

Miami defense attorney Ellis Rubin (b. 1925) has the relatively rare distinction of having been sent to jail rather than calling a witness who he believed was planning to perjure himself. Raised in Binghamton, New York, Rubin went to school with Rod Serling, who went on to create the acclaimed television series *The Twilight Zone*. Rubin encountered massive problems with stuttering throughout his childhood, but he was later able to overcome these in the courtroom. Rubin joined the navy, which sent him to Holy Cross College and he later graduated from the University of Miami Law School.

When Russell Sanborn told Rubin he was going to use a fabricated story to exonerate himself from the brutal killing of his wealthy girlfriend, Rubin asked the judge for permission to withdraw from the case, and was denied. Rubin subsequently spent thirty days in jail rather than commit what he regarded as an ethical violation (his client, defended by another appointed attorney who allowed him to testify, was convicted).

Rubin has had many sensational cases, most of which he has won. Rubin received great media attention when he unsuccessfully tried to argue that fifteen-year-old Ronny Zamora, who had robbed and shot an elderly neighbor, had done so because his addiction to television had caused him to be unable to distinguish between reality and fiction.

Rubin was more successful in defending Prentice Rasheed, a Miami businessman who, faced with numerous break-ins to his store, devised an electrical contraption that had the effect of electrocuting and killing, rather than simply shocking and deterring, an intruder. Rubin's defense before the grand jury is sometimes called the "Tutti-Frutti" defense because he used the example of his ferret named Tutti-Frutti, who chewed through an electrical cord with 115 volts and did not die to show that there was no way that his client could have anticipated the effects of his own contraption.

In another extraordinary case, Rubin used the "battered-woman syndrome defense" to exonerate Lisa Keller for the bludgeoning death of her father outside their condominium. Rubin showed that the petite Lisa (age twenty-nine) had suffered years of physical and sexual abuse at the hands of her father from age thirteen and that she had finally snapped on a night when her father had insisted that she, her mother, and he must all drink from the same glass at the dinner table.

In yet another case, Rubin was able to exonerate Charles Reynolds of Delaware for the strangulation death of his live-in girlfriend, Linda Palachios. Rubin had been recruited into the case by Reynolds's sister, Doris, who had come to him after an initial trial had resulted in a hung jury. After meticulous examination of photographs from the crime scene, Rubin was able to demonstrate that Palachios's death was not murder but was the result of autoerotic behavior, possibly compounded by an overdose of Advil.

Reference

Rubin, Ellis, and Dary Matera. *"Get Me Ellis Rubin!": The Life, Times, and Cases of a Maverick Lawyer*. New York: St Martin's Press, 1989.

system of religious education in public schools under which children desiring to participate in religious instruction are excused from their secular studies for a specified period weekly, while those children not participating in religious instruction remain under the jurisdiction and supervision of the public school for the usual period of secular instruction. The actual practice of released time began in 1913 in Gary, Indiana, and was a staple in the curriculum of the majority of American public schools by the 1940s. Pfeffer was intrigued by the assignment, since the released-time concept had led his parents to remove him from the New York City public schools as a youngster. The memorandum he prepared not only revealed his opposition to the idea of released time but also formed the basis of the AJC's Commission on Law and Social Action brief of amicus curiae in the U.S. Supreme Court case of *McCollum v. Board of Education* (1948).

The brief listed four reasons why the released-time scheme is unconstitutional. It argued that the program (1) preferred one religion over another while at the same time aiding all religions, (2) influenced and compelled children to attend instruction against their will and that of their parents, (3) rendered financial aid to sectarian instruction, and (4) constituted government participation in religious instruction. In delivering the opinion of the Court, Justice Hugo Black held that the state's practice of using public school buildings for the dissemination of religious doctrines "aided the sectarian groups through the use of state's compulsory public school machinery. This is not separation of church and state." According to Pfeffer, the significance of the Court's decision was its application of the "wall of separation" principle. In his concurring opinion, Justice Felix Frankfurter observed that the divergent amicus curiae briefs filed by different religious organizations showed that the program had been a divisive one. The Court sided with Pfeffer's position, ruling that released-time instruction, when it takes place on school premises, is unconstitutional. Pfeffer's important career as an advocate for religious freedom and church-state separation was off and running.

Pfeffer's involvement in church-state litigation proved to be prolific. His arguments in a range of cases were significant influences in shaping the Supreme Court's mostly "separationist" interpretations of the religion clauses. Although it was Thomas Jefferson's "wall of separation" metaphor that provided the vision for the American principle of separation of church and state, it was Leo Pfeffer who convinced the Court of the brilliance of that vision. In case after case, the high court sided with Leo Pfeffer. The issues in those cases involved primarily religious education in public schools and controversies over public aid to religious schools, both of which he argued under the establishment clause. In addition, there were the cases he called "clash of conflicting interests" involving the defense of new religions and the protection of Sabbatarians and conscientious objectors, which he argued under the free exercise clause. Generally speaking, Pfeffer did not see a clear-cut conflict between the two religious clauses. He maintained that when there is a government-created coercion to participate in religious conduct, both religion clauses are violated, but where there is a coercion to participate in secular conduct only, only the free exercise clause is abridged.

In 1952, four years after the *McCollum* case, Pfeffer represented before the Supreme Court a number of parents whose children attended the New York City public schools. The city had a released-time program, but it differed from the one in *McCollum* in that it released the students to off-campus sites for religious instruction rather than permitting the instruction to take place on school grounds. Pfeffer argued that the program was substantively no different from the one in *McCollum*. "The weight and influence of the school is put behind a program in religious instruction, which remains a violation of the Establishment Clause," he argued. But to no avail; much to Pfeffer's chagrin, the Court ruled in favor of the New York City school system.

Pfeffer filed an amicus curiae brief in the 1962 landmark case of *Engel v. Vitale*. The arguments of Pfeffer and his colleagues prevailed this time, convincing the Court that a twenty-two-word, nondenominational prayer written by the New York State Board of Regents for official use in the public schools was unconstitutional. The following year he filed an amicus brief in *Abington School District v. Schempp*, a case that considered the merits of daily recitations of the Lord's Prayer and Bible passages in public school settings. His side prevailed, convincing the Court that such practices violate the Constitution's requirement of neutrality toward religion. He also filed an amicus brief in *Stone v. Graham* (1980), asserting the unconstitutionality of a Kentucky law authorizing the display of the Ten Commandments on the walls of public school classrooms. The Court ruled the law unconstitutional.

During the civil rights era of the 1960s, many of the state governments initiated programs to fund private schools, which were in fact sectarian schools. Pfeffer participated in many of these cases, seeking to end public funding of religious schools (from the elementary to the college level). It was the incessant nature of the cases that led him to describe the situation as "a chess game with the Constitution." He elaborated on the strategy behind these cases:

> A game plan emerged. Pass a law providing aid to parochial schools and start paying immediately or as quickly as possible. Continue paying until the Supreme Court finally declares the law unconstitutional. It may take a year or more before a suit is started to challenge the law, and perhaps another two years until the case gets to the Supreme Court. In the meantime, keep paying.

When the law is finally struck down by the Supreme Court, rush some variation through the legislature and start over again. (Pfeffer, 1974, 282)

Among the recurrent cases in which he participated were *Board of Education v. Allen* (1968), *Flast v. Gardner* (1968), *Lemon v. Kurtzman* (1971), *Tilton v. Richardson* (1971), *PEARL v. Levitt I* (1973), *PEARL v. Nyquist* (1973), *Sloan v. Lemon* (1973), *Meek v. Pittenger* (1975), *Roemer v. Board of Public Works of Maryland* (1976), *PEARL v. Levitt II* (1977), *Wolman v. Walter* (1977), and *PEARL v. Regan* (1980). In the *Allen*, *Roemer*, and *Wolman* cases, Pfeffer, as special counsel for the AJC, filed briefs arguing that all aid to sectarian schools is a violation of the establishment clause. In his brief in the *Allen* case he challenged the "child benefit theory," which was first applied in the case of *Everson v. Board of Education* (1968). He sought to affirm the "no-aid" principle and show the unconstitutionality of a statute that allowed the loaning of public school textbooks to sectarian schools. He argued that the statute was fraudulent on the grounds that child benefit is the goal of *all* education and so would warrant state funding for all education, public or private. Although the case was decided for the (New York) Board of Education, it prepared Pfeffer to show in future cases that religion permeates all activities of religious schools.

In 1971, the Supreme Court simultaneously heard arguments in two similar cases, *Lemon v. Kurtzman* and *Earley v. DiCenso*. Both cases dealt with salaries or salary supplements paid to teachers of private religious schools from state funds. As counsel for plaintiffs/appellants in both cases, Pfeffer sought to show the extent of religious pervasiveness in church schools as well as the excessive entanglement of the state in the affairs of church schools. In addition to challenging the unconstitutionality of the legislative funding efforts, Pfeffer objected to the inclusion of private-school personnel on the committee that oversaw the administration of the funding statute. Pfeffer argued on the basis of *Schempp*'s two-prong test (legislation must have a secular purpose and cannot advance or inhibit religion), and the excessive entanglement principle announced in *Walz v. Tax Commission* (1970). The Court found in favor of the appellants and based its decision on these three principles which became known as the "*Lemon* three-prong test."

In that same year (1971), Pfeffer served as lead counsel for the plaintiff in *Tilton v. Richardson*. He challenged a law that provided state aid to church colleges to construct facilities to be used for secular purposes only. The law permitted the state to recover the funds if the facilities were used for religious purposes within twenty years. After twenty years, however, the restriction ceased and the property could be used for any purpose, secular or religious. The Court held that the twenty-year provision was unconstitutional but that the law did not otherwise violate the establishment clause. In arguing that the Court must consider the level of religiosity of colleges and universities in ascertaining whether or not facilities could actually be constructed for "secular" purposes, Pfeffer recommended considering six criteria: (1) the stated purpose of the college, (2) the college personnel, which included the governing board, the administrative officers, the faculty, and the student body, (3) the college's relationship with religious organizations and groups, (4) the place of religion in the college's program, (5) the result or "outcome" of the college program, and (6) the work and image of the college in the community. He argued that all of these criteria were present in *Tilton*, but the Court disagreed, holding that the college was not "pervasively sectarian" and that the state funding statute was therefore constitutional. A year later, however, in *PEARL v. Levitt I*, the Court, in striking down a New York statute that compensated church schools for expenses incurred in keeping records and conducting tests, used Pfeffer's six-category profile to find the church schools "pervasively sectarian" and thus incapable of receiving state funds. The "pervasively sectarian" rule remains in place today as the standard by which the constitutionality of government programs to aid religiously affiliated education is measured.

Finally, Pfeffer litigated numerous cases involving Sunday laws, Sabbatarian interests, new religious movements, and conscientious objectors. As noted earlier, these cases are what he termed "clash of conflicting interests." Among them were *Gallagher v. Crown Kosher Supermarket* (1961), a case that upheld Sunday closing laws; *Sherbert v. Verner* (1963), a Sabbatarian case that produced the all important "compelling state interest" test to measure violations of the free exercise clause; *U.S. v. Seeger* (1965), which recognized the right of conscientious objection to war; and *Torcaso v. Watkins* (1961), which struck down religious tests for holding civil office. Pfeffer filed briefs of amicus curiae in the *Crown Kosher*, *Sherbert*, and *Seeger* cases and argued as counsel in *Torcaso*. In these cases, Pfeffer based his argument on freedom of conscience, which the First Amendment guarantees. In his argument challenging the Sunday law, Pfeffer contended that the law imposes a "religious test for the right to receive unemployment benefit" and that "the grant of a privilege may not be conditioned upon the forfeiture of a right secured by the First Amendment." Although Pfeffer did not win his Sunday law cases, he did prevail in *Torcaso* and *Sherbert*.

Conclusion

Leo Pfeffer was indeed one of the premier advocates of church-state separation and religious liberty in U.S. history. Although many have praised Pfeffer for his enormous influence on the development of U.S. church-state law,

Gregg Ivers, in his book *To Build a Wall: American Jews and the Separation of Church and State*, delivered perhaps the highest accolade of all. He concluded that Pfeffer "was beyond doubt the most dominant and influential advocate of his generation (and quite possibly of all time) in the field of church-state law."

—*Derek H. Davis*

Sources and Suggestions for Further Reading

Holcomb, David J. "The Nexus of Freedom of Religion and Separation of Church and State in the Thought of Leo Pfeffer." Ph.D. dissertation, Baylor University, 1997.

Pfeffer, Leo. "An Autobiographical Sketch." In *Religion and the State: Essays in Honor of Leo Pfeffer*, edited by James E. Wood Jr. Waco, Tex.: Baylor University Press, 1985.

_____. *Church, State and Freedom*. Boston: Beacon Press, 1953. Revised, 1967.

_____. *God Caesar, and the Constitution: The Court as Referee of Church-State Confrontation*. Boston: Beacon Press, 1974.

_____. *Leo Pfeffer's Papers and Publications*. 22 vols. Compiled by the J. M. Dawson Institute of Church-State Studies, Baylor University, Waco, Tex., 1985.

_____. *Religion, State, and the Burger Court*. Buffalo, N.Y.: Prometheus, 1985.

_____. *This Honorable Court: A History of the United States Supreme Court*. Boston: Beacon Press, 1965.

Wood, James E., Jr., ed. *Religion and the State: Essays in Honor of Leo Pfeffer*. Waco, Tex.: Baylor University Press, 1985.

_____. "A Tribute to Leo Pfeffer." *Journal of Church and State* 35 (1993): 605–606.

PINKNEY, WILLIAM

(1764–1822)

WILLIAM PINKNEY WAS A DIS-
tinguished lawyer, diplomat, and
statesman. Born in Annapolis,
Maryland, to Jonathan Pinkney
and Ann Rind Pinkney, William
Pinkney had his education at
King William School interrupted when his parents' property was confiscated during the
Revolutionary War due to their
Tory sympathies. Pinkney, who
had joined the patriot cause,
subsequently took up the study
of medicine under a Doctor
Goodwin before turning to law
with the aid of Samuel Chase,
who later became a justice of the
U.S. Supreme Court.

WILLIAM PINKNEY
Library of Congress

Pinkney was admitted to the
bar in 1786, first practicing outside Baltimore and later moving
to Annapolis. Pinkney's deep
knowledge of real property and
special pleadings were quickly
recognized, and he quickly rose to the top of his profession. In 1789, he
married Ann Maria Rodgers, with whom he was to have ten children.

Pinkney held a variety of offices during his life. He was elected in 1790 to
the U.S. House of Representatives, although he did not subsequently serve.
He was elected as mayor of Annapolis and delegate to the Maryland legislature in 1785. From 1796 to 1804, he served as a diplomat to England, where
he served on a commission that helped resolve prize cases between Great
Britain and the United States under the Jay Treaty. He was the attorney
general of Maryland from 1805 to 1806. From 1807 to 1811, he was a minis-

ter to England. He served as U.S. attorney general from 1811 to 1814, during which time he was a Maryland militiaman and was wounded at the battle of Bladensburg (he resigned as attorney general when he was told that he needed to reside full time in the nation's capital, which would have limited his outside legal work). Pinkney served as ambassador to Russia and Naples in 1816; and he served as U.S. senator from 1819 until his death in 1822 (Sterling 1999, 548).

Pinkney was admitted to the bar of the U.S. Supreme Court in 1806, and, despite interruptions of his practice occasioned by his diplomatic assignments, he argued eighty-four cases before that body (Sterling 1999, 548). Many of the encomiums Pinkney received came from U.S. Supreme Court justices. Chief Justice JOHN MARSHALL is reported to have referred to Pinkney as "the greatest man he had ever seen in a Court of Justice" (Niles 1907, 177). Justice JOSEPH STORY noted that "his accurate and discriminating Law knowledge, which he pours out with wonderful precision, gives him in my opinion, a great superiority over every man whom I have known" (Niles 1907, 177–178). Noting that "it was worth a journey from Salem to hear it," Story said of Pinkney's arguments in *McCulloch v. Maryland* (1819) that "All the cobwebs of sophistry and metaphysics about States' Rights and State Sovereignty, he brushed away with a mighty besom" (Niles 1907, 211). Similarly, Chief Justice Roger Taney claimed that he had never seen another attorney before the Supreme Court who "was equal to him" (Niles 1907, 177).

When he was state attorney general, Pinkney argued the case of *Luther Martin v. The State*, in which he established that, as attorney general, MARTIN had received a fee to which he was not entitled (Niles 1907, 193). Much later, Pinkney delivered a three-day speech in the case of *McCulloch v. Maryland* (1819), in which he argued, in language from which Chief Justice John Marshall seems to have borrowed heavily (see White 1991, 248–250), for the constitutionality of the U.S. bank. *McCulloch* has been described as "the most important case of William Pinkney's legal career" and is possibly "his greatest speech before a court of law," and there is some evidence that the court might actually have been leaning against the bank prior to Pinkney's presentation (Ireland 1986, 181–186). Pinkney's arguments in this case displayed his usual use of analogies and allusion to classical learning:

> These miserable *State Jealousies*, which the learned counsel seems, in the language of Milton, to consider as "hovering angels, girt with golden wings"—but which, in my estimate of their character, attended like *Malignant Influences* at the birth of the Constitution, and have ever since dogged the footsteps of its youth—may be said to have been summoned by him to testify in this cause, to give this Court their hysterical apprehensions and delirious warnings, to affect

our understanding with the palsy of fear, to scream us, as it were, into a surrender of the last, the only fortress of the common felicity and safety, by capitulating with these petty views and local feelings which once assailed us, in the very cradle of our independence, as the serpents of Juno assailed the cradle of Hercules, and were then upon the point of consigning us to everlasting perdition. (Niles 1907, 209)

Although he died before he could argue either, Pinkney also developed the argument in *Cohens v. Virginia* (1821) that the U.S. Supreme Court had jurisdiction to hear the case, and he was initially retained in the historic *Gibbons v. Ogden* case (1824), dealing with navigation and interstate commerce. Pinkney was also involved in the *Nereid Case* (1816), in which he unsuccessfully argued that Argentine goods were subject to capture by American privateers. Pinkney frequently appeared in prize cases, arguing in more than one-third of ninety-three such cases argued before the U.S. Supreme Court from 1812 to 1822, "the golden age of prize law" (Ireland 1986, 95).

Pinkney was a powerful orator who could adorn his speeches with striking figures of speech. Renowned by contemporaries for his word painting, an acquaintance once remembered Pinkney's description of St. Paul's Cathedral to him as lingering in his memory "like a strand of the grandest music" (Ireland 1986, 230). Pinkney was also known for his prodigious preparation.

A more controversial quality, for which Pinkney was also known, was his practice of ruthlessly focusing on his opponent's weakest points and giving no quarter. After distinguishing "soft and persuasive" rhetoric from that which is "impetuous and overpowering," a nephew, in an otherwise rather fawning biography, notes that

> Mr. Pinkney's oratory was impetuous and overpowering. He could touch the tender chords with the hand of a master, and call forth, when he willed, the softest tones to melt and subdue the listener; but most commonly he spoke to command and bear down, and such was the might and majesty of his eloquence that it took captive every hearer at its will. It was masterful and victorious. (Pinkney 1969, 82)

So too, another biographer has noted that "One characteristic, however, of his arguments throughout his whole career, was the unmerciful way in which he would pounce down upon some weak point or careless argument of his adversary, and remorselessly hold it up as a target, while he riddled it with his logic" (Niles 1907, 188).

Perhaps because of the interruption of his earliest schooling, while serving abroad as a U.S. diplomat Pinkney became cognizant of his own educa-

Littleton Waller Tazewell

Few of the advocates before the John Marshall Supreme Court could have been less ambitious than Virginia's Littleton Tazewell (1774–1860). Born in Williamsburg to Henry Tazewell, an attorney, and Dorothea Waller, who died when Littleton was only three, Tazewell was largely raised by his maternal grandfather, Judge Benjamin Waller. The young Tazewell also attracted the attention of GEORGE WYTHE, who helped in his education before he graduated from the College of William & Mary and read law under John Wickham in Richmond, after his father unsuccessfully pressured him to consider diplomatic service.

Tazewell began practice in Williamsburg and was elected to the Virginia House of Delegates, during which service his father, then a U.S. senator, died. Tazewell would later serve as a member of the U.S. House of Representatives, a member of the Virginia General Assembly, a U.S. senator, a delegate to the Virginia Convention of 1829–1830, and as governor of Virginia, but he rarely sought office, and he resigned from a number of them. A Tazewell biographer notes that he did not consider public office as "a prize to be won" but "a duty to be borne" (Peterson 1983, 239). Tazewell once remarked, "If I know myself, there is no situation within the power of the government to bestow which I covet or desire, nor is there one which I would not accept, if the discharges of its duties by me was deemed necessary or useful to my country. I have no ambition to gratify, although I have duties to fulfill" (Peterson 1983, 94).

Drawing from his contemporaries, a modern scholar has identified Tazewell's key characteristics as a courtroom attorney. They were "a striking physical appearance [Tazewell was six feet tall and had striking blue eyes], a remarkable capacity to cut to the heart of an argument, a remorseless logic, and a competitiveness, and a seemingly greater interest in the mechanics of an argument than in the intrinsic rightness of the proposition he was arguing" (White 1991, 215).

Tazewell spent much of his life practicing law in Norfolk, where he developed interests in commerce and banking that sometimes distinguished him from other Virginia Republicans and where he developed commercial law as a specialty. He argued a number of prize cases before the U.S. Supreme Court, but his anticipated confrontation with William Pinkney in the *Santissima Trinidad Case* (1822) was forestalled when Pinkney died. Tazewell objected to a line in Justice JOSEPH STORY's opinion in this case that Tazewell thought was intended to give credibility to charges by Tazewell's political opponents, that he used subtlety to undermine his opponents' arguments; in what must surely be a relatively rare occurrence, Tazewell succeeded in having the language changed (White 1991, 223–224).

Although he lived until 1860, after resigning from the Virginia governorship in 1835, Tazewell ceased practicing before the U.S. Supreme Court and largely retired to private life, where he cultivated the life of a country gentleman. When others strove for glory, Tazewell pronounced himself content to "spend the balance of his days under the shade of his own fig tree" (Peterson 1983, 100).

REFERENCES

Peterson, Norma Lois. *Littleton Waller Tazewell*. Charlottesville: University Press of Virginia, 1983.

Van Atta, John R. "Tazewell, Littleton Waller." In *American National Biography*, edited by John A. Garraty and Mark C. Carnes. Vol. 21. New York: Oxford University Press, 1999.

White, G. Edward. *The Marshall Court and Cultural Change, 1815–1835*. Abridged ed. New York: Oxford University Press, 1991.

tional deficiencies and made serious, and apparently successful, efforts to attain a more powerful mastery both of classical literature and of the English language. Thereafter, Pinkney apparently made it a point to let fellow lawyers know how bothered he was by the grammatical infelicities of others. One memoir indicates that Pinkney was reported to be "writh[ing] as if in pain when listening to [Luther] Martin speaking in his slovenly way in broken sentences, using the most indefensible vulgarisms and sometimes mispronouncing his words" (White 1991, 241).

Pinkney enhanced his own reputation for verbal fastidiousness by dressing in a fashion that elicited the comments of his peers. Justice Story noted that Pinkney's personal appearance "was as polished as if he had been taken right from the drawer; his coat of the finest blue, was nicely brushed; his boots shone with the highest polish; his waistcoat, of perfect whiteness, glittered with gold buttons; he played in his hand with a light cane; in short, he seemed perfectly satisfied with himself" (White 1991, 241). Chief Justice Roger Taney indicated that Pinkney's dress "approached to dandyism" (White 1991, 241), and other contemporaries noted what they considered to be his excessive use of corsets and makeup.

Contemporaries often connected Pinkney's dress and his apparent claims to mastery of the facts in so many different areas—a friend is quoted as saying, "I never heard him allow that any man was his superior in anything; in field sports, in music, in drawing, and especially in oratory, in which his great ambition rested" (Niles 1907, 215)—to vanity. While they appreciated his ability to argue logically and to point out weaknesses in opponents' cases, colleagues often appeared to have less admiration for Pinkney's personal character, which many considered to be artificial and somewhat affected. Chief Justice Roger Taney observed that

> when replying to [opposing arguments] he took particular pleasure in assailing the weaker points, and dwelling upon them in a tone and manner that sometimes made the adversary ashamed of them, and sometimes provoked his resentment. . . . His voice and manner and intonations did not appear to be natural, but artificial and studied. . . . This want of naturalness in tone and manner was unpleasant to those who heard him for the first time. . . . But a man who, at the age of fifty, spoke in amber-colored doeskin gloves, could hardly be expected to have a taste for simple or natural elocution. (White 1991, 251)

Analyzing these and other comments by his contemporaries, a modern commentator has observed that "Pinkney was an especially formidable and annoying presence" (White 1991, 251). Pinkney once insulted THOMAS ADDIS EMMET by making a negative reference to his native country. An analyst of Pinkney's legal career also notes a "narrow escape" from a duel with

William Wirt and a "private altercation with Daniel Webster" (Ireland 1986, 130).

In 1789, Pinkney delivered a speech (later reprinted by abolitionists) in the Maryland legislature in which he attributed the downtrodden position of blacks to their station in life rather than to their inequality. In rhetoric typical of that he would later use in court, Pinkney observed,

> As well might you expect to see the bubbling fountain gush from the burning sands of Arabia, as that the inspiration of genius or the enthusiastic glow of sentiment should rouse the mind which has yielded its elasticity to habitual subjection. Thus the ignorance and vices of these wretches [the slaves] are solely the result of situation, and therefore no evidence of their inferiority. Like the flower whose culture has been neglected and perishes amidst permitted weeds ere it opens its blossoms to the spring, they only prove the imbecility of human nature unassisted and oppressed. (Niles 1907, 182)

Ironically, in the U.S. Senate, Pinkney, continuing to concede that slavery was "unchristian and abominable," argued that the Union had no authority to prohibit a state—in this case, Missouri—from preserving or instituting such an institution at its pleasure (Niles 1907, 212–213). His speech was one factor that led to the Missouri Compromise by which Missouri was admitted to the Union as a slave state and Maine as a free one.

Pinkney, who was scheduled to serve as counsel in twenty-two cases during the 1822 term of the Court (Ireland 1986, 222), died in February 1822. One week earlier, he had fainted after having apparently overexerted himself during a case and stayed up late during an illness. The U.S. Supreme Court adjourned in his honor, the first time in its history that it did such a thing, and about two hundred carriages accompanied his body to the grave (Ireland 1986, 224).

Pinkney, however, left a mixed legacy that enabled an early biographer, Henry Wheaton, to tell Chancellor Kent that Pinkney was one of the "brightest and meanest of men" (Ireland 1986, 226). A contemporary law professor, who says that Pinkney was "acknowledged to be the greatest advocate of his age," has identified Pinkney's central strengths as an attorney as "preparation, rigor, logic, competitiveness, presence, determination, [and] intimidation." Noting that these strengths were also "weaknesses," he went on to speculate that they were "part of a mask he fashioned to wear in the public gaze of a world he may well have feared and even hated" (White 1991, 254). Another sympathetic biographer, while noting Pinkney's "desire for applause," also observed that he was "perhaps, the most eloquent man of his age" (Niles 1907, 214).

—*John R. Vile*

Ireland, Robert M. *The Legal Career of William Pinkney, 1764–1822.* New York: Garland, 1986.

Niles, Alfred Salem. "William Pinkney." In *Great American Lawyers,* edited by William Draper Lewis. Philadelphia: John C. Winston, 1907, 2:177–220.

Pinkney, William. *The Life of William Pinkney.* New York: D. Appleton, 1853. Reprint, New York: Da Capo Press, 1969.

Sterling, David. "Pinkney, William." In *American National Biography,* edited by John A. Garraty and Mark C. Carnes. New York: Oxford University Press, 1999, 17:548–549.

White, G. Edward. *The Marshall Court and Cultural Change, 1815–1835.* Abridged ed. New York: Oxford University Press, 1991.

RANDOLPH, EDMUND

(1753–1813)

EDMUND RANDOLPH
Library of Congress

BORN NEAR WILLIAMSBURG, Virginia, to John Randolph and Ariana Jennings in 1753, Edmund Randolph, delegate to the U.S. Constitutional Convention and the first U.S. attorney general, was a member of one of the state's most prominent families. Both his father and grandfather served as king's attorneys in Virginia, and his mother's father, Edmund Jennings, served in this post in Maryland. Edmund's uncle, Peyton Randolph, served as president of the First Continental Congress. Like his forbears, Edmund would play a significant role in the history of his state and his nation, but when he died in 1813 he faced serious financial difficulties, and leaders of both political parties questioned his loyalty and his principles.

Randolph was educated at the College of William & Mary and subsequently studied in his father's law office before beginning practice at age twenty-one. As the American Revolution approached, Randolph's father and his family left for England, while Randolph found himself joining with his uncle Peyton, who took the patriot side. Edmund's own loyalty does not appear to be questioned; he took a job as an aide-de-camp to General George Washington, but he had to leave shortly thereafter to help his aunt cope with the unexpected death of his uncle.

Randolph was selected to serve in the Virginia State Convention in 1776. Although he was the youngest member, he helped write the influential Virginia Declaration of Rights. That same year, Virginia selected Randolph as the state's first attorney general (a position in which he would serve for about ten years), and Randolph married Elizabeth Nicholas, with whom he was to have six children (one of whom died in childhood and another of whom was stillborn).

Randolph's appointment as attorney general did not prevent him either from taking on private clients or from accepting other positions. In November 1776, he was elected mayor of Williamsburg; in 1777, he was chosen rector of William & Mary; in 1778, he was named clerk of the Virginia House of Delegates; and in 1779, the Virginia Assembly appointed Randolph as a delegate to the Continental Congress, a position from which he resigned due to pressing legal duties.

Randolph's private practice probably occupied more of his time than his work as state attorney general. Randolph's biographer believes that his practice was the state's largest and his income second only to that of Henry Tazewell (Reardon 1974, 70). As attorney general, Randolph argued the case of *Commonwealth v. Caton et al.* (1782), in which he successfully defended a pardon granted by the House of Delegates, even though it was arguably in conflict with the state constitution. President of the Court ED-MUND PENDLETON observed that Randolph argued the state's case "fully and learnedly" (Reardon 1974, 62). In another case, *Hite v. Fairfax* (1786), which Randolph argued as a private attorney, Randolph and John Taylor of Caroline (attorney John Marshall was on the other side) succeeded in defending Hite's claims to property in Virginia's Northern Neck against claims of Lord Fairfax. Randolph argued from principles of equity, and his outline in the case has been said to show an "impressive style and subtle coloring" (Reardon 1974, 72).

In 1786, the same year that he attended the Annapolis Convention—the body that issued the call for the Constitutional Convention—Randolph was selected as governor of Virginia. Randolph apparently believed that his new position was to be an end his career in law, and he did not seem disappointed in the prospect. Randolph, who on an earlier occasion had taken on some of Thomas Jefferson's clients, now turned over his own to JOHN MARSHALL (Reardon 1974, 88). Writing to Washington, Randolph noted that he was leaving a profession "which from the earliest moment of my life

I abominated, and from which I was determined to escape, as soon as I was possessed of a competence" (Reardon 1974, 88). In his capacity as governor, Randolph became head of the Virginia delegation to the Philadelphia Convention, and he appears to have played a key role in persuading George Washington to join the delegation.

As titular head of the Virginia delegation, Randolph was responsible for introducing the Virginia Plan, which appears to have been mostly written by James Madison, with whom Randolph had established a friendship in the Continental Congress. As a "moderate nationalist" (Bradford 1981, 168), Randolph was a defender of a stronger national government but grew increasingly concerned with the direction the convention took, favoring a plural executive and expressing concern over the powers that the smaller states had achieved. Ultimately hoping for another convention to propose amendments before the new document was ratified, Randolph (along with fellow Virginian George Mason and Elbridge Gerry of Massachusetts) was one of three remaining delegates who refused to sign the Constitution.

Back in Virginia, Randolph eventually supported the Constitution at the state ratifying convention when he was convinced that the only alternative was disunion—Randolph said that he would rather lose a limb than "assent to the dissolution of the Union" (Reardon 1974, 139). Not surprisingly, partisans on both sides attacked Randolph for what they perceived to be indecisiveness or an attempt to curry popular favor. In this and in future conflicts, Randolph would often find himself to be a man in the middle. After resigning as governor, Randolph was elected to the Virginia House of Delegates.

Nowhere was Randolph's role as a moderate more evident than in his service as the United States' first attorney general, an office that paid only half that of other offices, perhaps in part because it was expected that Randolph could continue private practice. Randolph appears to have been the first person sworn to practice before the U.S. Supreme Court (Reardon 1974, 192), but he initially had few cases to argue and served primarily to advise both the president and the Congress. In his first year of service, Randolph described himself as "a sort of mongrel between the State and the U.S.; called an officer of some rank under the latter, and yet thrust out to get a livelihood in the former,—perhaps in a petty mayor's or county court" (Baker 1992, 51). President Washington, who accepted the opinion of Treasury Secretary ALEXANDER HAMILTON, rejected Randolph's (and Secretary of State Jefferson's) advice on the unconstitutionality of the national bank, but Washington agreed with Randolph (and Jefferson) that a congressional reapportionment statute was unconstitutional and made this his first veto.

Randolph established the practice as attorney general of writing out formal opinions and of attending cabinet meetings. Perhaps more important than any legal opinion that he rendered, however, was Randolph's role as a presidential advisor. Caught between the partisan proclivities of Federalist Hamilton and Democratic-Republican Jefferson, Washington—who had long before received free personal legal advice from Randolph—increasingly turned to Randolph for advice, and Randolph complied with nonpartisan counsel that often carried the day but that endeared him to neither member. Jefferson, a former friend with whom Randolph most often still sided, would call Randolph "the poorest cameleon I ever saw, having no color of his own, and reflecting that nearest him" (Baker 1992, 53). Randolph took an increasing role in advising the president on political and diplomatic matters (including the treatment of the French diplomat Citizen Genêt) that did not necessarily flow from his office, and Jefferson's criticism was more directed to this extralegal advice than to his legal advice (Baker 1992, 54).

As attorney general, Randolph did argue two important cases. In *Hayburn's Case* (1792), he attempted to get circuit judges to perform an administrative task assigned by Congress, but Congress later revised this authorization after the judges questioned this authority on separation of powers grounds. Randolph also argued on behalf of the plaintiff in *Chisholm v. Georgia* (1793). Randolph engaged in a two-and-a-half-hour presentation designed to convince the Court that Georgia (which refused even to send a representative to Court) could be sued by an out-of-state citizen without its consent. Although Randolph won a divided opinion, the decision was extremely unpopular and was shortly thereafter modified by adoption of the Eleventh Amendment to the U.S. Constitution.

When Jefferson resigned from Washington's cabinet, Randolph was appointed secretary of state, but, despite some successes, this became a period of declining influence for him. After Federalists (aided by the release of communiqués that the British had captured) called Randolph's impartiality into question and he lost Washington's confidence, Randolph angrily resigned from the cabinet. He returned to Virginia, where he published two attempts to vindicate himself (one of which, in judgments Randolph later modified, was highly critical of George Washington) and resumed the practice of law. Randolph, who had previously resided in Williamsburg, now lived in Richmond so that he could argue cases before the Virginia Court of Appeals (state law prevented the lawyer who had argued a case in lower courts to handle appellate decisions).

Randolph appears to have had a successful practice, participating by 1800 in as many as half of the cases that appeared before this court (Reardon 1974, 348). Randolph's chief biographer believes that few of these cases held great interest for Randolph during the time in which he became "what he vowed he never would be—a professional lawyer" (Reardon 1974, 358). Randolph did take part in the case of *Turpin v. Lochet* (1804), in which the court evenly split over whether county overseers could sell property of the once-established Episcopalian church for the relief of the poor (the decision, which would have gone in Randolph's favor had Edmund Pendleton not died before he was able to give his opinion, left in place the lower court opinion permitting the sale and arguably striking a blow for disestablishment). Randolph, who at one time owned 101 slaves and who freed his own house slaves (Daniels 1972, 165), appears to have represented both slaves seeking their freedom and slaveholders. Randolph does not appear to have argued any cases before the federal courts during the latter part of his life, although he was one of six attorneys who defended Aaron Burr in his treason trial before the U.S. Circuit Court in Richmond in 1807 (Shepard 1999, 123). In a speech praised as "a masterpiece of invective," Randolph reportedly condemned Jefferson for commenting on Burr's guilt and noted that "if you cannot exorcise the demon of prejudice, you can chain him down to law and reason, and then we shall have nothing to fear" (Eckenrode 1946, 139).

In his latter years, Randolph was hounded by creditors, including the U.S. government, which accused him of improper disbursements of State Department funds. Although no one appears to think Randolph was guilty of embezzlement, his sloppy bookkeeping eventually led to a judgment of more then fifty thousand dollars against him, most of which was assumed by his brother-in-law Wilson Cary Nicholas. Randolph's wife died in 1810, and his own health declined. Randolph undertook to write his *History of Virginia*, which was not, however, published until many years after his death at the house of a friend near Millwood, Virginia, in 1813. An obituary in the *Richmond Enquirer* noted that "his history is blended with that of his country" (Reardon 1974, 365).

Randolph's contemporaries, who sometimes branded his moderation as a form of "trimming," did not always judge him positively, but he seems to have been motivated by nonpartisan ideals of citizenship. Never entirely at ease with his chosen profession, Randolph appears to have been good at it. A contemporary, Hugh Blair Grigsby, referred to "Randolph's reputation" for "exactness in statement, lucidity of language, and an impressive simplicity which allayed distrust" (Eckenrode 1946, 115). Similarly, after describing Randolph's physical features, WILLIAM WIRT noted that "his attitudes [were] dignified and commanding; his gesture easy and graceful; his voice perfect harmony; and his whole manner that of an accomplished and engaging gentleman" (Eckenrode 1946, 115–116). Randolph did much to shape the office of the nation's highest attorney, and, although it did not save him from financial worries and political misfortunes, the strength of his practice was tribute to the esteem with which his contemporaries viewed his legal talents.

—*John R. Vile*

SOURCES AND SUGGESTIONS FOR FURTHER READING

Baker, Nancy V. *Conflicting Loyalties: Law & Politics in the Attorney General's Office, 1789–1990*. Lawrence: University Press of Kansas, 1992.

Bradford, M. E. *Founding Fathers: Brief Lives of the Framers of the United States Constitution*. 2d ed. Lawrence: University Press of Kansas, 1981.

Daniels, Jonathan. *The Randolphs of Virginia*. Garden City, N.Y.: Doubleday, 1972.

Eckenrode, H. J. *The Randolphs: The Story of a Virginia Family*. Indianapolis: Bobbs-Merrill, 1946.

Shepard, L. Lee. "Randolph, Edmund." In *American National Biography*, edited by John A. Garraty and Mark C. Carnes. Vol. 18. New York: Oxford University Press, 1999, 121–123.

Randolph, Edmund. *History of Virginia*. Edited by Arthur H. Shaffer. Charlottesville: University Press of Virginia, 1970.

Reardon, John J. *Edmund Randolph: A Biography*. New York: Macmillan, 1974.

REEVE, TAPPING

(1744–1823)

TAPPING REEVE
Litchfield Historical Society

THE GREATEST LEGACY PRO-vided to the American legal profession by noted Connecticut lawyer, judge, and jurist Tapping Reeve was the "law school" that he established in Litchfield, Connecticut. Judge Reeve's Litchfield Law School was the first of its kind in the United States and can fairly be said to have inaugurated professional legal education in the United States. Reeve's Blackstone-based curriculum—lectures copied by students, and reinforced with occasional moot court exercises—would be a widely copied model for legal education until Christopher Columbus Langdell introduced the case method at Harvard in the 1870s.

Early Career

Tapping Reeve was born on Long Island, New York, in 1744, the son of a Protestant minister. He graduated in 1763 from the College of New Jersey (later Princeton University) and stayed on after graduation as a tutor until 1770. In 1771, Reeve moved to Connecticut and began the study of law in Hartford. About two years later, in late 1772 or early 1773, Reeve moved his practice to Litchfield, then an important seat for law and commerce in northwest Connecticut. Reeve spent the rest of his life there. Reeve brought with him his first wife, the sister of Aaron Burr. Burr himself was one of Reeve's first apprentices (McKenna 1986, 41).

Lyman Beecher, a prominent local clergyman, recalled in his *Autobiography* his sister's physical description of Judge Reeve. Reeve, she had written,

> had a pair of soft dark eyes of rare beauty, a beaming expression of intelligence and benevolence, while his soft gray hair fell in silver tresses to his shoulders in a style peculiar to himself. His figure was large and portly, and his manners gentle and dignified. His voice was singular, having failed from some unknown cause, so that he always spoke in a whisper, and yet so distinctly that a hundred students at once could take notes as he delivered his law lectures. (Cross 1961, 162)

Another admirer also emphasized his calm demeanor, his somewhat unruly hairstyle, and his weakened voice: "I seem, even now, to see his calm and placid countenance shining through his abundant locks as he sat, pouring [*sic*] over his notes in the lecture room, and to hear his shrill whisper, as he stood when giving his charge to the jury" (Kilbourn 1909, 27).

Reverend Beecher remembered Reeve as "distinguished for his piety, and interest in all benevolent operations, as much as for his learning" (Cross 1961, 151). Another admirer wrote that Reeve

> loved the law as a science, and studied it philosophically. He considered it as the practical application of religious principle to the business affairs of life. He wished to reduce it to a certain, symmetrical system of moral truth. He did not trust to the inspiration of genius for eminence, but to the results of profound and constant study, and was never allured by political ambition. (Kilbourn 1909, 27)

Others also remembered Reeve as an ardent opponent of slavery, who worked to end the practice in New England and thereafter put his legal services to the defense of fugitive slaves (Kilbourn 1909, 44, 329). Beecher's sister, in a letter to him that Beecher reprinted in his autobiography, recalled that "the judge was known for his chivalrous devotion to women both in and out of the domestic circle. . . . He was a great admirer of female beauty and also of female talent, and various anecdotes were current of his chivalrous sayings" (Cross 1961, 162). Indeed, Reeve's devotion to women was reflected in his treatise on domestic relations, *The Law of Baron and Femme* (1816), which was notable for its advanced views on sexual equality and calls for reform of legal disabilities imposed on women (Siegel 1998, 2017–2018).

Reeve the Advocate

By all accounts, Reeve quickly established a reputation as an effective (if a somewhat eccentric and absent-minded) courtroom advocate. In a speech recalling the greatness of the Litchfield bar at that time, Reeve was remembered as having "engaged in almost every case of importance tried in Superior Court at Litchfield, and never failed to argue every one in which he was engaged, if argued at all" (Kilbourn 1909, 42). During the American Revolution, Reeve's eloquence was employed in the service of the patriot cause. Reeve was dispatched by the Connecticut Assembly as part of a committee whose charge was "to rouse and animate the people" of the state, encouraging them to volunteer for General Washington's army (McKenna 1986, 43). Reeve's biographer wrote that "his deportment at the bar, his treatment of judge, jury, and witnesses . . . furnished an example worthy of imitation, and had an elevating influence on other practitioners" (McKenna 1986, 36). Reeve was known equally for his eloquent extemporaneous speeches in court, as well as his occasional lapses in grammar and syntax, when the ardor of his cause got the better of him. Nevertheless, his performances seem never to have failed to make an impression on those who heard them.

One witness, a Litchfield attorney named David Boardman, to Reeve's eloquence at the bar recalled:

> I saw him . . . during nine sessions of the Superior Court, and never failed to listen to him, if I could avoid it, with unqualified love and admiration through every speech he made, to its conclusion. . . . As a reasoner, he had no superior within the compass of my observation of forensic performances. I mean true, forcible and honest reasoning. In sophistry, he was too honest to indulge, and too discerning to suffer it to escape detection in the argument of an adversary. (Kilbourn, 1909, 42–43)

Reeve was remembered as ordinarily being "exceedingly ardent, and the ardor he displayed appeared to be prompted by a conviction of the justice of the cause he was advocating." Occasionally, Reeve himself was evidently swept away by the moral force of his argument:

> His ideas seemed often, and indeed, usually, to flow in upon him faster than he could give utterance to them, and sometimes seemed to force him to leave a sentence unfinished, to begin another,—and in his huddle of ideas . . . he was

careless of grammatical accuracy, and though a thorough scholar, often made bad grammar in public speaking. Careless as he was of his diction and thoughtless as he was of ornament in ordinary cases, yet some elegant expressions and fine sentences would seem, as if by accident, to escape him in almost every speech. But in such cases as afforded the proper field for the display of eloquence, such as actions of slander, malicious prosecution, etc., and in that part of such cases as usually prompt to exertions of the kind, his hurried enunciation and grammatical inaccuracies, all forsook him, and then he never failed to electrify and astonish his audience. (Kilbourn 1909, 43)

This same observer once heard Reeve "burst forth into such a strain of dignified and soul-searching eloquence, as neither before nor since, has ever met my ear. . . . I was perfectly entranced during its delivery, and for an hour afterwards I trembled so that I could not speak plain. His manner was as much changed as his language, and to me he looked a foot taller than before." The young admirer later approached Reeve for a copy of his closing argument. "He said he would try, but he did not know whether he could recall it to memory, for there was not a word of it written before hand. A day or two after he saw me in Court, behind his seat, and beckoned me to him and said he had tried to comply with my request, but it was so gone from him that he could make nothing of it" (Kilbourn 1909, 43). Though Reeve would largely give up private practice when he began to educate future lawyers in earnest, his powerful forensic talents seem undisputed.

The Litchfield Law School

Although Reeve's skills at the bar won him praise from contemporaries and secured for him pride of place in remembrances at annual Connecticut bar association dinners, his contributions to legal education have earned him a place in the history of American legal education. Until Reeve established his school, legal education was largely undertaken by the apprenticeship method. A member of the bar often took in one or two students, who would perform administrative tasks, such as copying documents; would observe the elder lawyer in court; and, in quiet times, would study the canonical texts—usually Blackstone's *Commentaries* and perhaps Coke's edition of the *Institutes*. After some period, often prescribed by law, the apprentice would be eligible to sit for an examination, on successful completion of which he would be "called to the bar." Although through the apprenticeship method future lawyers obtained an appreciation of legal practice in fact, it meant that an attorney was usually able to take only a small number of aspiring lawyers at any one time. Judge Reeve revolutionized this system by instituting a series of lectures that large numbers of students could attend.

Reeve's first student, whom he took in 1774, was his brother-in-law, Aaron Burr. "By 1782, Reeve had organized his legal material and was delivering detailed lectures to the young men congregating around his office" (Siegel 1998, 2003). Two years later, to provide respite to his ailing first wife, Reeve built a freestanding schoolhouse beside his residence; as a result, many date the official establishment of the "Litchfield Law School" to 1784 (Siegel 1998, 2003). Thereafter, the school grew from ten to fifteen students a year in the 1780s and 1790s, to forty or fifty at its peak in the first quarter of the nineteenth century. In 1797, after the death of his first wife, Reeve was appointed to Connecticut's highest court. To help with the school, he enlisted the services of a former student, James Gould, who would operate the school with Reeve until Reeve's retirement in 1820, and afterwards until 1834, when the school closed.

Students at Reeve's school saw their education gradually become more regimented, marked by a routine schedule and a prescribed curriculum. Five or six mornings a week, Reeve or Gould would lecture to the students for ninety minutes on a predetermined area of law. In addition to the "black-letter" rules, both teachers would often illustrate with applications or hypotheticals (Siegel 1998, 2006). A complete set of lectures was delivered over the course of fourteen to eighteen months, but students wandered in during different times of the year. After the morning lecture, students would retire to the impressive law library that Judge Reeve had accumulated and read treatises and cases cited in the morning's lectures. Having supplemented the morning's lectures, students would then spend the afternoons copying their lecture notes into the handsome leather volumes that would be their primary reference works once in practice (Siegel 1998, 2007). Although there were no formal grades, since Litchfield conferred no diplomas, it became standard practice for either Reeve or Gould to "examine" students on Saturday, by asking them questions on the week's lessons (McKenna 1986, 85; Siegel 1998, 2007). "Students received a further opportunity to impress their teachers during moot court exercises, held once a week" (Siegel 1998, 2008).

In addition to the legal education that students received, there was an ideological component, as well, that was believed to be just as important. Litchfield was a Federalist stronghold in Connecticut; after the French Revolution and the election of Thomas Jefferson in 1800, Federalists sought to create a redoubt of sorts in the legal profession and the judiciary from which to combat the swelling tide of Francophilia and "mobocracy" that threatened to wash away the old order. "It was through law that the Federalists hoped to inculcate and protect their core social values: order, hierarchy, and benevolence" (Siegel 1998, 2012–2013). This social vision naturally influenced the form and the substance of Reeve's and Gould's lectures.

In the end, Litchfield, lacking as it did an affiliation with a major college or university, was destined to go the way of many other proprietary law schools. Although Gould was able to keep the school going after the retirement of Reeve in 1820, the numbers of students steadily dwindled as Harvard, Yale, and Columbia began to offer law degrees. But this is not to say that Litchfield did not leave a substantial mark. One of the founders of the law school that eventually became the Yale Law School was probably one of Judge Reeve's students. In addition, "at least 101 Litchfield graduates sat in the United States House of Representatives, while at least twenty-eight [including John C. Calhoun] sat in the Senate. . . . Fourteen state governors and six members of the national cabinet owed their legal training to Reeve and Gould. Thirty-four sat on state supreme courts, three earned places on the U.S. Supreme Court, and dozens more served as . . . court reporters, lower court judges, and law professors" (Siegel 1998, 2020–2021).

Last Years

Although he would see his school continue after his retirement, Judge Reeve's last years were not happy ones. There was a bitter split with Gould in 1820. Some say Reeve was pushed from the school; Gould's partisans maintained that Reeve's mental and teaching capacities had been much diminished. Reeve was then beset with financial difficulties. Some of his former students tried to alleviate Reeve's difficulties by sending out a letter asking Litchfield alumni to contribute to a fund to support Reeve in his old age. Illness also plagued Reeve, and he died on December 13, 1823, at age seventy-nine. His old friend Lyman Beecher delivered a twenty-two-page oration at Reeve's funeral, and he was buried beside his first wife and his son, Aaron Burr Reeve, who was also one of his students (McKenna 1986, 164–165).

—*Brannon P. Denning*

Sources and Suggestions for Further Reading

Cross, Barbara M., ed. *The Autobiography of Lyman Beecher*. Vol. 1. Cambridge: Belknap Press of Harvard University Press, 1961.

Kilbourn, Dwight C. *The Bench and Bar of Litchfield County, Connecticut, 1709–1909*. Litchfield, Conn.: privately printed, 1909.

McKenna, Marian C. *Tapping Reeve and the Litchfield Law School*. New York: Oceana, 1986.

Siegel, Andrew M. "Note, 'To Learn and Make Respectable Hereafter': The Litchfield Law School in Cultural Context." *New York University Law Review* 73 (1998): 1978–2028.

"Tapping Reeve." In *Dictionary of American Biography*, edited by Dumas Malone. New York: Scribner, 1935, 8:468.

ROBERTS, OWEN J.

(1875–1955)

OWEN J. ROBERTS
Library of Congress

OWEN JOSEPHUS ROBERTS WAS a prominent Philadelphia corporate lawyer who served as a prosecutor in the Teapot Dome scandal. Impressed by Roberts's performance and his solid Republican credentials, President Herbert Hoover appointed him to the Supreme Court in 1930.

Roberts was born in the Germantown section of Philadelphia on May 2, 1875. His father, Josephus R. Roberts, was a wealthy hardware merchant. His mother's maiden name was Emma Elizabeth Lafferty.

He attended private schools and graduated from the Germantown Academy in 1891. Roberts received an A.B. degree in 1895 from the University of Pennsylvania, where he majored in Greek and was a member of Phi Beta Kappa. He considered a career as a professor of Greek but chose to attend law school at the University of Pennsylvania, where he was considered a brilliant student, receiving his LL.B. with highest honors in 1898. During the 1897–1898 academic year, he was an associate editor of the law review, *The American Law Register*. One of his law professors, George Wharton Pepper, was later elected as a Republican to the U.S. Senate and remained a lifelong influence. Roberts was admitted to the Pennsylvania bar in 1898 and began the private practice of law in Philadelphia as a solo practitioner. Roberts was disappointed that a large law firm did not offer him a position. To supplement his income, he joined the faculty of the University of Pennsylvania law school as an instructor. He offered courses in bankruptcy, contracts, damages, and property. He taught part time at the law school until 1918, reaching the rank of professor in 1907. After 1903, his only course was real property.

On June 15, 1904, he married Elizabeth Caldwell Rogers of Fairfield, Connecticut. They had one child, a daughter, Elizabeth, who later married and became Mrs. Roger Hamilton. Roberts was a devout Episcopalian, a church trustee, and president of the House of Deputies in 1946. Roberts joined the Pennsylvania Bar Association in 1898 and became its president in 1947.

In the three years following law school, Roberts had few clients and only an adjunct position as a law professor. He took his first full-time job in 1901 when Philadelphia district attorney John C. Bell appointed Roberts first assistant district attorney for Philadelphia County, a post he held until 1904. Roberts tried cases against several fraudulent contractors and achieved local fame as an able prosecutor. Bell drove his small staff mercilessly, and Roberts learned to work into the evenings to meet pressing deadlines. In 1903, he published an article on the question of whether Private Wadsworth, a member of the Pennsylvania National Guard who had shot and killed a peaceful civilian during a coal strike in 1902, should be tried in a civilian or military court. Roberts argued that martial law cannot exist in times of peace and that Wadsworth must be tried in a civilian court for murder. The article brought Roberts statewide notoriety for the first time.

With his reputation as a litigator growing, a large law firm, White & White, finally took in Roberts in 1903. One of his principal clients was the Philadelphia Rapid Transit Company, whom he defended before juries in accident cases. In 1912, he formed a partnership with William W. Montgomery and Charles L. McKeehan. In 1923, the firm became Roberts & Montgomery. He practiced a variety of law, including criminal cases as a private prosecutor, personal injury cases representing both plaintiffs and defendants, probate cases, suits against building contractors representing the defendant, and taxation suits. One of his best-known cases from this period was a contract dispute between wholesale grocers and sugar refiners in which the grocers had orally agreed to pay inflated prices for sugar. Roberts successfully argued that under the Statute of Frauds such contracts must be in writing in order to be enforceable. Roberts believed that it was the obligation of an attorney to represent any client who requested counsel as long as he did not already represent the other side. No case was too large or too small.

His first stint as a federal prosecutor came in May 1918 when the U.S. attorney general appointed him special deputy attorney general to represent the U.S. government in the prosecution of cases in the Eastern District of

Pennsylvania arising under the Espionage Act of 1917 during World War I. He obtained several convictions and jail sentences against the editors and publishers of two foreign-language newspapers who were charged with publication of sedition.

Roberts was a gifted trial attorney. He often quipped that the only speeches he made that were any good were those he was paid to make. Roberts was a striking figure in the courtroom. He stood six feet three and a half and weighed two hundred pounds. He was energetic, with well-defined features, a square face, penetrating blue eyes, determined jaw, thick brown hair, and a strong, persuasive voice. He was a master of clear and concise English. His memory and self-confidence were such that he examined and cross-examined witnesses without notes. Arguing cases before a jury was what he loved most. He was equally successful before appellate tribunals, and many lawyers asked him to argue their clients' cases on appeal. By 1930, Roberts had established a reputation as one of the outstanding litigators in the nation.

Roberts spent nearly all his waking hours working. He labored into the evening every day except Sunday. When interviewing applicants for positions in his law firm, his first two questions were "How robust is your health?" and "Are you willing to work at night?" When preparing a case for trial or appellate hearing, he became completely absorbed in the task and pushed all personal and social pursuits aside. For relaxation, he would make sudden trips to the Pocono Mountains in Pennsylvania or the Maine woods or visit his farm near Valley Forge. At the farm every Sunday he enjoyed adjusting the time on his large collection of clocks to coincide with the Naval Observatory clock at the Philadelphia Navy Yard.

Roberts first came to national attention in February 1924 when President Calvin Coolidge appointed him and former U.S. Senator Atlee Pomerene, an Ohio Democrat, special U.S. attorneys to prosecute individuals suspected of wrongdoing in the Teapot Dome scandal that occurred during the administration of Warren Harding. Senator Pepper had urged Roberts's appointment on the president. Coolidge told Roberts and Pomerene that he wanted a thorough and nonpartisan legal inquiry into the scandal. Roberts faced opposition from Senator Thomas Walsh, a Democrat from Montana, who headed the Senate inquiry into the scandal, but the Senate confirmed his appointment two days after approving Pomerene's appointment. Roberts left for Washington with two junior associates borrowed from his law firm. He estimated that their work would take two or three months. Over the next six and half years, they would complete two civil suits, two contempt cases, and eight criminal trials. He personally argued every Teapot Dome case from beginning to end. Roberts remained special counsel until June 1930, when he received his nomination to the Supreme Court.

Sullivan & Cromwell

Although this book focuses on the contributions that important individuals have made to American law, law firms, like individuals, often have their own unique identities. Few firms have been more influential than the firm of Sullivan & Cromwell, which was founded in New York City by William Nelson Cromwell and Algernon Sydney Sullivan in 1879 and went on to become one of the largest and most powerful Wall Street firms, handling complicated matters of finance for more than a century.

Leading partners in this firm became known for their internationalism and established offices in a number of foreign countries. Cromwell is largely credited with eliminating the legal barriers for the United States to assume the work that the French had begun in building the Panama Canal. Later, John Foster Dulles (1888–1959), who cultivated extensive—and, in retrospect, highly questionable—financial ties in Germany between the two world wars, moved from a position as managing partner of Sullivan & Cromwell to become an advisor to Republican presidential candidate THOMAS DEWEY, a U.S. senator representing New York, and secretary of state under President Dwight D. Eisenhower. Dulles, a Presbyterian minister's son who was known for making highly moralistic pronouncements as secretary of state, advanced the doctrine threatening massive nuclear retaliation against Communist aggression as an economical way of providing deterrence. His brother Allen, also a one-time Sullivan & Cromwell partner, simultaneously served as director of the Central Intelligence Agency, a position that he kept into the John F. Kennedy administration.

Harlan Fiske Stone, later chief justice of the U.S. Supreme Court, served for a time at Sullivan & Cromwell, as did Ronald Dworkin, who, rejecting what he considered to be the firm's emphasis on working to the exclusion of a healthy family life, subsequently went on to establish a career as a prominent legal philosopher. Sullivan & Cromwell turned down Richard Nixon for a job in 1937 (David Hawkins, the Sullivan & Cromwell administrator who interviewed Nixon, noted his shifty eyes), and future justice William O. Douglas professed to have been so disgusted with the pomposity of John Foster Dulles during a job interview with him in 1926, in which Dulles helped Douglas put on his coat, that he gave Dulles a quarter tip! (Lisagor and Lipsius 1988, 101).

REFERENCE

Lisagor, Nancy, and Franki Lipsius. *A Law unto Itself: The Untold Story of the Law Firm Sullivan & Cromwell, 100 Years of Creating Power & Wealth.* New York: William Morrow, 1988.

In 1921, President Harding transferred supervision of the naval oil reserve from the navy to the Department of the Interior. In 1921 and 1922, the secretary of the interior, Albert B. Fall, secretly leased the Teapot Dome, Wyoming, reserves to Harry F. Sinclair, head of the Mammoth Oil Company, and reserves located at Elk Hills and Buena Vista, California, to Edward L. Doheny of Pan American Petroleum Company. In exchange for the leases, Fall received large gifts of cash and no-interest loans. The secretary of the navy, Edwin Denby, signed each of the leases, believing that they were legal. When the affair became public, President Harding became disillusioned and exhausted and died.

Roberts moved slowly to gather the evidence against the accused. Liberals criticized him for not moving quickly. A $100,000 payment by Doheny to Secretary Fall was disclosed during the Senate hearings into the scandal, but a $230,500 bribe paid to Fall by Sinclair remained unknown until Roberts's investigation. Roberts convened several grand juries to issue subpoenas to compel testimony and documents. When a key witness refused to testify on Fifth Amendment grounds against self-incrimination, Roberts persuaded Congress to modify the statute of limitations so as to immunize his testimony. Roberts finally prosecuted Fall, Doheny, and Sinclair. Denby, he concluded, had been foolish but had done nothing criminal.

Fall's bribery case was the most important of the twelve trials. It began on October 7, 1929. Roberts faced defense attorney Frank J. Hogan of Washington, D.C., who had won an acquittal for Doheny in his criminal conspiracy trial. Hogan was short and wily. He was a natty dresser and had an Irish temper, a slight lisp, and a manner ingratiating with juries. Cocky and belligerent, Hogan was one of the most successful criminal lawyers in the country. He had worked his way up from poverty, and his fee from Doheny was one million dollars. Believing that public opinion would affect the jury's attitude toward his client, as soon as evidence favorable to Fall was offered in court, Hogan shared it with the press. Hogan's strategy to achieve victory was to play on the jury's sympathies by making Fall look old, frail, and sickly. A doctor and nurse and Fall's wife and daughter attended to him constantly in view of the jury.

By contrast, Roberts was large, boyish, and somewhat awkward. He came across as sincere but conservative and lacked the fiery oratory of Hogan. On the trial's first day Roberts argued that the jury should not witness Fall's entrances and exits in a wheelchair. Subsequently the judge allowed the jury into the courtroom only after Fall had been lifted from his wheelchair and placed in a stuffed green chair brought into the courtroom just for the defendant. In his closing argument, Roberts told the jury that the defendant's physical condition was of no concern to them. Roberts said that the government had proved all that was necessary to justify a conviction. The evidence showed, he said, that Doheny paid a $100,000 bribe to Fall. Fall had a criminal intent in soliciting and accepting the money. Doheny's intent was immaterial, since only Fall was on trial. Fall was charged with accepting a bribe; Doheny was not charged with making the payment. Hogan took more than a day to present his closing argument to the jury. He presented Fall as a patriot who had built oil storage tanks for the navy at Pearl Harbor at little profit to himself. He described Fall as a sick old man who had had a long friendship with Doheny. Money exchanged between friends, he suggested, was not a bribe.

To Roberts's relief, the District of Columbia jury convicted Fall of accepting a bribe. The maximum possible penalty was three years in prison and a fine of $300,000. The judge, however, citing his physical condition and the jury's recommendation for mercy, sentenced him to one year in prison and to pay a fine of $100,000. For the sentencing, Fall walked into the courtroom with the wheelchair nowhere in sight. The *New York Times* wrote that the verdict showed "that justice, even when leaden-footed, at last overtakes the criminal" and would "put fear in the hearts of any public officials tempted to betray their trust" (Werner and Starr 1959, 285). Different juries, however, acquitted Fall, Doheny, and Sinclair of criminal conspiracy and Doheny of offering a bribe. Because the statute of limitations had run out, Sinclair could not be charged with bribery. Roberts, well versed in the peculiarities of the jury system, nevertheless was perplexed by the paradoxical outcomes. Sinclair, however, spent six and a half months in jail for contempt of court and contempt of the U.S. Senate. Roberts obtained a contempt conviction and fine against H. M. Blackmer, president of the Midwest Refining Company, who refused to return to the United States from France to testify.

Roberts had more success in the civil suits and contempt cases than he did in the criminal prosecutions. He made an impressive showing, however, during all the Teapot Dome trials. During the civil trial brought by the federal government against Sinclair to cancel his lease to the Teapot Dome reserves, someone pointed to Roberts and said, "That's one of the government counsel." Sinclair replied, "One of them? Hell, that's all of them!" (Werner and Starr 1959, 202). Congress ordered the president to cancel the leases and, in a case brought by Roberts, the Supreme Court declared them fraudulent and Harding's transfer of authority from the navy to the Interior Department illegal. The scandal failed to harm the Republican party, however, and Coolidge was elected to a full term as president in November 1924. As a result of the publicity surrounding the trials, Roberts earned for himself a great reputation.

In 1929, Roberts represented Pennsylvania in a suit brought by New Jersey against New York under the Supreme Court's original jurisdiction to enjoin the defendant from diverting huge amounts of water to New York City from the New York tributaries of the Delaware River. The Court allowed Pennsylvania to enter the suit as an intervener, and the Court's final judgment accommodated Pennsylvania's interests in the dispute.

When the Senate rejected Herbert Hoover's nomination of a southerner, John J. Parker of North Carolina, to the Supreme Court, Hoover nominated Roberts. The Senate confirmed him unanimously in 1930. During his fifteen years as an associate justice, Roberts wrote more opinions than any other justice. In favor of a mandatory retirement age for Supreme Court justices, Roberts resigned from the Court in 1945 when he turned seventy. Roberts is best remembered for changing his mind about the constitutionality of President Franklin Roosevelt's New Deal program. Roberts was a committed opponent during Roosevelt's first term, 1933–1936. However, following Roosevelt's reelection by a landslide in November 1936 and the introduction of his plan to pack the court with six new liberal justices in February 1937, Roberts, along with Chief Justice CHARLES EVANS HUGHES, became a consistent supporter of the president's policies, rendering the court-packing scheme unnecessary.

Although he was a Republican, Roberts strongly opposed isolationism. After the surprise attack by Japanese imperial forces on the U.S. fleet anchored at Pearl Harbor on December 7, 1941, President Roosevelt appointed Roberts to head a commission of inquiry into the disaster. The commission issued its report in 1942. The report exonerated the president of any wrongdoing and laid full blame upon the army and navy commanders in Hawaii. After his retirement from the Supreme Court, Roberts devoted himself to the cause of world government. He worked in favor of an Atlantic Union, or federation of the United States and the countries of Western Europe, as a first step.

Roberts's reputation as a master litigator and prosecutor was not matched by his career as a judge. His strength was in the practice, not the theory, of law. He had no coherent judicial philosophy, swinging frequently from left to right on constitutional questions, and he did not get along well with his brethren on the Supreme Court. Feelings were so strong that he did not even receive the customary farewell letter on his retirement in 1945.

Roberts's best-known book is *The Court and the Constitution* (1969), the published version of his Oliver Wendell Holmes lecture delivered at the Harvard Law School in 1951. The subject of the work is the evolution of American federalism. Roberts also contributed essays under the pseudonym Publius II, along with John F. Schmidt and Clarence K. Streit, to *The New Federalist*, a work devoted to the desirability of an Atlantic Union.

Roberts received honorary degrees from Beaver College, Ursinus College, the University of Pennsylvania, Lafayette College, the Pennsylvania Military College, Dickinson College, Trinity College, Williams College, Princeton University, Temple University, and Oxford University.

Roberts died of a heart attack on May 17, 1955, at age eighty, at his country home, Bryncoed, in West Vincent Township, Chester County, Pennsylvania. He was respected and honored.

—*Kenneth M. Holland*

Leonard, Charles A. *A Search for a Judicial Philosophy: Mr. Justice Roberts and the Constitutional Revolution of 1937*. Port Washington, N.Y.: Kennikat Press, 1971.

McCracken, Robert T. "Owen J. Roberts—Master Advocate." *University of Pennsylvania Law Review* 104 (1955): 322–331.

The New Federalist, by Publius II (Owen J. Roberts, John F. Schmidt and Clarence K. Streit). New York: Harper, 1950.

Roberts, Owen J. *The Court and the Constitution: The Oliver Wendell Holmes Lectures 1951*. Port Washington, N.Y.: Kennikat Press, 1969.

"Roberts, Owen Josephus." In *Dictionary of American Biography*, edited by John A. Garraty. Supplement 5, *1951–1955*. New York: Scribner, 1977, 571–577.

Werner, M. R., and John Starr. *Teapot Dome*. New York: Viking Press, 1959.

ROBINSON, SPOTTSWOOD W., III

(1916–1998)

SPOTTSWOOD WILLIAM ROBINSON III

Spottswood Robinson (left) and Oliver W. Hill Jr. shown arriving at federal court for the hearing before federal judge Albert V. Bryan on a plea of thirty Negro children for an order permitting them to attend several previously all-white Arlington schools, 2 August 1958. (Bettmann/Corbis)

NOTED CIVIL RIGHTS ATTORney Spottswood William Robinson III was born in Richmond, Virginia, on July 26, 1916. His father, Spottswood William Robinson Jr., was a lawyer and businessman. His mother was Inez Clements Robinson. At age twenty, Spottswood III married Marian B. Wilkerson. The couple ultimately had two children, Nina and Spottswood IV.

Robinson attended Richmond's Armstrong High School and then Virginia Union University, where he received his bachelor's degree in 1936. He immediately entered Howard Law School, where he graduated magna cum laude in 1939, finishing first in his class with the school's highest grade-point average to that time.

In *Simple Justice*, author Richard Kluger called Robinson "the finest legal technician Howard law school had ever produced" (Kluger 1975, 2:728). However, it is Howard law professor James Nabrit who probably comes the closest to capturing the essence of Robinson. As Nabrit put it, Robinson "was the best student of law I ever taught. He was a superb pleader and writer and yet a modest man. He didn't have much of a voice, but he did well in court. He was always reading, always thinking, and worked harder than anyone I have ever known" (Kluger 1975, 2:598).

Robinson was not a gifted orator. In point of fact, he was blade thin, soft-spoken, and unassuming in posture, suggesting more of a scholar than an advocate. Yet, it was his superb mind and incredible drive that ultimately allowed him to become a highly distinguished litigator.

Considered to have a brilliant legal mind, he taught law for twenty years at Howard University Law School and ultimately became its dean and later a trustee. Yet, beyond teaching the law, he was also an accomplished practitioner. Besides practicing realty law and establishing a successful real estate business, he also served on the U.S. Civil Rights Commission under President John Kennedy and was later appointed as a federal judge, serving on the district court and the U.S. Circuit Court of Appeals for the District of Columbia. He was the first African-American to serve on the Washington, D.C., Court of Appeals. Yet, he was best known for his tireless work battling for civil rights in America's courtrooms.

Robinson was absolutely relentless in his legal assault on the Jim Crow laws that relegated African-Americans to the position of second-class citizenship. In the area of education, for example, with the possible exception of THURGOOD MARSHALL, no lawyer of his time logged more hours toward achieving better schools for African-Americans. His long hours were legendary. For example, he was known to continue to work ten to twelve hours per day even past age seventy.

Very cautious and a perfectionist, Robinson would spend untold hours writing and rewriting his briefs and then preparing for court. As a case in point, he spent two weeks refining the language of the Brown v. Board of Education pleading. He also noted that he learned from National Association for the Advancement of Colored People (NAACP) legend CHARLIE HOUSTON "to read over the (entire) record the night before arguing a case, so (you) might have all the facts and rebuttal arguments at (your) fingertips in the courtroom" (Kluger 1975, 2:246).

As Virginia NAACP executive secretary Lester Banks described him in 1948, "He is the most thorough, most methodical man in the world. . . . If he was going to cut a board ten inches long, he'd measure it fifteen times to make sure it was right. He'd think nothing of sitting up to three or four in the morning to search out a point of law he needed. He was always looking for just the right case in every situation. He was a terrific worker with a wonderful mind" (Kluger 1975, 2:599).

After his graduation from law school, and again after his successful foray into realty law, Robinson spent much of the 1940s and 1950s with Rich-

Clifford J. Durr, Southern Defender of Civil Liberties

Clifford J. Durr (1899–1975) was born to an old southern family in Montgomery, Alabama, and always considered himself a son of the South, but his work in Washington, D.C., in the service of the law eventually led him to question the institution of segregation. Educated in the law at a Milwaukee law firm after having previously graduated from the University of Alabama and going to England as a Rhodes scholar, Durr (a brother-in-law to senator and justice Hugo Black) returned to Alabama to practice law before being invited to Washington during the Great Depression.

Durr occupied a number of positions, including service with the Reconstruction Finance Corporation and the Defense Plant Corporation before serving on the Federal Communications Commission, where he established a record of standing up for the public interest and of resisting investigations that he thought unfairly impugned the integrity of other officials. Af-

ter leaving the Federal Communications Commission and establishing a reputation for defending those whose loyalty was questioned, Durr served for a time as president of the National Lawyers Guild and later as president of the National Farmers Union.

After returning to his native Alabama, Durr found that his work on behalf of civil rights increasingly alienated him from friends and family in the area. Still deeply conservative in many ways, Durr continued to adhere to his beliefs, convinced that the cause of civil rights for African-Americans was essential to establishing civil liberties for all Americans.

REFERENCE

Salmond, John A. *The Conscience of a Lawyer: Clifford J. Durr and American Civil Liberties, 1899–1975*. Tuscaloosa: University of Alabama Press, 1990.

mond law partner Oliver W. Hill and Lester Banks challenging Jim Crow laws in cities and counties across Virginia. These laws were attacked as violations of U.S. constitutional rights such as the guarantees of due process and equal protection under the law.

In 1948, Robinson was named special NAACP counsel in Virginia, and his focus turned primarily to racial inequalities in education. Setting out to survey African-American schools in the state, by this time he and his legal cohorts were logging some thirty thousand miles per year. They would argue before school boards and then file federal lawsuits after the expected rebuffs occurred, with Robinson doing most of the courtroom work. At one point, they had active lawsuits filed against seventy-five different Virginia school districts.

Needless to say, their efforts met with considerable resistance, some of it bordering on violence. For example, in King County they faced farmers with pickaxes who opposed voluntary school desegregation. Similarly, in Cumberland County, a school board member stood up and said, "The first little black son of a bitch that comes down the road to set foot in that school, I'll take my shotgun to, and blow his brains out" (Kluger, 1975, 2:601).

Nevertheless, Robinson and his colleagues persevered, winning a series of breakthrough decisions in federal court as early as 1948. For example, they won equalization of African-American and white educator salaries in Chesterfield County as well as the equalization of expenditures for African-American and white high schools in King George County. They also won additional funding for improving African-American schools in Gloucester County; and they even won a contempt citation against a white school board when that board opted to make only token improvements.

Initially they pursued the more conservative route, arguing within the "separate but equal" precedent of *Plessy v. Ferguson*, simply asking that separate be more equal. But striking Moton High School students in Prince Edward County would not relent in their demand for legal desegregation. Robinson and Hill met with the students, and, when a sizable number of parents also signed on, a much more revolutionary federal lawsuit was filed on May 23, 1951. This was one month after the students began their school walkout in Farmville, initially protesting school conditions, including leaking roofs and poor heating.

The case was *Davis v. County School Board of Prince Edward County*, with Davis being Dorothy Davis, daughter of a local farmer, who happened to be first on the list of 117 plaintiffs. In their pleading, they asked for equal educational spending on African-American students as well as a finding that Virginia's school segregation law was unconstitutionally discriminatory.

Case evidence, presented by Carter, Hill, and Robinson, included a comparison between the county's white and African-American high schools. The white school was in a quiet neighborhood, whereas the African-American school was next to a highway. The former had a far more attractive physical plant valued at more than four times that of the all-black Moton High School. In addition, asphalt floors made the white high school easier to keep clean, besides the fact that it had a host of facilities that Moton did not, such as an industrial-arts shop, a gymnasium, an auditorium, and a cafeteria. Faculty at the white school averaged eleven years of teaching experience to four years at Moton. And where fifteen buses were assigned to transport 854 white students, there were only nine buses for 811 African-American students, six of which were hand-me-downs from the white system. Robinson and company also put on professional testimony about the negative psychological and learning effects caused by such inequality as well as by segregation itself.

Yet despite the mounds of evidence, things did not go well at the trial level. Richard Kluger describes Robinson's opening statement as "short and dry" and his closing summation as "brief and cold" (Kluger 1975, 2:617, 639). In the end, they lost and would have to appeal.

Meanwhile, Robinson became one of the primary attorneys for the NAACP's Legal Defense and Educational Fund. It was in this capacity that he worked closely with the likes of the Fund's lead attorney, Thurgood Marshall. Kluger concludes that Robinson's "balanced judgment, scrupulous care, clarity of expression, and remarkable recall made him Marshall's most valuable all-around associate" (Kluger 1975, 2:815). His efforts were integral in the Fund's success at achieving major legal change from the federal courts, and especially the U.S. Supreme Court.

Arguably the most famous of these changes was set down in the U.S. Supreme Court's 1954 *Brown v. Board of Education* opinion. Consolidating cases from Virginia and four other states, Robinson was joined by William Coleman, Judge WILLIAM HASTIE, and Thurgood Marshall in crafting the *Brown* challenge. Robinson was most directly involved in the Virginia school segregation case. The frustrations of trying to get truly equal schools in Virginia was a key foundation in the *Brown* challenge to *Plessy*. Yet, once the consolidated cases worked their way onto the docket of the Supreme Court, they had to be argued twice before the justices finally handed down their final *Brown* decision, the second time being to determine remedies and pace of remediation.

In the first *Brown* case, Robinson's argument in the Virginia portion was "able, but rather listless and somewhat obscure . . . not very well organized . . . almost submissive (in style)" (Kluger 1975, 2:728). He belabored details of the case, dwelt on inequalities, and then made a weak argument for complete school desegregation by drawing on the logic of *Gaines v. Canada*, a marginally related precedent in which Missouri was forced to provide a law school African-Americans could attend rather than paying for them to go out of state. Yet, as Kluger describes it, Robinson did better in rebuttal. He noted that Virginia was still spending only sixty-one cents on its African-American students for every dollar spent on white children in the state. But more importantly, he was seen as arguing "genteelly" and with an "impressive command of legal history and scholarship" that Virginia's segregation laws were created initially to limit access to education by African-Americans, quoting earlier Virginia legislators to establish that legal intent to discriminate (Kluger 1975, 2:730).

Despite some flaws in the presentation of the case, the Supreme Court found for Robinson and the Fund, barring racial discrimination in public education. The legal principle of "separate but equal," which had been the accepted rule of the land since the *Plessy v. Ferguson* decision in 1896, had now been overturned. "Separate but equal" was now deemed to be "inherently unequal." This ruling had revolutionary implications not only for segregated education but for many other Jim Crow laws as well. Yet local resistance would remain strong, making implementation excessively slow. Consequently, the second *Brown* case presented the opportunity to attempt to accelerate implementation.

In an internal NAACP memorandum to Jack Weinstein, Robinson pressed for acceleration of action, stating, "absent circumstances of an extraordinary character, desegregation of a public school system can be accomplished by school officials acting diligently and in good faith within a maximum of one calendar year" (Kluger 1975, 2:911). To do otherwise was seen as blatantly unfair to children currently in school. Then, before the U.S. Supreme Court in the 1955 *Brown v. Board of Education* case, Robinson was considerably better in making his arguments. According to Kluger, Robinson argued "briskly and forcefully" that state-imposed caste laws violated the "broad purpose" of the Fourteenth Amendment, as embraced in the 1866 Civil Rights Act (Kluger 1975, 2:843–844). Marshall, who also saved some of his time for an effective rebuttal, followed. Their combined arguments ultimately helped prompt the Supreme Court's compromise language in its 1955 *Brown* decision, which required school desegregation efforts to proceed "with all deliberate speed."

Besides school desegregation, other major legal victories for Robinson and the Fund included gaining African-Americans the right freely to buy property, to travel equally on public transportation, and to enjoy equal use of public recreational facilities. In *Shelley v. Kramer* (1948), for example, the U.S. Supreme Court outlawed the state practice of allowing racially restrictive covenants to be written into the deeds of homes, essentially precluding the homes from being sold to African-Americans. In *Morgan v. Virginia* (1946), the Court struck down state travel laws requiring segregated seating on interstate bus travel; and in *Gayle v. Browder* (1956), the justices supported the position of the Montgomery, Alabama, bus boycott by ruling city bus segregation laws to be unconstitutional as well. In *Baltimore v. Dawson* (1955) and *Holmes v. Atlanta* (1955), the Court also ended racial segregation at public beaches and parks.

Nevertheless, despite his many successes, Robinson experienced his share of setbacks as well. For example, he was part of the Fund team that unsuccessfully defended the Martinsville Seven, seven African-American men accused of raping a white woman in Martinsville, Virginia, in 1947. That legal defense spanned a three-year period from 1949 to 1951. The defendants were ultimately convicted, sentenced, and executed.

Robinson also ventured into the political arena in a limited way on occasion, in his pursuit of racial justice in the United States. In 1970, for example, he joined a host of black leaders in condemning the Nixon administration at the sixty-first annual meeting of the NAACP. Characterizing that administration as "anti-black," they noted the administration's policies of signing defense contracts with firms that discriminated on the basis of race, retreating on school desegregation, continued attempts to dilute the Voting Rights Act, and nominating Harold Carswell and Clement Haynesworth to serve on the U.S. Supreme Court, despite their histories of insensitivity to African-Americans.

During the course of his lifetime, Robinson's honorary recognitions were numerous. Besides receiving an honorary doctorate from his alma mater, Virginia Union University, in 1955, he was also named to the Richmond African-American Honor Roll. He received a testimonial of merit in jurisprudence from the Phi Phi Chapter of Omega Psi Phi and from the National Bar Association. Howard University gave him a distinguished alumnus award, and the Beta Gamma Lambda chapter of Alpha Phi Alpha gave him a Non-Member Citizenship Award. He received the Social Action Achievement Award from Phi Beta Sigma and a citation of merit from both the Beta Theta Sigma Chapter of Delta Sigma Theta and the Richmond Chapter of Frontiers of America.

—*Marcus Pohlmann*

Sources and Suggestions for Further Reading

Kluger, Richard. *Simple Justice.* 2 vols. New York: Alfred A. Knopf, 1975.

Lowery, Charles, and John Marszalek, eds. *Encyclopedia of African-American Civil Rights: From Emancipation to the Present.* New York: Greenwood Press, 1992.

Ploski, Harry, and James Williams, eds. *The Negro Almanac: A Reference Work on the African American.* Detroit: Gale Research, 1989.

Wexler, Sanford. *An Eyewitness to History: The Civil Rights Movement.* Facts on File, 1993.

ROGERS, EARL

(1870–1922)

FEW AMERICAN TRIAL LAWYERS have enjoyed the success in the courtroom of Earl Rogers, who obtained more than 183 acquittals in criminal cases and lost fewer than 20 (Snow 1987, 96). Although criminal law was not his original pursuit, it soon became Rogers's passion. Few of the murder cases he defended were individually notable, but throughout the course of his career, Rogers had a significant influence on modern trial advocacy and the techniques that accompany it. Unlike some of his peers, Rogers rarely, if ever, expressed compunction about defending the guilty, and he often stretched acceptable defense tactics to the limit, if not the breaking point.

Rogers was born in 1870 in Perry, New York, the son of a gifted mother who introduced him to foreign languages and music and a father, Lowell L. Rogers, who combined careers as a Methodist evangelist, college professor, and real estate developer. Although his father brought the family west, Earl followed his footsteps at Syracuse University before his father's financial re-

EARL ROGERS
Library of Congress

verses forced him out of college and back to California. He brought with him his beautiful wife, Hazel Belle Green, with whom he would have four children and with whom he would long have a tempestuous relationship that finally ended in divorce, remarriage, and divorce again. Rogers's second marriage to Teddy Landers ended with her death from influenza in 1919, three years before his own passing.

After a short stint as a newspaper reporter, Rogers became increasingly interested in the law, a career he entered after studying in the office of Judge W. P. Gardiner and Senator Stephen M. White, one of the state's most highly regarded attorneys, whom Rogers would later beat in one of his early cases. Indeed, in that case, Rogers reputedly preyed on White's penchant for drinking by going to lunch with him, buying him an extra drink, and hurrying back to the courthouse. Rogers quickly put the vulnerable defendant (whom he expected White to cross-examine mercilessly) on the stand and questioned him only in a perfunctory fashion so that White's unprepared assistant would have to conduct the cross-examination before White arrived back in the courtroom.

Curiously, Rogers appears to have emulated White's own drinking habits, well aware of the possible consequences. In a later case, Rogers would formulate what his daughter described as "the first alcoholic insanity defense" (St. Johns 1962, 220) in acquitting Colonel Griffith J. Griffith of shooting his wife in the head. During cross-examination, Rogers exhibited great kindness to Griffith's wounded wife. In the process, he effectively converted her into a defense witness. He did so by allowing her to maintain her own dignity and spare her husband's life by leading her to indicate that she had tried to conceal her husband's drinking and concluding that he must have been insane to shoot her after falsely accusing her of having an affair and of trying to poison him.

Although some observers believe that Rogers's desire to win cases drove him both to use questionable tactics and to shy away from cases that he thought he could not win, he nonetheless won many cases that were thought to be unwinnable and in which he himself believed his clients to be guilty. In addition to saving numerous individuals from the death penalty, Rogers guided the defense of CLARENCE DARROW against charges that he had attempted to bribe jurors.

Rogers was a courtroom innovator known for dressing meticulously and for cross-examining witnesses mercilessly. Rogers, who could use the tone of his voice to make ordinary witnesses appear despicable, often pulled out his trademark gold lorgnette (eyeglasses on a long handle) for effect. Rogers was also known for his ability to disguise the questions to which he was really seeking answers amid many others that were unimportant; for his willingness to stage dramatic scenes—often involving himself—to bait the opposing attorneys and to divert attention from a concession made by a witness; and for his colorful recreations of crime scenes and the introduction of other dramatic evidence in court. Rogers was renowned for his grasp of medical knowledge (he lectured on the subject of medical jurisprudence in Los Angeles–area colleges) and ballistics, which he is credited for introducing into U.S. courts from German scientific sources (which he first read in that language). Rogers also had a reputation for introducing newly discovered (or planted?) weapons and other evidence at trials and, in at least one case, for helping to destroy evidence. Rogers conducted meticulous investigations, amassed a remarkable knowledge of potential jurors, and had an ability to make emotional connections with them. He could use humor to ridicule opponents and witnesses; make outrageous suggestions in court that he knew could not be true but which might plant reasonable doubt in the jurors' minds (for example, the suggestion that a defendant might have an identical twin); and was in general a real showman. Rogers generally went for all or nothing, almost always putting the defendant on the stand, and he generally looked with contempt on criminal lawyers, including Clarence Darrow, who settled for reduced pleas.

Rogers forged alliances with police officers (a number of whom he had successfully defended against murder charges in an early case), with prostitutes and pimps, with members of the Chinese community, and with actresses. Rogers also cultivated goodwill among journalists who, in exchange for tips about dramatic trial developments, could often be counted on to give him inside information and to help him in the arena of public opinion. Although, like good actors, Rogers usually succeeded in making his performances appear effortless, he was also known for his intense drive and his meticulous preparation. The strain of the trial often sapped his energies during trial and, along with the responsibility of defending human life (and he did lose some death-penalty cases), arguably helped drive him to alcohol.

The biographies of Rogers, one of which was penned by his adoring daughter, an accomplished journalist, agree that Rogers reveled in the drama and spectacle of trial work as well as in the publicity that his accomplishments brought. Although he was involved in politics, the law was always his primary preoccupation. Rogers was often cheered as a celebrity at baseball games and other athletic events, where fans would yell "kill the umpire, we'll get Earl Rogers to defend you" (St. Johns 1962, 107). One who profited from this advice was Patrick Calhoun, the head of the United Railroads, whom Rogers helped exonerate on charges of bribing the San Francisco Board of Supervisors.

Rogers clearly enjoyed his own notoriety, but he carelessly spent the extensive fees that came his way. Moreover, he did little to hide his drinking escapades (some with his friend novelist Jack London), and he eventually fell casualty to alcohol, which increasingly disrupted his practice and sometimes found him inexplicably absent from the courtroom. Through most of his life, a potential client's observation that "I'd rather have Earl Rogers drunk defending me than any other lawyer sober" (Kornstein 1987, 131) was true, but, in a rare occasion where Rogers found himself on trial, he had to put his own daughter on the stand to keep himself from being committed to a sanitorium. In the end, Rogers died alone of alcoholism in a cheap Los Angeles rooming house.

Many of Rogers's trials would be fitting subjects for movies. Early in his career in the aforementioned case against Senator White, Rogers defended William Alford for the murder of Jay E. Hunter by demonstrating that Hunter had provoked retaliation by beating Alford with a cane. Bringing Hunter's intestines to court in a jar filled with formaldehyde, Rogers purported to show that the wound had been inflicted from below, as the defendant was being beaten, rather than from above, as the prosecutor had argued. On another occasion, Rogers was able to comb through voluminous testimony to focus on an expert's use of the term "return spray" to suggest that his client, a well-known gambler, had shot and killed his mistress in self-defense *after* she had first thrown acid at him—a story that led some to believe that Rogers, who had apparently received the first telephone call about the incident, had actually advised his client to put acid on his own face (St. Johns 1962, 335).

In another case, Rogers defended a prostitute who murdered her boyfriend after she discovered that he was spending money she had given him to buy an engagement ring for another woman. When Rogers's daughter later told the story in "The Red Kimono," the defendant successfully sued a movie producer for including her name in the recreation of the story, and the resulting case of *Melvin v. Reid* became a stepping-stone in the development of the right of privacy (Kornstein 1987, 128).

In a case that showed Rogers's willingness to use trickery to question eyewitness testimony, Rogers had an assistant switch chairs and hats with the defendant seated beside him, eliciting a false identification of his assistant as a horse thief. In a case defending Charles F. Mootry for the death of his wife, for whom he had been a pimp, Rogers evoked jurors' own happy memories of being in love. Although arguing that this was a case of suicide and denying that any such man could have killed his wife, when the jury brought an acquittal, Rogers refused to shake Mootry's hand, telling him that he was "as guilty as hell" (Cohn and Chisholm 1934, 59). This incident led Rogers's upright father, who was otherwise pleased with his son's defense of the needy, to counsel him about crossing the line into unethical behavior (St. Johns 1962, 101–104).

On one, and apparently only one, occasion, Rogers teamed up with the prosecution to send a man to his death for the killing of the wife of a millionaire friend, who apparently feared that the killer would go free if Rogers were to defend him. Rogers succeeded in his role as a special prosecutor, and the man was sentenced to hang. Rogers's daughter reports that her father was remorseful about the outcome and even joined the medical examiner in performing an autopsy on the killer in the unfulfilled hope that he might find that he had acted under the impulse of a mental disorder brought about by a blow to his head. (St. Johns 1962, 213–215). Like Darrow, Rogers became a strong opponent of the death penalty.

There were times when Rogers's presence in the courtroom and his relentless cross-examination were almost hypnotic. Indeed, Francis Wellman, author of a book on cross-examination, said that "Earl Rogers invented the art of cross-examination as it is now practiced" (Kornstein 1987, 130). In the *Catalina Island Murder* case, involving a shooting in a card game, which Rogers meticulously recreated by bringing props into the courtroom, Rogers appeared to have gotten a witness for the prosecution to admit to having gone to the washroom to wash off gunpowder stains on his own hands. In this same case, Rogers actually pulled a gun on the chief opposition witness in the courtroom to demonstrate that he was lying about how he had reacted when he claimed that the same thing had happened during the card game.

Rogers demonstrated his cross-examination skills in a case in which he was defending a Chinese immigrant named Wong She, who had been charged with engaging in prostitution, against deportation. In addition to making jokes at the witness's own expense, Rogers was able to show that a seemingly perfect witness, a straitlaced missionary, was in fact basing his information on hearsay, which is severely limited under U.S. law:

Q. You say this child is a prostitute?
A. She most certainly is.
Q. You know for a fact that Wong She was a prostitute?
A. I do indeed.
Q. Of your own knowledge?
A. Yes, indeed of my own knowledge.
Q. But doctor, you are a married man. I thought your position . . .
A. Don't you try to make something of it. Of course no such thing happened.
Q. Then how can you know of your own . . . you peeped!
A. I did no such thing.
Q. You said you knew of your own personal knowledge.
A. Everybody in Chinatown knows about this woman. Her reputation is notorious.

Q. But that, my dear sir, is hearsay.

A. It is now, it's the truth and everybody in Chinatown knows it.

Q. Well, now we are getting somewhere, sir. Everybody in the world once knew it was flat, you recall. (Kornstein 1987, 131–132)

Rogers's defense of Clarence Darrow for bribery is still the subject of scholarly debate. Although Darrow had established a reputation as a labor lawyer, he had not yet defended his most important cases, so his defense had an important impact on history. Darrow was on trial for bribing jurors in the case of the McNamara brothers, who were accused of having bombed the *Los Angeles Times* building, killing twenty men—a case that Darrow (who had come to realize that the men were guilty) unexpectedly settled out of court after collecting large sums of money from labor organizations and promising a vigorous defense. Darrow had been in the immediate vicinity when cash had been given to a juror. Although Rogers accepted the case, he became extremely agitated with Darrow's abject demeanor, which Rogers thought contributed to an impression of Darrow's guilt, during much of the trial. Rogers, who focused on individuals and had few apparent ideological predispositions, also objected to Darrow's seeming willingness to justify his actions in ideological terms. Not surprisingly, Darrow in turn wanted greater control over his own case and worried about Rogers's drinking. Darrow's wife was also unimpressed with Rogers. Rogers helped obtain a hung jury in the first case, in which his daughter claims that he was extremely influential in crafting Darrow's final plea to the jury, which has been justly praised as a masterpiece. Rogers did not play as significant a role in the second trial, which also resulted in a hung jury (albeit by a closer margin) and Darrow's promise to leave the state and never return.

Toward the end of his life, Rogers became convinced that the increased regulation and the displacement of attorneys by other professionals was destroying the practice of law (see Cohn and Chisholm 1934, 282–287). Although Rogers decried the way that the public perceived lawyers, he seemed to make little connection between his own willingness to engage in courtroom antics and such a reputation. Clearly, Rogers, the loner, would be quite uncomfortable in modern firms employing hundreds of attorneys, and Rogers the actor could not have stood for assembly-line justice. It is unlikely that modern courts would have allowed Rogers the same leeway he had during his day, but he might continue to find himself at home cross-examining witnesses and be pleased at the role that expert witnesses and scientific evidence continue to play in modern trials.

—*John R. Vile*

Jake Ehrlich

Much like EARL ROGERS and Jerry Giesler (with whom he worked in defending Alexander Pantages against charges of rape), Jake Ehrlich earned a reputation as one of California's outstanding defense attorneys. Dubbed "the Master" by his friends and acquaintances, Ehrlich, born in Maryland in 1900 and educated at Georgetown University and at the San Francisco Law School, defended fifty-six individuals accused of murder and never lost one to the executioner.

Although his murder defenses made him famous, they constituted only 3 percent of his practice. He earned most of his money in more routine civil matters.

Ehrlich's celebrated cases included his defense of Jean Collins for killing her pimp; his defense of singer Billie Holliday for illegal drug possession; his defense of Gertrude Morris (a woman who wanted to be executed) for the shooting death of her husband; his defense of drummer Gene Krupa for possession of drugs; his defense of Alfred Leonard Cline, who had married many women whom he was accused of poisoning and then cremating (the defendant refused to talk to his attorney or to the court, but Ehrlich succeeded in having him sentenced to prison for forgery rather than for murder); his defense of the movie *The Outlaw* for what was alleged to be revealing clothing worn by Jane Russell; and a defense of Sally Rand against charges that her fan dance was obscene.

Ehrlich, who was a meticulous dresser especially known for his large cufflink collection, could be particularly dramatic in the courtroom, especially in closing arguments, in which he literally took on the persona of the individuals he was defending, and in which, like Earl Rogers, he liked to use visual displays. Disclaiming that he pulled from a bag of tricks, however, Ehrlich claimed to adapt to the circumstances of each case (Nobel and Averbuch 1955, viii).

When in an early case a judge accused another lawyer named Christensen of sending in Ehrlich as "a mere beardless youth," Ehrlich showed his adaptability by saying that "if Mr. Christensen had known Your Honor attached such importance to whiskers, I am sure he would have sent over a billygoat!" (Nobel and Averbuch 1955, 28). In another case, Ehrlich won a verdict when the witness identified him, rather than the defendant he was representing, as her rapist! (Nobel and Averbuch 1955, 34).

Like other high-profile defense attorneys, reporters have used many adjectives to describe Ehrlich. His biographers have listed the following: "cynical, steely, brilliant, impudent, grasping, boisterous, maudlin, urchin, cocky, generous, sly, shrewd, ruthless, profane, flamboyant, gregarious, sentimental, egotistical, and tender" (Nobel and Averbuch 1955, 5). Such adjectives help confirm Ehrlich's ability to adapt his strategy to the situation at hand.

REFERENCE

Noble, John Wesley, and Bernard Averbuch. *Never Plead Guilty: The Story of Jake Ehrlich the Brilliant Criminal Lawyer*. New York: Farrar, Straus & Cudahy, 1955.

Cohn, Alfred, and Joe Chisholm. *"Take the Witness!"* New York: Frederick A. Stokes, 1934.

Cowan, Geoffrey. *The People v. Clarence Darrow: The Bribery Trial of America's Greatest Lawyer.* New York: Times Books, 1993.

Kornstein, Daniel. *Thinking under Fire: Great Courtroom Lawyers and Their Impact on American History.* New York: Dodd, Mead, 1987.

Robinson, W. W. *Lawyers of Los Angeles.* Los Angeles: Los Angeles Bar Association, 1959.

Snow, Richard F. "Counsel for the Indefensible." *American Heritage* 38 (February/March 1987): 96–97.

St. Johns, Adela Rogers. *Final Verdict.* Garden City, N.Y.: Doubleday, 1962.

ROOT, ELIHU

(1845–1937)

ELIHU ROOT, CORPORATE AT-torney and U.S. secretary of state and senator was born February 15, 1845, to Oren Root and Nancy Buttrick Root in Clinton, New York. At that time, his father served as principal and his mother was a teacher at the local academy. Oren Root would later teach mathematics at Hamilton College. Elihu Root was greatly impressed with and influenced by his paternal uncle, Philander Sheldon Root, an attorney and county judge in Utica. Root was also influenced by his father's love of botany, geology, and music. Growing up in the midst of an educational environment also affected young Root. Although his father and mother were often too busy to read to him, Root began reading at a very early age.

Root enrolled at Hamilton College in 1860, before he was sixteen years old, and was the youngest in a class of fifty-four freshmen. It was during the spring of Root's sophomore year that President ABRAHAM LINCOLN issued a call for volunteers for the Northern Army to fight in the Civil War. Although he tried to enlist, Root

ELIHU ROOT
Library of Congress

was rejected because of his frail physique. During his junior year, a series of revival meetings were held at the new College Church, and Root was among the converts. His religious zeal often displayed itself in later years through his devotion to the church and the Young Men's Christian Association (YMCA).

Although he was a strong student, Root was not a strong speaker. His voice had a high pitch, which he would continue to consider a handicap throughout his life. Root graduated Phi Beta Kappa in 1864 at age nineteen with a B.A. degree.

What compelled Root to study law is not clear. It is likely that there were multiple influences, including the attorneys and judges who were affiliated with Hamilton College and, of course, his paternal uncle. His maternal uncle and his older brother, Oren Jr., were also attorneys.

Root spent a short time teaching at the Rome Academy. During this time he also enrolled as a private in the New York State Militia. In July 1865, Root traveled to New York City and worked out his rent by teaching Latin to his landlady's son. He attended the New York University School of Law. As he read and studied the law, Root also taught history at the Graham School on Fifth Avenue. He received his LL.B. degree in the summer of 1867. At the time, earning the degree was all that was required to practice law, which he began to do at the well-respected firm of Mann & Parsons. Root stayed there for one year, apprenticing without pay. On leaving the firm, he formed a partnership with John H. Strahan.

Root quickly discovered that he preferred and excelled at trial work. His first case was a criminal matter, in which he represented a man accused of accepting $10 in exchange for a false affidavit. The client was convicted, but Root successfully worked for the client's pardon. In his first year of practice, Root searched titles, argued a motion in federal court, won a suit for $36.00, and settled other claims for $241.66 and $212.36.

A major financial breakthrough for Root's law office came when he was recommended to teach Latin to John J. Donaldson, who was credit officer for the dry goods firm of H. B. Claflin & Co., and who would soon serve as president of the Bank of North America. Impressed with Root's abilities, Donaldson began giving him legal work. Root handled Donaldson's personal legal matters, as well as corporate cases for the bank. The largest among the earliest cases was a judgment for $6,712.45.

When the bank reorganized under a state charter, Root was given the responsibility of handling the legal aspects of the change. His outstanding work for the Bank of North America earned him the similar responsibility of changing the charter of the Pacific National Bank, for which he received a fee of $1,000. On October 31, 1869, the firm of Strahan & Root balanced its own books and calculated its income at $10,386.95.

Root soon changed his professional affiliation and formed a partnership with Alexander T. Compton, whom he had known in law school. Compton had represented James Ingersoll, who became one of the defendants in the William M. Tweed prosecutions. Not being a trial lawyer, Compton asked Root to handle the matter, which involved charges of bribery and fraud. During the trials, Root primarily assisted Tweed's lead counsel, David Dudley Field, although Root was also involved to some extent in conducting voir dire of jurors and cross-examining witnesses. In the end, the jury convicted the defendants on 204 of the 220 counts of the indictment. A portion of the criminal penalties was overturned on appeal, but Root was not involved in those proceedings. Root's chief client, Ingersoll, was convicted and sentenced to five years and seven months in prison; however, the governor later pardoned him.

Along with other counsel, Root continued through 1875 to participate in the defense in the many civil lawsuits against the "Tweed Ring" defendants. Root's total fee for the matter was approximately $15,000. The local press's reporting led the public to believe that Root was an intimate advisor to Tweed himself, which was not true. Nevertheless, the high-profile nature of the cases spotlighted Root's practice and established new contacts with important members of the bar.

The firm of Compton & Root became increasingly busy. Compton handled the office matters, and Root attended to all litigation. During the 1870s, Root's cases primarily focused on bank matters, railroad cases, wills, estates, and municipal government matters. In all of his cases, Root was a master of detail. He strove to know more about an opponent's case than did the opponent himself. His style in the courtroom was not flamboyant, but rather was serious and thorough. Root continued to handle collection cases for the Bank of North America and for H. B. Claflin. He also became involved in litigation that included the Erie Railroad.

Root married Clara F. Wales, daughter of Salem Wales, who was the editor of *Scientific American*. Over the course of time, they would have three children: Edith, Elihu Jr., and Edward. Although the postwar depression had set in, Root was financially sound. Although he was never wealthy enough to be considered a philanthropist, Root took great care to share his material possessions with those in need around him. He often provided pro bono legal work for family and friends.

In February 1878, Root defended General Oliver L. Shepard, who had been court-martialed for misappropriation of funds. The general was convicted, despite Root's competent representation. In 1879, Root traveled to Kansas City to represent famous restaurateur Charles Delmonico, who had been defrauded in a mining venture. The appeal of this case was Root's first to the U.S. Supreme Court. He was admitted to the Supreme Court bar on

November 14, 1881, but the case was settled to Delmonico's satisfaction before oral arguments were held.

The Delmonico case had taken Root to Denver, Colorado, in 1880, where he made several important contacts with the owners of large mining companies. Several such companies would place Root in charge of all their interests in the New York area. It was during this period that one of the associates in Root's office, Robert Strahan, became heavily involved in local and state politics. In Root's view, this involvement ruined an otherwise capable attorney. According to Root, witnessing Strahan's transformation convinced him always to place the practice of law above all other considerations.

However, it was also during this period that Root became involved in the local Republican party. Fellow Republican party members convinced him to seek the party's nomination for judge of the court of common pleas in 1879; Root was thirty-four years old at the time. As was typical for contemporary New York Republican candidates, Root lost the election. In later years, some Root supporters would charge that he was unfairly discriminated against because of his involvement in the *Tweed* cases. However, the media did not make an issue of *Tweed*, and Root's loss seems more properly attributable to the lack of strength of the Republican party in New York at that time.

Root also became a close friend and strong ally of Chester A. Arthur. In fact, when the Garfield/Arthur ticket won the presidential election of 1880, Root was invited to Washington for the inauguration and traveled there by special palace car. Seven months later, Root was with several friends at Vice-President Arthur's New York home when the telegram arrived announcing the death of the president and asking that Arthur take the oath of office at once. Root and a friend retrieved Judge Brady of the New York Supreme Court and witnessed as Brady administered the oath of office to Arthur. Many believed that Root would soon be appointed to a cabinet position. However, Arthur knew that Root did not desire such a position, and no offer was made.

Root continued an active practice of law, including the representation of several sugar importers and refiners. His representation of the Hannibal & St. Jo Railroad continued through two different company presidents. By that time, Root's legal abilities were widely known and respected. He continued to represent a wide variety of corporations, never considering becoming a full-time, in-house counselor for any one of them.

Root's involvement in New York City matters began when he defended Joel Erhardt, a police commissioner, in a termination proceeding against all the commissioners. Due in large part to Root's legal prowess, the mayor withdrew the demand for their dismissal. In 1878, Root successfully defended fifteen aldermen on misdemeanor charges, which turned out to be a politically motivated matter. He continued to serve as counsel for the police commissioners and was successful a second time in preventing their termination by a political foe. However, when the issue arose again in 1881, both the public and the press seemed to favor the mayor's position that the commissioners' alleged neglect of duty (specifically the unclean state of the city streets) made them unworthy to continue in their positions. The judge held in favor of the mayor, but Root gained the actual victory. He had drafted a bill relieving police commissioners of street sanitation duties, which was introduced by a friend in the state legislature and passed by the Republican majority. Root's corporate work also continued; he conducted twenty-eight lawsuits on behalf of Claflin & Co. against insurance companies and successfully established the insurance companies' liability for a fire loss.

In 1880, the Havemeyer Sugar Refining Company retained Root as counsel. At that time, no sugar monopoly existed and his representation was limited to debt collection and advice concerning how to avoid needless litigation. The Sugar Trust was established in 1887, but it is not known whether Root had any involvement in its creation. It was in 1890 that New York courts declared the Sugar Trust illegal. The Havemeyers turned to Root for advice. Aware of more favorable corporate statutes in New Jersey, he suggested reorganizing there. Highly successful, the new American Sugar Refining Company soon controlled 98 percent of the national output. Root did not represent the Sugar Trust during its successful defense against the government's suit under the Sherman Anti-Trust Act.

Root also represented the Whitney-Ryan traction syndicate, which involved the consolidation of Manhattan street railways. His corporate involvement, especially as counsel for trusts and syndicates, reveals Root's deep belief that all clients deserved vigorous representation. Never willing to perform in an unethical manner, Root did take advantage of every benefit the law and ethical rules would afford his clients.

In the fall of 1881, Root served as a delegate to the Republican State Convention. He was very active in the nomination to the State Assembly of a young politician named Theodore Roosevelt. In 1882, Root became a member of the Republican Central Committee.

In 1883, President Arthur suggested that Root be appointed as U.S. attorney for the Southern District of New York. At that time, the position did not require full-time devotion to political duties, and Root was free to continue his private practice. Root accepted the appointment and usually spent mornings in the district attorney's office and afternoons in his private law office. While meeting the staff of the district attorney's office, Root was introduced to a clerk who would soon be leaving for law school; the clerk's name was CHARLES EVANS HUGHES, who would later be chief justice of the United States. Root's legal background well equipped him to run the office, and he quickly initiated new policies that greatly lessened the office's over-whelming backlog of cases.

As district attorney general, Root was involved in many cases involving international law, as well as several tax cases and cases involving private postal systems. Probably the most well-known case was Root's prosecution of James C. Fish, president of the Marine National Bank. Fish was indicted on charges that he embezzled bank funds. Root prepared for the trial for six weeks, which included deposing former U.S. president Ulysses S. Grant (whose son had been Fish's partner). The trial lasted one month; Fish was convicted and sentenced to ten years in prison. Root retired as district at-torney after Grover Cleveland was elected president.

In 1886, after he refused to run for the office himself, Root directed Theodore Roosevelt's unsuccessful mayoral campaign against Abram S. Hewitt and Henry George. Two years later, Root single-handedly preserved Roosevelt's eligibility to seek the office of governor.

Root was also a very valuable ally of President William McKinley. In fact, McKinley asked Root to travel to Madrid in 1897 to take part in negotia-tions concerning that year's Cuban controversy. Root declined, citing his lack of experience in diplomatic matters. However, Root accepted McKin-ley's 1899 nomination as secretary of war. He served in that capacity through 1904. During that time, Root planned the U.S. Army War College and also reorganized the administrative system of the department. In addi-tion, he was also the primary author of the Foraker Act of 1900, which pro-vided for civil government in Puerto Rico. Root also established U.S. au-thority in the Philippines.

In 1905, then-president Theodore Roosevelt appointed Root secretary of state, a position he held through 1909. During this time, Root concluded treaties of arbitration with more than twenty nations. He was chief counsel for the United States before the Hague Tribunal, which settled the contro-versy between the United States and Great Britain over the North Atlantic coast fisheries. He also served as honorary president of the Pan-American Congress in 1906.

Root successfully ran for the U.S. Senate in 1909. He served until 1915 and declined to be a candidate for a second term. While in the Senate, Root served as both chair of the Committee on Expenditures in the Depart-ment of State and chair of the Committee on Industrial Expositions. Root supported the Allies at the outset of World War I, and he criticized Woodrow Wilson's policy of neutrality. His greatest honor was bestowed in 1912, when he was awarded the Nobel Peace Prize for his international peace efforts.

Root traveled to Russia in 1917 as head of a special diplomatic mission. He was appointed a member of the League of Nations committee to revise the World Court Statute in 1929. President Warren G. Harding also appointed Root in 1921 to serve as one of four U.S. delegates to the International Conference on the Limitation of Armaments. His writings include *Latin America and the United States* (1917), *Russia and the United States* (1917), and *Men and Policies* (1924). Elihu Root died in New York City, February 7, 1937.

—*Chris Whaley*

Sources and Suggestions for Further Reading

Jessup, Philip. *Elihu Root*. New York: Archon Books, 1964.
Leopold, Richard W. *Elihu Root: The Conservative Tradition*. Boston: Little, Brown, 1954.

SPENCE, GERRY

(1929–)

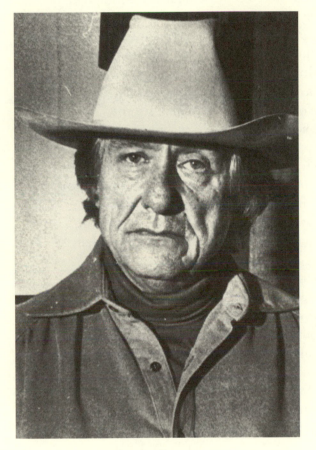

GERRY SPENCE
Bettmann/Corbis

IF ONE SUGGESTS THAT GERRY Spence has mastered the craft of "lawyering," Spence is almost certain to be offended. If, however, one insists that Spence is accomplished in the *art* of storytelling, Spence will surely smile. Spence is some artist. He has not lost a jury trial since 1969, including several of the most high-profile civil and criminal cases in the twentieth century.

Although Spence is one of the United States' greatest trial attorneys, his life has also been a fascinating series of contradictions. For instance, he deeply loved his mother, but her suicide when he was a young man engendered a lengthy and deep depression predicated on feelings of personal guilt. He finished law school at the top of his class, yet he was the school's first graduate to fail the state bar examination. He ran for the House of Representatives as a conservative Republican, and yet, later in life, he gravitated toward a combination of socialism and libertarianism. He was so angry with the way his father was treated by insurance companies that he grew up determined to make these companies pay for their callousness and cruelty. However, for several years he flourished as a defense attorney for the very same insurance companies.

Although Spence's life and career are often enigmatic, his record as a civil and criminal litigator over the last quarter century would be hard to equal. In 1974, he gained national prominence with his performance in a suit by the family of Karen Silkwood against the Kerr-McGee Corporation—a case in which a jury awarded his client a verdict in excess of ten million dollars. After this victory, he won a series of multimillion dollar verdicts, including one for fifty-two million dollars against McDonald's, a twenty-six-million-dollar verdict against *Penthouse* magazine on behalf of Kimberli Pring (a former Miss Wyoming), and a verdict of more than forty-five million dollars against Aetna Insurance Company. As a special prosecutor in the late 1970s, he secured a death penalty conviction against Mark Hopkinson, who bombed the home of a prominent Wyoming attorney. As a defense attorney, Spence obtained acquittals for such celebrated clients as Imelda Marcos and Randy Weaver.

Gerald Leonard Spence was born to Gerald Milner Spence and Esther Sophie Spence on January 8, 1929, in Laramie, Wyoming. Both his parents were college educated. Spence's father moved his bride from Colorado to Wyoming and accepted a position as a chemist. When Gerry was just a little boy, the family left Laramie to live in Sheridan, a small town more than three hundred miles to the north.

Growing up in northern Wyoming meant that Spence enjoyed hunting and fishing, crafting homemade slingshots, and raising pet sheep and cattle. Spence did not simply play cowboy like most American boys. He had an opportunity to *be* a cowboy, and worked, as a teenager, on several Wyoming ranches. However, life for Spence also meant that he arrived at school in clothes that his mother made from softened deer hide—a source of amusement for the other students—and that the animals he nurtured so carefully were eventually slaughtered and eaten. In Sheridan, his baby sister Peggy died at age three of meningitis. Her death proved to be traumatic both for Spence and for his parents' marriage.

His parents influenced young Spence greatly. As a boy, Spence learned how to flourish in the outdoors from his father. Although his father was indeed a "man's man," he was also tender and honest and provided for his family despite the obstacles put in his path by those with money and power. Spence grew up determined to make those responsible pay for the way they treated such men.

Spence's mother also profoundly influenced his life. A deeply committed Christian, Esther Spence instilled basic values in her son. She took him to church and taught him to pray. She encouraged him to have compassion for those suffering financially during the Depression and World War II. She helped him to see that it was senseless to judge others by their race. She urged her precocious child to be humble because "nobody likes a smarty." When Peggy died, Esther dedicated her boy to God. She wanted him to be a minister and avoid the fleshly vices—smoking, drinking, gambling, and premarital sex. Despite his deep affection for his parents, though, young Spence was a rebellious teenager. He started working early and often was employed at jobs that brought him into contact with hard men and even rougher women. At a young age, Spence became sexually active. He visited prostitutes. He smoked, drank, and learned to play poker with professional gamblers.

The family moved back to Laramie when Spence was in high school. Spence decided he wanted to be a lawyer. One day he walked over to the law school and announced his plans to the dean. The dean administered him an aptitude test, on which Spence's score was the highest the dean had ever seen. Encouraging Spence to enroll in law school after graduation, he predicted that Spence would be a great lawyer. This prediction certainly did not stop the teenager's rebellion. In fact, midway through his senior year, he earned enough credits to graduate from Laramie High School and promptly quit school, preferring instead to leave Wyoming with a friend bound for California, where the two young men spent a summer at sea working as deckhands. By the time Spence enrolled at the University of Wyoming, his life experiences made him a rather unusual student.

In 1948, while Spence was a nineteen-year-old student at the University of Wyoming, he married Anna Fidelia Wilson of Cheyenne. A year later, he received his bachelor's degree and entered the University of Wyoming College of Law. During Spence's first year of law school, his mother committed suicide. Spence, who assumed that his rebellion was responsible for the depression that triggered his mother's suicide, would not unburden himself from this guilt for decades.

Spence was a successful law student who graduated at the top of his class in 1952. Ironically, the area where Spence failed to excel in law school was in the courtroom in a trial practicum course and in moot court competition. During a law school mock trial, a judge in Laramie told him, "You will *never* become a trial lawyer, Mr. Spence. You may just as well face that fact now. I am doing you a favor by being brutally honest with you" (Spence 1996, 249). After graduation, Spence earned another dubious distinction. He became the school's first graduate who flunked the bar examination. In 1952, Spence passed the bar on his second attempt.

After graduating and successfully passing the bar, Spence went to work in Riverton, Wyoming, with an attorney named Franklin Sheldon for two hundred dollars per month. He discovered that he was woefully ill-prepared to practice law. Although trained to "think like a lawyer," he was not ready to do even the simplest legal assignments. As a result, he harbored a deep resentment against the kind of training given to prospective attorneys within the law schools.

After Sheldon left his practice to become a judge, Spence partnered with Frank Hill. The two attorneys found it difficult to build a lucrative practice in western Wyoming. Snubbed in his efforts to do legal work for the county attorney, Spence decided to run for that office. He was elected Fremont County attorney in 1954 and took office determined to clean up the county. He made some substantial enemies in doing so, but the voters agreed that he had kept his campaign promises, and Spence was reelected in 1958. After two terms as the county prosecutor, Spence ran for the House of Representatives in 1962. After incumbent William Henry Harrison soundly defeated him, Spence resumed his private legal practice.

After his failed bid for Congress, Spence's legal career can be divided into three phases. During the first interval, he became an important civil litigator and criminal defense attorney in Wyoming who aimed to help those he has described as the "little" or "ordinary" people. In the 1960s, Spence compiled some of the most impressive victories in Wyoming's legal history. He won a number of verdicts of more than one hundred thousand dollars for his clients and even a million-dollar verdict on behalf of a woman who was infected with gonorrhea by a wealthy, local playboy (a verdict subsequently set aside by the Wyoming Supreme Court).

Despite his courtroom success, Spence felt that he did not command the wealth, security, or prestige of Wyoming's leading attorneys who worked for the large corporations. As a result, Spence moved into the second phase of his postpolitical legal career when he started to represent insurance companies. Once again, Spence was an enormously successful civil litigator. For instance, he was once brought into a Denver courtroom as outside counsel for St. Paul Insurance Company. The company faced a multimillion dollar judgment, and it looked very much like the plaintiffs would collect. By the time Spence finished cross-examining the plaintiff, the jury returned a verdict awarding the plaintiffs twelve thousand dollars. Ecstatic, the insurance company paid the plaintiffs one hundred thousand dollars rather than allowing them to venture forward on appeal.

Although many now regarded Spence as the best trial attorney in Wyoming, his marriage was in trouble. In 1968, he began an affair with a woman named Imaging. A few months into their affair, Spence was plagued by guilt and grew determined to salvage his marriage. Having achieved some renown locally as a painter, Spence sold all of his Wyoming property, including his interest in his law practice, and enrolled in a graduate program in art at San Francisco State University. However, he could not shake his love for the law, Wyoming, and Imaging. Shortly after his arrival in San Francisco, he dropped out of graduate school, left his family on the west coast, and returned to resume his life and career in Wyoming. Within days of his divorce from Anna, Spence married Imaging, initiating nuptials that have endured more than thirty years.

His marriage to Imaging helped Spence to put his personal life back on track and prompted him to revisit the direction of his professional life. He no longer felt comfortable representing large corporations. During his final trial for an insurance company, Spence's skillful cross-examination of the plaintiff helped to secure a verdict for his client. The plaintiff, an old man who had been hit by a drunk driver, walked away from the courtroom without compensation for his substantial physical pain. Pleased with his performance, Spence and Imaging went to the store to purchase the fixings for an opulent celebration dinner. While standing in line, Spence noticed that the older chap ahead of them looked remarkably like his own grandfather. When the man turned around, Spence recognized him as the plaintiff. Spence mumbled that he was sorry about the outcome of the old man's case. "You don't need to be sorry, Mr. Spence," the old man said. "You were just doing your job" (Spence 1996, 424).

Earlier in his career, Spence realized that the law gave attorneys power. In fact, he surmised, it gave them the authority to kill people. The killing occurred in the courtroom, where Spence and other gifted litigators turned the hallowed legal arena into a place of death. Spence observed,

> Men die in the courtroom from words that send them to the executioner's gurney or to the gas chamber. They die when their names or their fortunes are taken from them, die as their children are wrenched from them, die when they walk the long walk, in chains, to dark concrete places where living men cannot abide. When I walk into a courtroom, I am the hunter. When I step into the arena, I feel as if I step into eons of history, of bloody duels, of misery and killing. And fear. (Spence 1996, 99)

The old man was right. Spence was indeed just doing his job. However, he could not shake the fact that, in this case, he harmed an aged plaintiff who was simply seeking justice from a drunk driver and her insurance company. Spence vowed never to represent corporations again.

Likening himself to Robin Hood, Spence entered the third phase of his postpolitical legal career determined to champion the powerless. The courtroom is still a place of killing, Spence surmised, but since the killing is for the right reasons, the killing itself is honorable. Absent an overriding public issue at stake, Spence returned exclusively to representing the "little/ordinary" people. In this phase of his legal career Gerry Spence began to achieve national prominence. He made his mark with the *Silkwood* decision. Victories against McDonald's, *Penthouse*, and *Hustler* magazine only solidified his national reputation as an effective hired gun.

Spence's success in the courtroom can be attributed, at least in part, to a particular rhetorical style. First, Spence's trademark is his use of the narrative. For Spence, the way to make a case come to life for a jury is to tell stories. "It is all about story telling—nothing more," notes Spence. He believes that effective use of the narrative is a lost art in the American courtroom largely because of the way students are prepared in law school. "The art of advocacy," Spence observes, "has become necrophilic at the hands of academicians. We have sent our young off to the morgues for training, to the morticians of the profession, to those who hate the art and who themselves abandoned it" (Spence 1986, 64–65). When Spence puts together a story for trial, the component parts are fairly straightforward. He places a premium on the beginning of the story (his opening argument) and how he believes the story must end (often voiced in both the opening and closing arguments). He develops a thesis for his story and uses a specific theme to crystallize the narrative. Like all good storytellers, Spence relates the facts of the story, anticipates his opponent's argument, and concedes points when he believes his opponent's case has merit (Spence 1995; Rodriguez and Doherty 1996).

He is a master storyteller who boils the complex legal problem down to a story of good against evil, with his client as the good guy. Spence appears in the stories as a narrator who guides the jury through the tale of woe and as the gladiator fighting for good. By positioning himself as a participant in the drama, Spence is able to extend the story. The tale did not end when Kerr-McGee leaked plutonium, when Mark Hopkinson bombed the home of Vincent Vehar, when *Penthouse* magazine published a vicious lie about Kim Pring, the former Miss Wyoming. No, Spence reminds the jury that the battle is still unfolding in the courtroom. Thus, Spence brings the jury into the story. He works to convince them that they are crucial if justice is to be achieved (Gill 1988).

Spence has transformed the rhetoric in the courtroom into an art form. Furthermore, Spence is a master of rhythm in his presentation. For centuries, people passed down their traditions from one generation to the next orally by learning to tell the stories to their audience's ears rather than to their eyes. Like such storytellers, Spence uses techniques such as repetition, a concise theme, and alliteration (Gill 1988).

In addition, Spence is willing to play a bit fast and loose with the rules of evidence in order to communicate with a jury. During his early experiences in the courtroom, Spence had difficulty directing a witness. His opponent repeatedly objected to his questions because Spence was consistently leading his witness. Initially, this was embarrassing. However, over time Spence discovered that the jury listened to his questions even when the judge sustained the objections of opposing counsel. Also, he found that the jury listened when he offered what the court later determined to be irrelevant materials. Thus, he took a weakness in his courtroom presentation and turned it into a strength. The judge might apply the rules of evidence, but the judge could not keep him from talking to the jury.

Finally, Spence prides himself on hard work. For most lawyers, substantial preparation means extensive legal research. For Spence, it might mean that he will pack up and move in with a client for a few weeks. While in the home of a client who, as the result of an accident, is a paraplegic, he can watch the client try to navigate around the home. He is there when the client endeavors to bathe or use the bathroom. He observes the client who might need to secure a specially enlarged spoon in order to eat his oatmeal. Spence can tell the jury in gripping detail just what the client has lost (Spence 1998).

Spence's work in the courtroom ranks beside that of CLARENCE DARROW at the beginning of the century. His performance is likened to Justice ROBERT JACKSON's prosecution of war criminals in the Nuremberg trials, or VINCENT BUGLIOSI's success in the Manson Family murder trial (Lief, Caldwell, and Bycel 1998).

In the *Silkwood* trial, Spence developed a central theme: "If the lion gets away, Kerr-McGee must pay." He used a principle of the common law to allow the jury to cut through the complicated, technical information by likening the corporation to a man in an ancient English community who brought a caged lion into the village. Concerned for his safety and the well-being of his neighbors, the man used the strongest cage, the best lock, and most able guards to secure the lion. Suppose, Spence argued, that the lion got away and killed a child. Citing his precautions, the man tells his neighbors that it cannot be his fault. The town's people acknowledge all the precautions. However, they deem the owner responsible for the lion's damages because *he* brought the lion into the town. Likewise, Spence noted in *Silkwood* that Kerr-McGee was responsible for plutonium leakage because it brought the "lion," plutonium, into the town. And, as Spence repeated often, "if the lion gets away, then Kerr-McGee must pay."

At the end of this case, Spence told the story of an old wise man and the challenge he faced from a younger man determined to better him. The young man captured a bird and cupped it in his hands. Approaching the old man, he asked, "Old man, will the bird live or die." The young man decided that if the old man announced that the bird would live, he would crush the bird. Likewise, if the old man guessed that the bird would die, he would free it. Instead, the old man simply acknowledged the obvious. "The bird," he proclaimed, "is in your hands." Spence reminded members of the jury that, like the bird, the decision was in their hands.

Now in his seventies, Spence remains quite active. He is senior partner in the firm Spence, Moriarty & Schuster. A prolific writer, Spence is the author of several books, including *Gunning for Justice* (1982), *Of Murder and Madness* (1983), *Trial by Fire* (1986), *Popular Mechanics: With Justice for None* (1989), *Freedom from Slavery* (1995), *How to Win an Argument* (1995), *The Making of a Country Lawyer* (1996), *O.J.: The Last Word* (1997), and *Give Me Liberty* (1998). He is in demand as a speaker and has hosted *The Gerry Spence Show* on the cable network CNBC. As a frequent guest on television, he is often asked to comment on a wide range of subjects.

Spence, who once unsuccessfully sought a teaching position at the University of Wyoming College of Law, founded the Trial Lawyer's College in western Wyoming. Every summer, he invites a small number of attorneys to study in a month-long course. The attorneys learn from some of the most celebrated trial attorneys in the United States, including Roy Black, Phil Corboy, MORRIS DEES, Judy Clark, RICHARD "RACEHORSE" HAYNES, Nancy Hollander, and Nfilton Grimes. The students take classes in drama and workshops in storytelling. They learn how to become gladiators in the courtroom. Spence's only requirement is that they not work as prosecutors or use their talents to represent corporations.

—*Frank Guliuzza III*

SOURCES AND SUGGESTIONS FOR FURTHER READING

"Gerry Spence's Summer Camp." *National Law Journal* 20 (December 1993): 6.

Gill, Ann. "The Oral Tradition of Gerry Spence in *Pring v. Penthouse*." *Southwestern University Law Review* 17 (1988): 693–706.

"*Keenan v. Spence:* Judge Holds the Reigns Tightly." *Manhattan Lawyer*, May 1990, 24.

Lief, Michael, H. Mitchell Caldwell, and Benjamin Bycel. *Ladies and Gentlemen of the Jury: Greatest Closing Arguments in Modern Law*. New York: Scribner, 1998.

Maravillosa, Sunni. "Please Don't Give Me Liberty!" *Laissez Faire City Times*, 21 December 1998.

Moss, Debra, and Daniel Kennedy. "Trial College and Tribulations." *American Bar Association Journal* (November 1994).

Nachman, Sherrie. "True Lies, Starring Gerry Spence." *The American Lawyer*, September 1994, 13.

Riccardi, Michael. "Spence: 'Justice for Sale.' 'Cowboy Lawyer' Tells City Slickers Standard Legal Training Is Bunk." *The Legal Intelligencer*, 2 February 1996, 1.

Rodriguez, Carmen, and Rebecca Doherty. "The Art of Arguing." *South Texas Law Review* 37 (1996): 365.

Spence, Gerry. "Art of the Argument: Beyond the Shouting." *American Bar Association Journal* (January 1995): 8.

_____. "How to Make a Complex Case Come Alive for a Jury." *American Bar Association Journal* (1 April 1986): 62.

_____. "Let Me Tell You a Story." *Trial*, February 1995, 73.

_____. *The Making of a Country Lawyer*. New York: St. Martin's Press, 1996.

_____. "Profits of Injustice." *Trial Lawyers Quarterly* 21 (1990–91): 18.

_____. "The Sale of the First Amendment." *American Bar Association Journal* (March 1989): 52.

_____. "Winning without Trying." *Trial*, April 1998, 24.

Spence, Gerry, and Anthony Polk. *Gunning for Justice*. New York: Doubleday, 1982.

STARR, KENNETH W.

(1946–)

IF A PERSON EVER SEEMED destined to don the robe of a U.S. Supreme Court justice it was Kenneth Starr. During the latter half of the twentieth century, Starr compiled one of the most impressive résumés in the history of U.S. jurisprudence and in the process gained a reputation as one of the country's most intellectually gifted appellate lawyers. Although he is primarily recognized for his role in the impeachment of President William Jefferson Clinton, there is much more to Kenneth Starr's career than his tenure as independent counsel for the White-water investigation.

KENNETH STARR

Independent Counsel Kenneth Starr holds a copy of his report while testifying on Capitol Hill, 19 November 1998, before the House Judiciary Committee's impeachment hearing. (AP Photo/Doug Mills)

Kenneth Winston Starr was born in Vernon, Texas, on July 21, 1946. His father, William Douglas Starr, was a Church of Christ minister and barber. His mother, Vannie, stayed at home to raise Kenneth's two older siblings—brother Jerry and sister Billie Jean—and him. The Starrs were devout Christians whose faith greatly shaped the character and development of their youngest child. To this day, Kenneth Starr remains a deeply religious man.

From the beginning of his scholastic career, Starr excelled in the classroom. He attended Sam Houston High School in San Antonio, Texas, where he was class president during his junior and senior years, a member of the National Honor Society, and chosen as the "most likely to succeed" by his peers. After high school, he spent a year and a half at Harding University, a small, Church of Christ–affiliated school in Searcy, Arkansas. At Harding, Starr continued his record of scholastic achievement by making the dean's list every semester. He also wrote a column for the college newspaper, won a seat on the student government council, and was actively involved with the Young Democrats. He transferred to George Washington University in Washington, D.C., midway through his sophomore year and graduated in 1968 from the school's honors political science program. While attending George Washington, Starr served as a congressional aide to Bob Price, a "libertarian" republican from his home state of Texas. After college, Starr attended Brown University as a university fellow, receiving a master's degree in political science from the school in 1969. Thereafter, Starr decided to attend law school at Duke University. At Duke, Starr was selected for the prestigious Order of the Coif, served as the Note and Comment editor for the school's law journal, and was president of the International Law Society. Starr graduated from law school in 1973 with highest honors and was named the Hughes Inn Graduate of the Year for his class.

After passing the California bar, Starr moved to Miami to clerk for David W. Dyer, a judge with the U.S. Court of Appeals for the Fifth Circuit. He then worked briefly as an associate with the Los Angeles law firm of Gibson, Dunn & Crutcher before accepting an offer to serve as Chief Justice Warren E. Burger's law clerk. At the conclusion of his clerkship on the nation's highest court, Starr rejoined Gibson, Dunn & Crutcher. It was during this time that he became a confidant of William French Smith, who, after the election of 1980, was selected by President Ronald Reagan to be U.S. attorney general. After receiving his appointment, Smith asked Starr to return to Washington to serve as counselor and as chief of his immediate staff. Starr accepted Smith's offer just three weeks after being named the youngest partner in the history of his law firm. As counselor, one of Starr's more notable assignments was shepherding Sandra Day O'Connor's nomination to the Supreme Court through the U.S. Senate. He did not walk in lockstep with Smith on every issue, however, and he angered fellow conservatives by opposing the Reagan administration's decision to defend tax exemptions for religious institutions that discriminated against minorities. Ironically, as counselor, Starr was also intimately involved with the administration's effort to challenge the constitutionality of the independent counsel statute.

On October 11, 1983, Kenneth Starr, at age thirty-seven, became the youngest judge ever appointed to "the second most important court in the nation," the U.S. Court of Appeals for the District of Columbia Circuit. Judge Robert Bork, who also served on the D.C. circuit bench, noted that as a judge, "Starr established a reputation for intelligence, diligence and un-failing courtesy to counsel and his fellow judges" (Bork 1998, 8). Liberal public interest groups also praised Starr for his willingness genuinely to consider their arguments and to rule in their favor "when he thought the law compelled him to" (Masters 1995). His opinions were generally conservative, but they occasionally displayed an "independent streak that pleased civil libertarians."

On May 27, 1989, Judge Starr reluctantly gave up his lifetime appointment to become President George Bush's solicitor general. The solicitor general is primarily responsible for supervising and conducting the executive branch's litigation before the Supreme Court. It is the only position in the federal government that requires the officeholder to be "learned in the law." The solicitor general's influence with the Supreme Court is so great that the person acting in this capacity is commonly referred to as the "tenth justice." Many in the legal community saw Starr's meteoric ascension to this post as a stepping-stone to an eventual appointment to the Supreme Court.

Kenneth Starr argued twenty-five cases before the Supreme Court during his tenure as solicitor general. Although many deserve mention, this essay will focus on three of the most highly publicized decisions in which he participated.

The "right to die" case of *Cruzan v. Director, Missouri Department of Health* (1990) marked the first time in our nation's history that the Supreme Court addressed the constitutional rights of dying medical patients. It was also Starr's first high-profile case as solicitor general. The issue before the Court in *Cruzan* was whether states could require the parent or guardian of a dying patient to demonstrate, by clear and convincing evidence, that the patient, while competent, expressed a desire not to be given life-sustaining medical treatment in the event of an irreversible medical condition. The Court's answer to this question hinged on whether the Constitution provides a fundamental right to dying patients, which would prohibit state involvement in such a decision. Starr agonized over the position his office would advocate on this extremely sensitive issue. He met with a representative from the family of Nancy Cruzan, and he visited Walter Reed Army Medical Center to discuss with doctors the ethical dilemmas they face in treating patients similarly situated. In his oral argument, Starr contended that although individuals might have a right to refuse unwanted medical treatment, the Constitution's silence on the issue required that "the due process clause . . . be interpreted to provide the states and the federal government with wide latitude . . . to develop approaches that reflect reasonably the values of the people." The Supreme Court agreed, holding that a state could require its citizens clearly to express their desire to refuse life-sustaining medical treatment, in the event of a terminal illness, prior to the time in which they become incompetent.

On May 14, 1990, Starr publicly weighed in on one of the most highly charged political issues in recent history: flag burning. The question before the Supreme Court in *United States v. Eichman,* however, was not political but constitutional: Does Congress have the authority to enact a federal statute criminalizing desecration of the American flag? The Court had recently addressed the issue in *Texas v. Johnson,* striking down a similar state law as a violation of free speech. Nevertheless, Starr defended the constitutionality of the federal law vigorously, and forced the reconsideration of *Johnson* by invoking the statute's expedited review provisions. Starr argued that the American flag was a unique national symbol, and as such, Congress had a legitimate interest in protecting its integrity. He maintained that flag burning did not convey a "particularized message" and therefore was not entitled to First Amendment protection. He also contended that flag burning was akin to other categories of communication that the Court had previously held were not forms of protected speech (e.g., "fighting words"). Starr emphasized that the statute in question was not aimed at deterring offensive expressive conduct, but was instead directed at preventing all forms of flag mistreatment. A narrow majority of the Supreme Court rejected Starr's argument, holding that "although the Flag Protection Act contains no explicit content based limitation on the scope of prohibited conduct, it is nevertheless clear that the Government's asserted interest is 'related to the suppression of free expression.'"

On January 21, 1992, the Supreme Court granted certiorari in the case of *Planned Parenthood of Southeastern Pennsylvania v. Casey.* The constitutional and political stakes in *Casey* were extremely high. The official question before the Court was whether various Pennsylvania regulations (e.g., parental consent for minors) violated a woman's constitutional right to an abortion. The much larger issue, however, was whether the Court would overrule one of its most controversial precedents, *Roe v. Wade* (1973). In *Roe v. Wade,* the Supreme Court held that women have a fundamental, constitutional right to have an abortion. Many legal commentators believed that the question was no longer whether *Roe* would be overruled, but rather when and by what means the reversal would occur

Casey was, without question, the biggest case of Kenneth Starr's career as solicitor general. Oral argument began with a passionate defense of *Roe* by acclaimed American Civil Liberties Union (ACLU) attorney Kathryn Kolbert. Kolbert made it clear to the justices, in her opening remarks, that she would be satisfied with nothing less than a complete reaffirmation of the Court's holding in *Roe.* Several justices attempted to persuade, or badger, Kolbert into softening her stance, but she refused. After a rough outing by

Clark Clifford, Washington Fixer

Few contemporary lawyers have achieved the respect and acclaim of Clark Clifford (1906–1998). Born in Kansas and reared in St. Louis, Clifford earned his law degree at Washington University and began clerking for a local firm. Determined to master the art of litigation, Clifford served as an appointed counsel for indigents, losing his first fourteen cases but constantly improving his skills in the process. Clifford's future cases would include appearances before the U.S. Supreme Court on behalf of well-known clients and businesses, but he was far better known for the advice he gave, for the political levers he pulled, and for his ability to court key members of the press than for his litigation skills.

The strikingly handsome Clifford enlisted in the navy during World War II and became an assistant naval aide in the Harry Truman White House, where he became Truman's private legal counsel and an advisor on important matters of both domestic and foreign policy, including approaches to the Cold War and strategies for Truman's reelection in 1948. After Dwight Eisenhower was elected to office in 1952, Clifford decided to set up practice in Washington, D.C., where elected officials with whom he was acquainted often directed business his way and where his services were in high demand among big businesses and others who needed to maneuver through the capital's many legal minefields. Clifford was highly regarded as an "insider's insider" who could discreetly work both legal and political levers. In addition to representing numerous business clients, Clifford's firm also looked after the personal interests of Supreme Court Justice William O. Douglas and incoming president John F. Kennedy, for whom he helped craft a transition strategy.

(*continues*)

Pennsylvania's attorney general, Starr rose to argue as a friend of the court in support of the state regulations. He began by addressing the standard to be utilized by the Court in reviewing the abortion restrictions. Starr argued that state regulations on abortion should be upheld so long as there was a rational basis for their existence. The underlying premise of his position was evident: abortion was not a fundamental, constitutional right to which women were entitled, and *Roe* and its progeny should be expressly, or implicitly, overruled. The liberal wing of the Court, led by Justice John Paul Stevens, went after Starr with a vengeance, attempting to sidetrack him with questions about whether a fetus should be considered a "person" for purposes of the Court's analysis. Starr responded that the United States did "not have a position on that question" and that the issue did not bear on whether the regulations in question were constitutional. The Court eventually returned to the issue of the appropriate standard of review, and Starr was then questioned as to whether the "rational basis" test would permit

(*continued*)

Clifford and fellow attorney ABE FOR-
TAS were close advisors to President Lyndon Johnson, and Clifford's connections to
government continued to bring in lucrative business until Clifford became secretary of defense in 1968. In that role, Clifford is credited with helping to persuade
President Johnson that further escalation
of the U.S. role in the Vietnam War would
be counterproductive; at the end of his
term, Johnson awarded Clifford a Medal of
Freedom.

Unsuccessful in his hopes of becoming
either president or secretary of state, Clifford rejoined his firm; his law practice continued to prosper as he took on diplomatic
roles during the Jimmy Carter administration. Driven by an insatiable appetite for
work and achievement, Clifford accepted
the presidency of the Bank of America,
long after the age that most people retire.
This ultimately resulted in Clifford's greatest embarrassment, when it was discovered
that, contrary to his own public assurances, stock in the bank was illegally
owned by the Bank of Credit and Commerce International (BCCI), in which
Clifford owned stock and which his firm
represented. BCCI was a foreign-owned
corporation engaged in unethical and illegal practices.

One of Washington's "wise men" was
now indicted along with a much younger
law partner, Richard Altman (husband of
actress Lynda Carter, of Superwoman
fame). Eventually exonerated of the
charges, Clifford's near godlike reputation
had nonetheless been tarnished, an example of the difficulties faced by lawyers who
go through the "revolving door" between
government service and private practice.

REFERENCES

Clifford, Clark, with Richard Holbrooke.
Counsel to the President: A Memoir. New
York: Random House, 1991.

Frantz, Douglas, and David McKean. *Friends in
High Places: The Rise and Fall of Clark Clifford.* Boston: Little, Brown, 1995.

states to ban abortion under any circumstance. Starr surmised that a complete prohibition of abortion would not be sustainable under "rational basis" scrutiny unless an exception existed for situations in which the life of
the mother was threatened. He also reminded the Court that under a "rational basis" review, a state may not "proceed in an arbitrary or capricious
fashion."

On June 29, 1992, the Court handed down its decision, and, in a surprising move, three justices—O'Connor, Anthony Kennedy, and David
Souter—jointly authored the majority opinion. A 5–4 majority of the
Court held that a woman has a constitutional right to an abortion. A different 5–4 majority, however, upheld all but one of the Pennsylvania regulations by using the less rigorous, newly adopted "undue burden" standard.
Casey has been heavily criticized as a political compromise that is constitutionally groundless. The net effect of the decision, however, was a substantial shift in the Court's abortion jurisprudence. *Roe,* as it had previously ex-

isted, was no more. State restrictions on abortion are now evaluated by the Supreme Court with far less scrutiny, and a woman's "right to choose" can, in the post-*Casey* era, be significantly curtailed.

As solicitor general, Kenneth Starr established himself as one of the top appellate lawyers in the United States. His intellect and integrity were widely respected within the legal profession, and he was praised for de-politicizing the solicitor general's office. His work ethic was, according to coworkers, of "mythic proportions," even by Washington standards (Winerip 1998). Starr exhaustively prepared for cases before the Supreme Court by staging moot court rehearsals and studying videotapes of his per-formances. His colleagues marveled at his ability to give attention to the smallest detail in even the most complex of cases. Despite his sterling repu-tation, however, he was twice passed over by the Bush administration for an appointment to the Supreme Court. His candidacy was apparently extin-guished at the crossroads of law and politics. It was, ironically, Starr's love for the law that ultimately proved to be his undoing. Many conservatives, while preaching the virtue of judicial neutrality, were agitated with Starr's steadfast adherence to the principle. Liberals, on the other hand, were furi-ous with him for challenging the constitutionality of *Roe v. Wade*. In the end, these strange political bedfellows indirectly worked together to deny the extremely qualified Starr his dream job: a seat on the Supreme Court of the United States.

On January 20, 1993, shortly after President Clinton's election, Kenneth Starr left the solicitor general's office with enviable credentials. Although he had not been in private practice for twelve years, Starr's experience as solicitor general made him immensely attractive on the open market. After considering many lucrative offers, Starr decided to sign on with the legal powerhouse Kirkland & Ellis for a reported seven-figure salary. Shortly thereafter, he began feverishly building his corporate litigation practice, working seventy- to eighty-hour weeks. His colleagues recall that although Starr enjoyed many aspects of private practice, he yearned to return to pub-lic service. He did return, albeit briefly, when Judge Thomas Penfield Jack-son, of Microsoft antitrust fame, appointed him as a special master in the widely publicized dispute between the Senate Ethics Committee and Sena-tor Bob Packwood. As special master, Starr's job was to determine how much of Senator Packwood's personal diaries and tapes could be used in the ongoing investigation against him for sexual misconduct. Starr also dabbled in politics, and, in 1994, he briefly considered opposing Oliver North for the Republican nomination to one of Virginia's U.S. Senate seats in 1994.

On August 5, 1994, a three-judge panel appointed Kenneth Starr as the independent counsel charged with investigating whether President Clin-ton, first lady Hillary Clinton, and other individuals engaged in criminal conduct through their involvement in a failed real estate transaction known as "Whitewater." Several prominent Democrats immediately criticized Starr's appointment, alleging that he was too partisan to oversee the investigation. These initial criticisms were muted when members of both sides of the political aisle rushed to his defense. This bipartisan support, however, ended as Starr's investigation quickly shifted from bank fraud to allegations of a cover-up by President Clinton and his aides of a sexual affair that the president had engaged in with a subordinate. The circumstances surrounding the affair were politically explosive and involved some of the most intimate and personal details of the president's private life. After thoroughly investigating the matter, Starr's office prepared a 453-page impeachment referral for Congress, which alleged that the president, in attempting to cover up the affair, committed perjury, obstructed justice, and tampered with the testimony of witnesses. The national news media portrayed Starr as an overly zealous, puritanical prosecutor whose actions were fueled by his disdain for the president. For his part, Starr maintained that his investigation was not driven by personal ideology, stating, "our job is to get at the truth, and the truth will speak for itself."

Lost in the vitriolic rhetoric surrounding Starr's performance as independent counsel are his considerable achievements in the courtroom. His office obtained fourteen convictions or guilty pleas during the course of its investigation, and Starr personally won each of the twenty-one legal questions that he argued at the appellate level. The most highly publicized appeal concerned whether his office could require members of the U.S. Secret Service to testify before the federal grand jury investigating President Clinton. Before the appeal, Clinton ordered Lewis Merletti, his secret service director, to research the question of whether its officers were legally permitted to assert a "protective function" privilege when being questioned about anything they witnessed while guarding the president. Notwithstanding the lack of any legal precedent for such a position, Merletti directed his officers to assert this novel privilege if called to testify. The basis for the assertion of this privilege was that "the continued absolute protection of the President of the United States depends on his faith and trust in the Secret Service members who constantly surround him." Starr filed a motion to compel the testimony of several officers, and the district court granted his request. A three-judge panel for the D.C. Circuit Court of Appeals unanimously affirmed the district court's decision, and the Supreme Court refused to grant the Secret Service's request to review the matter.

Although many still frequently criticize Starr's actions as independent counsel, others consider his role in the impeachment of President Clinton as a valiant defense of the "rule of law." As a result of the *Starr Report,* the House of Representatives impeached a president for only the second time in the history of the United States. Although the Senate failed to remove President Clinton from office, only his most ardent supporters question the truth of Starr's findings. Two significant postimpeachment events have gone a long way toward vindicating the legitimacy of Starr's investigation. On April 12, 1999, Judge Susan Webber Wright, a Clinton appointee, held the president in contempt for giving "false, misleading and evasive answers" during the course of the *Paula Jones* litigation. On June 30, 2000, an Arkansas Supreme Court committee filed a complaint for disbarment against President Clinton, alleging that he had conducted himself "in a manner that violates the model rules of professional conduct." As time passes and political passions wane, it appears more probable than not that the legacy of Starr's investigation will not be one of prosecutorial overreach, but rather the idea that no one is above the law, not even the president.

Since resigning as independent counsel, Kenneth Starr has begun work on a book that will address the Supreme Court's effect on Americans' lives. He is also serving as an adjunct professor at New York University Law School and as a distinguished visiting professor at George Mason University. Speculations run rampant on how history will judge Kenneth Starr, but the tide appears to be shifting toward a more thoughtful and balanced view of his career (Schmidt and Weisskopf, 2000; Charen, 2000; Frolik, 2000). Within his own profession, however, there is no question that Starr is still greatly admired by his peers. Judge Griffin Bell, a former U.S. attorney general, sums up this sentiment nicely: "Kenneth Starr is, without a doubt, one of the top appellate lawyers in the country. He is a gentleman, a scholar, and the consummate professional. Simply put, he is the best that the legal profession has to offer" (Starr 2000). The conventional wisdom is that, notwithstanding his impeccable credentials, Starr will never be appointed to the Supreme Court. For his part, he has openly stated that he would not shy away from a confirmation fight. Regardless of what the future holds for Kenneth Starr, his place among the greatest American lawyers of his time is secure.

—*Stephen Louis A. Dillard*

Sources and Suggestions for Further Reading

Bork, Robert H. "Man of the Year: Ken Starr." *Human Events* 54, no. 49 (1998): 8.

Charen, Mona. "The Vindication of Ken Starr." *Orange County* (CA) *Register,* 7 May 2000, G05.

"FBA Member Spotlight: U.S. Solicitor General Kenneth W. Starr." *The Federal Lawyer* 45, no. 4 (1998): 12.

Frolik, Joe. "Examination Shows Starr Motivated by Principle." *Plain* (Ohio) *Dealer,* 29 April 2000, E1.

Lewis, Neal A. "Washington at Work: Solicitor General's Career Advances at Intersection of Law and Politics." *New York Times*, 1 June 1990, A16, col. 1.

Masters, Kim. "Kenneth Starr, Supernova? He Hurled across the Legal Universe into Whitewater and, Perhaps an End to His Burning Ambition?" *Washington Post*, 10 January 1995, E1.

Nellis, Kevin. "So Who the Hell Is Kenneth Starr?: A History Profile of the Life and Times of the Man That Could Finish a President." <http://www.thehistorychannel.co.uk.topstory/starr.htm>.

Ogletree, Charles J., Jr. "Personal and Professional Integrity in the Legal Profession: Lessons from President Clinton and Kenneth Starr." *Washington & Lee Law Review* 56 (1999): 851.

Pressley, Sue Anne. "The Roots of Ken Starr's Morality Plays." *Washington Post*, 2 March 1998, C1.

Rosen, Jeffrey. "Kenneth Starr Trapped." *New York Times*, 1 June 1997, sec. 6, p. 42, col. 1.

Schmidt, Susan, and Michael Weisskopf. *Truth at Any Cost: Ken Starr and the Unmaking of Bill Clinton*. New York: HarperCollins, 2000.

Starr, Kenneth. Personal interviews with the author, 12 November 1999, 31 January 2000, and 10 April 2000.

Winerip, Michael. "Ken Starr Would Not Be Denied." *New York Times*, 6 September 1998, sec. 6, p. 36, col. 1.

ST. CLAIR, JAMES DRAPER

(1920–)

A DISTINGUISHED TRIAL AT-
torney involved in several nationally prominent cases, James
Draper St. Clair participated in
the Army-McCarthy hearings,
defended Yale chaplain William
Sloane Coffin on charges stemming from his antidraft activities
during the Vietnam War era, and
represented President Richard
M. Nixon in proceedings arising
from the Watergate scandal.

James St. Clair was born April
14, 1920, in Akron, Ohio, to
Clinton Draper and Margaret
Glenn St. Clair. He served in
the navy during World War II after graduating from the University of Illinois in 1941. He graduated from Harvard Law School
in 1947, was admitted to the
Massachusetts bar, and began
work at Hale & Dorr, the most
prominent law firm in Boston.
He remained with Hale & Dorr
throughout his entire legal ca-

JAMES DRAPER ST. CLAIR

*James D. St. Clair (2d from left), President Nixon's lawyer,
arriving to attend a closed session of the House Judiciary Committee, tells newsmen he hopes the impeachment panel will
summon Charles W. Colson and predicted that Colson's testimony would aid the President's defense. (Bettmann/
Corbis)*

reer as an associate, a junior partner, and a senior partner from 1956 until
his retirement in 1995. St. Clair married Asenath Nestle on November 25,
1944, and they had a daughter and two sons.

St. Clair was heavily engaged in educational and professional activities in
addition to his legal practice. He lectured at Harvard Law School for
twenty-five years, was a member of the American Bar Association's Council
on Litigation, the Boston Bar Association, the American Law Institute, the

American College of Trial Lawyers, the National Advisory Council for the Practicing Law Institute, and the advisory council of the New England Law Institute. He was involved in many civic and philanthropic activities as well: he served for ten years as president of Horizons for Youth, a nonprofit group dedicated to the needs of underprivileged children; he was a long-term trustee for the Walker Home for Children; and he was a member of the boards of directors of both the Boston Opera Association and Massachusetts General Hospital.

Although St. Clair typically represented corporate clients, most recently in the high-technology industry, he also was involved in a number of high-profile cases. His first national exposure occurred in 1954 when Joseph N. Welch, a senior attorney at Hale & Dorr, asked him to assist in representing the army during the Army-McCarthy hearings. Senator Joseph R. McCarthy chaired a Senate subcommittee that conducted a number of so-called investigations aimed at exposing Communist infiltration of the federal government. The army was one of the governmental institutions targeted by McCarthy, and throughout the autumn of 1953, the senator had pressed the Defense Department for access to confidential files on loyalty and security (Griffith 1987, 244). Perhaps the most important problem facing the subcommittee was the role of McCarthy himself (Griffith 1987, 252).

The Army-McCarthy hearings extended nearly two months and featured typical McCarthy tactics such as cropped photographs and phony letters. His assertions during the hearings were credible only to "diehards on the Far Right" (Reeves 1997, 636). After the hearings had concluded, President Dwight Eisenhower privately congratulated Welch and St. Clair. Welch observed that if the hearings had accomplished nothing else, the army had been able to keep McCarthy on television "long enough for the public to get a good look at him" (Reeves 1997, 636). Before the hearings ended, a resolution ultimately leading to McCarthy's censure was introduced in the Senate (Griffith 1987, 265).

After the hearings, St. Clair returned to Hale & Dorr, resuming his litigation practice. Most of his cases with high profile were local—visibility was largely confined to the Boston area. For example, in 1962 he served as special investigator in the case of Leo J. Sullivan, Boston police commissioner. A television report suggested that the police under Sullivan's command were "out of control." St. Clair agreed and recommended that Sullivan be replaced, an action taken subsequently by Massachusetts governor John Volpe. A few years later, St. Clair led an effort to clean up the corrupt Rivers and Harbors Commission. Reform of the commission was determined to be impossible, and it eventually was placed within the Massachusetts Department of Public Works. As with the Sullivan investigation, St. Clair's services were provided pro bono (Montgomery 1992).

Another of St. Clair's more visible cases involved the federal government's prosecution of Yale chaplain William Sloane Coffin on charges of conspiring to counsel young men to violate the draft laws. Dr. Benjamin Spock was one of the four codefendants, who with Coffin were called the Boston Five. Those close to Coffin recommended that St. Clair conduct his defense. They assured Coffin that St. Clair was well suited to represent him, but they acknowledged that he was a "Wellesley Hills Republican" and that no one seemed to know where he stood on the war. Coffin was reminded that St. Clair had participated in the Army-McCarthy hearings in the 1950s. More important, St. Clair had a reputation as a superb trial lawyer. Coffin had misgivings, however, saying St. Clair sounded like one of those lawyers who's "all case and no cause," but chose him nonetheless (Coffin 1977, 266–267). During the lengthy pretrial conversations between Coffin and St. Clair, it seemed to Coffin that his lawyer knew of none of the people associated with the antiwar movement, and he tired of hearing St. Clair asking "Who's that?" every time he mentioned a name. Coffin said, "Look St. Clair, you know none of the cast of characters in this play and you can't even pronounce conscientious objection. How in hell do you propose to defend me?" According to Coffin, St. Clair was not the least perturbed and reminded him that the trial was still some time off, and "because you have to explain all this to me I'm exactly the man to explain it to the jury" (Coffin 1977, 268).

The Boston Five considered taking a Gandhian civil disobedience approach and pleading guilty. Instead, they chose to mount a full-scale legal defense, using what the media called a "battery of top-notch lawyers" (Mitford 1969, 74–75). Even after the decision to contest the government's charges at trial, counsel for the various defendants did not approach defense in the same way. Spock's lawyer undertook a Nuremberg defense, arguing that it is unjust to compel a citizen to choose between violating a federal law and participating in an international crime (Mitford 1969, 81–83). St. Clair, by contrast, filed a motion for severance of the cases seeking a separate trial for Coffin. It was St. Clair's view that there is an inherently prejudicial impact on the jury in a joint conspiracy trial; the defendants *look* like coconspirators, sitting together in court (Mitford 1969, 84).

St. Clair sought to establish that Coffin did not try to persuade young men to refuse induction into the military, but that he provided support to those who had already decided to turn in their draft cards (Mitford 1969, 141). Throughout the trial, St. Clair attempted to disengage the war and draft as issues in the trial, focusing instead on the sufficiency of the evidence the government offered supporting criminal charges (Mitford 1969, 179). Coffin and three of his codefendants were convicted. At the sentencing hearing a month later, St. Clair characterized Coffin as an "upstanding, honorable man, a family man." He also suggested that Coffin was a leader in a substantial public debate on a substantial public issue and that his actions did not have demonstrably harmful results. He urged the court to suspend Coffin's sentence (Mitford 1969, 206). The trial court was unpersuaded and sentenced Coffin to two years in federal prison. Execution of sentence was waived pending appeal. The convictions were set aside on appeal because of prejudicial statements by the judge to the jury. Acting on a motion from the Justice Department, a federal court judge in Boston agreed on April 22, 1970, to drop government draft-conspiracy charges.

Some of St. Clair's more visible cases reinforce Coffin's "all case and no cause" observation. His clients have been quite diverse. In 1958, he defended a Harvard professor who allegedly sympathized with Communists. While representing the Boston School Committee, a group attempting to forestall racial balancing in the Boston public schools, he defended Randolph Lewis, one of a gang of young African-American youths indicted for attacking Richard Poleet, a white Boston-area resident. Despite extensive brain surgery, Poleet died six weeks after the assault without regaining consciousness (McNamera 1981). Two weeks before the attack on Poleet, an African-American businessman was beaten severely by white youths attending an antibusing demonstration at City Hall. As a result, racial tensions were unusually high, and St. Clair received death and bomb threats because he was Lewis's defense counsel. He required a police escort virtually everywhere he went (Montgomery 1992). St. Clair argued in a motion for a new trial that he should have been allowed to question two prosecution witnesses about their own criminal records. The Massachusetts appeals court concluded that failure to allow a thorough cross-examination had denied Lewis a fair trial, but he was never retried, as the state dismissed charges against him. St. Clair also defended Frank J. Pilecki, president of Westfield State College, on charges of sexually assaulting two students. A Suffolk County Superior Court jury eventually acquitted Pilecki on both counts of indecent assault and battery in June 1984. Two jurors said the jury believed there was consent by the alleged victim. Michael Engel, Westfield State's faculty union president, said the incident was certainly unethical, if not criminal, and commented that "having a rich man's lawyer to make the prosecution's witnesses look silly certainly does help" (Curwood, 1987, 2).

In 1991, the *Boston Globe* wrote a series of highly critical articles about the Boston Police Department, and Mayor Raymond Flynn appointed a special commission headed by St. Clair to examine the management of the department after publication of the *Globe* series (Ellement and Rezendes 1991, 1). The *Globe* reported that the department's Internal Affairs Division appeared to have ignored vital evidence while investigating seven cases in which officers were accused of misconduct. The commission examined confidential police records to determine whether police had adequately investigated citizen complaints of police brutality. In some cases, confidential reports appeared to indicate that the Internal Affairs Division had not contacted witnesses who disputed the police account of a beating or shooting.

After a six-month investigation, the commission's work ended in January 1992. It was estimated that St. Clair contributed upwards of $250,000 of his professional time to the investigation and the writing of the final report. The commission made a number of recommendations focusing on improving the department, including a comprehensive overhaul of the Internal Affairs Division. Removal of Police Commissioner Francis (Mickey) Roache, a close friend of Mayor Flynn, was recommended as well. The Flynn administration received the commission's report and formally ended its operations. Top police officials reported that the department had implemented many of the commission's recommendations and would implement several more (Ellement and Murphy 1993). The three recommendations rejected by Mayor Flynn and the police department were considered by many to be the most important ones: replacing Roache, not placing lower-ranking officers on the command staff, and transferring the former commander of the police academy back to the academy. Changes were made in the Internal Affairs Division, including naming experienced detectives to the division and promising that their careers would not suffer because they investigated fellow police officers (Ellement and Murphy 1993, 1). Commissioner Roache dismissed the scathing critique of Roache's management of the department, disparaging St. Clair as a "downtown lawyer" (Black 1993, 13).

St. Clair's highest-profile client was, of course, President Richard M. Nixon. A break-in of the Democratic National Committee's offices in the Watergate complex occurred on June 18, 1972, and a number of people from Nixon's White House and campaign staff were eventually indicted. The following summer, it was disclosed that Nixon had secretly taped all conversations in the Oval Office. The Watergate special prosecutor was appointed, first ARCHIBALD COX and then LEON JAWORSKI; both were interested in obtaining the tapes as possible evidence.

The Watergate case presented several legal problems for Nixon, including potential criminal liability as a party to attempt to obstruct justice by covering up the crimes linked to the break-in. Watergate also presented significant political problems for Nixon, including his possible impeachment. St. Clair was engaged to lead the Nixon defense for all the Watergate-related matters, replacing J. Fred Buzhardt and Leonard Garment, who had headed the Nixon defense team until that time. The special prosecutor subpoenaed a number of tapes, and although some tapes were delivered, the

White House resisted turning over a number of other tapes on executive privilege grounds.

The Supreme Court eventually entertained Nixon's executive privilege claims. St. Clair argued that for the presidency to function, communications between top officials and advisers had to be kept confidential. He also argued that the separation of powers doctrine conferred legal immunity to the president that gave him the right to withhold the tapes. The Supreme Court disagreed in *United States v. Nixon,* 418 U.S. 683 (1974). The Court accepted St. Clair's contention that executive privilege was a legitimate shield for the executive branch but ruled that the privilege was not absolute. The president's need for complete candor and objectivity calls for great deference from the Court, but absent a claim of need to protect military, diplomatic, or sensitive national security secrets, the Court was not convinced that presidential communications would be significantly diminished by production of the tapes. Indeed, recognizing such a broad claim of executive privilege could seriously compromise the criminal process.

Shortly after the Supreme Court decision, St. Clair learned that one of the sixty-four tapes in question, the June 23 tape, included a conversation between Nixon and his chief of staff, H. R. Haldeman, in which Nixon sought to stop the Federal Bureau of Investigation from investigating the Watergate burglary. The conversation, which took place only five days after the break-in, was the so-called "smoking gun" proving Nixon had obstructed justice (Lukas 1976, 456). *U.S. v. Nixon* was a devastating blow to the president's position in Congress as well as in the courts. Impeachment resolutions charged Nixon with assisting in the Watergate cover-up, abusing his powers, and failing to honor committee subpoenas for the White House tapes.

After reading the Supreme Court's opinion, Nixon asked if there was "any air" in the decision—any way around it. St. Clair answered "no." The more frantically the president sought an avenue of escape, the more emphatic St. Clair became, warning that the country would not understand an outright defiance of the Supreme Court and that such defiance would ensure his impeachment by the House and his conviction by the Senate (Lukas 1976, 546). The timetable for the president's resignation was a series of decisions by St. Clair, Haig, and Buzhardt, driven to large degree by their own growing jeopardy. The June 23 tape showed Nixon's awareness of the cover-up five days after the Watergate burglary. The June 23 tape completely contradicted the version of events St. Clair had given the House impeachment inquiry. St. Clair, and Buzhardt and Garment before him, had continually asserted that Nixon first learned of the Watergate cover-up in March 1973. After release of the June 23, 1972 tape, the contention of

Nixon's ignorance was no longer available, and they had no further room to maneuver (Doyle 1977, 343).

St. Clair was never informed as to the true extent of the president's involvement in the Watergate cover-up, and when the June 23 transcript was released, he threatened to resign unless Nixon made it clear that St. Clair had not known about this evidence. Both St. Clair and Haig insisted that the statement be unequivocally clear that they had known nothing about the June 23 conversations (Lukas 1976, 551). Nixon complied, and in his August 5 statement said, "I did not inform my staff or my counsel of it, or those arguing my case. . . . This was a serious omission for which I take full responsibility ("Nixon Friends," 1974, 2115). St. Clair would later say that Nixon's resignation was in the public interest. Until release of the June 23 tape, St. Clair thought Nixon would not be impeached. He speculated that had he prevailed before the Court on the absolute privilege point, no impeachment resolution against Nixon would have emerged from the House (Micciche, 1984).

St. Clair was regarded as a brilliant courtroom tactician and a methodical trial advocate. Associates of St. Clair said that although he was not flamboyant in the courtroom, he had remarkable recall of minutiae. He was a scrupulously thorough pretrial planner who routinely compiled elaborate trial books before the start of a case and was rarely surprised by courtroom developments. St. Clair was seen as "all case and no cause" by some. It was intended as a pejorative description, but it came as flattery to those who preferred a lawyer committed to the work at hand rather than to philosophy.

—*Peter G. Renstrom*

Sources and Suggestions for Further Reading

Black, Chris. "Roache Says FBI Wanted Him to Run Police." *Boston Globe*, 14 August 1993.

Coffin, William Sloane, Jr. *Once to Every Man: A Memoir*. New York: Atheneum, 1977.

Curwood, Steve. "Pilecki Acquitted of Assault: Ex President of College Still Faces Second Trial." *Boston Globe*, 29 January 1987.

Doyle, James. *Not above the Law: The Battles of Watergate Prosecutors Cox and Jaworski*. New York: William Morrow, 1977.

Ellement, John, and Sean Murphy. "St. Clair Panel Expires; Police Defend Charges." *Boston Globe*, 23 January 1993.

Ellement, John, and Michael Rezendes. "Police Rip Globe Series; Flynn Picks Panel." *Boston Globe*, 8 May 1991.

Griffith, Robert. *The Politics of Fear: Joseph R. McCarthy and the Senate*. Amherst: University of Massachusetts Press, 1987.

Kutler, Stanley I. *The Wars of Watergate: The Last Crisis of Richard Nixon*. New York: Alfred A. Knopf, 1990.

Lukas, J. Anthony. *Nightmare: The Underside of the Nixon Years*. New York: Viking Press, 1976.

McNamera, Eileen. "Release of Poleet Suspect to be Sought." *Boston Globe*, 8 November 1981.

Micciche, S. J. "James St. Clair Looks Back on Nixon and Watergate." *Boston Globe*, 9 August 1984.

Mitford, Jessica. *The Trial of Dr. Spock: The Rev. William Sloane Coffin, Jr., Michael Ferber, Mitchell Goodman, and Marcus Raskin*. New York: Alfred A. Knopf, 1969.

Montgomery, M. R. "St. Clair: The Trials of a Lawyer." *Boston Globe*, 18 January 1992.

"Nixon Friends: Maybe the Enemies Fared Better." *Congressional Quarterly Weekly Report*, 10 August 1974, 2115.

Reeves, Thomas C. *The Life and Times of Joe McCarthy: A Biography*. Lanham, Md.: Madison Books, 1997.

Woodward, Bob, and Carl Bernstein. *The Final Days*. New York: Simon & Schuster, 1976.

STEUER, MAX

(1871–1940)

THE TRUTH ABOUT MAX Steuer, garnered from very sparse sources—and sources, it must be said, that are so fawning in their assessment of his career as to be of limited value—leaves the author of this essay with the notion that Steuer is to be included in a list of "lawyer greats" because of one very famous (and very successful) cross-examination of a witness in the criminal prosecutions stemming from the Triangle Shirtwaist Company fire. This is certainly not to say that Steuer was not a highly publicized and well-respected attorney practicing in New York during the first three decades of the twentieth century, during which he is reputed to have made one million dollars per year at the height of his career ("Steuer, Max David" 1940).

MAX STEUER

Joseph M. Schenck, film mogul (left), in federal court with his lawyer, Max Steuer, to plead not guilty in the government's income tax fraud case, 12 June 1940. (UPI/Corbis-Bettmann)

It is also not to say that Steuer was not a lot of things to a lot of people: son, immigrant, child entrepreneur on the Lower East Side, college student, law student, postal worker, Tammany Hall politico, civil lawyer, criminal lawyer, special prosecutor, and much more (Boyer 1932, 13–15; Steuer 1950, 7–10). By all accounts, whatever Steuer attempted, he generally successfully attained, and if he was not entirely popular (he was the subject of unsuccessful disbarment proceedings initiated by one of his many enemies), he was certainly respected and praised.

His inclusion in this book of great attorneys seems to suggest that Steuer handled many notorious cases or at least exemplified *in extremis* the traits and skills that attorneys and lay people have long associated with attorneys. Diligent work, copious preparation, industrious investigation, and an ability to relate to all types of people are characteristics of perhaps all professions but most particularly the legal profession. Although Max Steuer seemed possessed of an adequate level of these qualities, his true skills seemed to be his strong personal will, his intuition, and his sense of showmanship (Boyer 1932, 25–27).

Certainly his reputation as a great trial strategist and teacher would not be based on his stated and often cited list of things that attorneys should never do. For example, his admonitions that attorneys should "not be late for court," "not make a long opening speech," "not use big words in front of a jury" and "not eat a big meal during a court recess" (Boyer 1932, 41) are sound and make pretty decent common sense, but they do not hint at the musings of a great scholar or intellect.

On the other hand, his intuition about how the public perceived the bar, even in the early part of the twentieth century, was significant and perhaps radical. Included in the same "do not" list were some interesting nuggets over which today's trial lawyer should pause. For example, his notion that attorneys should not guard their case file or papers, but rather let them "wander" all over counsel table (Boyer 1932, 40), is at first a peculiar thought. This notion, however, based on the idea that jurors should think that the attorney has nothing to hide, is clever and useful and has practical application.

Some of Steuer's notions about how to try a case fly directly in the face of every first-year law school's trial advocacy course. Steuer preached to attorneys to refrain from making notes of the witness's testimony and never to take notes to cross-examine a witness (Boyer 1932, 40–41). This advice is contrary to much of the training most young attorneys have been exposed to for the last twenty-five years. The idea that a lawyer would attempt to cross-examine a witness without notes is heresy to most. An attorney would always want to have a clear idea of the points and topics that are critical in a particular witness's cross-examination, and most modest craniums when tested in the heat of battle need the security of notes or an outline to do just that.

Even his most famous cross-examination, discussed in greater detail below, violates two of the cardinal rules of cross-examination—do not allow a witness to use cross-examination simply to give direct testimony to the jury once again, and do not ask open-ended questions ("Tell us what happened, Mr. Witness" type questions), which allow the witness to narrate and delve into many areas that otherwise would and should be limited.

Although sometimes trite and countertraditional, Steuer's methods and rules of practice worked for him. Perhaps it took a figure like Steuer to make clear a point that is often ignored during the lengthy conditioning and apprenticeships that most students endure on the way to becoming attorneys. That is, Steuer showed that success is in large measure an unquantifiable commodity, coming as much from timing, intuition, guesswork, fear, boldness, and maybe, as much as anything, luck. Max Steuer in many respects defied convention and—through his will, his risk taking, and his youthful immigrant spirit that continued throughout his life—forged a successful career that often bordered on celebrity.

Steuer was born in Homino, Austria (later Czechoslovakia), to Aaron and Dinah (Goodman) Steuer in 1871 (some sources say 1870), and the family immigrated to the United States when he was six. As was the custom for most Jewish immigrants, the Steuer family then settled in the Lower East Side of Manhattan. Steuer's youth was devoted to school, where his early efforts showed no particular forecasting of greatness, and to his entrepreneurial endeavors. He was a paperboy who took many of his earnings and invested in the purchase of taxless matches, which he then sold to restaurants and coffee shops along Second Avenue. He attended City College and worked at the post office (Steuer 1950, 4–8).

It was at Columbia Law School that Steuer began to excel academically. By all accounts, he was an enthusiastic student who loved the "case method" of study, loved the research, and actually won cash prizes for his excellence in his academic work (Steuer 1950, 9).

Despite his noteworthy law school career, Steuer was rejected for all clerkships for which he applied and ended up—with little money and no business background—taking a huge risk and opening his own office on the East Side. For the next twenty years, Steuer became not only the trial counsel for the East Side but a well-known figure throughout the city. He got there primarily through bold perseverance. It is legend that he did not reject any client who walked through his door; he handled civil cases, criminal matters, and cases before administrative and review boards. No case was too small or too grand for him (Steuer 1950, 13–14).

One of his early cases, which typified his involvement in local community matters that did not generate huge fees, was a matter concerning a funeral procession for a beloved local rabbi. It seemed that a police inspector had ordered the funeral procession dispersed before its conclusion. When the mourners resisted and pleaded to be allowed to continue, they were beaten and arrested. Some of those arrested filed charges against the officer. Those charges were heard before the police commissioners, a majority of whom were Tammany Hall members well versed in the politics of violence.

The officer retained two of New York's finest members of the bar, and Steuer pursued the case on behalf of the petitioners (Steuer 1950, 14–15).

Steuer's successful prosecution of the officer is a testament not only to his skill at the time, but to his enthusiasm for cases that other attorneys avoided. It does appear, however, that his decision to tackle the police and Tammany Hall in that case stemmed as much from his efforts to establish his name and reputation as from any political convictions or deeply held moral beliefs about power. Steuer was just as easily at home in his career taking cases representing the other side—men and women with money and power—and in fact he became lawyer to many of Tammany Hall's power elite and was considered as something of an in-house counsel for that political machine for many years (Boyer 1932, 93).

Steuer represented throughout his lengthy career as many corrupt judges as poor neighbors from the East Side. For every case in which he successfully defended an indigent person charged with a crime, he represented someone like Queens borough president Maurice E. Connally, accused of defrauding the city of millions of dollars in a sewer scandal. It appears quite clearly that what drove Max Steuer was the thrill of the courtroom drama, the power that being a skilled and much-demanded attorney gave him, and the desire to drift as far from his poverty-laden immigrant childhood as he was able.

Steuer's success in the courtroom likely did not stem from his overwhelming physical presence. He was a small man (five feet six inches, 160 pounds), his voice was low and conversational, his manner was informal and polite, and he spoke using simple and old-fashioned terms (Steuer 1950, 21–22). In Steuer's jargon, for example, a woman had limbs, not legs. What Steuer did possess was a memory that was photographic, a trap for facts and figures and nuggets of testimony. His ability to remember small details from a witness's testimony helped him assemble effective cross-examinations and summations and impress the judges and jurors who witnessed such skill (Boyer 1932, 32).

In one published account, the author points to a famous instance where Steuer's memory served to end a rancorous exchange in a trial and put everyone in his place. During a summation in a criminal case, the district attorney objected to a comment about some testimony that Steuer was making. The attorney asserted that Steuer was going outside the record and telling the jury something that was not true. In defending his position and his recollection of the events, Steuer not only proceeded to advise the court of the exact context of his rendered statement, but advised the court reporter and all present of the page number of the transcript that contained the disputed testimony (Steuer 1950, 23).

Tocqueville's View of American Lawyers: A Natural Aristocracy?

Alexis de Tocqueville, who visited the United States in the 1830s to study the prison system, penned one of the most perceptive books ever written about the United States. In the course of his visit, Tocqueville authored *Democracy in America* (1838), which is still being studied for its insights into U.S. institutions and mores.

Tocqueville, himself a lawyer, thought that American lawyers had an especially important role in moderating "the tyranny of the majority" that he thought to be endemic to American democracy. Tocqueville noted that the study of law led to "habits of order, something of a taste for formalities, and an instinctive love for a regular concatenation of ideas" that were "strongly opposed to the revolutionary spirit and to the ill-considered passions of democracy" (Tocqueville 1969, 264).

Tocqueville noted how British and U.S. laws both emphasized adherence to precedents and how lawyers in these nations accordingly combined "a taste and respect for what is old with a liking for regularity and legality" (Tocqueville 1969, 267). He noted that, "If you ask me where the American aristocracy is found, I have no hesitation in answering that it is not among the rich, who have no common link uniting them. It is at the bar or the bench that the American aristocracy is found" (Tocqueville 1969, 268).

Tocqueville would not have been surprised at how many U.S. statesmen have been drawn from the ranks of lawyers. He noted that as "the only enlightened class not distrusted by the people," lawyers were "naturally called on to fill most public functions." As he noted, "The legislatures are full of them, and they head administrations; in this way they greatly influence both the shaping of the law and its execution" (Tocqueville 1969, 269). Alluding to judicial review, the power of U.S. judges to overrule legislation judged to be unconstitutional, Tocqueville noted that "there is hardly a political question in the United States which does not sooner or later turn into a judicial one," and that, as a consequence, "the language of everyday party-political controversy has to be borrowed from legal phraseology and conceptions" (Tocqueville 1969, 270).

REFERENCE

Tocqueville, Alexis de. *Democracy in America*, translated by George Lawrence, edited by J. P. Mayer. Garden City, N.Y.: Anchor Books, 1969.

Max Steuer's most famous courtroom moment came in the Triangle Shirtwaist Company criminal case, which originated when the district attorney charged the officers of the company with criminal negligence in their role in one of the most horrendous industrial accidents in U.S. history. On March, 25, 1911, a ten-story loft building on the edge of Greenwich Village owned by the Triangle Shirtwaist Company caught fire and erupted in moments in a conflagration that claimed the lives of most of the five hundred women and girls employed there. The public reaction to the accident was loud and clear: Someone had to pay for the deaths of the employees. The question of culpability, however, was not that clear. The cause of the fire itself was never clearly ascertained. The owners of the building were found to have been in compliance with existing codes (Steuer 1950, 83–110).

It fell to the district attorney's office to pursue an investigation that led to a theory of criminal responsibility on the part of the company's officers. The theory on which any hope of a conviction lay was that the Triangle Shirtwaist Company had not ensured that the exit doors from the factory were unlocked and clear in the event of an emergency. Once this was established, coupled with a showing that the locked doors contributed to the deaths of the employees, the criminal responsibility was complete—actually for purposes of criminal culpability, all that needed to be shown was that the locked door was the legal cause of one death.

The prosecutor saved for the dramatic conclusion of the trial a witness named Kate Alterman, an employee of the company who took the stand in an effort to prove that as she witnessed the confusion and chaos of the disaster, she observed the escape attempts of a girl named Margaret Schwartz. Alterman would establish that Schwartz died in flames as she was putting her whole strength into an effort to pull open one of the unyielding escape doors. Steuer's successful defense of the corporate executives rested on his ability to discredit Alterman's dramatic testimony concerning the locked door.

Kate Alterman testified in great detail about what she witnessed as the fire broke out in the factory. The testimony was lengthy and very specific and included phrases like "Bernstein (another of those trying to escape) was throwing around like a wildcat" and "the door was a red curtain of fire" (Steuer 1950, 90). Steuer's famous cross-examination began with a series of seemingly innocuous questions designed to allow the jury to know that this witness had met on numerous occasions with the district attorney to go over her testimony.

Then, Steuer asked the question that all first-year law students are trained not to ask: "Now, I want you to tell me your story over again just as you told it before." The witness then told the story again in the same detail. This time, however, the witness left out the specific phrases "throwing around like a wildcat" and "red curtain of fire." Steuer's next question (statement) was "It looked like a wall of flame?" Alterman's answer: "like a red curtain." Steuer's next question (revealing his strategy): "Now there was something in that that you left out, I think, Miss Alterman. When Bernstein was jumping around, do you remember what that was like? Like a wildcat, wasn't it?" Her answer: "Like a wildcat" (Steuer 1950, 96–99).

Steuer at other points during the cross-examination came back to his strategy and had the witness narrate again and again what had transpired on the day of the fire. On both those occasions, the witness related in close detail her prior testimony, including the phrasing that Steuer found unusual (Steuer 1950, 99–103).

The acquittal of the defendants was suggested by court critics and spectators then, and is regarded today, as the obvious result of Steuer's magic in the courtroom, the only logical verdict the jury could return based on the obviously rehearsed testimony of the chief witness, Alterman. Steuer's "magical" cross-examination, however, deserves critical investigation. His prelude to the essence of the questioning succeeded in establishing that the witness had communicated with, indeed, had practiced her testimony with the assistance of, the district attorney. Although this might be worth a passing comment in a trial as part of an overall defense strategy, its significance is overrated. Most jurors would not only imagine but assume that witnesses from both sides of a dispute will have prepared their testimony with their attorneys—especially in an important criminal case with as much at stake as the Triangle fire. It would be incompetent and perhaps unethical for attorneys to parade an unprepared witness into court, and their attempt to avoid this would certainly not shock anyone.

In addition, the fact that a witness would give virtually the identical version of her recollection time after time speaks just as forcefully to the witness's veracity as it does any other suggestion. A witness who has lived with a traumatic experience and has gone over it with his or her advocate would certainly be inclined to relate the facts in much the same way. At least the material elements of the version would be substantially similar. Maybe the characterizations of those elements would vary, and that is exactly what transpired with Alterman. The fact that she omitted or, more properly, recharacterized a description of an event as a "wall of flame" and not a "curtain of fire" is not a shocking example of a witness who is manufacturing her testimony any more than it is of a witness who in good faith under much pressure is attempting to recreate a traumatic event in the distant past.

Those who cite this famous cross-examination seem to focus on Steuer's prized intuition at knowing just exactly on whom of the several possible "major" witnesses to employ this strategy. Perhaps Steuer's notion that Alterman, as a poor, lower-class laborer with a meager vocabulary, could not devise the term "red curtain of flame" on her own rang true with the jury, and it was Steuer's cultivation of a cloak of trust with that body that perhaps lay at the heart of his genius.

There were many other legal battles that Steuer fought, many of which contributed to his aura as the epitome of the American success story, the rags-to-riches journey from steerage to the high-priced and high-powered New York litigator. Many, such as the successful defense of Senator Frank Gardner on bribery charges, established Steuer as the man to see if one was in major trouble (Boyer 1932, 44). Some of the battles found Steuer himself as the subject of the litigation, as in his messy disbarment proceedings over allegations (ultimately unproven) that he had counseled a witness in a civil case to commit perjury.

But it was Steuer's successful defense in the Triangle Shirtwaist case that has forever cemented his reputation as a great trial attorney. If his methods were unorthodox and his motivations often unclear, it is impossible to discount his results. He was fearless in his choice of cases and opponents and seemingly immune to public and political pressure. It was perhaps his great will to succeed that set him apart from his colleagues at the bar in the early twentieth century.

—*William Shulman*

Sources and Suggestions for Further Reading

Boyer, Richard Owen. *Max Steuer, Magician of the Law*. New York: Greenberg, 1932.

Steuer, Aaron. *Max D. Steuer, Trial Lawyer*. New York: Random House, 1950.

"Steuer, Max David." In *Current Biography, Who's News and Why 1940*. New York: H. W. Wilson, 1940, 763.

STORY, JOSEPH

(1779–1845)

WHEN EVALUATING THE RELA-
tively short history of American jurisprudence, the imprimatur left by
Joseph Story stands in stark contrast
to the contributions of other prominent lawyers. Although he is best
known for his brilliant tenure as a
justice on the U.S. Supreme Court,
he was also a prolific legal scholar,
beloved law professor, reluctant
politician, patriotic statesman, and,
for ten years, a remarkable lawyer.

Joseph D. Story was born in the
small fishing village of Marblehead,
Massachusetts, on September 18,
1779. His father, Elisha Story, was a
prominent Boston physician who
served with George Washington in
the Campaign of 1777, participated
in the Boston Tea Party, and was
one of the Sons of Liberty. Elisha
Story practiced medicine in Boston
until 1770, when he decided to
move his family to Marblehead. His
first wife, Ruth Ruddock Story, died

JOSEPH STORY
Library of Congress

in 1777 while giving birth to their eighth child, who, tragically, died as
well. Elisha Story was now a widower with seven children. In the fall of
1778, he married Mehitable Pedrick, the nineteen-year-old daughter of a
local "opulent merchant" (Story 1971, 1:2). Joseph was the first of eleven
children produced by this marriage, and by all accounts was his parents'
favorite.

Marblehead's public education was "primitive and sporadic" (Burns 1839,
11). Joseph Story, however, was fortunate enough to attend the town's only

established academy. He received a solid education from Marblehead Academy, but his academic success was largely the result of his own efforts outside of the classroom. During Story's final year at the academy, a heated exchange with another student led to his early withdrawal from the school. This placed the young scholar in quite a conundrum. The academy was the only school in town with a college preparatory curriculum, and he wanted to apply for early admission to Harvard. Fortunately, the town's principal schoolmaster agreed to oversee his studies for the remainder of the year, and he began diligently studying to pass the college's entrance examination.

In the fall of 1794, Story traveled to Cambridge, confident that he would gain early admittance to Harvard. His confidence, however, was short-lived when the president of the school informed him that before he could be enrolled he would have to be examined "not merely in the previous preparatory studies, but in all studies which the freshman class had been pursuing for the last six months" (Story 1971, 1:15). With only six weeks to prepare, he returned to Marblehead, depressed but determined to meet the challenge before him. Fueled by unbridled ambition and an enormous amount of self-discipline, he was able to cover the necessary materials in three weeks. He spent the remaining time mastering the subjects and ended up passing the entrance examination with great ease.

Story joined the freshman class at Harvard in January 1795. Compared to Marblehead, Cambridge was "a delightful new world" (Dunne 1970, 34) that brought him into contact with "a large circle of young men engaged in literary pursuits" who were "warmed and cheered by the hopes of future eminence" (Story 1971, 1:43–44). His classmates were initially skeptical of the "newcomer" and made fun of him on several occasions. In a few short weeks, however, they came to admire Story for his "good nature," intelligence, and self-deprecating humor. Story graduated from Harvard in 1798 with "second honors" and thereafter immediately obtained a legal apprenticeship with Samuel Sewell. Sewell was a well-respected Marblehead attorney, a prominent Federalist, and a member of Congress. Story, like his father, was a staunch Republican, but he prudently decided to avoid politics during his time as an apprentice, devoting himself entirely to the study of law.

Story's studies began with an examination of the "theory and general doctrines" of English common law. His first exposure to the law was the elegant prose of Blackstone's Commentaries on the Laws of England, which he enjoyed immensely. His next assignment, Coke upon Littleton, proved to be much more difficult, and he shed "bitter tears" attempting to understand the intricacies of real property law. He eventually mastered Coke and remarked that thereafter he "breathed a purer air" (Story 1971, 1:73–74). Story's victory over Coke marked the turning point of his legal education. He now had a "new power," and the remaining treatises and case reporters he studied seemed elementary by comparison. The greatest challenge he now faced was determining which part of the English common law was still authoritative in U.S. courts. Legal systems in the United States were just being developed, and there were no widely available treatises or case reporters on U.S. law. To assist him in this endeavor, he compiled a formbook to keep track of key distinctions between English precedent and leading U.S. cases.

Story's study habits were fueled by unquenchable ambition, and he routinely read for fourteen hours a day "to the point of nervous exhaustion" (Story 1971, 1:73). The theoretical, however, eventually gave way to the practical, and he was able to gain a great deal of experience as an apprentice. After a year of study, he was able to draft pleadings, enter actions, and learn the business side of a law practice. The citizens of Marblehead held the young apprentice in such high esteem that in February 1800 he was chosen to deliver the town's eulogy of George Washington. After a year of study, his mentor, Sewell, was appointed to the Massachusetts Supreme Court, and Story moved to Salem to finish his apprenticeship with Samuel Putnam.

At the outset, Story's law career in Salem looked bleak. A self-professed Jeffersonian Republican, he was seeking to practice law in a state that had only four or five lawyers "who *dared* avow themselves republican" (Burns 1839, 14). The Essex County bar was one of the most prestigious in the country at the time he sought admittance, and it had very strict requirements. To be admitted, an attorney needed a college education, a three-year legal apprenticeship, and "the consent and recommendation of the bar." The Essex County bar was completely Federalist, and its members sought to maintain this unanimity by preventing Story from joining their ranks. This effort, however, proved to be unsuccessful, and he was admitted in 1801.

Joseph Story was an exceptional lawyer at both the trial and appellate levels. In a relatively short period of time he became a prominent member of the bar and "was engaged in nearly all the cases of importance" (Story 1971, 1:116). In 1804, his stature among the citizens of Salem had grown as well, and he was asked to deliver "the annual oration on the 4th of July." Later that year, he married Mary Lynde Oliver, "a refined and accomplished woman," and the daughter of a local minister (Story 1971, 1:112). By 1805, Story's law practice was flourishing. His first significant book of law, *A Selection of Pleadings in Civil Actions*, was published that same year and was "received favorably by the profession." The publication of this treatise only enhanced Story's growing reputation as a scholarly lawyer. In 1806, Story had become so popular within the bar that he was asked to help oversee the admission of its new members. The tragic death of his wife on June 22,

1805, and of his father two months later, however, overshadowed these accomplishments. Story sought refuge from "painful thoughts by severe and exclusive labor in his profession" (Story 1971, 1:116). His personal life, however, "reawakened" in 1808 when he married Sarah Waldo Wetmore, the daughter of William Wetmore, a judge with the court of common pleas in Boston. They were married thirty-seven years and had six children. Sadly, four of the their children died early in life, and only Mary and William grew to see adulthood.

Story approached his clients' causes with characteristic zeal and energy, and he was considered "sagacious in the management" of the cases entrusted to him (Colton 1846, 70). His client base represented a true cross-section of the community. From carpenters and painters to some of the most influential families and businesses in the community, Story's practice was diverse and wide-ranging. Most of his cases involved debtor-creditor relations, but he also had a steady stream of probate business, as well as "chamber" and appellate work. One of his more interesting cases was a defamation action in which he successfully defended a client accused of maligning the reputation of another by associating him with Aaron Burr and Benedict Arnold.

Story was quick on his feet at trial, "ready in attack or defense," and he was noted to have "great eloquence of expression." Juries responded to his courtroom disposition, describing him as persuasive, ingenious, and "earnest and spirited" (Newmyer 1985, 64). Story's case preparation was "cautious and scrupulous" (Story 1971, 1:116). Prior to each of his court appearances, he meticulously examined the underlying facts and applicable law "never relying on first views and general knowledge" (Story 1971, 1:116). In his first appearance before the Supreme Judicial Court of Massachusetts, Story dazzled the court with citations from both English and Continental law to demonstrate that a certain individual was an alien/ and therefore not permitted to vote in a town election. Judges at both the state and federal level were amazed at the depth of Story's understanding of the law and by his brilliant oratorical abilities.

Story's ability as a lawyer is perhaps best illustrated by examining the case of *Rust v. Low*, 6 Mass. 90 (1809). *Rust v. Low* was a replevin action in which the plaintiff sought return of cattle that had "strayed" from his land onto the defendant's. The cattle caused damage to the defendant's property and were "being held hostage" by him in lieu of monetary damages. The salient question before the court was "whether, in the absence of any covenant or prescription, the tenant of a close [an enclosed piece of land] is bound to fence against the cattle of strangers, or only against such cattle as are rightfully on the adjoining land" (Story 1971, 1:117). The plaintiff was represented by William Prescott, a lifelong friend of Story's and one of the most respected lawyers of the period. Story, along with co-counsel Nathan Dane, represented the defendant and faced a seemingly uphill battle. Sir Matthew Hale, the lord chief justice of the King's Bench in England from 1671 to 1676, had written a "note" on the issue, which opined that in such a situation the plaintiff was entitled to the return of the cattle. This established precedent gave Story's adversary great confidence, and Mr. Prescott informed him, in no uncertain terms, "we shall beat you, Lord Hale is against you" (Story 1971, 1:117). Story was well aware of the note, but he thought that Lord Hale misunderstood the law. In preparation for the appeal, Story translated "nearly thirty cases from Year Books" to support his position. At the outset of his argument, Story informed the court that "I think I shall satisfy the court that Lord Hale is mistaken." Theophilus Parsons, chief justice of the Massachusetts Supreme Court, was taken aback by such a bold assertion, "What, Brother Story, you undertake a difficult task." Story, undeterred by the justice's obvious lack of confidence in his position, calmly responded, "Nevertheless, I hope to satisfy your Honor, that he [Lord Hale] has misapprehended the authorities on this point" (Story 1971, 1:117). Story's presentation of the law was so forceful that at its conclusion, William Prescott, while still advocating the note on stare decisis grounds, conceded that Hale's interpretation of the law was indeed erroneous. Before announcing his opinion, Justice Parsons contacted Story and requested that he once again explain his refutation of Lord Hale's note. Some time had passed, and Parsons apparently could not glean from his notes the nature or basis for Lord Hale's error. Story obtained the books that he had used to fashion his argument, and dutifully reargued the point in chambers, with Parsons taking copious notes all the while. Shortly thereafter, the court issued a judgment in favor of the defendant. Justice Parsons's opinion prominently noted Lord Hale's error and tracked all of the authorities that Story had provided. Notwithstanding the magnitude of the decision, and the young lawyer's brilliant performance, Parsons failed to give Story even the slightest amount of credit. A "manuscript note," in Story's handwriting, is included in his copy of the *Massachusetts Reports* volume containing *Rust v. Low,* and it sarcastically notes, "I well remember that this mistake of Lord Hale was first noticed and explained by Story, of counsel for the defendant, in the original argument, and that the authorities were cited and commented on by him in illustration. It is not a little remarkable that not one word is suggested either by the reporter or the Court on this fact. From aught that appears, the Court was the sole discoverer of all this nice learning. Is this right?" (Story 1971, 1:118). Because of cases like *Rust v. Low,* Story's reputation as a lawyer reached well beyond the boundaries of his home state. As a result, he was able to try several cases in nearby states, holding his own against some of the finest attorneys of his time, including Jeremiah Mason.

The highlight of Story's legal career was undoubtedly his participation in *Fletcher v. Peck* 1810). *Fletcher v. Peck* was the first case to appear before the Supreme Court involving the contract clause of the U.S. Constitution. The question before the Court was the constitutionality of a Georgia statute that repealed a grant from the state authorizing the sale of tracts of property in the "Yazoo area" (now known as Mississippi and Alabama) to land speculators. The circumstances surrounding the issuance of the grant certainly seemed to justify its repeal. Virtually every member of the Georgia legislature was bribed to vote for the grant, and as a result the state sold thirty-five million acres of land for the astonishingly low price of five hundred thousand dollars. The citizens of Georgia were outraged, and in 1796 they elected an entirely new legislature that, in turn, immediately repealed, and ceremoniously burned, the "corrupt" grant. In the meantime, however, several tracts of land were subsequently sold to third parties who, allegedly, had no knowledge of the scheme. In May 1803, Robert Fletcher brought suit against John Peck, in the federal circuit court in Boston, seeking rescision of the sale of a tract of the disputed land.

Story's first involvement with this case came as a result of his lobbying efforts as a federal congressman on behalf of the New England Mississippi Land Company. The shareholders of this company purchased several tracts of the Yazoo land and were seeking to have Congress enact a "compensation law" to indemnify them for losses they incurred as a result of the repeal. The Southern members of Congress, however, resoundingly quashed these efforts. Thereafter, Story succeeded JOHN QUINCY ADAMS as Robert Goodloe Harper's co-counsel in *Fletcher v. Peck*.

On February 15, 1810, Story appeared before the U.S. Supreme Court and eloquently argued that Georgia's repealing statute violated the contracts clause of the U.S. Constitution. A prominent Story biographer, R. Kent Newmyer, believes that Story's appearance before the Court may have been a contributing factor in his subsequent elevation to its ranks (Newmyer 1985, 66). On March 16, 1810, the Court announced its opinion holding that the original grant was a contract amounting to "a extinguishment of the right of the grantor [Georgia], and implies a contract not to reassert that right." The broader implication of the decision was the Court's use of the contracts clause as "an instrument of judicial nationalization"(Dunne 1970, 75). The direct effect this case had on Story's jurisprudential philosophy is uncertain, but there is no doubt that at some point he and Jefferson parted ways, and Story remained a Republican in name only.

Story's reputation as a lawyer was greatly enhanced by his legal scholarship and public service. In addition to his authorship of *A Selection of Pleadings in Civil Actions*, Story also penned or edited the following books as a practicing lawyer: *American Precedents of Declarations* (1802), Joseph Chitty's *A Practical Treatise on Bills and Exchange* (1809), Charles Abbott's *A Treatise of the Law Relative to Merchant Ships* (1811), and Edward Lawe's *A Practical Treatise on Pleading in Assumpit* (1811).

Shortly after he began practicing, President Jefferson offered to appoint him as a bankruptcy commissioner (1802) or a naval officer (1803), but Story declined to accept either post "without hesitation" and expressed his "determination to devote my life to the law" (Story 1971, 1:102–104). While eschewing federal appointments, he was willing to sit on local committees charged with revising city ordinances and overseeing public education. In 1805, at age twenty-six, he was elected to represent Salem in the Massachusetts legislature. He also agreed to serve as Essex County's attorney in 1807. Story served in the state legislature until the fall of 1808, when he was elected to represent "Essex South" in Congress for the remaining year of Jacob Crowninshield's term. He returned to Salem after only one session, and, after declining to run for reelection, was immediately reelected to the state legislature. In January 1811, he became the speaker of the house and served in that capacity until his appointment to the Supreme Court later that year.

On November 18, 1811, the U.S. Senate confirmed President James Madison's appointment of Story to the Supreme Court. Story was only thirty-two at the time of his senate confirmation, and he is the youngest person ever elevated to the Court. His appointment had more to do with luck than ability, although Story's ability was considerable. Madison had little choice but to select a lawyer from New England to fill the vacancy. During this period, Supreme Court justices, in addition to their traditional duties, spent most of their time traveling the "circuits" handling both original actions and intermediate appeals. The justice filling this seat would be charged with handling the First Circuit, a territory covering the states of Massachusetts, New Hampshire, Rhode Island, and Maine. It was also necessary for Madison to maintain the sectional balance of the Court. It was therefore imperative that the appointee be from one of these states. Madison's choices were further limited by political considerations. Federalists dominated the First Circuit, and there were very few Republican lawyers of any renown from whom to choose. Story was selected only after two of Madison's choices declined to serve and the Senate overwhelmingly rejected another. Nonetheless, it was Story's reputation as a lawyer that placed him in a position to be appointed to the Supreme Court at such a young age.

Story spent thirty-three years as an associate justice, and it was during this time that he left an indelible impression on the fabric of the American republic. As "the thinking man's JOHN MARSHALL" (McClellan 1971, vii), Story's legal scholarship, in both his opinions and his treatises, provided the foundation for the nation's constitutional jurisprudence. He authored more than two hundred opinions as a justice of the Supreme Court, and from 1832 to 1845, Story wrote nine exhaustive "commentaries" on the law. His *Commentaries on the Constitution of the United States* is still considered by many to be the greatest exposition on the history and text of the federal Constitution ever written.

For all of his accomplishments, Joseph Story was most proud of his title as the Dane Professor of Law at Harvard University, a distinction bestowed on him in 1829. He simply wished to be remembered as a "teacher of jurisprudence." Story's jurisprudential vision, however, was formulated during his thirteen years as an apprentice and practicing attorney. His experience as a lawyer was inextricably connected to his performance as a justice and legal scholar. It was as an attorney that he began his love affair with the law, and as a result the landscape of U.S. law was forever changed. Joseph Story died on September 10, 1845; he is buried in the Mount Auburn Cemetery in Cambridge, Massachusetts. The Sunday after his death, the Reverend R. C. Waterston offered a eulogy on the life of Joseph Story, stating, "Within a few days our country has lost one of its greatest and best men,—one who was universally respected and beloved" (Waterston 1845, 1). The United States had also lost one of its greatest lawyers, but there is little doubt that Story's "spirit continue[s] to inspire a love for the science of law" (Sumner 1846, 35).

—*Stephen Louis A. Dillard*

SOURCES AND SUGGESTIONS FOR FURTHER READING

Burns, James. *Beauties of Story*. Boston: James Burns, 1839.

Colton, George H. "Biographical Notice of Mr. Justice Story." *The American Review: A Whig Journal of Politics, Literature, Art and Science* 13 (January 1846).

Dunne, Gerald T. *Justice Joseph Story and the Rise of the Supreme Court*. New York: Simon & Schuster, 1970.

"Joseph Story." *The Green Bag* 9 (1897): 49–51.

McClellan, James. *Joseph Story and the American Constitution: A Study in Political and Legal Thought with Selected Writings*. Norman: University of Oklahoma Press, 1971.

Newmyer, R. Kent. *Supreme Court Justice Joseph Story: Statesman of the Old Republic*. Chapel Hill: University of North Carolina Press, 1985.

Schofield, William. "Joseph Story." In *Great American Lawyers*, edited by William Draper Lewis. Vol. 3. Philadelphia: John C. Winston, 1908.

Story, William W., ed. *Life and Letters of Joseph Story, Associate Justice of the Supreme Court of the United States, and Dane Professor of Law at Harvard University.* 2 vols. 1851. Reprint, Freeport, N.Y.: Books for Libraries Press, 1971.

Sumner, Charles. *The Scholar, the Jurist, the Artist, the Philanthropist.* Boston: William B. Ticknor, 1846.

Waterston, R. C. *A Discourse upon the Life and Character of the Hon. Joseph Story, LL.D.* Boston: William Crosby and H. P. Nichols, 1845.

White, G. Edward. *The American Judicial Tradition: Profiles of Leading American Judges.* New York: Oxford University Press, 1976.

TIGAR, MICHAEL E.

(1941–)

MICHAEL E. TIGAR

Michael Tigar, attorney for Terry Nichols, with associates behind him, responds to a question during a news conference in Denver on Tuesday, 9 April 1996, during a recess at a hearing for Oklahoma City bombing suspects Timothy McVeigh and Terry Nichols. (AP Photo/David Longstreath)

MICHAEL EDWARD TIGAR is a law professor and defense attorney noted for representing controversial defendants. Tigar was born on January 18, 1941, in Glendale, California, the son of Charles and Elizabeth Tigar. Charles Tigar, who died when his son was fifteen, was an executive secretary of Local 727 of the Machinists Union at Lockheed.

Michael Tigar attended the University of California at Berkeley, graduating with a B.A. degree in 1962. While an undergraduate at Berkeley, he was an early leader in the 1960s protest movements. He opposed the House Un-American Activities Committee, attended a leftist youth conference in Helsinki, and demonstrated against segregation. Tigar continued his education at Boalt Hall, as the law school at the University of California, Berkeley, is known. Tigar served as editor-in-chief of the law review. In 1966, he graduated first in his law school class.

Soon after receiving his law degree, Tigar moved east with his wife and two children to Washington, D.C., to accept a clerkship with Supreme Court Justice William J. Brennan. Justice Brennan, under pressure from several other justices and Federal Bureau of Investigation (FBI) director J. Edgar Hoover, asked Tigar's permission to release a list of the young lawyer's political activities. Tigar refused to permit release of the list, so Brennan fired him on the day the new clerk reported for work. Shortly before his death, Justice Brennan admitted that he often had second thoughts about firing Tigar.

Instead of working at the U.S. Supreme Court, the young lawyer landed a position at Williams & Connolly, the Washington-based law firm headed by EDWARD BENNETT WILLIAMS. Admitted to the District of Columbia bar in 1967, Tigar was a member of the legal team headed by Williams defending Lyndon Johnson aide Bobby Baker. Despite a spirited defense, Baker was convicted of tax fraud. Tigar remained an associate at Williams & Connolly until 1969, when he returned to California to teach.

His tenure as an acting professor of law at the University of California at Los Angeles (UCLA) was marked by controversy. He was jailed briefly during the 1969 *Chicago Seven* trial. Tigar had attended pretrial hearings to aid in the defense, but he did not wish to participate in a long trial. In an attempt to force their presence, U.S. district judge Julius J. Hoffman issued warrants for the arrests of Tigar and three other defense attorneys. Judge Hoffman wanted the lawyers to step in as primary defense counsel after another attorney became ill. Tigar and a second attorney were jailed for contempt. The lawyers were released after Judge Hoffman, under pressure from civil libertarians, relented.

In 1969, Tigar argued his first case before the U.S. Supreme Court, defending a war protester whose name had been moved up the induction list by the Selective Service because of his antiwar protest activities. The Supreme Court found the Selective Service's practice to be unconstitutional in *Gutknecht v. United States*, 396 U.S. 295 (1970). While he was an associate at Williams & Connolly, Tigar founded a publication called the *Selective Service Law Reporter*. The journal was a "repository of legal information for draftees and their counselors and lawyers" (Toobin 1996, 51).

Tigar left UCLA and moved to France to practice law in 1972. While in France, Tigar researched and wrote *Law and the Rise of Capitalism*, which he published in 1977. The book examines the role of lawyers in developing the European economy from a system of feudalism to capitalism. Tigar argued that lawyers played a central role in the social changes that resulted in the economic transformation. The book was criticized for its heavy reliance on Marxist thought.

Tigar returned to the United States and Williams & Connolly in 1974. Williams asked Tigar to come back to the firm to assist in John Connally's defense. The former Texas governor and secretary of the treasury was alleged to have accepted ten thousand dollars from milk producers who wanted Connally to speak with President Nixon about increasing milk price supports. Williams, with Tigar's assistance, won an acquittal for Connally. The Texan rewarded Tigar with four pregnant purebred heifers. According to one account, the lawyer gave one of the offspring to a Cuban agricultural cooperative (Toobin 1996, 51).

Another case handled by Michael Tigar in the mid-1970s brought him back to his student radical roots. Cameron David Bishop was a leader in the Students for a Democratic Society who was charged with dynamiting four high-voltage transmission towers in Colorado in 1969. The goal of sabotage was to disrupt the military-industrial complex aiding the war effort in Vietnam. After evading capture for a number of years, Bishop was arrested and brought to Denver for trial in 1975. Bishop was convicted of three of the four charges, but he was saved from jail by Tigar's legal ingenuity. On appeal to the U.S. Court of Appeals for the Tenth Circuit, Tigar argued that Bishop's original indictment was invalid. He had been charged with committing sabotage during a time of "national emergency," but the only national emergency found to exist in 1969 was the Korean conflict. The appeals court agreed, and Bishop's conviction was reversed (*United States v. Bishop*, 555 F.2d 771 [1977]).

Tigar left Williams & Connolly in 1977 to form his own practice in Washington, D.C. His partner was another Washington attorney, Sam Buffone. All lawyers working for the firm were required to devote a third of their time to pro bono work. One of the significant cases handled by Buffone and Tigar involved the politics of the South American country of Chile. In September 1976, Orlando Letelier, the Chilean ambassador to the United States, was killed by a car bomb in Washington. Letelier's family hired Buffone and Tigar to prove that the Chilean government, led by President Augusto Pinochet, had arranged the bombing (*Letelier v. Republic of Chile*, 748 F.2d 790 [1984]). For two decades, Buffone, aided on a regular basis by Tigar, who had left the firm, pursued the case, eventually winning more than one million dollars for the victims' families. In January 1999, Tigar was present in a courtroom in London when a British court refused to grant immunity to Pinochet. For his work in pursuing the bombing plotters, Tigar was awarded the Letelier-Moit Memorial Human Rights Award in 1992.

Michael Tigar returned to legal academe in 1983, taking a position as professor of law at the University of Texas at Austin. In 1987, he was named Joseph D. Jamail Centennial Professor of Law. While teaching and writing as an academic, he continued to practice law. Most of Tigar's cases in the 1980s and 1990s followed a common theme, one of protecting defendants from an overbearing government. In the early 1990s, Tigar took the case of John Demjanjuk, a retired Cleveland autoworker, who after being accused of being a Nazi concentration camp guard was stripped of his citizenship and extradited to Israel to stand trial. A court in Israel found Demjanjuk

Roy Black

Few contemporary cases have received the attention garnered by the rape charges leveled against William Kennedy Smith, a nephew of Edward Kennedy. The Miami trial before six jurors, which resulted in a verdict of not guilty, was broadcast around the world for eleven days, catapulting defense attorney Roy Black (1945–) into the headlines.

Black was born to Richard and Minna Black in 1945, but his parents divorced, so Black got to know his stepfather—an English executive and former Grand Prix race-car driver for Jaguar—better than his birth father, an electrical engineer. At an early age, his mother read Perry Mason stories to her son, despite her mother's fears that he would grow up to be a murderer (Jordan 1991). Black's stepfather moved the family to Jamaica, where Black attended an English school. He subsequently received a swimming scholarship to the University of Miami and went on to enroll in the law school there, after which he received the highest score on the 1970 Florida bar examination.

Black began his career as a public defender and subsequently went into private practice. The six-foot, three-inch Black is said to have "the air of a country gentleman" and is often called "the Professor" (Jordan 1991) for his calm and unassuming manner that enables him to bond easily with juries—indeed, he is now married to one of the jurors he met in the *Smith* case. The *Palm Beach Post* once noted that Black had "the bedside mannerisms of a kindly country doctor and the heart of an assassin" (Carlson 1997).

Black is known for meticulous preparation. Defending his law partner, Frank Furci, for shooting a neighborhood sheep dog, Black is said to have taken an aerial photograph of the area, deposed seventeen witnesses, had an autopsy performed on the animal, and located national experts before having charges dropped (Jordan 1991). Black notes that it is not so much the will to win that results in victory, "It's the will to prepare that makes the difference" (Pesce and Puente 1991).

A fellow Miami attorney has called Black "the Michael Jordan of criminal defense lawyers in America" (Carlson 1997). Black is more modest about his abilities, but he admits to having been inspired not

(continues)

guilty and sentenced him to death. Before he could be executed, additional evidence was discovered, a result of the collapse of the Soviet bloc in Eastern Europe and the fall of the Soviet Union. Israel's Supreme Court dismissed the conviction. Working pro bono, Tigar in 1993 argued before the U.S. Court of Appeals for the Sixth Circuit that the government had withheld evidence that could have helped Demjanjuk fight his 1986 extradition to Israel. The appellate court agreed and overturned its extradition in *Demjanjuk v. Petrovsky*, 10 F.3d 388 (1993). As the century ended, Michael Tigar, joined by his wife, Jane Blanksteen Tigar, continued to represent Demjanjuk as he tried to clear his name.

(*continued*)

only by his mother's reading of Perry Mason but also by his readings of Louis Nizer's *My Life in Court* and of everything he could find about Clarence Darrow (Carlson 1997).

Black, who is frequently interviewed about contemporary cases by national news networks, has detailed four of his prominent courtroom victories in a recent book. The first was his defense of Luis Alvarez, a Hispanic police officer charged with negligent homicide in the shooting death of an African-American man in Overtown, Miami. The second was his attempt to show that court-appointed attorneys for a vicious killer named Thomas Knight had not adequately presented the court with the extenuating circumstances (including the fact that he witnessed his father rape his sister) in his childhood. The third was his demonstration that Stephen Hicks had not intentionally murdered his live-in girlfriend but had killed her by accident when he grabbed a gun away from her. The fourth was his defense of a Hispanic banker, Fred De La Mata, against charges that he had used his bank to hide drug transactions.

Black rails against prosecutors who offer deals to prisoners to snitch against individuals accused of crime. He often tells his juries the story of the American Indian who finds a frozen rattlesnake in the winter and gets ready to kill it. The snake (who just happens to talk) persuades the Indian to save its life, promising that it will never bite him. As soon as it is taken to the Indian's tent and warmed, it strikes the Indian. When asked why it broke its promise, the snake responds, "When I made that promise, you already knew that I was a snake." Likening snitches to snakes, Black exhorts the jury, "Snakes have their own morality. Never blame a snake for acting in character; it's our fault if we trust them" (Black 1999, 301).

References

Black, Roy. *Black's Law: A Criminal Lawyer Reveals His Defense Strategies in Four Cliffhanger Cases*. New York: Simon & Schuster, 1999.

Carlson, Peter. "Roy Black Wins on Appeal; Marv Albert's Lawyer May Be Nice, but He's Not Last." *Washington Post*, 22 September 1997.

Jordan, Mary. "Willie Smith's Dogged Defender." *Washington Post*, 2 December 1991.

Pesce, Carolyn, and Maria Puente. "Victory Elevates Black to Elite." *USA Today*, 12 December 1991.

Tigar argued a significant First Amendment case before the U.S. Supreme Court in 1991. In *Gentile v. State Bar of Nevada*, 501 U.S. 1030 (1991), the Court decided the scope of lawyers' First Amendment rights to talk about their cases outside the courtroom. Because of public statements he had made in advance of the trial of a client, the Nevada State Bar had privately reprimanded Las Vegas criminal defense attorney Dominic Gentile. The Nevada bar prohibited attorneys from making out-of-court statements if a lawyer knew, or should have known, that the remarks could affect the judicial proceedings. Tigar attacked the constitutionality of the rule, arguing that unless the public remarks presented a clear and present danger to a fair trial, lawyers should not be punished for speaking outside the courtroom. The Court, finding that the rule was too vague, reversed the Nevada Supreme Court's decision to uphold the reprimand, and Gentile was not punished for his statements.

Despite his leftist credentials, Michael Tigar has defended noted conservatives, including former Treasury Secretary Connally and Republican U.S. Senator from Texas Kay Bailey Hutchison. A Travis County, Texas, grand jury indicted Senator Hutchison on four felony counts and one misdemeanor count of official misconduct, tampering with government records and tampering with physical evidence. The charges stemmed from her tenure as state treasurer. Hutchison argued that Democrats who did not want her to be reelected to the Senate seat she had taken from Senator Bob Kruger, a Democrat, in 1993 drove the investigation and charges. Kruger had been appointed to the seat when Democratic Senator Lloyd Bentsen was named to President Bill Clinton's cabinet. Through some legal and political maneuvering, Hutchison was acquitted of the charges in 1994.

Tigar is a staunch opponent of the death penalty. He was responsible for bringing the Texas Resource Center to Texas in 1988. The Texas Resource Center, a federally funded program, provided training for lawyers to conduct postconviction appeals in capital punishment cases. Tigar was chairman of the center's board from 1988 until 1993. He unsuccessfully represented Texas death row inmate Gary Graham before the U.S. Court of Appeals for the Fifth Circuit and the U.S. Supreme Court (*Graham v. Collins*, 506 U.S. 461 [1993]). A Harris County jury convicted Graham for killing a Florida man in a Houston parking lot in 1981. Graham was seventeen at the time of the murder. His appeal to the U.S. Supreme Court argued that the jury as a mitigating circumstance should have considered his age during the penalty phase of the trial. The opinion of the Court was that a new rule governing mitigating circumstances did not apply to Graham because he was convicted before the rule took effect. After a series of stays, Graham was scheduled to be executed in the summer of 2000. The Texas Resource Center lost most of its funding in 1995 when the new Republican majority in Congress reduced appropriations for legal services.

Michael Tigar gained a reputation for representing notorious defendants, but no defendant had the notoriety of Terry Nichols. Nichols was accused of assisting Timothy McVeigh in planning the 1995 bombing of the Murrah Federal Building in Oklahoma City. The blast destroyed the building and resulted in the deaths of 168 people. Tigar was appointed by U.S. District Judge David Russell of Oklahoma City to represent Nichols after a number of other lawyers refused the case. The core of Tigar's defense was very similar to those used in the Demjanjuk case and other cases: The government, specifically the FBI, broke the rules in pursuing Nichols. Although the jury was not convinced by Tigar's defense and found Nichols guilty in December 1997, the attorney was able to keep Nichols off death row. After the jury deadlocked during the sentencing phase of the trial, U.S. District Judge Richard Matsch sentenced Nichols to life in prison with no chance of parole.

While preparing Nichols's defense, Tigar took a leave from the University of Texas law school. In 1996, he took some time away from the bombing case to defend a female Air Force officer charged with sodomy and conduct unbecoming an officer. A civilian, Pamela Dillard, had accused twenty-two-year veteran Major Debra Meeks, Dillard's landlord, of threatening her with a gun. When an investigation found that the threat had not occurred, Dillard stated that she had been involved in a lesbian relationship with Meeks for two years. This relationship violated the military's 1993 "don't ask, don't tell" directive regarding homosexuality. Attacking the government's modes of investigation, Tigar was able to direct attention away from his client's behavior and toward the behavior of the government. The defense worked; Meeks was acquitted on all charges on August 16, 1996.

Tigar often portrays his clients as victims of an overbearing government. In his textbooks, he tells readers that every defense needs a theme, a simple statement that the jury can understand. The theme in John Demjanjuk's defense was that the government, in its extradition procedures, "hoodwinked the court" (Toobin 1996, 52). In the Terry Nichols trial, the defense contended that the government had the wrong man and that the FBI investigation was conducted incorrectly and was incomplete. Tigar has been accused of playing to the jury. Defending Major Meeks, Tigar was able to convince the military jury that his client was one of them—a professional soldier under attack by a deranged civilian. Tigar often quotes from Scripture or classic Greek epics in court, but he can adopt a folksy style that appears to endear him to the juries. He also has been accused of being a show-off (see Abbott 1997). In short, Michael Tigar treats the courtroom as it if were a stage with the jury as the audience.

Tigar married Jane Blanksteen on August 22, 1996. Blanksteen, a writer seeking a second career, became interested in public interest law as a Columbia University law student and, seeking an internship, posted her résumé on the Internet. Tigar saw the résumé and invited her to work at the Texas Resource Center. Blanksteen refused the invitation, indicating that she was not interested in the death penalty or moving to Texas. In 1995, she called Tigar after learning that he was defending Terry Nichols in the Oklahoma City bombing case. A course required her to do forty hours of pro bono work, and she offered the time to Nichols' defense team. Tigar accepted, and the two lawyers eventually fell in love. Blanksteen is Tigar's third wife; he has three children from his previous marriages.

Tigar left the University of Texas law school in 1998 to take a position at American University's Washington College of Law. His move was spurred by two considerations. First, his wife practices law in Washington, D.C. Second, an attempt to become dean of the Texas law school was unsuccessful. In addition to his duties as a law professor in the United States, Tigar teaches at the faculty of law in Aix-en-Provence every year.

In addition to being a legal academic and practitioner, Tigar has maintained an active publishing schedule. He has written numerous articles for legal publications, including a regular column in the *National Law Journal* and essays published under the pen name "Edward Michaels." Tigar also has written several textbooks introducing students to his techniques as a litigator. The books, *Examining Witnesses* (1993), *Persuasion: The Litigator's Art* (1999), and *Federal Appeals: Jurisdiction and Practice* (1999) (written with his wife), are replete with examples from Tigar's own cases.

Tigar also is a playwright. His play, *The Trial of John Peter Zenger,* was first performed at the Waldorf Astoria Starlight Roof on August 10, 1986. The *Zenger* trial served as the background for the First Amendment's freedom of the press. The play was commissioned by the American Bar Association's Section of Litigation, which Tigar chaired in 1989 and 1990. The second play, *Haymarket: Whose Name the Few Still Say with Tears* (first performed by the Remains Theater in Chicago in October 1987), features Tigar's hero Clarence Darrow, who represented the Haymarket strikers. Tigar earned critical acclaim for both plays due to his ability to weave compelling stories out of the legal record.

Michael Tigar has been criticized throughout his career for agreeing to represent unpopular and notorious clients. His defense of alleged concentration camp guard John Demjanjuk attracted particular scorn from the legal community. Tigar's response to the criticism can be found in the following story. When he was eleven or twelve, Tigar informed his father that he wanted to be a lawyer. The elder Tigar went to his room and returned with a copy of Irving Stone's *Clarence Darrow for the Defense*. Tigar's father told him, "This is the kind of lawyer you should be. He fought for people's rights" (Tigar 1993, xvii). Tigar patterned his career on Darrow's example. He has earned a reputation for fighting for people's rights.

—*John David Rausch Jr.*

SOURCES AND SUGGESTIONS FOR FURTHER READING

Abbott, Karen. "Lawyer's Fire Still Burning: Public Defender Michael Tigar's Passion for Justice, Stellar Reputation Precede Him." *Denver Rocky Mountain News*, 29 September 1997, A4.

"Jane Tigar Took Long Road to Law Career before Joining Nichols' Team." *Dallas Morning News*, 17 November 1997, A18.

Romano, Lois. "A Man of Independent Means; Attorney Michael Tigar Is Putting His Leftist Leanings to Work for Terry Nichols." *Washington Post*, 29 September 1997, D1.

Tigar, Michael E. *Examining Witnesses*. Chicago: Section of Litigation, American Bar Association, 1993.

———. *Law and the Rise of Capitalism*. New York: Monthly Review Press, 1977.

———. *Persuasion: The Litigator's Art*. Chicago: Section of Litigation, American Bar Association, 1999.

Tigar, Michael E, and Jane B. Tigar. *Federal Appeals: Jurisdiction and Practice*. 3d ed. St. Paul: West, 1999.

Toobin, Jeffrey. "The Man with Timothy McVeigh." *New Yorker*, 30 September 1996, 48–54.

TRIBE, LAURENCE H.

(1941–)

LAURENCE TRIBE IS ONE OF the leading constitutional litigators, scholars, teachers, and rights advocates of the twentieth century. Tribe was born in Shanghai, Republic of China, October 10, 1941, to George and Paulina Tribe, and moved to San Francisco in 1947. After attending public school in San Francisco, Tribe entered Harvard College, graduating summa cum laude in mathematics in 1962. While at Harvard College, Tribe was a national intercollegiate debate champion in 1961, demonstrating the qualities that would make him one of the most important advocates for individual rights ever to appear before the Supreme Court. Since 1978, Tribe has appeared before the Supreme Court at least thirty times as lead counsel in cases raising some of the most important constitutional questions of his times.

In 1966, he received the J.D. degree from Harvard Law School. After law school, Tribe clerked for Justice Mathew O. Tobriner of the California Supreme Court in 1966–1967, and Justice Potter Stewart of the U.S. Supreme Court in 1967–1968. Since 1968, he has been at Harvard Law School. In 1982, he was named the Ralph S. Tyler Jr. Professor of Constitutional Law. Tribe has been a member of the California bar since 1966, and the U.S. Supreme Court bar since

LAURENCE TRIBE

Laurence Tribe, lawyer for former Vice-President Al Gore, speaks to reporters gathered outside the U.S. Supreme Court after making arguments in the case of the hand-counted Florida ballots that helped decide who would win the presidency. (Reuters NewMedia Inc./Corbis)

1978. He also is a member of the bars of numerous U.S. circuit courts and the state of Massachusetts. Tribe married Carolyn R. Kreye of New Haven, Connecticut, in 1964 and has two children: a son, Mark, born in 1966, and a daughter, Kerry, born in 1973.

Tribe's stature as a constitutional litigator, scholar, and teacher is demonstrated by the numerous honors he has been awarded. He was elected as a Fellow to the American Academy of Arts and Sciences in 1980, and he was named by *Time* magazine as "one of the ten most outstanding law professors" in the United States in 1977.

Tribe has received honorary degrees from the following universities: Hebrew (1998), Colgate (1997), Illinois Institute of Technology (1988), American (1987), University of the Pacific (1987), and Gonzaga (1980). The range of Tribe's interests and accomplishments are truly unmatched in his generation. Tribe's accomplishments are seen in the following reasons stated by universities when awarding an honorary doctor of laws degree: The Illinois Institute of Technology noted Tribe's "profound and far-reaching influence on the understanding and development of constitutional law." American University awarded the honorary degree for his "scholarship, writing and advocacy showing a stunning breadth of expertise . . . from mathematics to . . . technology assessment . . . demonstrating a sensitivity to a world undergoing massive technological change." Gonzaga University awarded the honorary degree for "producing the leading treatise on American constitutional law" and "do[ing] much to build a bridge between law and technology."

In the 1970s, Tribe was an important interpreter of science to the legal community and of the law to scientists. In the 1980s and 1990s, Tribe's technical expertise was used to further groundbreaking lawsuits for damages against tobacco and asbestos producers, in which he sought to demonstrate that these producers were responsible for the deaths and medical costs associated with the use of their products. Since the 1980s, Tribe has been an advocate of the weak and politically unpopular in a period in which the Supreme Court has been reticent to expand individual rights. To reach the wider public, he has appeared before congressional committees thirty-one times and has written more than seventy-one magazine articles and op-ed essays.

Tribe has presented numerous named lectures: the Alexander Meiklejohn Lecture at Brown University, 1998; the First Annual Louis D. Brandeis Lecture at the Israel Academy of Science and Humanities in Jerusalem, 1994; the Keynote Lecture at the Bill of Rights Bicentennial at the U.S. National Archives, 1991; the Forty-third Annual Cardozo Lecture to the Association of the Bar of the City of New York, 1989; the Inaugural Lecture of the Richard Salomon Distinguished Lecture Series at the New York City

Public Library, 1988; and the Tanner Lecture on Human Values at the University of Utah, 1986.

As a legal advocate, Tribe has received awards from the groups whose causes he has championed. For his work in support of gay and lesbian rights, he received the Eleventh Annual "Honoring Our Allies" Award from the National Gay and Lesbian Task Force in 2000, and the Distinguished Lifetime Achievement Award from the National Gay Rights Advocates in 1988. In 1985, he received the Legal Achievement Award from the Bay Area Lawyers for Individual Freedom and the prestigious Roger Baldwin Award of the Massachusetts Civil Liberties Union Foundation.

Tribe is a world-renowned constitutional expert. He was a constitutional consultant to Chief Justice Valery Zorkin of Russia in 1992, a member of the United States–European Committee on Revision of the Czechoslovak Constitution in 1990–1991, and a Fulbright Distinguished Lecturer in Brazil in 1982 and in India in 1991. He helped the Marshall Islands draft a new constitution in 1978–1979 and was chairman of the Marshall Islands Judicial Service Commission in 1979–1980.

It is as lead counsel in important cases before the U.S. Supreme Court that Tribe has proved himself a brilliant litigator. Tribe has won eighteen of the twenty-nine cases he litigated before the Supreme Court. It is rare for a person other than the solicitor general of the United States to appear before the Supreme Court in so many cases, and so many cases that resulted in landmark decisions. What is impressive about Tribe as a litigator is both the number of appearances before the Supreme Court and the range and complexity of constitutional questions that he has brought to the Court as lead counsel. There are four major areas of cases that Tribe has brought to the Court. The first group involves constitutional questions affecting whether individuals and government will be able to use state and federal courts to redress grievances due to the health effects of products that corporations produce. The second group of cases center on key First Amendment issues. The third group of cases (all of which Tribe lost) involve cutting-edge issues of the right of privacy. A fourth group of cases covers a wide range of policy areas and centers on the power of local and state governments to limit the nationalizing effects of federal law and constitutional principles, which in many instances further the interests of corporations and limit those of citizens as consumers.

Tribe has been a leader in ensuring that those seeking damages for the wrongs of corporations get their day in court. In *Pennzoil v. Texaco*, 481 U.S. 1 (1987), Tribe was successful in getting the Supreme Court to agree that federal courts may not interfere with state court enforcement of a multibillion-dollar judgment for Pennzoil against Texaco. Tribe supported

Pennzoil's claim that lower federal courts should have abstained from enjoining payment under the rules of court deference to state courts. This allowed Pennzoil to collect a multibillion-dollar judgment. More important, it helped keep federal courts open as venues to limit unfair business practices that are very costly to consumers.

Perhaps the most important impact of Tribe as a litigator was his leadership in efforts to make the tobacco industry pay to individuals and governments the costs of smoking, which he argued should be paid because the tobacco industry covered up what they knew were the full risks of smoking. This case was key to the use of state courts to secure multibillion-dollar punitive damage awards against the tobacco industry. In *Cipollone v. Liggett*, 505 U.S. 504 (1992), Tribe was successful in getting the Supreme Court to agree that the Federal Cigarette Labeling and Advertising Act of 1965 did not preempt state-law damage actions. The required warnings on cigarettes do not foreclose additional obligations by manufacturers under state law. State claims of conspiracy among manufacturers or claims of an express warranty are not preempted by the 1965 law. In the 1990s, the lack of federal preemption in such cases opened the way to successful multibillion-dollar lawsuits won by states for the health costs associated with diseases from smoking, and for direct payments to smokers and their families. The rancor with which business viewed Tribe's work in the tobacco cases can be seen in a *Forbes* magazine article on lawyer's fees that stated, "Media-savvy Harvard law professor Laurence Tribe is representing Florida, Massachusetts, and Mississippi, pro bono, (at no fee), but he stands to collect $2,000,000 in 'juicy consulting fees from the Texas lawyers'" (www.forbes.com, 6 November 1995).

In *TXO v. Alliance Resources*, 509 U.S. 443 (1993), Tribe got the Supreme Court to affirm a state court award and declare that the $10 million punitive damage award in a case whose regular damage award was only $19,000 was not so grossly excessive as to be violative of the due process clause of the Fourteenth Amendment. The Court said the dramatic disparity between the actual and punitive damages is not controlling, or a per se violation of the Constitution.

In *Amchem Products, Inc. v. Windsor*, 521 U.S. 591 (1997), the Supreme Court invalidated a $1.3 billion asbestos class-action settlement because it included an improperly certified class of citizens under Rule 23 (b)(3). Tribe led the fight against efforts by Amchem Products and some of those hurt by the asbestos it produced to limit the class of individuals with health effects, including death, from asbestos poisoning. The class would preclude nearly all individuals who had not previously participated in the class action but were injured by the products of this company. The Supreme Court emphasized that Rule 23 (e) inquiries by a court must protect unnamed class members from unjust or unfair settlements agreed to by faint-hearted or self-interested class representatives.

Ortiz v. Fibreboard Corp., 119 S. Ct. 2295 (1999), is a follow-up case to *Amchem*. As lead attorney, Tribe succeeded in getting the Supreme Court to invalidate a $1.53 billion asbestos class-action settlement because the class improperly either failed to provide funds or provided too little funds for parties hurt by asbestos exposure. The record of the district court demonstrated that funds were limited by agreement of the parties, rather than through fact-finding on the needs of those exposed to asbestos (but not part of the suit) and on the resources of the company.

In a case that also ensured that individuals get a their day in court and that damage cases get the best information on which to make decisions, *Baker v. General Motors*, 522 U.S. 222 (1998), the Supreme Court said that the full faith and credit clause of the Constitution does not require Missouri courts to honor a Michigan court's ruling that enjoined Ronald Elwell, a former General Motors employee, from testifying against General Motors in claims of product liability. Michigan's injunction need not be enforced, because blocking Elwell's testimony would violate Missouri's public policy that shielded from disclosure only privileged information or otherwise confidential information.

In *Adams Fruit Co. v. Barrett*, 494 U.S. 638 (1990), Tribe succeeded in getting the Supreme Court to support the power of migrant farm workers to sue a fruit company for whom they were working for intentional violation of the motor vehicle safety provisions of a federal law, the Migration and Seasonal Agricultural Protection Act, even though they received benefits under Florida's workers' compensation law for injuries they suffered in an automobile accident while traveling to work in the fruit company's van.

Tribe lost two cases in which he sought to help cities secure damages for wrongful actions. One involved government, the other a corporation. In *Schweiker v. Chilicky*, 487 U.S. 412 (1988), Tribe sought to secure the right of a person whose disability benefits were terminated because of due process violations to sue one Arizona and two federal officials individually for emotional distress and for the loss of necessities proximately caused by the application of government policies. The Court said there is no damages action for wrongful denial of social security disability benefits. In *Honda Motor Co. v. Oberg*, 512 U.S. 415 (1994), Honda Motor Company successfully argued that Oregon's constitution, which prohibits judicial review of the amount of punitive damages by a jury "unless the court can affirmatively say there is no evidence to support the verdict," violates the Fourteenth Amendment's due process clause. In that case, Dean ERWIN GRISWOLD of Harvard Law School filed an amicus brief opposing Tribe's position.

These cases demonstrate Tribe's mastery of constitutional principles, technical data, judicial procedure, and how justices of quite different judicial philosophies will react to arguments. These cases also demonstrate Tribe's belief that damage awards and ensuring claimants their days in court are important ways to protect citizens from the negative effects of corporate power.

Tribe also appeared in some of the most important First Amendment cases to be brought to the Supreme Court since 1978. In *Boston v. Anderson*, 439 U.S. 951, 1389 (1978), Tribe's first appearance before the Supreme Court, he succeeded in convincing the Court to protect the power of the city of Boston to spend funds to influence the result of a state referendum even though the Supreme Judicial Court of Massachusetts had held that a city may not appropriate such funds. In *Larkin v. Grendel's Den*, 459 U.S. 116 (1982), Tribe succeeded in getting the Supreme Court to find unconstitutional a Massachusetts law that had vested to the governing bodies of schools and churches the power to prevent the issuance of liquor licenses to premises within a five-hundred-foot radius of the church or school by simply objecting to the license. The Court found that this law violated the First Amendment, which does not allow states to establish religion. This law substituted the reasoned decision making of a public body to make zoning decisions, based on evidence and guided by standards, with the unilateral and absolute power of a church. This law enmeshed churches in the processes of government and created the danger of political fragmentation and divisiveness along religious lines.

In *Board of Education of Oklahoma City v. National Gay Task Force*, 470 U.S. 903 (1985), Tribe successfully protected First Amendment speech rights of gay teachers. He was able to get the Supreme Court to affirm a Tenth Circuit Court decision that had found unconstitutional an Oklahoma school board policy that allowed teachers to be fired for "advocating, soliciting, imposing, encouraging public and private homosexual activity" without a finding of incitement and the presence of imminent lawless action, which is required before political speech can be limited. *Richmond Newspapers v. Virginia*, 448 U.S. 555 (1980), was a very important case that established the right of the press and public to attend criminal trials, as implicit in the press guarantees of the First Amendment.

In *Sable Communications Co. v. FCC*, 492 U.S. 115 (1989), Tribe won a case that restricted Congress from prohibiting the use of telephones for indecent, but not obscene, "dial-a-porn" services. Although the Federal Communications Commission (FCC) could limit interstate transmission of obscene commercial telephone messages, the Court found that the ban on indecent, but not obscene, telephone messages violated the First Amendment.

Lowell J. Myers

Few contemporary trials have been more dramatic or raised thornier legal issues than the trials of Donald Lang. Lang was an African-American deaf-mute from Chicago who was known in his neighborhood as "Dummy." Lang was accused of the murder of Ernestine Williams (1965) and Earline Brown (1971), both prostitutes.

Lang, who had fallen through the cracks in the educational system and had never received formal schooling when he was first accused of murder at age twenty, largely communicated through grunts and crude gestures. He had never learned to sign, to read or write, or to read lips, although he was a good worker who had been able to hold a job loading and unloading trucks and often seemed to have a good sense of what was going on around him. He was also known to use the services of prostitutes and to have been with Williams, and later Brown, on the dates of their violent deaths.

In the first case, courts ruled that Lang (whom police had no way of informing of his legal rights) was physically incompetent to stand trial. The state had nonetheless confined him in various institutions for about five years until the Illinois Supreme Court, responding to petitions filed by Lang's attorney, had ruled that he was entitled to a trial. When this trial was finally ordered, key witnesses had died and evidence had been destroyed. The state prosecutor decided not to prosecute, and Lang was released to his father and stepmother and returned to his old job.

Months later, Earline Brown's body was found in a motel closet a day and a half after she and Lang had been seen together there. This time the police investigation and laboratory follow-up was more thorough, and, although the case was circumstantial, Lang was convicted and sentenced to incarceration.

In both cases, Lowell J. Myers (1930–) represented Lang. Like Lang, Myers, who was white, was also deaf, but because he lost his hearing later in life, he was able to speak to the judge and jury. After earning degrees at Roosevelt University and the University of Chicago in business and accounting, Myers had later gravitated toward the law, completing a law degree at night at John Marshall Law School, where he was second in his class (Tidyman 1974, 29). Myers helped secure passage of a law requiring court interpreters for deaf-mutes and allowing deaf people to drive in Illi-

(continues)

Tribe lost two important First Amendment cases. In *Heffron v. International Society for Krishna Consciousness*, 452 U.S. 640 (1981), the Supreme Court allowed the state of Minnesota to restrict speech and solicitation on state fairgrounds. In *Timmons v. Twin Cities Area New Party*, 520 U.S. 351 (1997), Tribe was not successful in getting the Supreme Court to invalidate a Minnesota law that banned a candidate from appearing on a nominating ballot of more than one political party. The ban on fusion candidates was said by Tribe to violate the New party's associational rights under the First and Fourteenth Amendments. The Supreme Court feared that nomination

(continued)

nois. Myers wrote a book for deaf children about their legal rights, as well as a book entitled *The Law and the Deaf* (1967) for attorneys and judges (Tidyman 1974, 30–31).

Myers, who was adept at lip reading and sign language, and was for a time the only Illinois lawyer with knowledge of deaf-mute language (Tidyman 1974, 29), undoubtedly devoted more time, effort, and understanding to Lang's defense than many other court-appointed attorneys would have done. He was particularly adept at cross-examining experts in the field and questioning their views of Lang's competence. In the first case, Myers eventually succeeded in establishing the principle, never before established in a U.S. court, that the state could not continue to incarcerate an individual who was not insane and whom it was unable to bring to trial because of physical incapacities. In the second case, Myers at one point had to request that his own client—who could hear nothing and whose conduct often appeared threatening to the jury—be removed from the courtroom.

Although Myers lost the second case, observers agreed that he did his best to raise reasonable doubt in a case in which circumstantial evidence was relatively strong. An observer of both cases has estimated that Myers's payment as a court-appointed attorney in his first defense—one thousand dollars—amounted to less than two dollars an hour (Tidyman 1974, 169).

As someone who was deaf, Myers undoubtedly understood Lang's difficulties in communicating in a way that other lawyers did not. By contrast, some police investigators and prosecutors continued to believe that Lang's demeanor in the courtroom was all an act designed to elicit sympathy and hide his own culpability.

Evidence from Lang's trial, as well as his experience at various institutions where he was incarcerated, seems to suggest that he was much more comfortable and self-controlled in dealing with men than with women. Although his motives may never be known for certain, it appears that Lang may have become enraged when Brown took his money without intending to provide her services. Asked his opinion at the end of the second trial, Myers said, "If Donald had been given a little education *at the proper time* it would have made all the difference in the world" (Tidyman 1974, 275).

REFERENCE

Tidyman, Ernest. *Dummy*. Boston: Little, Brown, 1974.

of major parties' candidates by minor parties might enable minor parties to blur the message of the major party and help them bootstrap their way to major-party status in the next election and thereby circumvent the state's nominating-petition process.

The third group of cases involves issues of the right to privacy, with regard to the right of abortion choice, the right of sexual intimacy for homosexuals, and right to physician-assisted suicide. Tribe lost all three of the cases. In *Bowers v. Hardwick,* 478 U.S. 186 (1986), the Supreme Court found that there was no right of privacy for consensual sodomy among homosexuals. In *Rust v. Sullivan*, 500 U.S. 173 (1991), Tribe unsuccessfully argued against the constitutionality of the regulations made under Section 1008 of the Public Health Service Act, which prohibited federal funds to be used for counseling, referrals for, and activities advocating abortion as a method of family planning in federally funded clinics. The Court found that this regulation did not violate a woman's right to terminate a pregnancy under privacy rights granted by the Fifth Amendment's due process clause, which covers the federal government; nor did these regulations violate the First Amendment free speech rights of practice of doctors, fund recipients, their staffs, or patients by impermissibly imposing viewpoint-discriminatory conditions on government subsidies. In *Vacco v. Quill*, 521 U.S. 793 (1997), the Supreme Court refused to accept Tribe's argument that New York's law that makes it a crime to aid another to commit or attempt suicide, but permits patients to refuse even lifesaving medical treatment, violates the Fourteenth Amendment's equal protection clause. Because the statutes outlawing assisted suicide neither infringe fundamental rights nor involve classifications in the law that have been traditionally held suspect, like race classifications, the Supreme Court said they are entitled to a strong presumption of validity. The Supreme Court found that the distinction between letting a patient die and making that patient die is important, logical, rational, and well established. In this case, Tribe won a partial victory, since the Court did not speak to issues of limits on pain relief, which would hasten death. These cases, all losses for Tribe, show that he is willing to bring cases that are difficult to win to the Supreme Court in order to expand individual rights.

Finally, the fourth major group of cases in which Tribe appeared before the Supreme Court sought to limit the nationalizing effects of constitutional principles and federal law on citizens, cities, and states. In *Pacific Gas & Electric Co. v. California Resources Conservation and Development Commission*, 461 U.S. 190 (1983), Tribe was successful in getting the Supreme Court to agree that all state moratoriums on nuclear power plants are not preempted by the Atomic Energy Act of 1954. States continue to have authority over economic questions like the need for electric generation, while safety issues continue to be under federal law.

Tribe succeeded in getting the Supreme Court to agree that cities are not limited by the commerce clause of the Constitution and the Sherman Anti-Trust Act when they act as participants in the economic system. In *White v. Mass. Council of Construction Employers*, 460 U.S. 204 (1983), the Court said that the commerce clause does not bar cities from preferentially hiring their own citizens. The Court noted that when a state or city enters the market as a participant it is not subject to the restraints of the commerce clause. In *Fisher v. Berkeley*, 475 U.S. 260 (1986), Tribe got the Supreme

Court to accept the view that local rent control laws were not preempted by the Sherman Anti-Trust Act.

In *Northeast Bancorp v. Federal Reserve System*, 472 U.S. 159 (1985), the Supreme Court agreed with Tribe that states may limit bank mergers to banks in a several-state region without violating the commerce clause, compact clause, or equal protection clause of the Constitution. In another case that favored economic competition and the consumer, in *AT&T v. Iowa Utilities Board*, 119 S. Ct. 721 (1999), Tribe successfully got the Supreme Court to uphold Bell Operating Companies' challenge to FCC jurisdiction over interconnection with local exchange networks. In this case, Tribe fought to allow local telephone companies to buy elements outside the AT&T network and thereby overturn a rule made by the FCC. Finally, Tribe was lead counsel in *United States v. Chesapeake & Potomac Telelphone Co.–N.C.T.A. v. Bell Atlantic*, 516 U.S. 415 (1996), for local telephone companies in support of a lower-court decision that said Congress may not ban video programming by telephone companies, a case that was remanded below and mooted by the passage of the 1996 Telecommunications Act.

Tribe appeared before the Supreme Court in three other cases of note. In *Crawford v. Board of Education of Los Angeles*, 458 U.S. 527 (1982), Tribe lost a case in which he argued against the constitutionality of an amendment added to the state constitution by a public referendum that said state courts could not order mandatory pupil assignment and transportation unless a federal court would have been permitted to do so to remedy a violation of the equal protection clause of the Fourteenth Amendment. Tribe viewed the amendment as an unconstitutional racial classification. Tribe represented Hawaii in *Hawaii Housing Authority v. Midkiff*, 467 U.S. 229 (1984), in its efforts to sustain a state land reform law that forced landowners to sell land to occupants. The fact that the property taken by eminent domain was transferred in the first instance to private beneficiaries did not undermine the legality of such acts. Finally, in an effort to secure the greatest amount of time to gain passage of the Equal Rights Amendment, Tribe won the case of *NOW v. Idaho*, 445 U.S. 918 (1982), in which the Supreme Court said that federal courts may not interfere with Congress's time extension for ratification of the Equal Rights Amendment.

Laurence Tribe has gained a superb reputation for his ability to earn the respect of Supreme Court justices, many of whom do not share his views on the role of the Supreme Court as a venue for social change, nonoriginalist interpretive philosophy, and individual rights. His arguments before the Court are detailed, lively, and always directed at arguments that will sway a majority of justices while not enraging those with whom he disagrees. Tribe draws on his unmatched understanding of constitutional law and the Supreme Court as an institution to demonstrate to the Court that supporting his position will place the justices in line with principles—such as adherence to precedent and due process—that they hold deeply.

Tribe has commented on the most important and controversial news events with legal ramifications. *Time* magazine quoted Tribe as viewing the Immigration and Naturalization Service raid on the Gonzalez family home to capture Elián Gonzalez to return him to his father and to Cuba as "unlawful and unconstitutional" (Duffy 2000, 39). Tribe appeared on major news programs to discuss his view on the Gonzalez affair, a view with which the Bill Clinton administration, most liberals, and a majority of Americans disagreed.

Tribe took another position to which liberals have been opposed. *USA Today* reported that Tribe—"probably the most influential living American constitutional law scholar"—has received hate mail for writing in the second edition of his constitutional law treatise that the right to bear arms is an important political right that should not be dismissed as "wholly irrelevant." Tribe believes that the Second Amendment ensures that "the federal government may not disarm individual citizens without an unusually strong justification." Tribe argued in the edition that the Second Amendment gives citizens a right—"admittedly of uncertain scope"—to "possess and use firearms in the defense of themselves and their homes" (Mauro 1999, A4).

Tribe also was a leader in opposing the impeachment of President Clinton. On October 8, 1998, in the impeachment debate on the House floor, Democratic representative Patrick Kennedy of Rhode Island quoted Laurence Tribe as stating that this Congress was "twisting impeachment into something else, instead of keeping it within its historical boundaries. And our nation and its form of government are in peril as a result. . . . [We are] losing sight of the constitutional wreckage that this vote will cause as we lay down historical precedent that a president of the United States can be impeached for something other than official misconduct as president of the United States" ("Transcript" 1998). As reported by CNN, Senator Edward Kennedy referred to Laurence Tribe's testimony to the House Subcommittee on the Constitution that to impeach Clinton would "rewrite" the impeachment clause, when Kennedy's closed-door impeachment statement was released to the *Congressional Record* on February 12, 1999 ("Sen. Kennedy's" 1999).

Tribe is a prolific scholar. His brilliant treatise *American Constitutional Law*, which was published in 1978, received the triennial Order of the Coif Award, which is awarded for the outstanding work of legal scholarship, and the Scribes Award for the Outstanding Legal Publication. The book is one of the most cited of all twentieth-century legal treatises. The first volume of a two-volume third edition of the treatise was published in 2000. It is rare that a litigator of Tribe's stature is also a scholar of international reputation.

Tribe's early scholarship centered on technology and the law, with an emphasis on issues of the assessment of environmental damage and its reduction. In 1969, Tribe wrote *Technology: Processes of Assessment and Choice*, which was prepared for the House Committee on Science and Astronautics (National Academy of Sciences 1969). His next two books were *Environmental Protection* (Tribe and Jaffe 1971) and *Channeling Technology through Law* (1973). Tribe also co-edited *When Values Conflict: Essays on Environmental Analysis, Discourse, and Decision* (Tribe et al. 1976).

In 1985, Harvard University Press published *Constitutional Choices*. In this book we see Tribe the constitutional litigator melding with Tribe the constitutional scholar. In sixteen superb essays, Tribe argued against the trend of the day, grand constitutional theory. He writes,

> Much of what constitutional scholars write these days either focuses so closely on constitutional doctrine, or looks to matters so distant from doctrine, as to bear no real resemblance to *doing* constitutional law—to constructing constitutional arguments and counterarguments or exploring the premises and prospects of alternative constitutional approaches to concrete settings. Such constitutional *problem solving*, I recognize, is in less academic vogue nowadays than is discussion of constitutional *voice*: what it means for judges to expound the Constitution, how the vulnerability of judges relates to their authority. . . . The core of my concern is the making of constitutional law itself—its tensions and tendencies; its puzzles and patterns they make; its limits as a form of activity; in a word, its horizons. (Tribe 1985, x)

Tribe describes the themes that cut across the essays: the domination of constitutional theory and practice by "the dangerous allure of proceduralism," "the paralyzing seduction of neutrality," "the morally anesthetizing imagery of the natural," "the hidden tilt of various constitutional doctrines towards the perpetuation of unjust hierarchies of race, gender and class," and "the potential of various forms of constitutional argument to deflect judicial responsibility from crucial substantive choices onto external circumstances or remote actors" (Tribe 1985, ix).

For Tribe, both Robert Bork's focus on original intent and John Hart Ely's nonoriginalist constitutional theory, which emphasizes keeping the political system open for minorities, do not provide sufficient rights protections for the politically weak and unpopular. In contrast to *Constitutional Choices*, Tribe describes his treatise as a "global effort; it was an attempt to roll the constitutional universe into a ball and show it as a unified whole" (Tribe 1985).

The strength of *Constitutional Choices* is that it demonstrates the foremost constitutional litigator of his age working out how (and why) the Supreme

Court should interpret the Constitution. Tribe would like the Supreme Court to make affirmative choices about the effects of economic, social, and political power on institutional power and individual rights, rather than trying to resort to what he considers to be falsely neutral categories in the law. If such affirmative choices are made, then constitutional law will not replicate, or increase through law, the inequalities that already exist in our nation.

Since the publication of *Constitutional Choices* in 1985, Tribe has concentrated on books for a more general readership. In these works, Tribe has addressed some of the key constitutional questions facing our nation. *God Save This Honorable Court: How the Choice of Supreme Court Justices Shapes Our History* (1985) argues that it was just and proper for the Senate to reject President Reagan's nominee to the Supreme Court, conservative jurist and scholar Robert Bork. *Abortion: The Clash of Absolutes* (1990) is a superb argument for why the right of abortion choice should be constitutional and why *Roe v. Wade* (1973) should stand. One can see a superb litigator, as scholar, presenting the history of abortion here and overseas, arguing why the right to abortion choice is in the Constitution, that the presence of a fetus does not automatically negate the "private" character of the abortion decision, and that it does not matter whether the fetus is a person or not. *On Reading the Constitution* (Tribe and Dorf 1991) argues against an originalist interpretation of the Constitution.

Laurence Tribe's scholarship is not without its critics, in part because it is about how to litigate specific constitutional questions, not grand theory. Perhaps the most pronounced critic of Tribe's scholarship is Robert Bork, who writes,

> Laurence Tribe's constitutional theory is difficult to describe, for it is protean and takes whatever form is necessary for the moment to reach a desired result. This characteristic, noted by many other commentators, would ordinarily disqualify him for serious consideration as a constitutional theorist. But Tribe's extraordinarily prolific writings and the congeniality of his views to so many in the academic world and in the press have made him a force to be reckoned with in the world of constitutional adjudication." (Bork 1990, 199)

Tribe's stature as a leading constitutional scholar and adjudicator was enhanced by his arguments before the U.S. Supreme Court in the first case of *Bush v. Gore*, 531 U.S. _____, 2000, involving the presidential election results in the state of Florida.

Laurence Tribe's involvement in the most important constitutional and political issues of his times, including his opposition to Judge Bork's appointment to the Supreme Court, and his work as lead counsel in some of the most controversial cases that have ever come before the Supreme Court, makes him perhaps the most gifted constitutional litigator and scholar who has little chance of appointment to the Supreme Court.

— *Ronald Kahn*

Sources and Suggestions for Further Reading

Bork, Robert H. *The Tempting of America: The Political Seduction of the Law*. New York: Free Press, 1990.

Duffy, Michael. "The Raid in Replay." *Time*, 8 May 2000, 39.

www.forbes.com/forbes, 6 November 1995.

Mauro, Tony. "Scholars Views on Arms Rights Anger Liberals." *USA Today*, 27 August 1999, A4.

National Academy of Sciences Panel on Technology Assessment. *Technology: Processes of Assessment and Choice*. Washington, D.C.: U.S. Government Printing Office, 1969.

"Sen. Kennedy's Closed-Door Impeachment Statement. Released into Congressional Record." Allpolitics.com, 12 February 1999. http://www.cnn.com/ALLPOLITICS/stories/1999/02/12/senate.statements/kennedy.html>.

"Transcript: House Debate on Launching Impeachment Inquiry." Allpolitics.com, 8 October 1998, 2. <http://www.cnn.com/ALLPOLITICS/stories/1998/10/08/-impeachment.advancer/transcript2.html>.

Tribe, Laurence. *Abortion: The Clash of Absolutes*. New York: W. W. Norton, 1990.

_____. "The Abortion Funding Conundrum: Inalienable Rights, Affirmative Duties and the Dilemma of Dependence." *Harvard Law Review* 99 (1985): 330.

_____. *American Constitutional Law*. 2d ed. Mineola, N.Y.: Foundation Press, 1988.

_____. *American Constitutional Law*. 3d ed. Vol 1. New York: Foundation Press, 2000.

_____. *Channeling Technology through Law*. Chicago: Bracton Press, 1973.

_____. *Constitutional Choices*. Cambridge: Harvard University Press, 1985.

_____. "The Curvature of Constitutional Space: What Lawyers Can Learn from Modern Physics." *Harvard Law Review* 103 (1989).

_____. *God Save This Honorable Court: How the Choice of Supreme Court Justices Shapes Our History*. New York: Random House, 1985.

_____. "Taking Text and Structure Seriously: Reflections on Free-Form Method in Constitutional Interpretation." *Harvard Law Review* 108 (1995): 1221.

Tribe, Laurence, and Michael C. Dorf. *On Reading the Constitution*. Cambridge: Harvard University Press, 1991.

Tribe, Laurence, and Louis L. Jaffe. *Environmental Protection*. Chicago: Bracton Press, 1971.

Tribe, Laurence, Corinne S. Schelling, and John Voss, eds. *When Values Conflict: Essays on Environmental Analysis, Discourse, and Decision*. Cambridge: Ballinger, 1976.

VAN BUREN, MARTIN

(1782–1862)

BEST KNOWN AS THE EIGHTH president of the United States, Martin Van Buren also enjoyed great success as a lawyer. Van Buren's legal career stretched from 1796, when he was first apprenticed to a lawyer, until 1828, when he stopped practicing law and became a full-time politician. In that period, Van Buren gained a reputation as one of New York's finest attorneys, known especially for his work in the appellate courts. Moreover, Van Buren's biographers agree that his legal work greatly influenced his political career.

Van Buren was born on December 5, 1782, in Kinderhook, New York, a small Dutch town near Albany. His parents, Abraham and Maria Van Buren, operated a small tavern in their home and farmed. Farming had been the way of life for the Van Burens in America for six generations, but Maria Van Buren had other aspirations for her children. As she had done with her two sons from a previous marriage, Maria encouraged Martin to become an attorney. She also helped foster in him a love of politics.

MARTIN VAN BUREN
Library of Congress

686

Van Buren received his only formal education at the village school in Kinderhook. Van Buren long felt inadequate because of his meager schooling, and he tried to make up for it through hard work and self-study. His family's modest means prevented him from attending college. In 1796, the fourteen-year-old Van Buren decided to pursue a legal career and signed on as an apprentice with Francis Silvester, a Kinderhook lawyer.

Few details are known about Van Buren's legal apprenticeship. In a typical arrangement, the apprentice's parents paid the master to train and house their son for a seven-year period. Silvester was known as a capable attorney, but the average small-town lawyer in that period did not own many law books. Van Buren put in long hours and demonstrated a knack for the law, and his mentor gave him increasing responsibility.

An active Federalist—as were most of Kinderhook's residents—Silvester pressured his promising student to join that party. At the risk of harming his career, Van Buren refused, maintaining the firm allegiance to republicanism he had inherited from his father. In 1801, Van Buren's increasing involvement in Republican politics led to a break with Silvester, and he was forced to find another mentor with whom to complete his legal studies. Nevertheless, years later Van Buren described Silvester as "a just and honorable man" (Van Buren 1920, 13).

Van Buren eventually found a position in the New York City law office of William P. Van Ness. Van Buren loved the legal and political activity of New York City, and he became active in the Aaron Burr wing of the Republican party. Beset by financial woes, however, Van Buren returned to Kinderhook in the spring of 1803 to study for the bar examination. On November 23 of that year, Van Buren was examined by three prominent lawyers in New York City. "They declared themselves perfectly and entirely" satisfied, Van Buren reported to a friend, and Van Buren was admitted to the bar thirteen days before his twenty-first birthday (Mushkat and Rayback 1997, 22).

Van Buren then accepted an offer from his half brother, James Van Alen, to join him as a partner in his well-established legal practice in Kinderhook. The practice flourished, and Van Buren's financial problems soon disappeared. Van Buren's skillful handling of cases in the justice of the peace courts, his ability to deal with all kinds of people, and his political activity all helped him attract clients.

In his early years as an attorney, Van Buren focused mainly on small civil cases and commercial transactions, but he also helped Van Alen draft briefs for the appellate courts. Van Buren's small stature (he stood about five feet six inches) and unimpressive voice hampered him in the courtroom, and he was not a particularly eloquent speaker. He compensated for these problems, however, through exhaustive research, careful preparation, and his analytical abilities. His attractive features, erect posture, and sharp dress also enhanced his courtroom image. Van Buren continued his political involvement, earning the approval of DeWitt Clinton, one of New York's leading Republicans. Still, Van Buren made his legal career his top priority during this period, and he was pleased to be earning a nice living.

In 1806, Van Buren won his first public office when the citizens of Kinderhook named him a "fence viewer," which entailed overseeing the boundaries and fences between farms. That same year, Van Buren became licensed to practice before the state supreme court. In November 1806, he argued and won two cases before that court. In 1807, Van Buren married his cousin and childhood sweetheart, Hannah Hoes. The couple had four sons.

In 1808, Van Buren's partnership with Van Alen, who had won election to the U.S. House of Representatives, ended. The Van Burens moved to nearby Hudson, New York, the county seat of Columbia County and home to an array of talented lawyers. Van Buren quickly established a fine legal reputation, and he soon was appointed as county surrogate, the government official responsible for probate and related issues. Not only did this office enable Van Buren to deal with interesting legal issues, but it also put him in contact with many of the county's citizens.

In addition to serving as county surrogate, Van Buren vigorously pursued his own legal practice, including an increasing amount of work before the state's appellate courts. Van Buren faced in court some of the state's finest lawyers, including the noted Federalist attorney Elisha Williams, and he practiced in a variety of courts. His reputation grew so large that Williams and other Federalists sometimes asked him to be co-counsel.

In 1809, Van Buren was involved in a series of court actions on behalf of tenants on some of the large estates in the Hudson Valley. Two years later, he clashed with the powerful Van Rensselaer and Livingston families over the issue of landlord-tenant relations. Van Buren advised a group of tenants that the two families had fraudulently claimed land that really belonged to the state, and he wrote a lengthy report to support his position. Realizing that the courts would probably side with the landowners, Van Buren called on the state legislature to remedy the situation.

Van Buren's stance sparked a bitter political and legal debate, with both sides making public pronouncements and threatening lawsuits. Tensions ran so high that challenges for a duel were traded between Van Buren and John Suydam, a surveyor for the landowners (no duel ever took place). Although the legislature did not act and the issue was not settled until years later, Van Buren's work for the tenants, and against the wealthy landlords, was later used by his political supporters as proof of his affinity for the common man. This image helped him win election to the New York state senate in 1812.

Van Buren also had his eyes on another office—attorney general of New York. Partly because he believed the move would help him attain that office, he supported the 1812 presidential candidacy of DeWitt Clinton, who was then New York's lieutenant governor as well as mayor of New York City. Clinton was a controversial candidate, however, because he opposed the War of 1812 and was challenging an incumbent Republican, James Madison. Clinton won New York's electoral votes, largely because of Van Buren's efforts in the state senate, but he lost the election. Van Buren was not appointed attorney general.

In March 1813, when Van Buren sat as a judge on New York's court of errors (where state senators acted as judges), he issued an important decision in *Barry v. Mandell*, a case that dealt with imprisonment for debt. John W. Barry had been jailed for debt but was released on bond with the provision that he stay within certain boundaries. When Barry chased one of his cows a few feet beyond his boundary, his creditor, Mandell, sued for the amount of Barry's bond and won the case before the state supreme court. After carefully reviewing the case, Van Buren wrote a lengthy judgment criticizing the supreme court's decision and blasting imprisonment for debt, which he called "a practice fundamentally wrong" (Mushkat and Rayback 1997, 76). Debtors were jailed, Van Buren wrote, "for the misfortune of being poor; of being unable to satisfy the all-digesting stomach of some ravenous creditor" (Cole 1984, 25). The other members of the court agreed with Van Buren; the court overturned the supreme court's decision and ordered Mandell to pay Barry's costs.

Van Buren's involvement in *Barry v. Mandell* (which some mockingly referred to as the "cow case") prompted him to deal with the issue of debt in his political life. The month after the case, he introduced in the senate a bill designed to provide some relief for small debtors. The senate did not pass the measure, but Van Buren sponsored similar bills in later sessions and when he was a U.S. senator. His efforts reinforced his image as a man sympathetic to the common person.

In 1814, Van Buren served as a special judge advocate for the prosecution in the court-martial of General William Hull. The general, a hero during the American Revolution, had been called back into service when the War of 1812 began and was put in charge of the army in the West. His job was to invade Canada and protect Michigan, but his invasion failed and he ultimately surrendered Detroit to the British without firing a single shot. He was brought before the court-martial on charges of treason, cowardice, and neglect of duty.

The case drew great attention not only because it involved a military calamity, but because an acquittal for Hull would shift blame for the event to President James Madison and others. After he familiarized himself with the procedures of military justice, Van Buren performed his usual meticulous case preparation. He conducted the prosecution skillfully, presenting more than sixty documents and calling a variety of witnesses. In his summation, Van Buren discounted the charge of treason, calling it "unsupported and insupportable," but hammered Hull on the other charges. The court found Hull guilty and sentenced him to death by firing squad, but recommended that the president grant him clemency in light of his age and service during the Revolution; Madison concurred. Van Buren's work in the difficult case solidified his reputation as a courteous and highly skilled attorney. More important, he gained his first exposure as a national figure.

In the wake of the Hull trial, Van Buren renewed his efforts to be named New York's attorney general. Van Buren was better placed to achieve his desire than he had been two years earlier; he was more widely known because of his legal work and his strong support of the War of 1812 in the New York senate (he had severed his ties with the antiwar Clinton after the election of 1812). Van Buren was especially proud of the classification act he engineered; the measure authorized the state of New York to draft men for service in the war. In early 1815, Van Buren was selected as attorney general. The office enhanced both his legal and political careers, and it secured his position as one of the leading Republicans in New York.

Van Buren exercised a variety of functions as attorney general. His overall mandate, according to the state constitution, was to act as the state's attorney in "all cases where the people of this state shall be interested." Statutes gave the attorney general a range of more specific duties, including checking the state and local governments for malfeasance, ruling on the legality of bail set in certain cases, serving on several state boards, giving the state legislature legal opinions, preparing contracts for the state, and seeing that chartered corporations operated according to the law. His job entailed substantial trial work. These responsibilities, in addition to his continued service in the state senate (he was reelected in 1816) and his private legal practice and business interests, made Van Buren an extremely busy man. His hectic schedule forced him to end the legal partnership he had enjoyed with Cornelius Miller since 1810. He received valuable assistance, however, from his clerk, Benjamin F. Butler (Mushkat and Rayback 1997, 43, 101–103).

In 1816, Van Buren tried to ease his tremendous workload by moving his family to Albany, the state capital. The next year, he made Butler a partner in his private legal practice, which was suffering due to the heavy demands on Van Buren's time. Yet 1817 was a difficult year for Van Buren in both his legal career, because he lost an uncharacteristically high number of cases, and his political career, because DeWitt Clinton—by then a bitter political enemy of Van Buren—won election as governor of New York. Van Buren became the leader of the "Bucktails," Republicans who opposed Clinton.

With Clinton's position strengthened by the elections of 1818, Van Buren realized that he might be removed as attorney general. Nevertheless, he continued his frenetic pace in office. Perhaps his finest legal moment as attorney general came in 1818, when he used the quo warranto writ in an original way; he was the first lawyer to apply that type of writ against a corporation (Mushkat and Rayback 1997, 125–126).

Van Buren faced a series of devastating personal losses in this period. His father died in 1817, followed by his mother in 1818. Then, in February 1819, his wife, Hannah, died of tuberculosis. Van Buren admitted to Butler that Hannah's death had left him in a "delicate" condition (Cole 1984, 53). Van Buren never remarried. Soon after Hannah's death, Butler ended his legal partnership with Van Buren, a crippling blow to his private practice. Finally, in July 1819, Clinton ousted Van Buren as attorney general.

With Van Buren pledging to concentrate on his legal career, he and Butler (who later served as U.S. attorney general under Presidents Jackson and Van Buren) formed a new partnership based in Albany in 1820. Although he did not run for reelection to the state senate in 1820, Van Buren could not forsake politics for long. With the support of the Bucktails, who had become the dominant force in New York Republican politics, Van Buren was elected to the U.S. Senate in 1821.

Van Buren continued to practice law part-time throughout his tenure in the senate, but the time he devoted to the law decreased each year. He became an increasingly important player in national politics, eventually forming an alliance with Andrew Jackson and helping to form the new Democratic party. Van Buren's legal career ended in 1828, when he was elected governor of New York. Van Buren's political career soared; he became President Jackson's secretary of state in 1829, vice-president in 1833, and president in 1837.

Even though frequently preoccupied with politics, Van Buren had been a highly successful lawyer. He won almost 89 percent of his 255 appellate cases and successfully handled innumerable other cases of many types. He won 11 of 21 cases before the court of errors and, as a senator-judge on that court, he wrote 15 opinions. As attorney general, he won another 258 cases. Over the course of his twenty-five-year legal career, he faced hundreds of other attorneys and rose to the top of the crowded and talented New York legal profession (Mushkat and Rayback 1997, 179–180). Van Buren was probably the most accomplished lawyer among the twenty-five (of the first forty-one) presidents who practiced law at some point in their lives (Cole 1984, 25).

Moreover, his legal work facilitated his political career. It helped him achieve public visibility throughout his home state, it provided him with a large income that freed him to pursue politics, it enhanced his sense of security and self-esteem, and it allowed him to develop a sizable network of friends and supporters. More important, perhaps, it was as a lawyer that Van Buren's political ideology, a mixture of classical and liberal republicanism, evolved. Those republican principles—including a belief in limited government, individual liberty, equal opportunity, and antipathy to aristocracy—laid the groundwork for Jacksonian democracy (Mushkat and Rayback 1997, vii, 177–186). Thus, not only did Van Buren's legal career help him launch his political career, it ultimately influenced a movement that transformed the United States.

—*Mark Byrnes*

Sources and Suggestions for Further Reading

Cole, Donald B. *Martin Van Buren and the American Political System*. Princeton: Princeton University Press, 1984.

Mushkat, Jerome, and Joseph G. Rayback. *Martin Van Buren: Law, Politics, and the Shaping of Republican Ideology*. DeKalb: Northern Illinois University Press, 1997.

Niven, John. *Martin Van Buren: The Romantic Age of American Politics*. New York: Oxford University Press, 1983.

Van Buren, Martin. *The Autobiography of Martin Van Buren*. Edited by John C. Fitzpatrick. Washington, D.C.: U.S. Government Printing Office, 1920.

VANDERBILT, ARTHUR T.

(1888–1957)

ARTHUR T. VANDERBILT
Bettmann/Corbis

ALTHOUGH HE IS WIDELY known in American legal circles for his writings, for his work as a law professor and law school dean, for his efforts to bring about judicial reform, and for his service as chief justice of the New Jersey Supreme Court, Arthur T. Vanderbilt is less known for his skills as an attorney. However, his biographer has said that his main contribution to the law was "as a lawyer and not as a judge"; his biographer further referred to Vanderbilt as the "complete lawyer" (Gerhart 1980, 211). There can be little doubt that Vanderbilt's lawyerly skills contributed to his widespread success and that they have earned him a place among the United States' greatest attorneys.

Born in Newark, New Jersey, on July 7, 1888, to Louis and Ellen H. Leach Vanderbilt, Vanderbilt apparently grew up believing that his father—who was a telegraph operator for a railroad—lacked sufficient ambition. Arthur was, however, greatly influenced by his mother, whose Methodist background emphasized hard work and high goals.

Ephraim Tutt

Long before Erle Stanley Gardner invented Perry Mason, Arthur Train had been writing stories about Ephraim Tutt, described as "a combination of Robin Hood, Abraham Lincoln, Puck, and Uncle Sam" (Tutt 1944, xii). Tutt's persona was loosely based on a successful attorney by that name, who was born in Vermont in 1869, graduated from Harvard Law School, and practiced in rural New York and later in New York City.

In Tutt's autobiography, he tells of a case in which he was defending an Italian named Angelo Serafino who was charged with the murder of a man who had once jilted Serafino's wife and who subsequently professed still to be enjoying her favors. In jail, Serafino had bragged, "I killa him—I killa him again."

Tutt had almost no exonerating evidence to go on, and, faced with closing arguments, Tutt had wandered the streets until morning, when he had entered St. Patrick's Cathedral and fallen asleep on one of the back pews. All he could do the next day was to admonish the jury to acquit his client if they had any reasonable doubt.

As the jury deliberated, Serafino shrieked in open court, "I killa that man! He maka small of my wife. He no good—bad egg! I killa him once—I killa him again!"

Tutt's offer to enter a plea to second-degree murder was rejected, and he awaited the inevitable judgment. No one—except perhaps the judge and prosecuting attorney—was more surprised than he when his client was declared not guilty. An Irish juror, Patrick Henry Ross, whom Tutt had hoped to exclude from the jury, explained the verdict:

> At first we couldn't see that there was much to be said for your side of the case, Counsellor; but whin Oi sthepped into St. Patrick's on me way down to court this mornin' and spied ye prayin' there fer guidance, I knew ye wouldn't be defendin' a guilty man, and so we decided to give him the benefit of the doubt. (Tutt 1944, 398–400)

Train's version of this story is entitled "The Human Element" (Train 1940, 1–25).

References

Train, Arthur. *The Adventures of Ephraim Tutt: Attorney and Counsellor-at-Law*. New York: Scribner, 1940.

Tutt, Ephraim. *Yankee Lawyer: The Autobiography of Ephraim Tutt*. New York: Scribner, 1944.

Vanderbilt graduated from high school at age sixteen, and, after a year of work as a surveyor, he attended Wesleyan University in Middleton, Connecticut. There he participated in a variety of activities, including debate, managed the football team, edited the college paper, was active in Delta Kappa Epsilon (in which he would maintain a lifelong interest), served as student body president in his senior year, and won numerous academic awards while simultaneously pursuing his B.A. and M.A. degrees and being selected for Phi Beta Kappa. The college president described Vanderbilt as "the most unusual and gifted undergraduate I have known in all my college experience" (Vanderbilt 1976, 6). Vanderbilt subsequently began clerking for a civic-minded attorney named Frank Sommer, earned his law degree at Columbia Law School, and soon after began many years of teaching at New York University Law School. Unlike many other top students who remained in New York to practice, however, Vanderbilt moved back to Newark, New Jersey, where he was active in state politics until his death.

In 1914, Vanderbilt married Florence Althen, a high school sweetheart who had graduated from the Juilliard School of Music and gave piano lessons. Although he was in a number of early partnerships, Vanderbilt extolled the single practice but apparently worked best in what has been described as a "solar" system of practice, consisting of "a single bright sun, like Arthur T. Vanderbilt, surrounded by satellite young lawyers who are dependent on him and work with him" (Gerhart 1980, 25). In addition to being strongly influenced by his mother, Vanderbilt admired Henry Churchill King's inspirational book *Rational Living* (1905) and the self-help philosophy of Benjamin Franklin.

These influences helped Vanderbilt lead an extremely well-organized life, which enabled him to excel in multiple activities. Vanderbilt's first cases involved debt collection; he earned 5 percent of the seven hundred thousand dollars he collected, being prudent enough to aggregate all his collections together rather than allowing the attorney who hired him to change his fees (Vanderbilt 1976, 18–19). Vanderbilt continued his specialization in bank and insurance litigation and amassed an awesome record by winning all twenty-five cases that he argued before New Jersey's court of errors and appeals (the state's highest court) between 1928 and 1932. His biographer notes that he was soon "regarded as one of the foremost trial lawyers, not only in New Jersey, but in the East" (Gerhart 1980, 36). Other attorneys increasingly referred cases to Vanderbilt, who, between 1927 and 1937, argued more cases before state and federal courts than all but one other New Jersey attorney (Gerhart 1980, 41).

Vanderbilt's most notable win was probably the case of *State v. Butterworth* (1928), in which he defended leaders of a parade during a strike against charges of unlawful assembly. Challenged during his argument for pointing to evidence that was not otherwise in the record that the defendant had been accompanied by two "attractive girls carrying American flags," Vanderbilt quickly responded—to the apparent satisfaction of the court—that "I would assume that the Court would take judicial notice of the fact that any young, American girl leading a parade, carrying the American flag, is an attractive girl" (Gerhart 1980, 37). At age thirty-seven, Vanderbilt received $175,000 in fees for serving as a receiver of the Virginia-Caroline Chemical Company, and he used this money to move to an eighteen-room house in nearby Short Hills to accommodate his family of three girls (two of whom eventually married lawyers) and twin boys (both of whom later became attorneys).

Vanderbilt helped found and served as first president of the Essex County Republican League, an influential organization devoted to "clean government" in Newark and the surrounding Essex County. Noting that some attorneys "will doubtless sneer and say 'politics,'" his own view was that, called by whatever name, politics "represents the only process thus far devised by which society may permanently advance itself" (Gerhart 1980, 58). Successfully backing many candidates for state and local offices, Vanderbilt also served as counsel to Essex County from 1922 to 1947, a job that some regarded as a plum for political service but for which Vanderbilt clearly performed yeoman service (Vanderbilt 1976, 38–39). Vanderbilt was less successful in his role as founder of the Public Fire Insurance Company of Newark, which had a successful beginning but went bankrupt during the Great Depression.

Vanderbilt's participation in politics did not keep him from deepening his knowledge of the law. He served as chair of the New Jersey Judicial Council from 1930 to 1940 and was widely regarded for his expertise in insurance law and for his growing equity practice (Gerhart 1980, 77). Vanderbilt was also chosen as chairman of the National Conference of Judicial Councils and as the chairman for the National Committee on Traffic Law Enforcement. Vanderbilt served as president of the American Bar Association (ABA) from 1937 to 1938, and he flew more than seventy thousand miles during this tenure. The following year he served as president of the American Judicature Society.

As president of the ABA, Vanderbilt helped create the Section of Judicial Administration; Judge John J. Parker chaired this section and issued seven reports, which did much to advance the cause of efficient judicial administration. As ABA president, Vanderbilt also helped push for legislation that resulted in the creation of the Administrative Office of the United States Courts (Gerhart 1980, 131).

Although he was increasingly recognized for his political connections, an English client who hired Vanderbilt for his New Jersey influence only to find the venue changed to Philadelphia was happy when Vanderbilt won the case. The client remarked, "I thought I hired a politician but I am pleased to know I hired a lawyer" (Gerhart 1980, 81).

Vanderbilt was appointed as a member of the Constitution Commission to write a new New Jersey constitution. Although this proposal was rejected in 1944, Vanderbilt helped bring about the proposals that eventually resulted in the New Jersey Constitution of 1947. His successful work in unifying and systematizing the previously antiquated system of New Jersey courts—described as "a hydraheaded monster of confusion for litigants and a legal maze for lawyers" (Vanderbilt 1976, 79)—during this time has been compared to the work of England's Jeremy Bentham and that of New York's David Dudley Field and Roscoe Pound (Gerhart 1980, 85).

In the 1940s, Vanderbilt served as chairman of the advisory committee to draft rules of procedure for criminal cases being argued in U.S. federal district courts—work that eventually resulted in 1946 in the promulgation of the Federal Rules of Criminal Procedure. In 1942, he directed the first Annual Survey of American Law. Vanderbilt also continued his work as a litigator. In 1939, Vanderbilt successfully argued before the U.S. Supreme Court against the expulsion of socialist Norman Thomas from Jersey City in attempts to limit public meetings and union activities in *Hague v. CIO*. In 1945, Vanderbilt further succeeded in *U.S. v. Michener*, a case before a U.S. district court, in acquitting a defendant accused of criminal conspiracy relating to government contracts. Perhaps in part because of his prodigious efforts in this case, as well as his numerous other commitments, Vanderbilt suffered a stroke, which slowed, but did not stop, his work.

Vanderbilt continued to work for improvements in judicial administration. The highlights of the judicial system he proposed for New Jersey called for unification, flexibility, and control over the administration of justice (Gerhart 1980, 153). Vanderbilt also emphasized the importance of pretrial conferences. Many of Vanderbilt's ideas were expressed in his *Cases and Other Materials in Modern Procedure and Judicial Administration* (1952), one of the many books that he authored.

Vanderbilt had begun in 1914 as an instructor at the law school at New York University. By 1918, he was appointed as a professor, and from 1943 to 1948 he served as dean. Vanderbilt was particularly concerned about prelegal education, and he was convinced that lawyers needed to engage in continual "self-education." Citing Ben Jonson, Vanderbilt said that

"It is not growing like a tree. In bulk, doth make men better be." Knowledge is only worth while when it has been assimilated and thus made usable. The capacity to work hard, the ability to think straight, training in expressing oneself well both orally and in writing, the understanding and sympathy with people one meets, a social consciousness, a keen interest in life, are more important than any amount of knowledge. (Gerhart 1980, 264–265)

Despite his own emphasis on other roles, Vanderbilt noted that "lawyers carry on a wide variety of activities but in the final analysis the advocate representing his client in court typifies the profession, for it is in the courts and other tribunals that the rights which the law protects must be vindicated" (Gerhart 1980, 192). Vanderbilt is credited with inventing the concept of the "law center," emphasizing continuing education (the building that now houses this center at New York University, and for which Vanderbilt helped raise funds, now bears his name), and he also established honors courses at New York University.

After New Jersey adopted its new constitution, it was only logical that Vanderbilt would be asked in 1948 to serve as the state supreme court's first chief justice (the court had seven members), a position that required him to step down as dean at New York University. As would be expected, Vanderbilt issued a number of important decisions during his tenure as chief justice. The court's most controversial decision highlighted the fact that Vanderbilt's most important contribution as chief justice was in his continuing effort to promote sound judicial administration. The case, *Winberry v. Salisbury* (1947), involved the interpretation of the provision in the New Jersey state constitution granting the supreme court the power "to make rules governing the administration of all courts in the State and, subject to law, the practice and procedure of all such courts" (Gerhart 1980, 237). Although his decision appeared to be in conflict with the arguments he had made concerning the phrase "subject to law" when the constitution was being argued, Vanderbilt now argued that this phrase referred not to the power of the state legislature but to the supreme court itself. Thus ruling in favor of the power of his court, Vanderbilt ensured that the judicial branch would maintain its independence.

As chief justice, Vanderbilt sought to ensure that the *Canons of Judicial Ethics* were enforced throughout the state. Lower courts were required to establish uniform hours and to fill out what critics called judicial "report cards" indicating how quickly they were resolving cases. When a number of such judges suffered heart attacks, Vanderbilt was criticized for having driven them too hard. Asked whether Vanderbilt might be named as the replacement for Chief Justice Frederick Vinson on the U.S. Supreme Court (the position went to Earl Warren, to whom President Dwight Eisenhower had promised it), Justice Felix Frankfurter reflected the view that Vanderbilt was "a pompous martinet who treats his court as though it were a factory where men punch clocks" (Gerhart 1980, 231). The fact that one of the judges who worked on the New Jersey court with Vanderbilt was William Brennan, who later had such a distinguished career on the U.S. Supreme Court, is one indication that Frankfurter's critique, while reflecting elements of truth, was wide of the mark.

Just as he promoted judicial efficiency, so too Vanderbilt was willing to use his decisions to adapt the law to the times (Schwartz 1993, 496). Vanderbilt ruled on a fairly consistent basis that legal certainty, or stare decisis, should be subordinate to the need for social justice. A grandson has described the "common thread" running through Vanderbilt's decisions as chief justice as the attempt

> to make the substantive law of New Jersey suitable to contemporary conditions by pushing aside procedural or technical intricacies and discarding legal doctrines, no matter how ancient or revered, that were no longer compatible with a modern court system or with the economic and social realities of the new age. (Vanderbilt 1976, 198)

Vanderbilt appears to have been more conservative in adapting criminal laws than in adopting new rules of civil liability. Vanderbilt thus failed to extend the lawyer-client privilege to conferences believed to involve the defense of gangsters. This opinion led a biographer to observe that "many lawyers felt that on issues of this kind Vanderbilt let his noble desire to reach a particularly felicitous end of which he approved, dictate the law" (Gerhart 1980, 261).

Vanderbilt received many honors during his life, including thirty-two honorary degrees (including one from Princeton University in New Jersey), the American Bar Association Medal, the Gold Medal of the New York State Bar Association, the Golden Anniversary Award of the American Judicature Society, and the Columbia University Award. He was also named in 1950 as the Outstanding Citizen of New Jersey (Gerhart 1980, 262–263).

Vanderbilt's devotion to the law has been described as being "religious" in nature (Gerhart 1980, 277). Often called a "lawyer's lawyer" (Gerhart 1980, 285), Vanderbilt had an excellent memory for details, was well organized, prepared for cases thoroughly, had a deep sense of public service, and wrote briefs and opinions clearly. THOMAS E. DEWEY described Vanderbilt as

> a man with a twinkle in his eye—a man with two tough fists and a sharp tongue who could go in and fight harder and better than anybody else around him when it was necessary for a client or for a cause. He was a man who selected his causes with wisdom and then gave them a degree of vigor and imagination which has rarely been equaled in our history. (Vanderbilt 1976, xii)

Vanderbilt's motto has been described as "organize, delegate, supervise" (Gerhart 1980, 290). Had he not been able to follow this motto so closely, it is unlikely that he could have accomplished all that he did before dying on June 16, 1957, three days after rupturing his aorta. Former U.S. Supreme Court justice Lewis Powell noted that Vanderbilt's "contributions to the improvement of judicial administration . . . will rank among the great achievements of American lawyers" (Gerhart 1980, vii). Similarly, Justice

William Brennan, who had worked with Vanderbilt on the New Jersey Supreme Court, observed at his death that "his contribution toward improvement of judicial administration and substantive law are an imperishable monument to his memory" (Gerhart 1980, 296).

—*John R. Vile*

Sources and Suggestions for Further Reading

Gerhart, Eugene C. *Arthur T. Vanderbilt: The Compleat Counsellor.* Albany: Q Corporation, 1980.

Schwartz, Bernard. *Main Currents in American Legal Thought.* Durham, N.C.: Carolina Academic Press, 1993.

Vanderbilt, Arthur T., II. *Changing Law: A Biography of Arthur T. Vanderbilt.* New Brunswick, N.J.: Rutgers University Press, 1976.

WEBSTER, DANIEL

(1782–1852)

DANIEL WEBSTER
Library of Congress

DANIEL WEBSTER, BEST RE-membered for his powerful advocacy and staunch defense of the federal union, maintained a wide-ranging law practice. Webster played a major role in shaping constitutional jurisprudence, and at the height of his practice, from 1819 to 1827, he participated in many leading cases interpreting the contract clause and the commerce clause of the U.S. Constitution. He also litigated numerous private cases, dealing primarily with real property and commercial issues.

Webster's practice covered almost every class of case, including civil and criminal, law and equity, trial and appellate. He appeared in state courts at every level, as well as in federal district and circuit courts and the U.S. Supreme Court. Webster generally represented propertied interests and advocated national supremacy over state power. Many of his clients were corporations, such as insurance companies, banks, railroads, and shipping houses. The Bank of the United States kept him on annual retainer, as did other companies.

He viewed the judiciary as a necessary check on legislative power, and he even spoke against the doctrine of judicial self-restraint, urging that courts should not defer to legislatures because they had a duty to decide the validity of statutes.

Daniel Webster was born in January 1782 to Ebenezer and Abigail Webster. His father was a New Hampshire pioneer who raised a large family in Salisbury, New Hampshire, about twenty miles north of Concord. In 1796, at age fourteen, Webster attended Phillips Academy, studying Latin and Greek. The next year, he entered Dartmouth College, and after graduating in August 1801, he became a clerk in the law office of his father's neighbor in Salisbury, Thomas W. Thompson. This clerkship was interrupted in December 1801 when Webster helped to finance his older brother's college education. Webster left in early 1802 to teach at Fryeburg Academy in Maine. He returned to his clerkship in September 1802 to continue studying law.

In July 1804, Webster left Thompson's office to join his brother, Ezekiel, in Boston. There he secured a clerkship in the office of Christopher Gore, and in the spring of 1804, Webster was admitted to the Massachusetts bar. Soon after, he moved back to New Hampshire to open a law office in Boscawen, which was near his father's farm. His practice in Boscawen from 1805 to 1807 dealt primarily with debt collection and disputes over promissory notes. Webster primarily represented creditors. During this time, he also began to represent Boston merchants, a practice he continued throughout his professional life. When collecting debts for these merchants against local proprietors with failing businesses, he helped to create arrangements among creditors who claimed the same property of the debtor. His debt cases by nature involved property law, which became another continuing aspect of his practice.

In late 1807, Ezekiel took over the Boscawen office and Webster moved to Portsmouth, New Hampshire, taking his Boston clients with him. The first few years of his Portsmouth practice were similar to that of his Boscawen experience, consisting primarily of debt collections. But by 1816, he had begun to handle more contract litigation cases. These contract cases focused on express or implied agreements involving loans, goods, or services. Moreover, he started to handle maritime issues, naturally arising from Portsmouth's status as eastern New Hampshire's principal port, and from 1814 to 1819 he concentrated on admiralty cases.

Webster continued a strong maritime practice throughout his career. He argued cases dealing with prize issues, liability for cargo losses, and liability for accidents aboard ships. An important maritime case he tried in a lower federal court was *United States v. La Jeune Eugenie* (1822). A U.S. naval officer seized the ship off the coast of West Africa because it appeared to be equipped for transporting slaves. He sent the vessel to Boston, where the

French owners faced charges of participation in the slave trade, which the United States had outlawed. Webster, appearing on behalf of the United States and the captor, contended that slave trade was against the law of nature, which he asserted was part of the law of nations. Since the civilized countries of the world had banned such trade in humans, Webster argued that the French owners had violated international law. Justice Joseph Story, in the circuit court, agreed with Webster, castigated the international slave trade, and ruled that the vessel was subject to condemnation.

In 1816, Webster moved to Boston, where he continued to practice in both state and federal court, focusing on debtor-creditor issues. His early practice also included appearing for Boston merchants and insurance companies before the Spanish Claims Commission in Washington. In 1819, the United States and Spain signed the Adams-Onis Treaty, which arose partly as a result of claims concerning Spain's seizure of U.S. ships. The treaty provided for a three-member commission of U.S. citizens to resolve these U.S. claims. Webster filed more than two hundred claims with the commission during the its three-year existence from 1821 to 1824.

While maintaining his practice in commercial law, Webster began to handle property, marine insurance, corporate, and patent cases. An example of Webster's property law practice was *Drake v. Curtis* (1848). The defendant's predecessor had built a wharf on the plaintiff's shoreline property in Massachusetts. Curtis claimed title to the land by adverse possession. He had bought the land, including the wharf, from Jabez Hatch. Drake owned the adjoining land and eventually discovered that he held title to the land that Curtis had bought. Drake was sued to recover the land. The jury determined that Curtis owned the wharf and the immediately surrounding shore, but that the rest of the property described in Curtis's title belonged to Drake because Curtis had not "used" this land as required for adverse possession. Webster represented Curtis in his appeal to the Massachusetts Supreme Judicial Court. Webster's argument combined the facts that Curtis had partially occupied the land, that Drake had not attempted to occupy any part of it for thirty years, and that Drake had knowledge of Curtis's use and intent to possess, hoping that this combination of facts would be enough to prove title by adverse possession. However, the court affirmed the jury's verdict for Drake.

In addition to his law practice, Webster had an active career in public service. He was nominated for the presidency by Massachusetts Whigs in 1836, but he received electoral support only in New England. Twice appointed U.S. secretary of state, Webster served in that post from 1841 to 1843 and again between 1850 and 1852.

In November 1812, Webster was elected to the U.S. House of Representatives and served in this capacity from 1813 to 1817. He was a member of the Massachusetts House of Representatives in 1822, and returned to the U.S. House of Representatives in 1823 as a representative from Massachusetts, serving until 1829. He also represented Massachusetts in the U.S. Senate from 1827 to 1841 and from 1845 to 1850.

Webster maintained his practice of law while serving as a member of Congress, and he took advantage of being in Washington by arguing cases before the U.S. Supreme Court. In fact, he was admitted to practice before the Supreme Court in 1814 and made his first appearance in the same year. He argued 168 cases before the Supreme Court, winning about half of them.

The effectiveness of Webster's advocacy can be traced to several sources. He prepared arguments carefully, and he aimed his presentation to match the predilections of the judges before whom he appeared. Moreover, at a time when the Supreme Court had no time limit for oral argument, Webster's masterful oratory could hold the attention of the Court for hours. Twenty-four of the cases Webster argued before the Supreme Court raised constitutional questions. Of his Supreme Court practice, Webster's cases concerning the scope of the contract clause provide the most insight into his ability for creative legal argument.

The *Dartmouth College* case (1819), Webster's first well-known Supreme Court case, involved the contract clause. The college was founded during the colonial era with a royal charter. The New Hampshire legislature in 1816 enacted a law that changed the governmental structure of the college, transforming it into a state institution. The trustees of the original college brought suit in state court against a former trustee who had joined the newly created university for the return of the charter, records, and seal. Webster was one of the college's counsel, and he argued that Dartmouth was a private corporation. He maintained that the charter was a contract with the state, and thus the legislature had no power to amend its charter.

Acting as lead attorney before the U.S. Supreme Court on an appeal from an adverse state court ruling, Webster focused on corporate rights at common law. He emphasized that the state constitution's due process clause protected the property rights of the trustees and the president to govern the institution. He also asserted that the contract clause of the U.S. Constitution prohibited the New Hampshire legislation because the charter of a private corporation was a contract with the issuing state. Describing Dartmouth College, Webster famously declared: "It is, sir, as I have said, a small college. And yet there are those who love it" (Stites 1972, 1).

Vindicating Webster's position, Chief Justice JOHN MARSHALL held that the college was a private corporation and that New Hampshire had unconstitutionally impaired the obligation of the contract between the corporation and the state.

Daniel Webster as Mythological Hero

Daniel Webster most certainly ranks among America's greatest lawyer-statesmen. One measure of his fame is the manner in which he has been immortalized in a story by Stephen Vincent Benét entitled *The Devil and Daniel Webster* (Benét 1937).

The story describes a mythological case in which Webster defends New Hampshire citizen Jabez Stone. In the story, Stone had sold his soul to the devil in exchange for prosperity for his family and himself, and he now faces Scratch (the Devil) who comes to collect his part of the bargain. The contest is portrayed much as a contest of equals; at one point Satan is described as "the King of Lawyers" (Benét 1937, 38).

The exchange between Webster and the Devil goes relatively poorly for Webster (after all, Stone had signed a contract) until the Devil, noting his presence when Indians were first wronged and Africans were first loaded on ships to America, claims American citizenship. Webster then demands a jury trial; in what must be every lawyer's nightmare, the Devil literally brings in a jury from hell presided over by the most fanatical judge in the Salem Witch Trials.

Although the Webster of history is generally known for the overpowering intensity of his oratory, in Benét's story, Webster realizes just before he gives his closing statement that he will lose the case if he resorts to the devil's own tools and is motivated by hate (Benét 1937, 48). Just in time, Webster alters his strategy and speaks to the jury in a low voice of "the simple things that everybody's known and felt" (Benét 1937, 49) and especially about what it means to be a man. Thus managing to touch the hearts even of the judge and jury from hell, Webster gains a victory, albeit "not strictly in accordance with the evidence" (Benét 1937 55).

Reference

Benét, Stephen Vincent. *The Devil and Daniel Webster*. New York: Holt, Rinehart & Winston, 1937.

In *McCulloch v. Maryland* (1819), Webster served as counsel for the Bank of the United States. Maryland had levied a tax on all banks in the state that were not chartered by the legislature. The Baltimore branch of the Bank of the United States refused to comply, and the state sued the branch cashier. Webster argued that Congress had the authority to charter a bank, and that the state tax interfered with the execution of a national law. This contention prevailed. Chief Justice Marshall upheld the authority of Congress to create a national bank and relied on the U.S. Constitution's supremacy clause to invalidate the Maryland bank tax.

Another significant contract clause case handled by Webster was *Ogden v. Saunders* (1827). The issue was whether states had the power to enact bankruptcy legislation affecting future contracts. Webster contended that the national bankruptcy power excluded concurrent state bankruptcy power, and also argued that the state law was invalid due to its violation of the contract clause. Webster's position was that the contract clause forbade legislation whenever it discharged the debtor's liability to pay its debt. However, the Court held that the contract clause only applied retrospectively to protect existing contracts. Chief Justice Marshall, in his only dissent in a constitutional case, agreed with Webster's argument.

In *Charles River Bridge v. Warren Bridge* (1837), the Massachusetts legislature incorporated the Charles River Bridge Company to build a toll bridge, conferring on the company the right to collect tolls for forty years. Later, the legislature incorporated the Warren Bridge Company to build a free bridge. Webster argued the case in the Massachusetts Supreme Court for the Charles River Bridge Company, concluding that it had the exclusive right to a bridge over the river from Boston to Charlestown, under its charter. He classified the charter as a contract obligating Massachusetts not to effectively destroy the value of the plaintiff's right to collect tolls. Thus, the state had violated the contract clause. He also asserted that the state had taken the company's property without compensation, violating the eminent domain clause of the state constitution. The court was split on the validity of the statute granting the Warren Bridge charter. Webster appealed, but the U.S. Supreme Court rejected his argument and ruled that legislative grants should be strictly construed to preserve state police power.

Webster was counsel in several cases from 1824 to 1849 in which the courts analyzed the unsettled issue of the division of state and national power over commerce. He advocated maximum national power, preferably exclusive of state authority. Webster urged his views in *Gibbons v. Ogden* (1824), the first commerce clause case in constitutional history. Representing Gibbons before the Supreme Court, Webster opposed a New York state–granted steamboat monopoly in state waters that had been granted to two men, of which Aaron Ogden was an assignee. He insisted that national power to regulate interstate commerce was exclusive. Since Gibbons held a license under the Federal Coasting Act of 1793, Webster also argued that this license conferred a right freely to navigate the waters of the United States because federal statutes were superior to inconsistent state laws. Although the Supreme Court stopped short of endorsing Webster's claim of exclusive federal jurisdiction over interstate commerce, it construed the federal license to nullify the New York steamboat monopoly.

In *Smith v. Turner* and *Norris v. Boston* (1849), known as the *Passenger Cases*, Webster, along with RUFUS CHOATE, represented the plaintiffs against the states of New York and Massachusetts, which were represented by John Davis. The states had enacted laws to tax alien passengers arriving at their ports, with the intent to protect the eastern states from infiltration by undesirable persons. The western states viewed this as an unjustified regulation of foreign commerce, which prevented them from attracting immigrants. Webster based his argument on the federal commerce clause, maintaining that Congress had the exclusive power to regulate national commerce, and thus Massachusetts was interfering with national commerce by taxing passengers. Webster's arguments proved persuasive. The Court invalidated the statutes as violations of the commerce clause of the U.S. Constitution but had difficulty articulating the basis for its decision.

As his practice grew, Webster handled more cases dealing with property rights, including real property and intellectual property, and at least one state boundary dispute. In 1846, he successfully represented Massachusetts before the Supreme Court in a boundary dispute with Rhode Island. An important case involving real property ownership was *Johnson v. McIntosh* (1823). Webster represented the plaintiff, who had purchased land in Illinois from Indians, against the defendant, who had later purchased the same land from the U.S. government. The Court held that Johnson's title was invalid because the Indians' rights to land were subordinate to the title established by discovery of North America by European countries. A defeat for Webster, *Johnson* was the initial Supreme Court decision to define the relationship between Indians and the government.

In the later years of his practice, Webster represented patent and copyright claimants. In *Wheaton v. Peters* (1834), he handled Henry Wheaton's appeal before the Supreme Court. Peters planned to publish a condensed work of Wheaton's reports of U.S. Supreme Court cases. Wheaton asserted a copyright in his work, and Webster argued that English common law conferred such right on Wheaton. The majority rejected this argument and held that Wheaton had not complied with Congressional copyright laws and could not assert a common law copyright. The ruling established the principle that copyright protection rested solely on a statutory foundation. Similarly, in *Pennock v. Dialogue* (1829), Webster argued for broad protection for inventors, urging the Supreme Court to recognize the natural rights of inventors. The Court, however, held that claimants must comply with the federal statute to gain patent protection.

Webster gave his last full-scale oral argument in *Goodyear v. Day* (1852), a patent case in which Charles Goodyear, the inventor of a process for vulcanizing rubber, sought to enjoin an infringement of his patent. The defendant was represented by Rufus Choate, and the case was heard in the federal circuit court in Trenton, New Jersey. The court held for Goodyear and established a rule that was important for patent claimants generally. Webster convinced the court that instead of presenting the issue to a jury, the court, as a matter of equity practice, could make findings of fact and grant an injunction. Webster viewed this as a victory because he thought inventors' rights were better protected by judges than by juries sympathetic to assertions of monopoly power against patent holders.

Webster died in Marshfield, Massachusetts, on October 24, 1852.

—James W. Ely Jr.

SOURCES AND SUGGESTIONS FOR FURTHER READING

Baxter, Maurice G. *Daniel Webster & the Supreme Court*. Amherst: University of Massachusetts Press, 1966.

_____. *The Steamboat Monopoly: Gibbons v. Ogden, 1824*. New York: Alfred A. Knopf, 1972.

Ely, James W., Jr. *The Guardian of Every Other Right: A Constitutional History of Property Rights*. 2d ed. New York: Oxford University Press, 1998.

Stites, Francis N. *Private Interest & Public Gain: The Dartmouth College Case, 1819*. Amherst: University of Massachusetts Press, 1972.

Webster, Daniel. *The Papers of Daniel Webster: Legal Papers*. Vol. 1, *The New Hampshire Practice*, edited by Alfred S. Konefsky and Andrew J. King. Hanover, N.H.: University Press of New England, 1982.

_____. *The Papers of Daniel Webster: Legal Papers*. Vol. 2, *The Boston Practice*, edited by Alfred S. Konefsky and Andrew J. King. Hanover, N.H.: University Press of New England, 1983.

_____. *The Papers of Daniel Webster: Legal Papers*. Vol. 3, Parts 1 and 2, *The Federal Practice*, edited by Andrew J. King. Hanover, N.H.: University Press of New England, 1989.

WILLEBRANDT, MABEL WALKER

(1889–1963)

MABEL WALKER WILLEBRANDT
Library of Congress

MABEL WALKER WILLEBRANDT served as a U.S. assistant attorney general from 1921 to 1929 with jurisdiction over prohibition cases, federal income and estate taxes, prisons, and war risk insurance. Dubbed "Prohibition Portia," she focused primarily on enforcing prohibition laws by prosecuting major bootleggers. After leaving the Justice Department, Willebrandt turned her attention to defining and developing aviation law, serving as the Washington counsel for the Aviation Corporation and chairing the Committee on Aeronautical Law of the American Bar Association, the first woman to head an American Bar Association committee. At the same time, Willebrandt worked in communication law, another relatively new legal field, as well as international claims and tax law. Throughout the 1940s and 1950s, many of her clients were famous Hollywood actors, directors, and film executives.

Born Mabel Elizabeth Walker on May 23, 1889, the only child of Myrtle Eaton and David W. Walker, Willebrandt began life in the southwest Kansas frontier town of Woodsdale. Until 1902, when the family settled in Kansas City, they led a nomadic life, moving from Kansas to Putnam County, Missouri, to Blackwell, Oklahoma, and back to Putnam County. During these early years of Willebrandt's life, her father worked as a printer and newspaper editor, and both parents taught in local schools. Before the move to Kansas City, Willebrandt received little formal schooling; instead, her parents taught her to read, set type for the newspaper, and work on the farm. They worked to develop Willebrandt's character and relied on local church services to impart religious training. In Kansas City, Willebrandt completed grammar school and took some courses at Manual Training High School. In September 1906, she began further study at Park College and Academy in Parkville, Missouri, but she left in 1907 after disagreeing with the school's president on religious doctrine and resisting the strict rules of the Presbyterian-based school. She then moved with her family to Buckley, Michigan, so that her father could care for his ailing mother. During the next two years, Willebrandt passed the teachers' examination, taught in a nearby county school and in the Buckley grammar and high schools, and studied during the summer at Ferris Institute in Big Rapids, Michigan. On February 7, 1910, she married the school principal, Arthur F. Willebrandt, in Grand Rapids, Michigan, and moved with him to Arizona in his effort to regain his health after suffering from pneumonia and the threat of tuberculosis.

During two years in Arizona, Willebrandt earned a diploma from Tempe Normal School while she nursed Arthur back to health. In 1912, the couple moved to Los Angeles, where Mabel worked as both teacher and principal in area schools and, along with Arthur, studied at the College of Law of the University of Southern California. In 1916, she earned her LL.B. and was admitted to the bar, opened a private practice with law school friends Fred Horowitz and John Shepard, continued her earlier work as an assistant to the city's police court defender's office handling women's cases, and worked toward an LL.M., which she earned the following year. In 1916, she and Arthur also separated and eventually divorced in 1924.

In private practice, Willebrandt refused to take criminal or divorce cases, focusing instead on civil cases that tended to benefit the underdog. During World War I she won a sedition case when she defended an elderly woman accused of speaking against the government. She also offered legal advice and help in contacting family members to women arrested for vagrancy near the army camp established in Los Angeles during the war. Yet even in the early years of her practice, she also served as counsel for a bank, handling land ownership cases, mortgage foreclosures, damage suits, and guardianship cases. As a new lawyer, Willebrandt was not afraid to challenge authority, as evidenced by her request for and the granting of a change of venue when a well-known judge discussed details of the case with attorneys over lunch before the trial began.

Besides deciding early in her career the type of law she would practice, Willebrandt also determined that she had a special role to play as a woman attorney. She joined Phi Delta Delta, a legal fraternity begun by five women students at the College of Law shortly before she began her studies at the school. In 1918, Willebrandt was instrumental in founding the Women Lawyers' Club in Los Angeles County, a small but influential organization that expanded on the work of Phi Delta Delta and sought to help women lawyers in working with the traditional male-dominated Los Angeles courts. In keeping with her belief that she had a responsibility to participate in civic and political life, Willebrandt also joined a number of professional women's clubs that focused on legislative issues, including passage of a married woman's property bill. Although she opposed a political office for herself, Willebrandt's support of progressive Republican party politics in California throughout the 1910s earned her the appointment as a U.S. assistant attorney general in 1921. Serving under several attorneys general during her eight-year tenure, her most significant long-term impact occurred in the area of prison reform. There she oversaw the improvement of conditions in federal penitentiaries, provided for prison industries, and won authorization and appropriations for the first federal prison for women at Alderson, West Virginia.

Yet Willebrandt concentrated on upholding the Eighteenth Amendment, with over 50 percent of her division's forty thousand yearly cases dealing with prohibition. She led a multipronged approach toward making the country dry that included attempts to stop the illegal smuggling, production, and distribution of alcohol as well as illegal activities of corrupt politicians. She worked closely with the Treasury Department to arrest and prosecute smugglers and bootleggers for violating the Volstead Act and for income tax evasion. In 1923, she focused on ending the illegal activities of the biggest offenders, including "the King of the Bootleggers," Willie Haar, the leader of a four-family smuggling operation known as the Savannah Four. Although she did not personally argue the case against them, choosing instead White B. Miller, a southern lawyer, as prosecutor, Willebrandt worked carefully behind the scenes to win indictments from the grand jury against the Savannah Four. She followed the same procedure in pursuing bootleggers in the Mobile, Alabama, area when she chose Hugo Black from Birmingham to head the prosecution that resulted in the conviction of five members of the Mobile Big Six.

Willebrandt also sought to stop the illegal flow of alcohol from distilleries, breweries, and warehouses. Her most successful case in this effort was

Abortion Crusaders: Sarah Weddington and Linda Coffee

Great lawyers are often identified by the significance of the cases they argued. Most of the lawyers singled out for full essays in this volume have established their reputations through many cases, but there are some lawyers who have appropriately gained notoriety from a single important case.

Proponents and opponents of abortion rights would have to agree that there has been no more important case on the subject than *Roe v. Wade* (1973), in which the U.S. Supreme Court decided that women had the constitutional right of privacy, at least to the point of fetal viability, to seek abortions. This case was brought by Sarah Weddington, then a recent graduate of the law school of the University of Texas at Austin, and a former classmate, Linda Coffee, whom Weddington recruited to make up for her own lack of knowledge about making federal appeals. Weddington and Coffee took the case of Jane Roe (a pseudonym for Norma McCorvey), an unmarried woman with one child who was being raised by McCorvey's mother, and who was seeking an abortion—then prohibited by Texas law. After undergoing a religious conversion, Norma McCorvey now opposes abortion, but Weddington and Coffee continue to fight for what they believe to be an important right.

Weddington, the daughter of a Methodist minister who as a law student had obtained an abortion in Mexico at a time when the procedure was illegal in Texas, has written a book describing her role in this case and defending her pro-choice views. She has been the subject of a made-for-television movie (*Roe v. Wade*) that was first played in 1989, and she was among those who testified against the confirmation of Clarence Thomas as a Supreme Court justice.

REFERENCE

Weddington, Sarah. *A Question of Choice*. New York: Putnam, 1992.

---

the prosecution and conviction of George Remus, a Chicago lawyer, who oversaw an illegal alcohol distribution operation that netted him over $6 million in just a few years. In this case, Willebrandt insisted through an appeal that Remus be subject to the stiffer penalties for tax evasion on liquor sold for beverage purposes rather than the weaker Volstead statutes. In an October 1922 decision, the Supreme Court supported her argument.

Willebrandt participated more directly in the trials to prosecute corrupt politicians. In the case of Kentucky congressman John W. Langley, indicted and found guilty of conspiracy for bootlegging whiskey from a local distillery, Willebrandt cross-examined witnesses and addressed the jury in the trial's summation. In 1925, she prosecuted an Ohio conspiracy case that involved the state prohibition director and his assistant, and allegations that illegal money had ended up in the Warren G. Harding campaign fund. Believing "that the case was her responsibility," Willebrandt examined witnesses and presented an argument that not only won praise from both the judge and the defense lawyer but also gained her a guilty verdict (Brown 1984, 69).

Yet Willebrandt believed that winning cases was "much less important than clarifying the law." To this end, she argued more than forty cases before the Supreme Court, submitting 278 petitions for a certiorari by 1929 (Willebrandt 1929, 239). Willebrandt was instrumental in obtaining numerous decisions that represented "permanent gains in the government's huge task of enforcing the Eighteenth Amendment" (Willebrandt, 1929, 249). These included the *Grace and Ruby*, 283 F. 475 (1922), case, which allowed the U.S. government to seize a foreign vessel beyond the agreed-upon three-mile territorial limit if that vessel had made a "constructive entry" into U.S. territory through the use of smaller boats or dories, crew, and tackle to facilitate the landing of alcohol on U.S. shores. In an attempt to strengthen enforcement, Willebrandt also successfully argued before the Supreme Court in *Donnelley v. United States* (1928) that the prohibition law was intended to punish not only people who committed crimes against the law but also omissions by prohibition agents who failed to report and prosecute these crimes. In addition, Willebrandt, believing that she could deter bootleggers by punishing them financially and making crime less profitable, argued successfully in 1928 in *United States v. Manley Sullivan* that income tax was due on illegally gained money. She also argued and won *Carroll v. U.S.* (1925), a decision that determined that federal agents could stop and search a car if they "observed enough to be reasonably certain of its violation of law" (Willebrandt, 1929, 239). Although Willebrandt was ultimately proved wrong, she believed these various decisions provided the necessary foundation on which "orderly enforcement" of the prohibition law would be built. She considered them "a permanent contribution to the development of constitutional law" (Willebrandt, 1929, 249).

Similarly in the area of tax law, Willebrandt's division in the Justice Department sought to clarify the implications and limits of federal taxing power. Although most of her appearances before the Supreme Court on tax issues related to prohibition, she argued tax cases that she believed would set a new interpretation or extension of the relatively new tax laws. She eventually served as a member of the Taxation Committee of the American Bar Association, a reflection of her increasing knowledge in the field.

Throughout her tenure as an assistant attorney general, Willebrandt hoped for an appointment to a federal judgeship. When this failed to materialize by the time Herbert Hoover took office in 1929, Willebrandt, with an offer to serve as Washington counsel for the Aviation Corporation, resigned her position and left the Justice Department in June 1929. She quickly established a private legal practice with offices in both Washington, D.C., and California, serving a variety of clients. Her work for the Aviation Corporation focused first on aiding in the drafting of legislation to regulate the young air industry. The McNary-Watres Act resulted and dealt primarily with regulation of airmail rates and routes. In 1931, Willebrandt filed an amicus curiae brief for the Aviation Corporation in *Swetland v. Curtiss Airports Corp.* in the U.S. Court of Appeals for the Sixth Circuit. In her highly praised brief, she compiled the first comprehensive review of common law and state and national statutes on control of air space. Soon recognized as one of the leaders in the field of aviation law, Willebrandt chaired the American Bar Association Committee on Aeronautical Law from 1938 to 1942 (Brown 1984, 201–203).

Willebrandt also moved into the area of communication law after she left the Justice Department. She first served in an advisory position in cases dealing with patent law. Then in 1933 she successfully argued before the Supreme Court in *Federal Radio Commission v. Nelson Brothers Bond & Mortgage* that the Federal Radio Commission had the power to regulate broadcasting. In part because of her California connections and a long friendship with Louis B. Mayer, Willebrandt also represented Metro-Goldwyn-Mayer (MGM), focusing on federal regulation, tax issues, and public relations in Washington. Her association with MGM brought her many famous Hollywood clients, and in 1938 she represented the Screen Directors Guild in the organization's labor struggles with producers. Her association with the guild continued throughout the 1940s, and in 1950, in the midst of the Red Scare, Willebrandt drafted the guild's loyalty oath.

Although Willebrandt continued to follow a heavy work schedule throughout the 1950s, including active participation in Republican party politics, she focused much of her attention on her family life. After the death of her mother in 1938, Willebrandt spent more time with her aging father, sharing a home with him in Temple City, California, and carving out time to vacation with him. David Walker died in 1954. Willebrandt's daughter, Dorothy, whom Willebrandt adopted in 1925 when Dorothy was two years old, was married with a family of her own by the 1950s. Willebrandt kept in close contact with her daughter and son-in-law, Hendrick Van Dyke, and their three sons. During this time, Willebrandt's health steadily declined due in part to a chronic ear problem that increasingly affected both her balance and her hearing. She argued her last case in February 1962 and shortly afterward closed her law practice. Willebrandt died of lung cancer on April 6, 1963, in her home in Riverside, California.

—*Janice M. Leone*

Brown, Dorothy M. *Mabel Walker Willebrandt—A Study of Power, Loyalty, and Law.* Knoxville: University of Tennessee Press, 1984.

Harris, Mary Belle. *I Knew Them in Prison.* New York: Viking Press, 1936.

Martin, John S. "Mrs. Firebrand." *New Yorker*, 16 February 1929, 23–26.

Obituary. *Los Angeles Times*, 8 April 1963.

Obituary. *New York Times*, 9 April 1963.

Strakosch, Avery. "A Woman in Law." *Saturday Evening Post*, 24 September 1927, 17, 190–198.

"Who's Who—and Why." *Saturday Evening Post*, 27 September 1924, 74, 102.

Willebrandt, Mabel Walker. *The Inside of Prohibition.* Indianapolis: Bobbs-Merrill, 1929.

Winter, Alice Ames. "The First Lady in Law." *Ladies Home Journal*, June 1925, 39, 63.

WILLIAMS, EDWARD BENNETT

(1920–1988)

EDWARD BENNETT WILLIAMS was one of America's foremost attorneys. He established an early reputation in the field of criminal law and subsequently became known as "the man to see" among the rich and powerful.

Born in Hartford, Connecticut, the son of a department store floorwalker Joseph Williams and his wife Mary Bennett, Edward Bennett Williams was a man of contradictions. An Irish Catholic who went to Mass daily, could be prudish, and valued family life, Williams also drank heavily, enjoyed "going out with the boys," and loved parties and the company of showgirls. Williams could go into the courtroom and blast the gov-

EDWARD BENNETT WILLIAMS
Teamsters boss Jimmy Hoffa (left) with attorney Edward Bennett Williams (right), ca. 1957. (Bettmann/Corbis)

ernment use of wiretaps, and yet he argued behind closed doors for the Central Intelligence Agency's (CIA's) authority to bug foreign spies in the United States. Williams worked both to defend Senator Joseph McCarthy and to protect the reputations of some of the Hollywood figures and others whose reputations McCarthy sought to vilify. Williams pursued the only successful libel suit against columnist Drew Pearson on behalf of Norman Littell but successfully defended the magazine *Confidential* against censorship by the post office. Williams brilliantly defended a U.S. soldier, Aldo Icardi, falsely accused of a war crime in Italy (Williams, who showed that a

716

murder blamed on Icardi was committed by Communist partisans, got charges dismissed by showing that the congressional committee that had accused him of perjury had not been investigating with the intention of formulating new laws), but he also defended a Soviet spy, Igor Melekh, against whom the government dropped charges. Williams's fees could be among the highest of any attorney of his day, and yet he often worked free for clients (like ex-CIA Director Richard Helms) whom he admired. Williams enjoyed flying his own jet and owned a number of houses, but he was also generous to charities, especially Catholic universities.

Williams graduated in 1941 from Holy Cross College, where he had been a champion debater. After a brief and unsuccessful stint in the air force, he went to the Georgetown University Law School, where he graduated first in his class. He worked for four years in the firm of Hogan & Hartson in Washington, D.C. (marrying Dorothy Gilder, the granddaughter of the firm's founder, with whom he would adopt three children), and then set up his own practice in the nation's capital, which eventually grew to encompass nearly one hundred other attorneys. For much of his life, Williams was in partnership with Paul Connolly; for a time, Joseph Califano (who left the firm to join the cabinet in President Jimmy Carter's administration) was also a partner. Williams taught criminal law and evidence at Georgetown (among whose law students he developed a faithful following), and he also served as a guest lecturer at other universities, including Yale.

Williams's clients included mafia dons, cabinet members, members of Congress, and corporate leaders. Strongly competitive, Williams was early a master of the courtroom with an ability to use a nearly photographic memory to conduct relentless cross-examinations and to communicate effectively with jurors—it was said that he did "not so much address a jury as woo it" (Thomas 1991, 320). Williams also developed the art of the backroom deal. Particularly in later years, his successes often appeared to depend on the force of his own expansive personality and on friendships he had cultivated with the prosecuting team and with presiding judges.

Williams almost always demanded complete control of his cases and complete cooperation from his witnesses, and he had the most trouble defending those, like Joseph McCarthy, whose statements, especially out of the hearing room, he could not control. Williams encouraged defendants to take the stand in their own defense, and, although his pretrial conferences could be brutal, he was often also fairly creative in suggesting noncriminal explanations of their behavior to them that they could use on the stand. Williams attempted to give dignity to his role as a criminal defense attorney, distinguishing a "criminal lawyer" from a "trial lawyer who practices criminal law" (Thomas 1991, 123). Williams often cited the Sixth Amendment for the principle that everyone was entitled to a good defense and comparing a good attorney to a good doctor, who went about his business and left moral judgments to others. Still, there were clients (among them Richard Nixon and Benjamin Spock) that Williams himself refused, and, like other such attorneys, Williams sometimes seemed to have greater interest in those who were rich than those who were not. In a similar vein, although Williams could wax eloquent about constitutional rights, it has been said that "the liberty he really cared about was that of his clients" (Thomas 1991, 337).

Although Williams's early association with Senator Joseph McCarthy even caused Mafia don Frank Costello to worry about hiring him, Costello overcame this reluctance, and Williams successfully defended him against deportation after he had been convicted of income tax evasion. In another early case, Williams successfully defended Teamsters boss Jimmy Hoffa against bribery charges. Robert Kennedy, then working for a Senate committee, had been so certain that Hoffa would be convicted that he claimed he would jump off the Capitol building if the case was lost—Williams subsequently sent him a parachute.

In 1960, Williams defended the flamboyant New York congressman Adam Clayton Powell against charges of income tax evasion. Williams mastered an impressive array of facts and succeeded in obtaining a hung jury. At one point, an observer who noticed a look of "utter amazement" on Powell's face during Williams's defense reported that "he was shocked to find he was innocent" (Thomas 1991, 143).

Although best known for his trial work, Williams was also an effective appellate advocate. He argued a number of cases before the U.S. Supreme Court, including some pathbreaking cases on Fourth Amendment rights and (on behalf of a Catholic college) *Tilton v. Richardson* (1971), which involved the defense of federal grants to religious institutions. Justice William Brennan, a personal friend, identified Williams as one of the two or three best attorneys whose presentations he had witnessed before the Supreme Court (Thomas 1991, 175).

Williams often entertained Supreme Court justices and other politicians. Williams largely took on the defense of Bobby Baker, an aide to Lyndon Johnson, against fraud and tax evasion at the request of Justice ABE FORTAS and President Lyndon Johnson. Williams once told an interviewer that the difference between a good attorney and a bad one was only about twenty percent (Sheresky 1977, 24), but although he knew he could not win every case, Williams was extremely depressed, and even cried, when Baker was convicted and sent to jail.

Williams was more successful in defending financier Robert Vesco, *Playboy* magazine owner Hugh Hefner, and one-time cabinet member John Connally. Connally was tried for attempted bribery. Williams succeeded in

The Contradictions of Roy Cohn

Few contemporary lawyers have had a greater flair for publicity or been more loved and hated than Roy Cohn (1927–1986). The son of a New York Supreme Court justice and a doting mother, Cohn first came to prominence in 1953 with his appointment to the internal security section of the Department of Justice. Cohn and a colleague, David Schine, garnered extensive publicity by touring American libraries in Europe looking for "subversive" books. Roy subsequently beat out Robert Kennedy to become the chief counsel to Wisconsin Senator Joseph McCarthy and led McCarthy in the hearings that eventually resulted in McCarthy's disastrous confrontation with Joseph Welch, then representing the U.S. Army.

Cohn went on to establish a law practice in New York City, where he delighted in representing and associating with a diverse array of politicians, millionaires, and literary figures, and where he frequented a trendy nightclub known as Studio 54. Recognized for his brilliance and his capacity for friendship, Cohn cultivated numerous press outlets, where his own reputation and legal victories were lauded. Cohn successfully defended himself against three different prosecutions, most of which can be traced to Attorney General Robert Kennedy.

Cohn spent little time in preparation for court battles, preferring to resolve cases through personal influence and back-room dealings and to leave the courtroom to lawyers just out of law school. Cohn often seemed to do little for his clients once he received his retainer. Cohn was a lavish spender who traveled widely, threw magnificent parties, and maintained a yacht and a Rolls-Royce, but he boasted that he rarely paid his bills, even to the Internal Revenue Service. Moreover, although he remained a strong public defender of conservative family values, Cohn engaged in a vast number of homosexual affairs, and he eventually contracted acquired immune deficiency syndrome, which killed him.

Despite the favorable press that he received, Cohn was excluded from the Martindale-Hubbell directory of U.S. attorneys. Shortly before his death, Cohn was disbarred from the New York bar. Among the charges were that Cohn had refused to pay back a $100,000 loan to a client and that he had misrepresented this loan as a legal fee.

Cohn is a prominent example of how a lawyer's image before the public may be very different from the lawyer's reputation among members of the bar.

REFERENCE

von Hoffman, Nicholas. *Citizen Cohn: The Life and Times of Roy Cohn*. New York: Doubleday, 1988.

helping Connally put an innocuous face on his transactions, and he called in numerous character witnesses, including evangelist Billy Graham, on Connally's behalf.

Williams was close friends with columnist Art Buchwald and *Washington Post* editor Ben Bradlee—the threesome claimed to be members of an exclusive club, of which only they were members. Williams was also friends with Phil and Katharine Graham, owners of the *Washington Post* (Williams protected Katharine's interest when Phil, who was having mental problems and eventually committed suicide, tried to cut her out of his will), and his firm defended the *Post* in a number of cases. Williams, who had advised editor Bradlee to publish the *Pentagon Papers* despite government opposition, was arguing another case and thus did not defend the paper in its ultimately successful *Pentagon Papers* case. Just as Williams, especially in his early years, had a flair for positive publicity, on occasion, he was able to use his friendships with the editors to quash stories unfavorable to his clients or to himself. Williams succeeded in getting a 7–1 verdict written by Judge Kenneth Starr in a decision by a U.S. Circuit Court of Appeals in which Williams had defended the *Post* against libel charges. Arguing that a *Post* story accusing the president of Mobil Oil Corporation of easing the path of his son was largely true, Williams had told the judges that one would have to believe in "the tooth fairy" to believe that the son had risen in a single year from the position of clerk to 75 percent owner without such help (Thomas 1991, 443–444).

In defending ex-CIA director Richard Helms against perjury charges involving testimony he gave before the Senate Foreign Relations Committee, Williams perfected the strategy of "graymail" that he also used in other cases. Williams hinted at numerous other scandals that would be revealed if the government proceeded with its case, and Helms got by with a judicial slap on the wrist.

As his career progressed, Williams took on more and more corporate clients. He and his partners perfected the art of delay and often attempted to bury rival prosecutors in such mounds of arguments and motions that they would either give up or negotiate a relatively favorable outcome for Williams's clients. Williams lost his last jury trial defending Victor Posner, a corporate empire builder, against criminal tax fraud, but he got the verdict overturned and used his connections with the judge to get Posner's sentence reduced to community service and donations to a homeless organization. Junk bond tycoon Michael Milken had hired Williams to defend him, but, much to Milken's consternation, Williams died before he could do so.

Williams greatly admired fellow Washington attorney Clark Clifford and tried, especially in his later years, to cultivate a reputation like Clifford's for being a wise counselor and Washington insider. Williams had many close friends. He was often able to calm clients and persuade them that bringing a case of libel or the like was only likely to yield further negative publicity.

Williams, himself a mediocre sportsman, enjoyed the company of sports figures (especially baseball great Joe DiMaggio, whom he once defended) and the competitiveness of sports. Williams loved to attend boxing matches. He was a longtime part owner of the Washington Redskins football team, for whom he successfully recruited his friend Vince Lombardi as a coach, before Lombardi died of cancer. Williams often invited prominent Washingtonians to watch the games with him in his box, and he distributed free tickets to many others. Williams later became the majority owner of the Baltimore Orioles baseball team, which won the World Series once during the time he owned it.

Williams, who earned just under $2 million in the year he died, also owned a Washington motel. When Williams died in 1988 after a long-running battle with cancer, his estate was valued at more than $100 million. He left most of his estate to his second wife (his first wife died), former law associate Agnes Neill Williams, with whom he had four children. An old-style Catholic who had always loved fame and power, Williams noted when he knew his own death was imminent, "I'm about to see true power" (Thomas 1991, 493). More than two thousand mourners, including a host of dignitaries, attended Williams's funeral at St. Matthew's Cathedral in Washington. Although Williams was lauded by priests for his many accomplishments, a biographer, Evan Thomas, has said that Williams was the victim of what he called "the 'betrayal of success." As Thomas explained, as one who was "addicted to winning," Williams "could never quite satisfy his yearning" (Thomas 1991, 495).

On a number of occasions, Williams toyed with running for a Maryland Senate seat or even for the U.S. presidency, but he never did so. He did serve on the President's Foreign Advisory Board, and he was also treasurer for a time of the Democratic party—a position that did not keep him from later supporting the candidacy of Republican Gerald Ford. Williams turned down a request from President Lyndon Johnson to serve as mayor of Washington, and he twice turned down the directorship of the CIA, the first time in order to stay in control of his law firm and because of concern that he could not keep secrets (the job went instead to George H. W. Bush), and the second time because of ill health. Williams left an account of some of his cases in a book entitled *One Man's Freedom* (1982), but his primary focus in the book was on constitutional principles. Williams included chapters opposing capital punishment, urging more humane treatment for individuals who commit crimes because of mental illnesses, opposing discrimination on the basis of race, and advocating expanded jurisdiction for the world court—Williams had long hoped that the rule of law might be used to moderate international tensions.

Other lawyers from Williams's firm have also distinguished themselves. They include MICHAEL TIGAR, whom Williams had hired after Justice William Brennan let him go because of his association with radicals; Vincent Fuller, who conducted the successful insanity defense of John Hinckley in the attempted assassination of President Ronald Reagan; and Brendan Sullivan, who led the successful defense of Oliver North in congressional hearings dealing with the Iran-Contra scandal.

—*John R. Vile*

SOURCES AND SUGGESTIONS FOR FURTHER READING

Pack, Robert. *Edward Bennett Williams for the Defense*. New York: Harper & Row, 1983.

Sheresky, Norman. *On Trial: Masters of the Courtroom*. New York: Viking Press, 1977.

Thomas, Evan. *The Man to See: Edward Bennett Williams: Ultimate Insider; Legendary Trial Lawyer*. New York: Simon & Schuster, 1991.

Williams, Edward Bennett. *One Man's Freedom*. New York: Atheneum, 1982.

WIRT, WILLIAM

(1772–1834)

WILLIAM WIRT
Library of Congress

WILLIAM WIRT, THE LONGEST-seated attorney general in U.S. history, is equally well known for the many cases he argued before the U.S. Supreme Court in his private capacity. Among the 170 cases in which he appeared before the highest court are *Dartmouth College v. Woodward* (1819), *McCulloch v. Maryland* (1819), *Gibbons v. Ogden* (1824), *Cherokee Nation v. Georgia* (1831), and *Charles River Bridge v. Warren Bridge* (1831). Wirt also prosecuted Aaron Burr for treason and successfully defended the man who probably murdered George Wythe, chancellor of the Virginia courts.

William Wirt was born in Bladensburg, Maryland, on November 8, 1772, the youngest son of Jacob and Henrietta Wirt. Orphaned at age eight, Wirt spent the next eight years at boarding schools and studying in the home of the Reverend James Hunt in Montgomery County, Maryland. After two years as a tutor in Maryland and a visit to his sister in Georgia, in 1791 Wirt returned to Montgomery County and began his study of law in the office of William Pitt Hunt, son of his former teacher. In early 1792, Wirt crossed the Potomac River to Leesburg, Virginia, to continue his legal studies with Thomas Swann. In the fall of 1792, Wirt obtained his license to practice law in Virginia.

For the next three years, Wirt attended court in the counties around Culpeper Court House, his place of residence, taking any client who came his way. He found Albemarle County to his liking, and soon married into one of the established families there. His marriage to Mildred Gilmer, daughter of Dr. George Gilmer, brought the young lawyer to the attention of Thomas Jefferson, James Madison, and James Monroe, also residents of Albemarle. Although he kept an office near the courthouse in Charlottesville, Wirt's reading in Dr. Gilmer's library contributed more to his future legal career than the cases that came his way at that time. But the pleasures of Albemarle soon vanished with the sudden death of Mildred in 1799.

Within months, the twenty-eight-year-old widower moved to Richmond, Virginia, and with the endorsement of Jefferson and John Taylor of Caroline, was quickly elected clerk of the House of Delegates. In addition to performing his legislative recording duties, Wirt also took cases in the local and federal courts and soon found himself recruited by Governor Monroe as one of the defense attorneys for James Thomson Callender, a Republican journalist charged with violating the Sedition Act of 1798. Although the all-Federalist jury rendered a verdict of guilty, Wirt's argument before the domineering Supreme Court justice Samuel Chase (hearing the case as a federal circuit court judge) enhanced the young lawyer's reputation in Republican circles. In 1802, when the General Assembly of Virginia established two new chancery courts, Wirt received the appointment as judge of the High Court of Chancery for the Williamsburg District, a position he held briefly. While he was chancellor, he married Elizabeth Washington Gamble, daughter of prominent merchant (and Federalist) Robert Gamble, and resumed private practice in Norfolk, Virginia. In 1806, he acceded to his wife's wishes and returned to Richmond, where he practiced for the next decade.

Wirt had hoped for an important case to mark his return to the Richmond courts, and he found it when he agreed to join in the defense of George Wythe Swinney, who had been accused of poisoning his great-uncle, GEORGE WYTHE, longtime chancellor and judge and former professor of law at the College of William & Mary. The defense showed that Swinney had not been proven guilty beyond a reasonable doubt, and Wirt's argument was described as "eloquent and ingenious."

Within a year, Wirt was engaged in another sensational case, this time as one of the prosecutors of former vice-president Aaron Burr for treason. In a trial heavy with political overtones, Wirt is said to have "aenraptured [the audience] with an eloquence that has lived for a century." He reminded Chief Justice JOHN MARSHALL, sitting as a federal circuit court judge, not to be diverted by defense maneuvers to implicate Burr's codefendant Harman Blennerhassett. "Who is Blennerhassett?" Wirt began, and went on to describe him as an innocent man of letters living a peaceful life on an "enchanted island" in the Ohio River. But Blennerhasset's Eden was changed to hell by the arrival of the serpent Burr, "a soldier, bold, ardent, restless, and aspiring, . . . the contriver of the whole conspiracy." Although failing to convince the ardent Federalist Marshall, whose restricted definition of treason made conviction impossible, Wirt's speech was immensely popular with the public in attendance. It was immediately published and became the typical declamation of schoolboys throughout the nineteenth century.

By the 1810s, Wirt was recognized as one of the leading attorneys of the Richmond bar. He had represented Jefferson in several private matters, served briefly in the house of delegates, declined to run for Congress, and found the spare time to write three well-received collections of character sketches and a biography of PATRICK HENRY. In 1813, President Madison appointed Wirt federal district attorney for Virginia.

In addition to the duties of district attorney, Wirt continued his private practice and accepted young men in his office who worked as clerks and read law under his guidance. Wirt encouraged his students "to speak like Henry, to write like Jefferson, and to reason like Marshall." His personal forensic ideal balanced eloquence and reason, but by modern standards his speeches often sound emotional and overblown. At the time, they were considered impressive, with an appropriate blend of imagery and logic. Wirt himself believed his speech was too rapid: "I have been trying all my life to learn to speak in the time of Lady Coventry's minuet—but I began with a Virginia jig and shall go on shuffling all the days of my life." He was especially good in jury trials, in which he stood beside his trial table and addressed the jury at a distance. Like HENRY CLAY, his gestures, though practiced, were artfully elaborated, with his snuffbox held in his hand. In appellate argument he became known for the thoroughness of his legal presentation, which he supported with "the truths of philosophy, the experience of history, and the beauties of poetry" and a wit that on occasion demolished the argument (and composure) of his adversary.

In 1816, Wirt argued his first case before the U.S. Supreme Court, and in late 1817 he and his family moved to Washington, D.C., where he assumed the post of President Monroe's attorney general. Most of Wirt's more than 170 Supreme Court cases date to his years as attorney general, yet most of his appearances there were on behalf of private clients. Until well into the nineteenth century, the attorney generalship was a part-time job whose major duties consisted of conducting suits in the Supreme Court when the United States was a party and advising the president and department heads when required. Soon after he assumed office, Wirt complained that it was difficult to accomplish even these limited roles without a clerk, an office, or even furniture. While waiting for Congress to act, Wirt began his duties alone. He was the first attorney general to maintain official opinion and letter books, remarking to a friend in 1824 that publication of his opinions "would do me more honour than anything else I have ever done." By the end of his eleven years as attorney general, he had researched and written more than 370 formal opinions.

But it was as a private advocate that Wirt was best known. During his years in Washington (1817–1829) and Baltimore (1829–1834), Wirt argued with or against the best legal talent in practice: Joseph Hopkinson, THOMAS ADDIS EMMET, WALTER JONES, WILLIAM PINKNEY, LUTHER MARTIN, Roger Taney, and DANIEL WEBSTER. When Wirt and Webster appeared before the Supreme Court, the chamber filled with Washington political and social figures intent on hearing the best speakers of the era. They were rarely disappointed. Of the two, Wirt's powers were probably the less appreciated, partly because he chose not to serve in Congress, where a political forum would have provided further publicity. Wirt's Supreme Court arguments also appear to have suffered at the hands of court reporters and his own failure to publish them privately, a modesty not indulged by Webster. At the time, however, Wirt's advocacy was so admired that he had more than enough clients, averaging twelve cases in each Supreme Court term during his fourteen full years of attendance. And it was Wirt who was asked to deliver the congressional eulogy on the deaths of Thomas Jefferson and JOHN ADAMS in 1826.

Although Wirt's Republican sentiments can be easily identified with his early mentors, Jefferson, Madison, and Monroe, a personal legal philosophy is harder to find. Largely an appellate lawyer, Wirt accepted cases referred by other attorneys. Rarely did he have firsthand knowledge of his clients or a thorough grounding in the issues before accepting their causes. Like other lawyers, Wirt furthered the cause of each day's client but recognized that the next day's client could require arguing the other side of the same issue. Some of his earliest Supreme Court appearances—for example, the *Prize Cases* (1863)—provide evidence of these case-by-case shifts.

Another early case, *Dartmouth College v. Woodward* (1819), shows a less workmanlike side to Wirt's practice, for it was one of two cases in which he admitted he was unprepared. His opponent, Daniel Webster, also a neophyte before the Supreme Court bench, had represented the college at the hearing before the New Hampshire Supreme Court, where the college had lost. The appeal to the U.S. Supreme Court argued that the college charter was a contract within the meaning of the U.S. Constitution's prohibition of state impairment of the obligation of contracts (Article I, Section 10). Webster, hoping favorably to impress both the court and the representatives of his alma mater, argued the legal and policy points of his client for over four hours, ending on a highly sentimental note. Wirt, recently hired by the university (Woodward), and conducting his duties as attorney general without assistance, failed in the limited time available to him to rise to the challenge of either the issues presented by the case or Webster's rhetoric. However, the justices, while captivated by Webster's presentation, were not readily convinced, and their decision that the New Hampshire legislature had impaired the charter of the college was not forthcoming until 1819. By then Wirt was allied with Webster in one of the most important constitutional cases of the era.

Three weeks after Marshall announced the decision in *Dartmouth*, the Court heard arguments in *McCulloch v. Maryland* (1819), an appeal by the Bank of the United States (BUS) from a decision in Maryland courts that the state's tax on BUS banknotes was legal. The bank had retained Webster and William Pinkney; Wirt (also retained by the bank) appeared at the request of President Monroe in his official capacity as attorney general. Webster began the BUS argument, relying on the authorization of the necessary and proper clause (Article I, Section 8) to permit Congress to create the bank. He then denied the state's ability to tax federal institutions, claiming that the supremacy clause (Article VI) forced the Maryland tax law to yield to Congress's charter of the bank. Joseph Hopkinson for Maryland replied to Webster's argument, denying that the BUS was necessary.

In his argument the next day, Wirt insisted that Congress's powers to create the bank had been expressly given because the BUS was necessary to the fiscal operation of the government. Wirt believed "necessary" meant "useful," and Congress, not the Court, decided what was useful for carrying out its purposes. Wirt worried that if the Court found for Maryland, it would deny Congress the choice of how to execute its powers. On the matter of taxation, Wirt declared that the federal act creating the bank prevailed over the state tax.

Walter Jones responded for Maryland with an extended exposition on states' rights. He was followed by Luther Martin, also defending Maryland, who rambled for three days. Pinkney's three-day response elaborated Webster's and Wirt's arguments and brought them to a masterful conclusion. Marshall's decision, delivered three days later, reflected much of Pinkney's argument.

Five years later, Wirt and Webster again shared the appellant's table in *Gibbons v. Ogden* (1824), a case testing New York's grant of a monopoly to

George Sullivan

George Sullivan (1771–1838), who served for twenty years as the attorney general of New Hampshire, was the son of an earlier state attorney general, John Sullivan (a general in the Revolutionary War), and the father of another. Sullivan, a Federalist, served for a time in the U.S. House of Representatives and in the New Hampshire state legislature.

George Sullivan was ranked among the top attorneys in a state bar that included Daniel Webster and JEREMIAH MASON. Sullivan actually prevailed in the superior court in the famous *Dartmouth College* case when that court decided that the college was a public corporation whose charter the state could alter, but Daniel Webster prevailed when he argued the case before the U.S. Supreme Court.

Lawyers are often known not only for the famous cases they argued but also for the manner in which they treated colleagues. The author of a sketch of Sullivan noted that he worked among colleagues who yielded "no advantage" in the courtroom but forced opponents to "take the consequences" of their mistakes. By contrast, Sullivan was recorded as offering "no objection to any reasonable amendment" (Bell 1894, 672). Sullivan was described as a fine orator, whose speech, logic, and charm "rendered him the most attractive advocate of his time in the State" (Bell 1894, 672).

REFERENCE

Bell, Charles H. *The Bench and Bar of New Hampshire*. Boston: Houghton Mifflin, 1894.

---

the Fulton-Livingston steamboat interests (Ogden). Ranged against them were Thomas Oakley, former attorney general of New York, and Thomas Addis Emmet, a brilliant Irish-American lawyer. Webster began the argument on behalf of the rival New Jersey steamboat interest (Gibbons) by discussing Congress's power to regulate commerce (Article I, Section 8). According to Webster, if Congress had not exercised its commerce power, then the subject should be left free of restraint. Where states had appeared to regulate commerce, they had merely exercised their police powers, while Gibbons's federal coasting license gave him the right to freely navigate the waters of the United States.

Oakley and Emmet argued that the states had concurrent powers to regulate commerce based on their reservations protected by the Tenth Amendment. They denied that navigation by steamboats constituted "commerce," which they defined narrowly as trade, and therefore the state of New York could grant a monopoly without interfering with Congress's power under the commerce clause. Furthermore, the New York monopoly grant to Ogden pertained only to the internal waters of the state.

Wirt responded that navigation was commerce and the exclusive subject matter of Congress. He declared that once Congress had legislated, state interference with the subject was void. Congress had so legislated with the Coasting Act of 1793 under which Gibbons held his coasting license, and therefore the New York grant to Ogden, conflicting with the Coasting Act, was void. He closed with a rebuttal of Emmet's quotation of the hero's lament in Virgil's *Aeneid*, correcting Emmet's misquotation and thereby stealing Emmet's thunder. It was a typical Wirt flourish: classical scholarship in aid of legal eloquence. The audience was thrilled, and praise followed in newspapers around the country. Three weeks later, Marshall announced the unanimous decision of the Court, which paralleled Wirt's argument.

In late 1824, president-elect JOHN QUINCY ADAMS asked Wirt to serve as attorney general in the new administration. In accepting and completing this appointment, Wirt's eleven-year cabinet service under Monroe and Adams became the longest tenure of any attorney general in U.S. history. In 1826, Wirt was elected president and professor of law by the faculty at the new University of Virginia, an honor he declined, pleading financial concerns. In addition to his public duties as attorney general, Wirt continued to appear before the Supreme Court in private cases. Some of the more famous of his later years include *Ogden v. Saunders* (1827), *Willson v. Blackbird Creek Marsh Company* (1829), and the initial argument of *Charles River Bridge v. Warren Bridge* (1831), which was reargued and decided after his death.

By the early 1830s, Wirt's career had taken another turn. John Quincy Adams's failure to win reelection ended Wirt's tenure as attorney general, and he and his family moved to Baltimore, where he practiced before the state and federal courts, returning to Washington to argue before the Supreme Court during its winter sessions. Among the caseload of his last years was *Cherokee Nation v. Georgia* (1831) and *Worcester v. Georgia* (1832), which raised the issue of the legal status of Native Americans in the United States. President Andrew Jackson and Georgia (as well as other states) wanted the Indians, in these cases Cherokees, removed so that their lands would be available for white settlement. The Cherokees wanted to stay on their native soil. They hired William Wirt.

Wirt initially requested the governor of Georgia to join the Cherokees and submit their grievances to the arbitration of the Court, but the governor refused. Wirt then published in the major newspapers an extended position paper on behalf of the Cherokees. His circumspection was due to the legal concern about how to achieve standing for the Cherokees before the Supreme Court. In the meantime, Georgia officials arrested, tried, convicted, and hanged a Cherokee whose "crime," if he committed it, had taken place in Cherokee country. Forced to act immediately, Wirt and his co-counsel John Sergeant asked the Supreme Court for an injunction to restrain Georgia from executing its laws in Cherokee territory. Georgia refused to appear.

Nonetheless, the Court heard the Cherokees' arguments in the absence of Georgia. Sergeant spoke first, claiming that the Court had jurisdiction to grant relief. Wirt later discussed the same legal points but added an impassioned plea for Native American rights. The case turned on the status of the Cherokee Nation, which Sergeant and Wirt declared was a foreign state. Since the Cherokees had never been conquered, and had merely placed themselves under the protection of the United States, they had the right to sue Georgia. Their treaties with the United States reinforced their nationhood and their right to self-government and control of their lands. Those same treaties also limited Georgia, since the supremacy clause made federal laws and treaties supreme.

Marshall's majority opinion sympathized with the Cherokees' plight but denied their argument, finding them a "domestic dependent nation" with no right to sue in federal courts. Two concurring opinions went further still, finding the Cherokees a conquered people under the authority of Georgia. However, Justice Smith Thompson's dissent, joined in by Justice JOSEPH STORY, accepted the arguments of Sergeant and Wirt and found that the Court had jurisdiction to hear the case and that the remedy of an injunction against Georgia was appropriate.

In 1832, Wirt and Sergeant were again before the Supreme Court arguing for Cherokee rights in a new case, *Worcester v. Georgia*; once again Georgia failed to appear. Here the similarity to *Cherokee Nation* ended, for in the intervening year Marshall had changed his mind. Writing for a new majority, Marshall borrowed from Wirt's new argument and Justice Thompson's dissent in *Cherokee Nation* and found that the Cherokees were a nation able to enter into treaties. Therefore, the Georgia acts limiting Cherokee rights within Native American territory were clearly unconstitutional. The Cherokees had won the legal battle with the help of William Wirt, and Wirt's representation of them placed him in the political spotlight in opposition to President Andrew Jackson, whose policy was to remove Indians beyond the Mississippi River. Wirt was mentioned as a possible Whig vice-presidential running mate to Henry Clay, but instead, to the surprise of his family and friends, Wirt accepted the presidential nomination of the Anti-Masonic party and ran a distant third in the election of 1832.

William Wirt died after a brief illness on February 18, 1834. Characteristically he died while in Washington attending the winter session of the Supreme Court. Congress and the Court adjourned in honor of his service to the country, and President Jackson and many members of the government accompanied his body to National Cemetery.

—*Elizabeth Brand Monroe*

Sources and Suggestions for Further Reading

Burke, Joseph Charles. "William Wirt: Attorney General and Constitutional Lawyer." Ph.D. dissertation, Indiana University, 1965.

Kennedy, John P. Memoirs of the Life of William Wirt. 2 vols. Philadelphia: Lea & Blanchard, 1850.

Robert, Joseph C. "William Wirt, Virginian." *Virginia Magazine of History and Biography* 80 (1972): 387–441.

Thomas, F. W. *John Randolph of Roanoke and Other Sketches of Character, Including William Wirt together with Tales of Real Life*. Philadelphia: Hart, 1853.

White, G. Edward. *The Marshall Court and Cultural Change, 1815–1835*. Vols. 3 and 4 of *History of the Supreme Court of the United States*. New York: Macmillan, 1988.

WYTHE, GEORGE

(1726–1806)

ONE OF THE MOST SCHOLARLY and gifted attorneys in colonial Williamsburg (where tourists can still tour his stately two-story brick house), George Wythe went on to become one of the most venerated teachers, capable attorneys, and esteemed judges to serve in Virginia after the winning of independence.

Wythe was born in 1726 (some sources say 1727) in Elizabeth City County, Virginia, to Thomas and Margaret Walker Wythe, the second of three children. Thomas Wythe, a planter, served, like his Virginia father and grandfather before him, in a number of governmental positions but died when George was only three years old. His remarkable mother, the granddaughter of preacher and scholar George Keith, apparently took primary responsibility for her son's education (which included an introduction to Greek and Latin), and, at age sixteen, he became an apprentice to his uncle by marriage Stephen Dewey, the king's attorney for Charles City. Wythe was admitted to the bar in 1746, within a year of his mother's death. Wythe subse-

GEORGE WYTHE
Library of Congress

quently settled in Spotsylvania County, where he assisted attorney Zachary Lewis, the king's attorney there, and subsequently married his daughter Ann Lewis, who was about his age.

Ann died within eight months of the marriage, and Wythe moved to the colonial capital at Williamsburg. There, under apparent sponsorship of Ann's uncle, Benjamin Waller, he became clerk to a legislative committee of the House of Burgesses. Wythe subsequently served in a number of positions in the colony, including that of acting attorney general, mayor of Williamsburg, vestryman in the Bruton Parish Church, and elected member and, later, clerk of the House of Burgesses.

Wythe quickly established a reputation for integrity. Often compared to the Greek statesman Aristides "the Just," Wythe was identified by a contemporary clergyman as "the only honest lawyer I ever knew" (Brown 1981, 36). Unlike many lawyers who perceive it to be their obligation to defend anyone who comes to them, Wythe refused to take cases from clients whose causes he thought to be unjust. Wythe was even known to send money back to a client as he researched the client's case and decided that he was in the wrong. John Randolph of Roanoke would say that Wythe "lived in the world without being of the world, and . . . was a mere incarnation of justice" (Kirtland 1986, 166). When later serving as judge, Wythe returned even the smallest gift (a bottle of alcohol and an orange tree) to avoid the appearance of impropriety (Dill 1979, 59).

In 1755, Wythe's older brother died, leaving Wythe in possession of his family's considerable estate in Chesterfield and guaranteeing him relative financial independence. Wythe subsequently married Elizabeth Taliaferro, then about fourteen or fifteen, and her father, an architect and owner of Powhatan Plantation, designed and built an imposing house for them in Williamsburg. The couple had only one child, who died either at birth or in early childhood.

Wythe became close friends with the scholarly lieutenant governor, Francis Fauquier, College of William & Mary professor William Small (who taught natural philosophy and mathematics), and student Thomas Jefferson. After leaving William & Mary, Jefferson, for whom Wythe served much as a surrogate father, studied from three to five years under Wythe's direction before starting his own short-lived legal career and entering political service; the two men remained friends throughout their lives.

Wythe may have been one of the best-read and erudite lawyers of his day, and, like Jefferson (to whom Wythe would will some of his scientific equipment), he mixed a love for natural science with his love of law and languages. Wythe had numerous clients, including George Washington. As one of the few complete records of his cases revealed (see Schwartz 1997), he sprinkled his oral arguments and briefs with allusions to Roman and English law and Latin phrases, and he was an able courtroom advocate. Sitting on the board of examiners in 1760, Wythe had hesitated before giving Patrick Henry (who had spent but a few months in the study of law) a license.

In the courtroom, Wythe was often thwarted by EDMUND PENDLETON. Unlike Wythe, Pendleton was willing to take on all clients. Although Pendleton's knowledge was not as deep, he was more outgoing, and his oratorical skills and physical presence were more imposing. A contemporary observer thus noted that "Mr. Pendleton was the more successful practitioner, altho' Mr. Wythe was considered as the better lawyer" (Littleton Waller Tazewell, cited in Brown 1981, 69). The expansive Pendleton was often able to drive the more serious and pedantic Wythe to distraction with legal quibbles. Whereas Wythe was the master of the written brief, Pendleton was quicker in responding to oral arguments. One observer noted that

> as a speaker he was always able, often most impressive, and at times even eloquent. His preparations were made with conscientious care, and he was most successful in presenting his case in its best aspect; but he sometimes lost, under the skilled cross-fire of skillful opponents, his self-possession in reply, and not infrequently failed to rally until the day was lost. (Dill 1979, 11)

Wythe appeared to love law for its own sake, while Pendleton appeared to view law more as an instrument for advancing his own interests (Blackburn 1975, 71).

One noteworthy occasion when Wythe's quick thinking gained an advantage over Pendleton occurred when Pendleton (who was facing both Wythe and Robert Carter Nicholas) had moved for a continuance because of his client's delay in arriving at court. Governor Dunmore had told him, "Go on, sir, for you'll be a match for both of them." Much to the governor's embarrassment, Wythe rebuked the governor by rising and bowing toward Dunmore, saying, "with your Lordship's assistance" (Dill 1979, 18).

As tensions between the American colonies and England developed over taxation, representation, and other issues, Wythe was one of the early advocates of independence. Wythe was elected to the Virginia Committee of Safety, and when George Washington was appointed head of the Continental Army, Wythe was elected to the Second Continental Congress to replace him. He, or an authorized agent, subsequently signed the Declaration of Independence (his name heads that of the Virginia delegation), and, on returning to Virginia, where he arrived too late to effect Jefferson's plans for a new state constitution, he helped design the state seal urging resistance to tyranny and was assigned to the committee to revise the state's laws. Thomas Jefferson and he assumed primary work on this project, in which Edmund Pendleton also participated. Wythe and Jefferson prevailed in their belief that the existing laws should be incorporated wherever possible into the new system rather than starting completely anew, as Pendleton apparently favored. Not all their alterations were accepted, but those that were included the Virginia Statute for Religious Liberty, one of the three accomplishments that would be listed on Jefferson's tombstone.

After being elected speaker of the house of delegates, Wythe was subsequently appointed in 1778, along with his nemesis Edmund Pendleton and Robert Carter Nicholas, to the state's high court of chancery. This position was not viewed as being incompatible with service in a professorship—created in 1779 when Jefferson was governor—of law and police at the College of William & Mary. This was the first such professorship of law in America and only the second in the English-speaking world (the first was held by the English jurist William Blackstone).

Although Wythe resigned in apparent frustration with fellow professors in 1790 when the college was reorganized (his resignation may also have signaled his impending move to Richmond), Wythe was as successful in this position as his earlier tutelage of Thomas Jefferson might have suggested. Indeed, one scholar has observed that "if a teacher is to be judged by the success of his pupils, then George Wythe must certainly be ranked as the greatest teacher this nation has ever produced" (Brown 1981, 224). Wythe regarded his function as that of forming "such characters as may be fit to succeed those which have been ornamental and useful in the national councils of America" (Dill 1979, 2). Wythe's students included future chief justice JOHN MARSHALL—who appears to have been largely distracted by love for his future wife, Polly, during the six months he sat under Wythe's lectures; James Madison, cousin of the fourth president, future president of William & Mary, and first bishop of the Protestant Episcopal Church of Virginia; future secretary of state and president James Monroe, who, however, got most of his legal training from Thomas Jefferson; John Brown, one of Kentucky's first two senators; future Virginia judge Spencer Roane; and a host of others who would later serve as governors, state legislators, and members of Congress. Moreover, St. George Tucker—Wythe's successor at William & Mary—read law with him in the 1770s as Thomas Jefferson had done earlier, and, in later years, HENRY CLAY would also serve for a time as a clerk to Wythe. In addition to his lectures, Wythe successfully engaged the interests of his students through moot court and mock legislative sessions, for both of which he was able to draw on his own personal experience.

Wythe was elected as a delegate to the Constitutional Convention in 1787 but left for home out of concern for his wife's health after chairing the Rules Committee and leaving a proxy vote on behalf of a single executive. His wife died shortly thereafter at age forty-eight, and Wythe never remarried.

Is Thomas Jefferson among the Top Ten?

In a list of America's top ten attorneys, Professor Bernard Schwartz included one name, namely that of Thomas Jefferson (Schwartz, Kern, and Bernstein 1997), that is not included as a separate entry in this book, even though this book includes ten times as many lawyers. In part, this difference shows the difficulty implicit in any attempt at rankings; in part, it stems from the fact that this book, unlike Schwartz's list, focuses chiefly on lawyer litigators rather than on lawyer statesmen.

Certainly, it would be difficult to find a lawyer whose contributions to the nation have matched those of Jefferson. The primary author of the Declaration of Independence (which reads in part like a legal indictment against the English king, George III), Jefferson served as a governor of Virginia, a minister to France, the nation's first secretary of state under George Washington, the founder of the Democratic-Republican party, vice-president under JOHN ADAMS, and two-term president. He had a gift for languages, a facility and appreciation for music, and abilities as an architect, planter, educator, and political philosopher. President John F. Kennedy once told a distinguished group of Nobel laureates at the White House that there had never been a more gifted gathering there "with the possible exception of when Thomas Jefferson dined alone" (Schwartz, Kern, and Bernstein 1997, 24).

Jefferson attended the College of William & Mary. He subsequently studied from two to five years (estimates vary) under GEORGE WYTHE, who would later be appointed to the first chair of law at the College of William & Mary that Jefferson helped create when he was governor. By all accounts, Wythe was a Renaissance man who considered Jefferson much like he would a son.

Jefferson practiced law between 1767 and 1774 and for a brief six-month period in 1782 (Schwartz, Kern, and Bernstein 1997, 57, 67), but he spent the rest of his life in politics. Although he was a gifted writer, Jefferson was a mediocre speaker. During his time as an attorney, Jefferson appears to have been blessed with many clients and to have found practice to be reasonably financially rewarding.

Records of most of Jefferson's cases are lost, but one is not. The case, *Bolling v. Bolling* (1770–1771), involves a dispute between two brothers regarding a will written by a third. Jefferson left a 239-page manuscript in his handwriting and that of a friend, which is apparently the "most complete account in existence of the arguments made in a late eighteenth-century case" (Schwartz, Kern, and Bernstein 1997, 1). Jefferson's arguments demonstrate familiarity with a wide variety of legal sources, including both cases and statutes. He also demonstrated that he had learned how to assess these sources and argue for their validity against a veteran of many more years at the bar. And who was Jefferson's opponent in this case? It was none other than his mentor, George Wythe!

REFERENCE

Schwartz, Bernard, with Barbara W. Kern and R. B. Bernstein. *Thomas Jefferson and Bolling v. Bolling.* San Marino, Calif.: Huntington Library, 1997.

Wythe, who was elected without running for the position, played a key role in the Virginia convention that ratified the U.S. Constitution. On this occasion, he appears to have worked successfully with Pendleton, who served as president and appointed Wythe to chair the Committee of the Whole. Wythe's and Pendleton's support for ratifying the document before the adoption of a bill of rights or other amendments was quite influential in setting the convention's course and helped counter PATRICK HENRY's fiery oratory against such ratification.

In 1782, Wythe voted with the court of chancery in Richmond in the case of *Commonwealth v. Caton*, with John Marshall sitting in the audience. In dealing with the constitutionality of a pardon issued by a single house of the state legislature, Wythe clearly articulated the view that legislative acts were subject to constitutional restraints, a view that Marshall would later make justly famous at the national level in *Marbury v. Madison* (1803).

In 1788, the Virginia courts were reorganized. Wythe remained as a chancellor, with Pendleton and others joining a newly created court of appeals. Wythe continued to be known for pursuing justice, even in cases in which it went contrary to popular opinion. In 1793, in *Page v. Pendleton and Lyons*, Wythe ruled against a Virginia agreement (that would have hurt the financial interests of Pendleton) allowing individuals to repay debts to England in deflated currency. In *Hudgins v. Wright* (1806), Wythe, who had himself owned slaves, a number of whom he had freed, not only ruled that a woman claiming to be descended from an Indian mother and a slave father was free but went on to state that slaves were entitled to freedom "on the ground that freedom is the birthright of every human being, which sentiment is strongly inculcated by the first article of our 'political catechism,' the bill of rights" (Brown 1981, 191).

As it often did in such cases, the court of appeals accepted Wythe's verdict in the case while repudiating his expansive reasoning. Often frustrated by what he believed to be the appellate court's misinterpretation of the law in overruling and modifying his own precedents, in 1795 Wythe published a book airing his grievances with that court—and especially with Pendleton (Wythe 1852). Displaying Wythe's vast knowledge of the law, the book was above the heads of most lay readers and appears to have had little impact on most citizens, who probably attributed his attack to differences in personality between Wythe and Pendleton.

In 1791, Wythe moved to Richmond; it was there that Henry Clay served as his law clerk before later teaching at Transylvania and becoming Kentucky's premier statesman. Wythe headed several public meetings in Richmond during Washington's administration, served as an elector for Thomas Jefferson in the elections of 1800 and 1804, and took up the study of Hebrew with a local rabbi, apparently to be able to read the Old Testament in its original language.

Wythe, who had frequently allowed students he was tutoring to room at his house, had custody of his great-nephew (his sister Ann's grandson) George Wythe Sweeney, as well as of a mulatto boy named Michael Brown. Sweeney, who had amassed gambling debts and who had forged Wythe's signature on a number of checks, may or may not have realized that he was one of Wythe's heirs. In any event, he apparently obtained arsenic and put it in the household coffee. A freedwoman, Lydia Broadnax, who kept Wythe's house, was poisoned but survived, but the arsenic killed both Michael Brown and, after two weeks of suffering, Wythe himself. Wythe, who realized what his nephew had done, was able both to disinherit and forgive Sweeney during this time. When he died in Richmond in 1806 at age eighty-one, he was likely the most venerated attorney in the state of Virginia. Wythe appears to have embraced Christian (and not simply Deist) doctrine; his last reported words were "Let me die righteous!" (Dill 1979, 81).

Both because Virginia courts would not accept the eyewitness testimony of Wythe's African-American housekeeper and because there was no existing Virginia law against forgery, EDMUND RANDOLPH and WILLIAM WIRT successfully defended Sweeney, who disappeared from public view. There is some evidence that Sweeney's contemporaries may have believed him to be insane (Blackburn 1975, 141).

At his death, Thomas Ritchie, writing for the *Richmond Enquirer*, noted that "kings may require mausoleums to consecrate their memory; saints may claim the privilege of a canonization; but the venerable George Wythe needs no other monument than the services rendered to his country, and the universal sorrow that country sheds over his grave" (Brown 1981, 294). Jefferson wrote, "His virtue was of the purest tint; his integrity inflexible, and his justice exact; of warm patriotism, and, devoted as he was to liberty, and the natural and equal rights of man, he might truly be called the Cato of his country, without the avarice of the Roman; for a more disinterested person never lived" (Dill 1979, 82).

One difficulty in studying Wythe is that his lecture notes have been lost, relatively few of his papers survive, and many of his opinions were destroyed in various fires. One observer, who is somewhat critical of Wythe for not doing more to eliminate slavery in Virginia, has noted that "Wythe saw the law as a temple in which he functioned as a priest" (Noonan 1976, 32). Another more sympathetic student of Wythe's thought, who contrasts Wythe's exalted view of the law with what he considers to be Pendleton's more instrumentalist approach, has concluded that Wythe was an early exponent of "a government of law" rather than of men (Kirtland 1986, 52).

This same scholar notes that, shaped as he was by his defense of the American Revolution, Wythe was not impressed by English laws that had not been ratified by colonial legislatures and thought that English precedents should only be given the weight that their reasoning might warrant. He also argues that Wythe attempted to implement the plain meaning of statutes and was only willing to repudiate legislation through the exercise of judicial review when he thought it was in direct violation of the Constitution (Kirtland 1986, 215–216).

—*John R. Vile*

Sources and Suggestions for Further Reading

Blackburn, Joyce. *George Wythe of Williamsburg*. New York: Harper & Row, 1975.

Brown, Imogene E. *American Aristides: A Biography of George Wythe*. Rutherford, N.J.: Fairleigh Dickinson University Press, 1981.

Dill, Alonzo T. *George Wythe: Teacher of Liberty*. Williamsburg: Virginia Independence Bicentennial Commission, 1979.

Kirtland, Robert B. *George Wythe: Lawyer, Revolutionary, Judge*. New York: Garland, 1986.

Noonan, John T., Jr. *Persons and Masks of the Law: Cardozo, Holmes, Jefferson, and Wythe as Makers of the Masks*. New York: Farrar, Straus & Giroux, 1976.

Schwartz, Bernard, with Barbara W. Kern and R. B. Bernstein. *Thomas Jefferson and Bolling v. Bolling*. San Marino, Calif.: Huntington Library, 1997.

Wythe, George. *Decisions of Cases in Virginia by the High Court of Chancery with Remarks upon Decrees by the Court of Appeals Reversing Some of These Decisions*. 2d ed. Edited by B. B. Minor. Richmond: J. W. Randolph, 1852.

WYZANSKI, CHARLES E., JR.

(1906–1986)

CHARLES WYZANSKI WAS ONE of the five lawyers selected to argue the five cases that would decide the validity of the National Labor Relations Act. The Supreme Court's decisions in these cases would set the standard of review for all of President Roosevelt's New Deal legislation (Irons 1982, 182). These decisions were the beginning of a constitutional revolution that expanded the regulatory power of government and ended the Supreme Court's support of laissez-faire attitudes toward government's control of business.

Wyzanski was born in Boston, Massachusetts, to Charles and Maude Wyzanski on May 27, 1906. Charles was raised in the affluent Boston suburb of Brookline. He attended Phillips Exeter Academy and graduated from Harvard magna cum laude and Phi Beta Kappa in 1927.

On completion of his undergraduate degree, Wyzanski corresponded with Justice Oliver Wendell Holmes about his future plans. Justice Holmes replied,

However a man feels about his work, nature is likely to see to it

CHARLES E. WYZANSKI JR.
UPI/Corbis-Bettmann

that his business becomes his master and an end in itself, so that he may find that he has become a martyr under the illusion of self-seeking. . . . For your sake I hope that where your work seems to present only mean details you may realize that every detail has the mystery of the universe behind it and may keep up your heart with an undying faith. (Bok et al. 1987, 711)

This letter was framed and kept near his desk for a lifetime, as a caution and credo. Based on the encouragement of Justice Holmes, Wyzanski attended Harvard Law School.

During his law school education, Wyzanski came under the influence of Felix Frankfurter, legal scholar, advisor to President Franklin Roosevelt, and future Supreme Court justice. Wyzanski excelled at law school, serving on the *Harvard Law Review* and graduating magna cum laude.

After his graduation, Wyzanski, with assistance from Professor Frankfurter, obtained a clerkship with Judge Augustus N. Hand of the U.S. Court of Appeals for the Second Circuit, but rejected a second clerkship with Justice Louis Brandeis. Wyzanski began practicing corporate law with the firm of Ropes & Gray in 1931. His final clerkship was with Judge Learned Hand, who had a great influence on Wyzanski and his approach to the law and public service. Many have said that Judge Hand was the greatest American jurist not to serve on the Supreme Court, and the same comments were later made about Charles Wyzanski (Garraty and Carnes 1999, 96).

The New Deal and the country's many economic problems were the critical issues of the day when Wyzanski returned to private practice in 1933 with Roper & Gray. As an associate, he was confronted with a moral dilemma when he was asked to draft a brief challenging a state anti-injunction law that he believed to be desirable and valid. Wyzanski declined the assignment and was supported by several senior partners in the firm. This refusal came to the attention of President Roosevelt, probably through Wyzanski's mentor, Felix Frankfurter.

In 1933, Wyzanski was appointed to the post of solicitor of the Department of Labor, where he worked closely with Secretary Frances Perkins for two years (Bok et al. 1987, 711). During Wyzanski's time as the Department of Labor's solicitor he played an important role in drafting the public works provision and labor sections of the National Recovery Act as well as the charter of the International Labor Organization. He was instrumental in liberalizing the immigration laws, which were then under the Labor Department's jurisdiction (Garraty and Carnes 1999, 94).

The opportunities and experiences made available to Wyzanski during his time in Washington were extraordinary. He drafted legislation, lobbied for its passage, and eventually argued that the law was constitutional. In 1935, Wyzanski was transferred to the Department of Justice as special assistant in the legal defense of key New Deal programs, principally the National Labor Relations Act and the Social Security Act. This work culminated in Wyzanski's participation in the following cases: *National Labor Relations Board v. Jones & Laughlin Steel Corp.*, 57 S. Ct. 615; *National Labor Relations Board v. Fruehauf Trailer Co.*, 57 S. Ct. 642; *National Labor Relations Board v. Friedman–Harry Marks Clothing Co.*, 57 S. Ct. 645; *Washington, Virginia & Maryland Coach Co. v. National Labor Relations Board*, 57 S. Ct. 648; *Associated Press v. National Labor Relations Board*, 57 S. Ct. 650. All five decisions were handed down April 12, 1937 (Nathanson 1937, 196).

The National Labor Relations Act, which created the National Labor Relations Board (NLRB) and the procedures necessary to enforce the law, were signed into law on July 5, 1935. Approximately four months later, the NLRB began a fourteen-month-long campaign to accumulate sufficient cases to support its theory that the new law was valid through the commerce clause of the Constitution.

The NLRB was looking for companies that clearly engaged in business that would be viewed as interstate commerce. The board was also interested in a company engaged in manufacturing, which had interstate connections. For years the courts had viewed these types of businesses as intrastate endeavors and excluded them from governmental control under the commerce clause.

The two cases that provided the NLRB with the best opportunity to support their theory were the *Jones & Laughlin Steel* and the *Associated Press* cases. The facts concerning the unfair labor practices were fairly well documented in both cases. The *Associated Press* case dealt with the firing of Morris Watson, a political reporter and national vice-president of the American Newspaper Guild. The company's own personnel file contained documents showing the firing was motivated by Watson's union activities. The Associated Press clearly engaged in interstate commerce. The real issue to be decided by the Court was whether the government had the power to prevent discrimination against union activities from disrupting interstate commerce in transportation and communication (Irons 1982, 265, 284–285).

The *Jones & Laughlin* case involved the nation's fourth-largest steel corporation and a longtime antiunion company. It was an integrated steel manufacturer that owned iron ore, coal, and limestone properties in several states as well as railroads and large subsidiaries. It shipped approximately 75 percent of its products out of Pennsylvania. The company engaged in many antiunion activities, including creating a company union, threatening workers' employment if they did not vote for the company union, and firing union activists. The NLRB's regional director, Clinton Golden, expressed concerns about violence and potential strikes (Irons 1982, 260–262).

One Question Too Many

Because they take depositions prior to trial, in important cases attorneys often know the key points that witnesses will make before they put them on the stand. Trial advocacy professors accordingly often exhort lawyers not to ask questions, especially of witnesses on the other side, to which they do not know the answers. In a chapter devoted to legal anecdotes in *The Trial Lawyer's Art,* Sam Schrager allows attorney Boyce Holleman to report a story, attributed to Clarence Darrow, that illustrates what can happen when a lawyer forgets to follow this maxim.

This young lawyer was defending a fella. The charge was biting another fella's ear off in a fight. There was only one witness, and he had this witness on the stand. And after a number of questions, he got to the big question.

He said, "Did you see my client bite this man's ear off?"

[The witness] said, "No, sir, I didn't see that."

He oughta set down. But he didn't. He said, "Well, then, how is it you come here and tell this jury that he bit his ear off? How'd you know that?"

He said, "I saw him spit it out." (Schrager 1999, 203)

Edward Bennett Williams learned a similar lesson early in his career when he was cross-examining the son of a man who had been killed by a streetcar. Williams was convinced that the man was drunk and that his son, who had bent over him after the accident, had removed a bottle from his father's pocket. Williams questioned the son accordingly:

"You leaned over him, didn't you?" A. "Yes."

"You were sniffing for alcohol, weren't you?" A. "No, sir."

"You were reaching into his pocket for a bottle, weren't you?" A. "No, sir."

"Other witnesses have testified that they saw you bending over your father. Now why *were* you bending over him?" A. "Because he was my father, and I wanted to kiss him good-bye." (Thomas 1991, 44–45)

Not surprisingly, Williams asked for a recess, called the insurance company, and recommended that it settle.

References

Schrager, Sam. *The Trial Lawyer's Art.* Philadelphia: Temple University Press, 1999.

Thomas, Evan. *The Man to See: Edward Bennett Williams, Ultimate Insider; Legendary Trial Lawyer.* New York: Simon & Schuster, 1991.

The company took the position that its manufacturing of steel was performed within the state of Pennsylvania. Earl Reed, counsel for Jones & Laughlin Steel, argued that this made the company's activities intrastate and not subject to the jurisdiction of the NLRB. This argument had been used in the past to deny union organizing activity. The Supreme Court had ruled that intrastate business activity was not subject to governmental control. The board needed to convince the Supreme Court that the corporate structure of Laughlin Steel and its many subsidiaries constituted interstate commerce by a manufacturing entity under the law.

The other three cases that were decided by the board had similar fact patterns or dealt with similar issues contained in the *Jones & Laughlin* and *Associated Press* cases. The different appellate courts decided or reviewed the board's action in the spring and summer of 1936. The different parties filed their writs to the Supreme Court in the fall, and the petitions for writ of certiorari were granted on November 9, 1936. The five cases would be argued before the Supreme Court on February 9, 1937 (Irons 1982, 268–271).

The responsibility of preparing the board's brief to the Supreme Court fell on five young lawyers. The two lawyers from the NLRB were Tom Emerson and Philip Levy, and from the Department of Justice and the solicitor general's office came Charles Wyzanski, Charles Horsky, and Abe Feller. Wyzanski took the lead of this group, whose members shared government expertise, age, and Ivy League legal educations. The group worked well together on a personal level, but sometimes their institutional loyalties conflicted. The Justice Department and the NLRB differed in their approach to arguing these cases before the Court. The Justice Department's main focus was pushing the cases it believed it could win. The NLRB's focus was on obtaining the broadest interpretation of the National Labor Relations Act. The two interests were finally merged into a three-pronged approach to the difficult arguments.

The brief for NLRB began with an argument focused on the effect of labor strife in a "far-flung, integrated enterprise," which was "likely to spread to other enterprises for the purpose of stopping shipments out of all plants in order to bring pressure to bear upon the industry as a whole." In these larger-scale cases, the NLRB would presume an intent to directly obstruct interstate commerce. The second argument did not depend on the "magnitude" of the industry, but measured a company's size "in relation to the industry as a whole" and "whether it is within a stream or flow of commerce." The impact of labor strife in such cases would depend, not on the intent of the strikers to directly obstruct commerce, but on whether the potential curtailment of production would have the "necessary effect of burdening or obstructing interstate commerce." The third argument expressed the concern of Charles Fahy (from the general counsel of the NLRB) with the limitations of the first two. It would focus attention on "the prevention of certain activities, even though usually only of local concern, which recur with such frequency as to constitute an undue burden on commerce." The board would thus be able to deal with unfair labor practices in any industry "where those practices and burdens are reasonably found constantly to recur." What most distinguished this argument from the other two was its emphasis on the Wagner Act, dealing with labor relations, as a preventive rather than a remedial statute. This was an argument "which [was] advanced vigorously" as the best way to stretch the act to cover smaller industries with only a minimal involvement in interstate commerce, Levy said. As finally written, the briefs somewhat uneasily accommodated the positions of both sides, leaving the Court free to stop at any rung on the ladder (Irons 1982, 280–281).

The Supreme Court arguments on this historical case began on February 3, 1937, and the parties were allotted three days. The Court heard from eleven attorneys, seven representing the different business interests and four arguing the government's position. JOHN DAVIS argued the Associated Press's case and Earl Reed represented Jones & Laughlin Steel; both were considered the premier appellate attorneys for arguments before the Supreme Court. Charles Wyzanski argued the *Associated Press* and *Friedman–Harry Marks* cases with Charles Fahy.

The business interest represented in these cases took the traditional approach of laissez-faire ideology for labor relations between employer and employee. A century of business practices and court decisions kept the representatives of business from really dealing with the arguments presented by the government's counsel. Wyzanski's delivery, working without notes, was flawless as he argued before the Court. The performance was described as a tour de force by Tom Emerson, a coauthor of the Supreme Court briefs (Irons 1982, 283).

On the final day of arguments, Wyzanski artfully summarized the board's arguments and their application to the different-sized business entities represented in the five cases. He returned to the question of "whether or not this act may be so applied as to cover all industry and labor in this country" to distinguish among the three arguments advanced by the government. The steel corporation, due to its size and interest, would engender intentional interference with interstate commerce as a result of labor strife. The importance of Fruehauf to the transportation industry would support the board's "necessary effect" argument as the stream or flow of commerce and its effect on interstate commerce. Finally, the smaller businesses, like Friedman–Harry Marks, had to deal with labor strife on a recurring basis, and the board should have jurisdiction to deal with these problems and eliminate any danger to interstate commerce (Irons 1982, 285–286).

The Court announced its decision upholding the National Labor Relations Act on April 12, 1937, when the opinion of the Court was read by Chief Justice CHARLES EVANS HUGHES. This decision was a culmination of the efforts by the New Deal lawyers to recognize a national crisis and provide a mechanism through government agencies and administrative law to provide a solution. This decision provided Congress the ability to deal with problems created by a national economic system and level the playing field between the employer and the employee (Irons 1982, 285–286).

The Court's more liberal reading of the commerce clause and due process clause led to an almost unlimited approval of New Deal legislation. Wyzanski returned to the Supreme Court six weeks later to argue the constitutionality of the Social Security Act, specifically dealing with the unemployment taxes being imposed on employers. A second case was heard on the federal old-age pension program. Once again, Wyzanski went head to head against John W. Davis, who was representing the interest of business in these cases. Wyzanski's performance before the court was so stellar that his worthy opponent Davis said, "In my palmiest days I could not have matched that argument" ("Ceremonial Presentations" 1996, lxix).

After these successes, Wyzanski left government service to return to private practice with Roper & Gray. He remained in private practice until he was appointed to the U.S. district court, where he served nobly for the next forty-five years. Although his time before the bar as a litigator had ended, his influence on the trial process continued in his capacity as a federal trial court judge. Wyzanski's tenure on the court was a continuation of the principles and ideals set down by many of the great justices he had known in his lifetime—Holmes, Augustus Hand, Learned Hand, Brandeis, and Frankfurter—whose voices could be heard in Judge Wyzanski's court.

A summary of some of Wyzanski's more memorable decisions was made by Judge Mark L. Wolf on the occasion of Wyzanski's portrait being presented to the U.S. District Court after his death in 1986. Judge Wolf made the following statement:

> During his tenure, Judge Wyzanski brought the ideals articulated by his mentors on the Supreme Court to the firing line of the District Court. In 1953, he affirmed the vitality of Brandeis' commitment to competition by ordering the break-up of the United Shoe Company. Extending the tradition of courageous support for civil liberties that earned Holmes and Brandeis their reputations as the "Great Dissenters," in the 1960s Judge Wyzanski ruled that a sincere, but not religious, conscientious objector could not be drafted for combat in Vietnam because that individual's interest in not killing was more compelling than the country's need for him to do so. Earlier, however, with Justice Frankfurter's former law clerk Elliot Richardson as the prosecutor, Judge Wyzanski decided that the vital need to prosecute public corruption trumped an individual's claim of conscience in requiring a reluctant probationer to identify the official he had bribed. ("Ceremonial Presentations" 1996, lxviii)

The final case mentioned by Judge Wolf drew quite a bit of criticism, with which Wyzanski did not totally disagree. In dealing with the Watergate scandal in the early 1970s, Judge John Sirica successfully used a similar sentencing practice (Bok et al. 1987, 712).

Wyzanski was a strong supporter of his alma mater, Harvard University. He was president of the Harvard Board of Overseers and senior fellow of the Harvard Society of Fellows. He served as a trustee for twenty-five years on the Ford Foundation and from 1942 was councilor of the American Law Institute.

Wyzanski's inclusion in this book of great litigators is best explained by his work as special assistant in the Department of Justice protecting New Deal legislation. As he put it, he was "enrolled in [a] battle to bring to a successful conclusion the third great period in United States Constitutional development—a period in which 'ancient powers given to and preserved for Union' were 'invoked to make a democratic government function in a modern world'" (Irons 1982, 289). Wyzanski was always aware of the outside influences that affected the decisions made in the law. In responding to Felix Frankfurter about the Supreme Court's decision in the five NLRB cases, he made the following observation: "Right along I have said that the cases were won not by Mr. Wyzanski but either by Mr. Roosevelt or, if you prefer it, by Mr. Zeitgeist" (Irons 1982, 289 n55).

— *James Wagoner*

Sources and Suggestions for Further Reading

Associated Press v. National Labor Relations Board, 57 S. Ct. 650, 193 (1937).

Bok, Derek, Stephen Breyer, Paul Freund, Carl Kaysen, Edward Levi, and Elliot Richardson. "In Memoriam: Charles E. Wyzanski Jr." *Harvard Law Review* 100 (1987): 705–727.

"Ceremonial Presentation of the Portrait of the Honorable Charles E. Wyzanski Jr.," April 12, 1996. 937 Fed. Supp. lx–lxxv.

"Constitutional Law—Freedom of the Press—National Labor Relations Act Held Not to Violate the First Amendment." *Harvard Law Review* 51 (1937): 163–164.

"Constitutional Law—Scope of the National Spending Power—Validity of Federal Old-Age Benefit Appropriations under Social Security Act." *Columbia Law Review* 37 (1937): 1206–1208.

Finburg, Burton A. "Constitutional Law—Wagner Labor Act (National Labor Relations Act)—Labor Disputes—Interstate Commerce." *Boston University Law Review* 177 (1937): 710–724.

Garraty, John A., and Mark C. Carnes, eds. *American National Biography*. Vol. 24. New York: Oxford University Press, 1999.

Helvering v. Davis, 301 U.S. 619, 641 (1937).

Irons, Peter. *The New Deal Lawyers*. Princeton: Princeton University Press, 1982.

Jackson, Kenneth, Karen Markoe, and Arnold Markoe, eds. *The Scribner Encyclopedia of American Lives*. New York: Scribner, 1999.

Marquis. *Who Was Who in America*. Wilmette, Ill.: Macmillan Directory Division, 1989.

Nathanson, Nathaniel L. "The Wagner Act Decisions Studied in Retrospect." *Illinois Law Review* 32 (1937): 196–206.

National Labor Relations Board v. Friedman–Harry Marks Clothing Co., 57 S. Ct. 645 (1937).

National Labor Relations Board v. Fruehauf Trailer Co., 57 S. Ct. 642 (1937).

National Labor Relations Board v. Jones & Laughlin Steel Corp., 57 S. Ct. 615 (1937).

Thompson, Royal E. "Constitutional Law—Old Age Pensions—Titles II and VIII of Social Security Act—Power to Spend for the General Welfare Act." *Michigan Law Review* 35 (1937): 1370–1373.

United States v. United Shoe Machinery Corp., 110 F. Supp. 295 (D. Mass. 1953), aff'd per curiam, 347 U.S. 521 (1954).

Washington, Virginia & Maryland Coach Co. v. National Labor Relations Board, 57 S. Ct. 648 (1937).

Wyzanski, Charles E., Jr. *Whereas—A Judge's Premises*. Boston: Little, Brown, 1965.

Appendix A

Great American Lawyers
Listed by Year of Birth

Andrew Hamilton (1676–1741)
Edmund Pendleton (1721–1803)
James Otis Jr. (1725–1783)
George Wythe (1726–1806)
John Adams (1735–1826)
Patrick Henry (1736–1799)
Luther Martin (1744–1826)
Tapping Reeve (1744–1823)
Edmund Randolph (1753–1813)
John Marshall (1755–1835)
Alexander Hamilton (1757–1804)
Thomas Addis Emmet (1764–1827)
William Pinkney (1764–1822)
John Quincy Adams (1767–1848)
Jeremiah Mason (1768–1848)
Joseph Hopkinson (1770–1842)
William Wirt (1772–1834)
Walter Jones (1776–1861)
Henry Clay (1777–1852)
Joseph Story (1779–1845)
Martin Van Buren (1782–1862)
Daniel Webster (1782–1852)

James Louis Petigru (1789–1863)
Edward Bates (1793–1869)
Reverdy Johnson (1796–1876)
Rufus Choate (1799–1859)
Caleb Cushing (1800–1879)
David Dudley Field (1805–1894)
Salmon P. Chase (1808–1873)
Benjamin Robbins Curtis (1809–1874)
Abraham Lincoln (1809–1865)
Jeremiah Sullivan Black (1810–1893)
Judah P. Benjamin (1811–1884)
John Archibald Campbell (1811–1889)
Stephen A. Douglas (1813–1861)
Richard Henry Dana Jr. (1815–1882)
William M. Evarts (1818–1901)
Roscoe Conkling (1829–1888)
John Mercer Langston (1829–1897)
Belva Lockwood (1830–1917)
John Forrest Dillon (1831–1914)
Joseph H. Choate (1832–1917)
John Garner Johnson (1841–1917)
Elihu Root (1845–1937)

Attorneys born in the same year are arranged alphabetically rather than by birthday.

Louis Dembitz Brandeis (1856–1941)
Clarence Darrow (1857–1938)
William Dameron Guthrie
(1859–1935)
Charles Evans Hughes (1862–1948)
Homer Stille Cummings (1870–1956)
Earl Rogers (1870–1922)
Max Steuer (1871–1940)
John W. Davis (1873–1955)
Arthur Mullen (1873–1938)
Owen J. Roberts (1875–1955)
Francis Beverly Biddle (1886–1968)
William J. Fallon (1886–1927)
Arthur T. Vanderbilt (1888–1957)
Mabel Walker Willebrandt
(1889–1963)
Thurman Wesley Arnold (1891–1969)
Robert H. Jackson (1892–1954)
Samuel Simon Leibowitz (1893–1978)
Charles Hamilton Houston
(1895–1950)
Carol Weiss King (1895–1952)
John Marshall Harlan II (1899–1971)
Thomas E. Dewey (1902–1971)
Percy Foreman (1902–1988)
Louis Nizer (1902–1994)
Erwin Nathaniel Griswold
(1904–1994)
William Henry Hastie (1904–1976)
Leon Jaworski (1905–1982)
Charles E. Wyzanski Jr. (1906–1986)

Melvin Mouron Belli Sr. (1907–1996)
Thurgood Marshall (1908–1993)
Leo Pfeffer (1909–1993)
Abe Fortas (1910–1982)
Hayden C. Covington (1911–1978)
Archibald Cox (1912–)
Mary Metlay Kaufman (1912–1995)
Spottswood W. Robinson III
(1916–1998)
William M. Kunstler (1919–1995)
James D. St. Clair (1920–)
Edward Bennett Williams (1920–1988)
John Michael Doar (1921–)
Constance Baker Motley (1921–)
Jack Greenberg (1925–)
Richard "Racehorse" Haynes (1927–)
James F. Neal (1929–)
Gerry Spence (1929–)
F. Lee Bailey (1933–)
Ruth Bader Ginsburg (1933–)
Vincent T. Bugliosi Jr. (1934–)
Rex E. Lee (1935–1996)
Morris Dees Jr. (1936–)
Johnnie L. Cochran Jr. (1937–)
Alan Morton Dershowitz (1938–)
Marian Wright Edelman (1939–)
David Boies (1941–)
Michael E. Tigar (1941–)
Laurence H. Tribe (1941–)
Kenneth W. Starr (1946–)

Appendix B

GREAT AMERICAN LAWYERS LISTED BY CENTURY

Colonial and Revolutionary Times

John Adams (1735–1826)
Thomas Addis Emmet (1764–1827)
Alexander Hamilton (1757–1804)
Andrew Hamilton (1676–1741)
Patrick Henry (1736–1799)
John Marshall (1755–1835)
Luther Martin (1744–1826)
James Otis Jr. (1725–1783)
Edmund Pendeton (1721–1803)
Edmund Randolph (1753–1813)
George Wythe (1726–1806)

Nineteenth Century

John Quincy Adams (1767–1848)
Edward Bates (1793–1869)
Judah P. Benjamin (1811–1884)
Jeremiah Sullivan Black (1810–1893)
John Archibald Campbell (1811–1889)
Salmon P. Chase (1808–1873)
Joseph H. Choate (1832–1917)
Rufus Choate (1799–1859)
Henry Clay (1777–1852)
Roscoe Conkling (1829–1888)

Benjamin Robbins Curtis (1809–1874)
Caleb Cushing (1800–1879)
Richard Henry Dana Jr. (1815–1882)
John Forrest Dillon (1831–1914)
Stephen A. Douglas (1813–1861)
William M. Evarts (1818–1901)
David Dudley Field (1805–1894)
Joseph Hopkinson (1770–1842)
John Garner Johnson (1841–1917)
Reverdy Johnson (1796–1876)
Walter Jones (1776–1861)
John Marcer Langston (1829–1897)
Abraham Lincoln (1809–1865)
Belva Lockwood (1830–1917)
Jeremiah Mason (1768–1848)
James Louis Petigru (1789–1863)
William Pinkney (1764–1822)
Tapping Reeve (1744–1823)
Joseph Story (1779–1845)
Martin Van Buren (1782–1862)
Daniel Webster (1782–1852)
William Wirt (1772–1834)

Twentieth Century

Thurman Wesley Arnold (1891–1969)
F. Lee Bailey (1933–)

Melvin Mouron Belli Sr. (1907–1996)
Francis Beverly Biddle (1886–1968)
David Boies (1941–)
Louis Dembitz Brandeis (1856–1941)
Vincent T. Bugliosi Jr. (1934–)
Johnnie L. Cochran Jr. (1937–)
Hayden C. Covington (1911–1978)
Archibald Cox (1912–)
Homer Stille Cummings (1870–1956)
Clarence Darrow (1857–1938)
John W. Davis (1873–1955)
Morris Dees Jr. (1936–)
Alan Morton Dershowitz (1938–)
Thomas E. Dewey (1902–1971)
John Michael Doar (1921–)
Marian Wright Edelman (1939–)
William J. Fallon (1886–1927)
Percy Foreman (1902–1988)
Abe Fortas (1910–1982)
Ruth Bader Ginsburg (1933–)
Jack Greenberg (1925–)
Erwin Nathaniel Griswold
    (1904–1994)
William Dameron Guthrie
    (1859–1935)
John Marshall Harlan II (1899–1971)
William Henry Hastie (1904–1976)
Richard "Racehorse" Haynes (1927–)
Charles Hamilton Houston
    (1895–1950)
Charles Evans Hughes (1862–1948)

Robert H. Jackson (1892–1954)
Leon Jaworski (1905–1982)
Mary Metlay Kaufman (1912–1995)
Carol Weiss King (1895–1952)
William M. Kunstler (1919–1995)
Rex E. Lee (1935–1996)
Samuel Simon Leibowitz (1893–1978)
Thurgood Marshall (1908–1993)
Constance Baker Motley (1921–)
Arthur Mullen (1873–1938)
James F. Neal (1929–)
Louis Nizer (1902–1994)
Leo Pfeffer (1909–1993)
Owen J. Roberts (1875–1955)
Spottswood W. Robinson III
    (1916–1998)
Earl Rogers (1870–1922)
Elihu Root (1845–1937)
Gerry Spence (1929–)
Kenneth W. Starr (1946–)
James D. St. Clair (1920–)
Max Steuer (1871–1940)
Michael E. Tigar (1941–)
Laurence H. Tribe (1941–)
Arthur T. Vanderbilt (1888–1957)
Mabel Walker Willebrandt
    (1889–1963)
Edward Bennett Williams
    (1920–1988)
Charles E. Wyzanski Jr. (1906–1986)

Appendix C

GREAT AMERICAN LAWYERS LISTED BY BIRTHDATE, STATE, AND COLLEGE

Name[1]	Nation or State of Birth	Education[2]	Practice[3]
Andrew Hamilton (1676–1741)	Scotland	St. Andrews/ Read law[4]	VA/MD/PA/ DE
Edmund Pendleton (1721–1803)	VA	Read law	VA
James Otis (1725–1783)	MA	Harvard/Read law	MA
George Wythe (1726–1806)	VA	Read law	VA
John Adams (1735–1826)	MA	Harvard/Read law	MA
Patrick Henry (1736–1799)	VA	Read law	VA
Luther Martin (1744–1826)	NJ	Col. of NJ/Read law	MD
Tapping Reeve (1744–1823)	NY	Col. of NJ[5]/Read law	CT
Edmund Randolph (1753–1813)	VA	William & Mary/ Read law	VA
John Marshall (1755–1835)	VA	William & Mary	VA
Alexander Hamilton (1757–1804)	W. Indies	Kings College[6]/ Albany	NY
Thomas Addis Emmet (1764–1827)	Ireland	Trinity/Edinburgh/ I. Temple	Ireland/NY
William Pinkney (1764–1822)	MD	Read law	MD
John Quincy Adams (1767–1848)	MA	Harvard/Read law	NH/MA
Jeremiah Mason (1768–1848)	CT	Yale	CT/VT/NH

Joseph Hopkinson (1770–1842)	PA	U. PA/Read law	PA
William Wirt (1772–1834)	MD	Read law	VA/MD
Walter Jones (1776–1861)	VA	Read law	VA
Henry Clay (1777–1852)	VA	Read law	KY
Joseph Story (1779–1845)	MA	Harvard/Read law	MA
Martin Van Buren (1782–1862)	NY	Read law	NY
Daniel Webster (1782–1852)	NH	Dartmouth/Read law	MA
James Louis Petigru (1789–1863)	SC	Col. of NJ/SC College	SC
Edward Bates (1793–1869)	VA	Read law	MO
Reverdy Johnson (1796–1876)	MD	St. Johns	MD
Rufus Choate (1799–1859)	MA	Dartmouth/Harvard Law	MA
Caleb Cushing (1800–1879)	MA	Harvard/Harvard Law	MA
David Dudley Field (1805–1894)	CT	Williams/Read law	NY
Salmon P. Chase (1808–1873)	NH	Dartmouth/Read law	OH
Benjamin Curtis (1809–1874)	MA	Harvard/Harvard Law	MA
Abraham Lincoln (1809–1865)	KY	Read law	IL
Jeremiah Black (1810–1893)	PA	Read law	PA
Judah P. Benjamin (1811–1884)	St. Croix	Yale/Read law	LA/England
John Archibald Campbell (1811–1889)	GA	West Point/Read law	AL/LA
Stephen A. Douglas (1813–1861)	VT	Read law	IL
Richard Henry Dana Jr. (1815–1882)	MA	Harvard/Harvard Law	MA
William M. Evarts (1818–1901)	MA	Yale/Harvard Law	NY
Roscoe Conkling (1829–1888)	MA	Read law	NY
John Mercer Langston (1829–1897)	VA	Oberlin/Read law	OH/DC/VA
Belva Lockwood (1830–1917)	NY	Syracuse[7]/Nat. Law Sch.	DC
John F. Dillon (1831–1914)	NY	Iowa/Read law	NY
Joseph H. Choate (1832–1917)	MA	Harvard/Harvard Law	NY
John Garner Johnson (1841–1917)	PA	U. PA/Read law	PA

Elihu Root (1845–1937)	NY	Hamilton College/ NYU Law	NY
Louis Dembitz Brandeis (1856–1941)	KY	Germany/Harvard Law	MA
Clarence Darrow (1857–1938)	NY	Allegheny/Michigan/ Read law	IL
William D. Guthrie (1859–1935)	CA	Columbia Law	NY
Charles Evans Hughes (1862–1948)	NY	Colgate/Brown/Col. Law	NY
Homer Stille Cummings (1870–1956)	IL	Yale/Yale Law	CT
Earl Rogers (1870–1922)	NY	Syracuse/Read law	CA
Max Steuer (1871–1940)	Austria	City Col. NY/ Columbia Law	NY
John W. Davis (1873–1955)	WV	Wash. & Lee/W&L Law	WV/NY
Arthur Mullen (1873–1938)	Canada	U. Mich. Law	NE
Owen J. Roberts (1875–1955)	PA	U. PA/U. PA Law	PA
Francis Biddle (1886–1968)	France	Harvard/Harvard Law	PA
William J. Fallon (1886–1927)	NY	Fordham/Fordham Law	NY
Arthur T. Vanderbilt (1888–1957)	NJ	Wesleyan (CT)/Col. Law	NJ
Mabel Walker Willebrandt (1889–1963)	KS	Tempe Normal/ S. Cal. Law	CA/DC
Thurman Wesley Arnold (1891–1969)	WY	Princeton/Harvard Law	DC
Robert H. Jackson (1892–1954)	PA	Albany/Read law	NY
Samuel Simon Leibowitz (1893–1978)	Romania	Cornell Law	NY
Charles Houston (1895–1950)	TN	Amherst/Harvard Law	MA
Carol Weiss King (1895–1952)	NY	Barnard/NYU Law	NY
John Marshall Harlan II (1899–1971)	IL	Princeton/Oxford/NYU	NY
Thomas E. Dewey (1902–1971)	MI	U. MI/Columbia Law	NY
Percy Foreman (1902–1988)	TX	U. Texas, Austin	TX
Louis Nizer (1902–1994)	England	Columbia/Col. Law	NY
Erwin Griswold (1904–1994)	OH	Oberlin/Harvard Law	OH/NY
William Hastie (1904–1976)	DC	Amherst/Harvard Law	MA
Leon Jaworski (1905–1982)	TX	Baylor Law/G.W. Law	TX
Charles E. Wyzanski Jr. (1906–1986)	MA	Harvard/Harvard Law	TX
Melvin Mouron Belli Sr. (1907–1996)	CA	Berkeley/Boalt	CA

Thurgood Marshall (1908–1993)	MD	Lincoln/Howard U.	MD/DC
Leo Pfeffer (1909–1993)	Hungary	City College/NYU Law	NY
Abe Fortas (1910–1982)	TN	Southwest[8]/Yale Law	DC
Hayden C. Covington (1911–1978)	TX	San Antonio Bar Assoc.[9]	NY
Archibald Cox (1912–)	NJ	Harvard/Harvard Law	MA
Mary Metlay Kaufman (1912–1995)	GA	Brooklyn C./ St. Johns Law	NY
Spottswood W. Robinson III (1916–1998)	VA	VA Union/Howard Law	VA/DC
William Kunstler (1919–1995)	NY	Yale/Columbia Law	NY
James D. St. Clair (1920–)	OH	U. IL/Harvard Law	MA
Edward Bennett Williams (1920–1988)	CT	Holy Cross/ Georgetown Law	MD/DC
John Michael Doar (1921–)	MN	Princeton/U. CA	WI/DC/NY
Constance Baker Motley (1921–)	CT	Fisk/NYU/Col. Law	NY
Jack Greenberg (1925–)	NY	Columbia/Col. Law	NY
Richard "Racehorse" Haynes (1927–)	TX	Houston/Houston Law	TX
James F. Neal (1929–)	TN	Wyoming/Vanderbilt	TN
Gerry Spence (1929–)	WY	WY/WY Law/ Georgetown Law	WY
F. Lee Bailey (1933–)	MA	Harvard/Boston U. Law	MA/FL
Ruth Bader Ginsburg (1933–)	NY	Cornell/Harvard Law	NY
Vincent T. Bugliosi Jr. (1934–)	MN	Miami, FL/UCLA Law	CA
Rex E. Lee (1935–1996)	CA	Brigham Y./U. Chicago	AZ/UT
Morris Dees Jr. (1936–)	AL	U. AL/U. AL Law	CA
Johnnie L. Cochran Jr. (1937–)	LA	UCLA/Loyola L.A.	CA
Alan Dershowitz (1938–)	NY	Brooklyn/Yale Law	MA
Marian Wright Edelman (1939–)	SC	Spelman/Yale Law	MS/DC
David Boies (1941–)	IL	Redlands/N.western/ Yale Law	NY
Michael E. Tigar (1941–)	CA	Cal. Berkeley/U. CA Law/CA/France/	TX/DC
Laurence H. Tribe (1941–)	China	Harvard/Harvard Law	MA
Kenneth W. Starr (1946–)	TX	Harding/G.W./Brown/ Duke	CA/DC

[1]Attorneys born the same year are arranged alphabetically rather than by birth day.

[2] Schools attended are listed even when individuals did not receive a degree.

[3] Notable attorneys often take cases in other states. I have tried to identify the key state, or states, in which each attorney practices, but I have undoubtedly left out a number of such locales.

[4] Especially in early American history, most attorneys studied for the law by "reading law" in the office of an established practitioner.

[5] Now Princeton University.

[6] Now Columbia University.

[7] The college was then called Genese Wesleyan.

[8] This is now called Rhodes College.

[9] This is now St. Mary's.

Editor's Comments: In reviewing this list, it is noteworthy that eleven of one hundred great American attorneys identified were born abroad, just over half in Britain or its colonies. Close to half the states were birthplaces to the remaining outstanding lawyers, with New York, Massachusetts, and Virginia leading the list, in part because of their prominence in early American history.

Just over one-third of the attorneys read law in the offices of other attorneys. One-fifth of the attorneys in this book attended Harvard either as undergraduates and/or as law students. Columbia, Yale, Princeton, and New York University are the only other schools to have educated a handful or more of the attorneys covered in this book.

—*John R. Vile*

How Well Do You Know Your Great American Lawyers?

Which great American attorney:

- Helped direct the education of Thomas Jefferson? [George Wythe]

- Wrote "Hail Columbia"? [Joseph Hopkinson]

- Argued the *Zenger* case, and designed Pennsylvania Hall? [Andrew Hamilton]

- Served as secretary of war in the Confederate cabinet before moving to England and practicing law there? [Judah P. Benjamin]

- Helped defend the Scottsboro Boys against charges that they had raped two white women? [Samuel Leibowitz]

- Was imprisoned as an Irish revolutionary before coming to America? [Thomas Addis Emmet]

- Defended the Redcoats in the Boston Massacre Trial and later became president of the United States? [John Adams]

- Helped argue the *Amistad* case and served in the House of Representatives after having been president of the United States? [John Quincy Adams]

- Was the grandson of William Evarts and a long-time Harvard law professor who was ousted as Watergate special prosecutor in the "Saturday Night Massacre"? [Archibald Cox]

- Was known as "the Little Giant"? [Stephen A. Douglas]

- Was the first African-American ever appointed to the U.S. Supreme Court? [Thurgood Marshall]

- Brought the most important cases involving the rights of women to the U.S. Supreme Court before being appointed as a U.S. Supreme Court justice? [Ruth Bader Ginsburg]

- Prosecuted Charles Manson and wrote the book *Helter Skelter* about the experience? [Vincent Bugliosi]

- Won millions of dollars in judgments against the Los Angeles Police Department before helping to defend O. J. Simpson? [Johnnie Cochran]

- Had a type of legal brief citing voluminous studies and statistical data named after him? [Louis Brandeis]

- Led the U.S. prosecution of the Nuremburg trials of Nazis after World War II? [Robert Jackson]

- Helped as secretary of state to precipitate a case that later resulted in the establishment of judicial review of congressional legislation? [John Marshall]

- Served as a Harvard professor and Supreme Court justice and wrote one of the most influential works on the U.S. Constitution in the nineteenth century? [Joseph Story]

- Was said to have birthed the American Revolution when arguing against the hated Writs of Assistance? [James Otis]

- Authored the Gettysburg Address? [Abraham Lincoln]

- Defended Elvis Presley's doctor against charges that he had illegally prescribed drugs? [James Neal]

- Served as a de facto defender of Lee Harvey Oswald, was scheduled to defend Jack Ruby, and later advised James Earl Ray to plead guilty to assassinating Dr. Martin Luther King Jr.? [Percy Foreman]

- Is often credited with inventing the modern art of cross-examination and defended Clarence Darrow against bribery charges? [Earl Rogers]

- Delivered a famous speech in which he proclaimed, "Give me liberty or give me death"? [Patrick Henry]

- Brought over fifty cases (most of which he won) to the U.S. Supreme Court on behalf of Jehovah's Witnesses? [Hayden C. Covington]

- Was the key subject in a famous play by Steven Vincent Benét? [Daniel Webster]

- Often considered to be the greatest lawyer in American history, was the key subject in the play *Inherit the Wind* and a strong opponent of the death penalty? [Clarence Darrow]

- Is a Harvard law professor, specializing in appellate advocacy, who helped defend Leona Helmsley? [Alan Dershowitz]

- Is a Harvard law professor who unsuccessfully argued for gay rights in the case of *Bowers v. Harwick?* [Laurence Tribe]

- Resigned from the U.S. Supreme Court at the beginning of the Civil War and later served on the Confederate cabinet? [John Archibald Campbell]

- Dissented in the *Dred Scott* decision of 1857? [Benjamin Curtis]

- Created one of the most influential schools for training lawyers in the early nineteenth century? [Tapping Reeve]

- Was the first African-American to be appointed as a U.S. federal judge? [William Hastie]

- Served as the nation's first secretary of the treasury and helped found the Federalist party? [Alexander Hamilton]

- Was designated as "the King of Torts"? [Melvin Belli]

- Is best known for his cross-examination in the New York Triangle Shirtwaist Factory fire? [Max Steuer]

- Was a cabinet officer in the administration of Andrew Jackson who advocated a two-party system and later became U.S. president? [Martin Van Buren]

- Resigned from the U.S. Supreme Court to run unsuccessfully for president but was later appointed as chief justice? [Charles Evans Hughes]

- Achieved a reputation as a prosecutor and was incorrectly projected to beat Harry S Truman in the election of 1948? [Thomas E. Dewey]

- Was the grandson of the dissenter in the case (*Plessy v. Ferguson*, 1896) that established the doctrine of "separate but equal" who became almost equally well known for his own dissents as a justice on the Warren Court? [John Marshall Harlan II]

- Defended Clarence Gideon in the case (*Gideon v. Wainwright*, 1963) that established an indigent's right to appointed counsel in felony cases before being appointed to the U.S. Supreme Court by President Lyndon Johnson? [Abe Fortas]

- Authored *Two Years before the Mast?* [Richard Henry Dana]

- Has been identified by his biographer as "the most hated lawyer in America"? [William Kunstler]

- Formulated the key to success as "$IQ + WQ^2 = S$ or Intelligence Quotient plus Work Quotient squared equals Success"? [Louis Nizer]

- Was a former Teapot Dome prosecutor who, as a U.S. Supreme Court justice, is generally thought to be responsible for the "switch in time that saved nine" on the Supreme Court in 1937? [Owen Roberts]

- Argued the case of *Meyer v. Nebraska* (1932) and helped establish the right of parents and private schools to educate children? [Arthur Mullen]

- Represented President Richard Nixon in making his claims against the special prosecutors for executive privilege? [James St. Clair]

- Was the author of *The Folklore of Capitalism* who was said to be a combination of "Voltaire and the Cowboy"? [Thurman Arnold]

- First came into national prominence with his successful appeal of the *Sam Shepard* case and his work analyzing polygraph tests? [F. Lee Bailey]

- Was a descendant of Edmund Randolph and served as both solicitor general and attorney general of the United States? [Francis Biddle]

- Resigned from the U.S. Supreme Court and later argued for the butchers in the famous *Slaughterhouse Cases* that helped determine the interpretation of the Fourteenth Amendment? [John Archibald Campbell]

- Helped persuade the U.S. Supreme Court that the income tax was unconstitutional? [Joseph H. Choate]

- Attended Dartmouth College during the time that Daniel Webster represented the school before the U.S. Supreme Court? [Rufus Choate]

- Was a Kentucky senator who served as a key architect of the Missouri Compromise and the Compromise of 1850? [Henry Clay]

- Was told during a law school mock trial that he would "*never* become a trial lawyer"? [Gerry Spence]

- Defended leading American Communists after returning from prosecuting Nazis at Nuremberg? [Mary Kaufman]

- Was founder and president of the Children's Defense Fund? [Marian Wright Edelman]

- Was the subject of a movie, *Boomerang,* which described a prosecutor who brought out evidence favorable to a defendant? [Homer S. Cummings]

- Was America's longest-serving attorney general who helped defend George Wythe Sweeney against charges that he poisoned his uncle, George Wythe? [William Wirt]

- Was a U.S. solicitor general who served for a time after leaving the post as president of Brigham Young University? [Rex Lee]

- Was a key attorney for the NAACP's Legal Defense Fund who became the first African-American to serve on the Washington, D.C., court of appeals? [Spottswood Robinson III]

- Was one of the attorneys who argued before the U.S. Supreme Court for the validity of the National Labor Relations Act before serving for forty-five years as a U.S. district judge? [Charles E. Wyzanski Jr.]

- Used his role in the adoption of the Fourteenth Amendment to back his later claim that the amendment was designed to protect corporations? [Roscoe Conkling]

- Served as attorney general under James Buchanan, fought against congressional reconstruction, and successfully argued against governmental actions in *Ex parte Milligan* and *Ex parte McCardle?* [Jeremiah Black]

- Was appointed by President McKinley as secretary of war and by Theodore Roosevelt as secretary of state? [Elihu Root]

- Was the first woman to receive a degree from an American law school? [Belva Lockwood]

- Was the unsuccessful Democratic nominee for president in 1924 who later argued for upholding segregation in the case of *Brown v. Board of Education* (1954)? [John Davis]

- Was a law school dean and chief justice of the New Jersey Supreme Court who was America's greatest advocate of judicial reform? [Arthur T. Vanderbilt]

- Had the reputation in Washington, D.C., as an insider who was "the man to see"? [Edward Bennett Williams]

- Was the first African-American elected to public office in the United States and helped establish the law department at Howard University? [John Mercer Langston]

- Was the Virginia governor who offered the Virginia Plan at the Constitutional Convention, refused to sign the Constitution in September 1787, but later advocated its ratification in the Virginia Ratifying Convention and became the nation's first attorney general? [Edmund Randolph]

- Was a cofounder of the Southern Poverty Law Center known for formulating strategies by which the Ku Klux Klan could be sued for violent actions by its members? [Morris Dees Jr.]

- Served as director of the NAACP's Legal Defense Fund from 1961 to 1994 and for a time as dean of the Columbia Law School? [Jack Greenberg]

- Was the son of a Church of Christ minister best known for leading the Whitewater and Lewinsky investigations involving President Clinton? [Kenneth Starr]

- Was called "the Ajax or Agamemnon" of the Rockingham (New Hampshire) bar and often bested Daniel Webster in legal arguments? [Jeremiah Mason]

- Was known as "the attorney general for runaway slaves"? [Salmon P. Chase]

- Became known as "Prohibition Portia" for her role in enforcing prohibition as assistant U.S. attorney general from 1921 to 1929? [Mabel Walker Willebrandt]

- Argued more cases before the U.S. Supreme Court than any other American attorney in history? [Walter Jones]

- Described herself as a "he-woman with a heart" and helped defend accused American Communists against deportation? [Carol Weiss King]

- Was a longtime litigator for the NAACP's Legal Defense Fund who became the first African-American woman to sit in the New York Senate and as a U.S. district court judge? [Constance Motley]

- Was fired as a clerk to Justice William Brennan after refusing to release a list of his political activities? [Michael Tigar]

- Authored the influential *Commentaries on the Law of Municipal Corporations?* [John Dillon]

- Followed his service as dean of the Harvard Law School from 1946 to 1967 by serving as U.S. solicitor general from 1967 to 1973? [Erwin Griswold]

- As chief justice of a Virginia court of appeals often reversed decisions of Virginia's chancellor, George Wythe, whom he had frequently bested in arguments as a litigator? [Edmund Pendleton]

- Served as president of the American Bar Association before being selected as the second Watergate special prosecutor? [Leon Jaworski]

- Was a Texas attorney known for arguing over a thousand death penalty cases and losing only one defendant to the executioner? [Percy Foreman]

- Argued against the constitutionality of the national income tax, against extensive congressional powers under the commerce clause, and against the Oregon law prohibiting children from attending private schools at issue in *Pierce v. Society of Sisters* (1921)? [William Guthrie]

- Participated in more than 50 percent of the cases before the U.S. Supreme Court dealing with the establishment clause during his career, including the case that established the "Lemon Test"? [Leo Pfeffer]

- Was a prominent attorney for railroads in the late nineteenth and early twentieth centuries who was often called "the King of the American Bar" and who left an extensive art collection to Philadelphia? [John Garner Johnson]

- Was lead counsel in what has become known as the *Mississippi Burning* trial? [John Doar]

- Defended T. Cullen Davis against charges of murder and of plotting the assassination of a judge? [Richard "Racehorse" Haynes]

- Was a fastidious dresser who delivered an influential three-day speech on the constitutionality of the national bank in *McCulloch v. Maryland* (1819)? [William Pinkney]

- Although blinded in one eye by a ricocheted bullet and in the other by apparent eye strain, went on to argue the Southern case in *Dred Scott v. Sandford* (1857)? [Reverdy Johnson]

- Is generally credited with helping to gain President Andrew Johnson's acquittal in impeachment charges before the U.S. Senate? [William Evarts]

- Was the key nineteenth-century American proponent of codification and brother to an influential U.S. Supreme Court justice? [David Dudley Field]

- Served as attorney general under Lincoln? [Edward Bates]

Questions about the lawyers described in boxes rather than in full entries: Which American lawyer(s):

- Defended Eric and Lyle Menendez against charges that they murdered their parents? [Leslie Abramson]

- Successfully argued in *Wisconsin v. Yoder* on behalf of the Amish parents who did not want to send their children to public schools beyond the eighth grade? [William Bentley Ball]

- Is best known for his defense of William Kennedy Smith against rape charges? [Roy Black]

- Was known, along with Daniel Webster and Henry Clay, as one of the three great congressional leaders in the first half of the nineteenth century? [John C. Calhoun]

- Was an "insider's insider" who advised presidents from Truman to Lyndon Johnson? [Clark Clifford]

- Was Senator Joseph McCarthy's chief legal counsel? [Roy Cohn]

- Wrote *Constitutional Limitations?* [Thomas Cooley]

- Was called "the Napoleon of the Western Bar" and won nineteen acquittals in nineteen murder cases? [Delphin Michael Delmas]

- Although born to an old Southern family in Montgomery, Alabama, went on to serve as president of the National Lawyers Guild and the National Farmers Union and to work on behalf of civil rights? [Clifford J. Durr]

- Appears to have been the first woman lawyer to practice in America? [Margaret Brent]

- Was a "country lawyer" who became known for his role in leading the Senate Watergate investigation? [Sam Ervin]

- Headed up the Manhattan Sex Crimes Prosecution Unit that prosecuted assailants who participated in the gang rape of a Central Park robber? [Linda Fairstein]

- Was the law partner of Abraham Lincoln? [William H. Herndon]

- Was the fictional hero in *To Kill a Mockingbird?* [Atticus Finch]

- Was known for the defense of celebrities and defended Paul Wright for the murder of his wife and best friend after he discovered them in a compromising situation? [Jerry Giesler]

- Is known for writing a legal thriller each year, and who returned to the courtroom to win a substantial award for a client who had lost her husband in a railroad accident? [John Grisham]

- Was called "the Greta Garbo of the bar"? [Fanny Holtzmann]

- Helped draft the constitution of Texas and twice served as its president? [Sam Houston]

- Are perhaps the two best-known attorney scoundrels in New York and U.S. history? [William F. Howe and Abraham H. Hummel]

- Wrote the Declaration of Independence? [Thomas Jefferson]

- Wrote the "Perry Mason" series? [Erle Stanley Gardner]

- Defended a deaf-mute in a murder trial? [Lowell J. Myers]

- Wrote *Unsafe at Any Speed* before running for president of the United States? [Ralph Nader]

- Served two jail terms before becoming a lawyer in the Indian Territory and defending 342 accused murderers? [Moman Pruiett]

- Is said to have achieved acquittals for 99 percent of his clients in Minnesota courts? [Eugene A. Rerat]

- Resigned as U.S. attorney general rather than fire Archibald Cox? [Elliot Richardson]

- Went to jail rather than put a defendant on the stand who he thought was about to perjure himself? [Ellis Rubin]

- Helps head the Innocence Project to release individuals from jail when it can be proved through DNA evidence that they are not guilty of the crimes for which they have been incarcerated? [Barry Scheck]

- Was the inspiration for the Johnny Cash song, "A Boy Named Sue"? [Sue Hicks]

- Served as secretary of state under President Eisenhower? [John Foster Dulles]

- Served for twenty years as attorney general of New Hampshire and often argued against Daniel Webster? [George Sullivan]

- Once persuaded a Supreme Court justice to alter a reference made to him in an opinion? [Littleton Waller Tazewell]

- Was described as "a combination of Robin Hood, Abraham Lincoln, Puck, and Uncle Sam"? [Ephraim Tutt]

- Successfully argued the case of *Roe v. Wade?* [Sarah Weddington and Linda Coffee]

- Is credited with exposing Senator Joseph McCarthy during nationally televised hearings? [Joseph Welch]

- Is best known for his book *The Art of Cross-Examination?* [Francis L. Wellman]

Selected
Bibliography

Abramson, Leslie, with Richard Flaste. *The Defense Is Ready: Life in the Trenches of Criminal Law*. New York: Simon & Schuster, 1997.

Adams, Charles Francis, Jr. *Richard Henry Dana: A Biography*. 2 vols. Boston: Houghton Mifflin, 1890.

Adams, John. *Diary and Autobiography*. Edited by L. H. Butterfield. 4 vols. Cambridge: Belknap Press of Harvard University Press, 1961.

Alexander, James. *A Brief Narrative of the Case and Trial of John Peter Zenger*. Edited by Stanley Katz. Cambridge: Belknap Press of Harvard University Press, 1963.

Alton, Stephen R. "Loyal Lietuenant, Able Advocate: The Role of Robert H. Jackson in Franklin D. Roosevelt's Battle with the Supreme Court." *William & Mary Bill of Rights Journal* 5 (1997): 527–530.

Arnold, Thurman. *Fair Fights and Foul*. New York: Harcourt, Brace and World, 1965.

Axelrad, Jacob. *Patrick Henry: The Voice of Freedom*. Westport, CT: Greenwood Press, 1975.

Axelrod, Alan, Charles Phillips, and Kurt Kemper. *Cops, Crooks and Criminologists*. New York: Facts on File, 1996.

Ayer, Eleanor H. *Ruth Bader Ginsburg: Fire and Steel on the Supreme Court*. New York: Macmillan, 1994.

Aymar, Bryandt, and Edward Sagarin. *A Pictorial History of the World's Great Trials from Socrates to Eichmann*. New York: Bonanza Books, 1967.

Bailey, F. Lee, and Harvey Aronson. *The Defense Never Rests*. New York: Stein & Day, 1971.

Bailey, F. Lee, with John Greenya. *For the Defense*. New York: Signet, 1975.

Bailyn, Bernard, ed. *Pamphlets of the American Revolution*. Vol 1, *1750–1776*. Cambridge: Belnap Press of Harvard University Press, 1965.

Baker, Leonard. *John Marshall: A Life in the Law*. New York: Macmillan, 1974.

Baker, Mark. *D.A.: Prosecutors in Their Own Words*. New York: Simon & Schuster, 1999.

Baker, Nancy V. *Conflicting Loyalties: Law & Politics in the Attorney General's Office, 1789–1990*. Lawrence: University Press of Kansas, 1992.

Barrows, Chester L. *William M. Evarts: Lawyer, Diplomat, Statesman*. Chapel Hill: University of North Carolina Press, 1941.

Bass, Jack. *Unlikely Heroes*. New York: Simon & Schuster, 1981.

Baxter, Maurice G. *Daniel Webster & the Supreme Court*. Amherst: University of Massachusetts Press, 1966.

_____. *The Steamboat Monopoly: Gibbons v. Ogden, 1824*. New York: Alfred A. Knopf, 1972.

Beeman, Richard. *Patrick Henry: A Biography*. New York: McGraw-Hill, 1974.

Belknap, Michael R., ed. *American Political Trials*. Westport, CT: Greenwood Press, 1981.

Bell, Charles H. *The Bench and Bar of New Hampshire*. Boston: Houghton Mifflin, 1894.

Belli, Melvin M. *Dallas Justice: The Real Story of Jack Ruby and His Trial*. New York: McKay, 1964.

_____. *Modern Trials*. Indianapolis: Bobbs-Merrill, 1954.

Belli, Melvin M., with Robert Blair Kaiser. *Melvin Belli, My Life on Trial*. New York: William Morrow, 1976.

Bemis, Samuel Flagg. *John Quincy Adams and the Union*. New York: Alfred A. Knopf, 1956.

Benét, Stephen Vincent. *The Devil and Daniel Webster*. New York: Holt, Rinehart & Winston, 1937.

Ben-Veniste, Richard, and George Frampton Jr. *Stonewall: The Real Story of the Watergate Prosecution*. New York: Simon & Schuster, 1977.

Berkman, Ted. *The Lady and the Law: The Remarkable Life of Fanny Holtzman*. Boston: Little, Brown, 1976.

Berry, Dawn Bradley. *The 50 Most Influential Women in American Law*. Los Angeles: RGA, 1996.

Beyer, Barry K. *Thomas E. Dewey 1937–1947: A Study in Political Leadership*. New York: Garland, 1979.

Biddle, Francis B. *A Casual Past*. Garden City, NY: Doubleday, 1961.

_____. *In Brief Authority*. Garden City, NY: Doubleday, 1962.

Black, Chauncey F. *Essays and Speeches of Jeremiah S. Black*. New York: Appleton, 1886.

Black, Roy. *Black's Law: A Criminal Lawyer Reveals His Defense Strategies in Four Cliffhanger Cases*. New York: Simon & Schuster, 1999.

Blackburn, Joyce. *George Wythe of Williamsburg*. New York: Harper & Row, 1975.

Blackwell, Victor V. *O'er the Ramparts They Watched*. New York: Carlton Press, 1976.

Blaine, James G. *Twenty Years of Congress from Lincoln to Garfield*. 2 vols. Norwich, CT: Henry Bill, 1884.

Bland, Randall R. *Private Pressure on Public Law: The Legal Career of Justice Thurgood Marshall*. Port Washington, NY: Kennikat Press, 1973.

Blue, Frederick J. *Salmon P. Chase: A Life in Politics*. Kent, Ohio: Kent State University Press, 1987.

Bok, Derek, Stephen Breyer, Paul Freund, Carl Kaysen, Edward Levi, and Elliot Richardson. "In Memoriam: Charles E. Wyzanski, Jr." *Harvard Law Review* 100 (1987): 705–727.

Boyer, Richard Owen. *Max Steuer, Magician of the Law*. New York: Greenberg, 1932.

Bradford, M. E. *Founding Fathers: Brief Lives of the Framers of the United States Constitution*. 2d ed. Lawrence: University Press of Kansas, 1981.

Brigance, William N. *Jeremiah Sullivan Black*. Philadelphia: University of Pennsylvania Press, 1934.

Brookhiser, Richard. *Alexander Hamilton, American*. New York: Free Press, 1999.

Brown, Dorothy M. *Mabel Walker Willebrandt—A Study of Power, Loyalty, and Law*. Knoxville: University of Tennessee Press, 1984.

Brown, Imogene E. *American Aristides: A Biography of George Wythe*. Rutherford, NJ: Fairleigh Dickinson University Press, 1981.

Brown, Samuel Gilman. *The Life of Rufus Choate*. 3d ed. Boston: Little, Brown, 1879.

Bugliosi, Vincent. *Outrage: The Five Reasons O. J. Simpson Got Away with Murder*. New York: W. W. Norton, 1996.

Bugliosi, Vincent T., and Curt Gentry. *Helter Skelter: The True Story of the Manson Murders*. New York: W. W. Norton, 1974.

Bugliosi, Vincent T., and Bruce B. Henderson. *And the Sea Will Tell*. New York: Ballantine, 1991.

Bugliosi, Vincent T., and Ken Hurwitz. *Till Death Us Do Part*. New York: W. W. Norton, 1978.

Burke, Joseph Charles. "William Wirt: Attorney General and Constitutional Lawyer." Ph.D. dissertation, Indiana University, 1965.

Burns, James. *Beauties of Story*. Boston: James Burns, 1939.

Butler, Pierce. *Judah P. Benjamin*. New York: Chelsea House, 1980.

Calabro, Marian. *Great Courtroom Lawyers: Fighting the Cases That Made History*. New York: Facts on File, 1996.

Capers, Gerald M. *Stephen A. Douglas: Defender of the Union*. Boston: Little, Brown, 1959.

Caplan, Lincoln. *The Tenth Justice: The Solicitor General and the Rule of Law*. New York: Vintage Books, 1988.

Carrington, Paul D. *Stewards of Democracy: Law as a Public Profession*. Boulder, CO: Westview Press, 1999.

Carson, Clara N. *The Lawyers Statistical Report: The U.S. Legal Profession in 1995*. Chicago: American Bar Foundation, 1999.

Cartwright, Gary. *Blood Will Tell: The Murder Trials of T. Cullen Davis*. New York: Harcourt Brace Jovanovich, 1979.

Chase, Harold, Samuel Krislow, Keith O. Boyum, and Jerry N. Clark. *Biographical Dictionary of the Federal Judiciary*. Detroit: Gale Research, 1976.

Cheek, William, and Aimee Lee Cheek. *John Mercer Langston and the Fight for Black Freedom*. Urbana: University of Illinois Press, 1989.

Chidsey, Donald Barr. *The Gentleman from New York: Roscoe Conkling*. New Haven: Yale University Press, 1935.

Chroust, Anton-Hermann. *The Rise of the Legal Profession in America*. 2 vols. Norman: University of Oklahoma Press, 1965.

Clancy, Paul R. *Just a Country Lawyer: A Biography of Senator Sam Ervin*. Bloomington: Indiana University Press, 1974.

Clark, Gilbert J. *Life Sketches of Eminent Lawyers, American, English and Canadian to Which Is Added Thought, Facts and Facetiae*. Kansas City, Mo: Lawyer's International, 1895. Reprint, Littleton, CO: Fred B. Rothman, 1963.

Clarkson, Paul S., and R. Samuel Jett. *Luther Martin of Maryland*. Baltimore: Johns Hopkins University Press, 1970.

Clay, Thomas Hart. *Henry Clay*. Philadelphia: George W. Jacobs, 1910.

Clayton, Cornell. *The Politics of Justice: The Attorney General and the Making of Legal Policy*. Armonk, NY: M. E. Sharpe, 1992.

Clayton, Mary Black. *Reminiscences of Jeremiah Sullivan Black*. St. Louis: Christian, 1887.

Clifford, Clark, with Richard Holbrooke. *Counsel to the President: A Memoir*. New York: Random House, 1991.

Cochran, Johnnie L., Jr., with Tim Rutten. *Journey to Justice*. New York: One World, 1996.

Coffin, William Sloane, Jr. *Once to Every Man: A Memoir*. New York: Atheneum, 1977.

Cohn, Alfred, and Joe Chisholm. *"Take the Witness!"* New York: Frederick A. Stokes, 1934.

Cole, Donald B. *Martin Van Buren and the American Political System*. Princeton, NJ: Princeton University Press, 1984.

Conkling, Alfred R. *The Life and Letters of Roscoe Conkling: Orator, Statesman, Advocate*. New York: Charles L. Webster, 1889.

Connor, Henry G. *John Archibald Campbell: Associate Justice of the United States Supreme Court, 1853–1861*. Boston: Houghton Mifflin, 1920. Reprint, New York: Da Capo Press, 1971.

Cook, Charles M. *The American Codification Movement: A Study of Antebellum Legal Reform*. Westport, CT: Greenwood Press, 1981.

Coquillette, Daniel R. *Law in Colonial Massachusetts 1630–1800*. Boston: Colonial Society of Massachusetts, 1984.

Couric, Emily. *The Trial Lawyers: The Nation's Top Litigators Tell How They Win*. New York: St. Martin's Press, 1988.

Coway, Geoffrey. *The People v. Clarence Darrow: The Bribery Trial of America's Greatest Lawyer*. New York: Times Books, 1993.

Cummings, Homer S. *Selected Papers of Homer Cummings, Attorney General of the United States, 1933–1939*. Edited by Carl Brent Swisher. New York: Da Capo Press, 1972.

Cummings, Homer S., and Carl McFarland. *Federal Justice*. New York: Macmillan, 1937.

Curriden, Mark. "From Elvis To Exxon." *American Bar Association Journal* (November 1990): 65–68.

Curriden, Mark, and Leroy Phillips Jr. *Contempt of Court: The Turn of the Century Lynching That Launched a Hundred Years of Federalism*. New York: Faber & Faber, 1999.

Curtis, Benjamin R., ed. *A Memoir of Benjamin Robbins Curtis, LL.D.: With Some of His Professional and Miscellaneous Writings*. 2 vols. Boston: Little, Brown, 1879.

Cushman, Clare, ed. *The Supreme Court Justices: Illustrated Biographies, 1789–1993*. Washington: Congressional Quarterly, 1993.

Daniels, Jonathan. *The Randolphs of Virginia*. Garden City, NY: Doubleday, 1972.

Darrow, Clarence. *The Story of My Life*. New York: Scribner, 1932.

Davis, Deane C. *Justice in the Mountains: Stories & Tales by a Vermont Country Lawyer*. Shelborne, VT: New England Press, 1980.

Davis, Michael D., and Hunter R. Clark. *Thurgood Marshall: Warrior at the Bar, Rebel at the Bench*. New York: Birch Lane Press, 1992.

Dees, Morris, Jr., and James Corcoran. *Gathering Storm: America's Militia Threat.* New York: HarperCollins, 1996.

Dees, Morris, Jr., and Steve Fiffer. *A Season for Justice: The Life and Times of Civil Rights Lawyer Morris Dees.* New York: Scribner, 1991.

Dershowitz, Alan. *The Abuse Excuse.* New York: Little, Brown, 1994.

————. *The Best Defense.* New York: Random House, 1982.

————. *Reasonable Doubts.* New York: Simon & Schuster, 1996.

————. *Reversal of Fortune.* New York: Random House, 1986.

Desmond, Charles S., Paul A. Freund, Potter Stewart, and Lord Shawcross. *Mr. Justice Jackson: Four Lectures in His Honor.* New York: Columbia University Press, 1969.

Dewey, Frank L. *Thomas Jefferson, Lawyer.* Charlottesville: University Press of Virginia, 1986.

Dill, Alonzo T. *George Wythe: Teacher of Liberty.* Williamsburg: Virginia Independence Bicentennial Commission, 1979.

Dillon, John F. *Commentaries on the Law of Municipal Corporations.* Boston: Little, Brown, 1890.

Doar, John. "The Work of the Civil Rights Division in Enforcing Voting Rights under the Civil Rights Acts of 1956 and 1960." *Florida State University Law Review* 25 (1997): 1.

Donald, David H. *Lincoln.* New York: Simon & Schuster, 1995.

Dorman, Michael. *King of the Courtroom: Percy Foreman for the Defense.* New York: Delacorte Press, 1969.

Dorsen, Norman. "The Second Mr. Justice Harlan: A Constitutional Conservative." *New York University Law Review* 44 (1969): 249–271.

Doyle, James. *Not above the Law: The Battles of Watergate Prosecutors Cox and Jaworski.* New York: William Morrow, 1977.

Drachman, Virginia G. *Sisters in Law: Women Lawyers in Modern American History.* Cambridge: Harvard University Press, 1988.

Draper, Robert. "The Great Defenders." *Texas Monthly* 96 (January 1994).

Duff, John J. *A Lincoln: Prairie Lawyer.* New York: Rinehart, 1960.

Dunnahoo, Terry. *Before the Supreme Court: The Story of Belva Ann Lockwood.* Boston: Houghton Mifflin, 1974.

Dunne, Gerald T. *Justice Joseph Story and the Rise of the Supreme Court.* New York: Simon & Schuster, 1970.

Dyer, Brainerd. *The Public Career of William M. Evarts.* Berkeley: University of California Press, 1933.

Eckenrode, H. J. *The Randolphs: The Story of a Virginia Family.* Indianapolis: Bobbs-Merrill, 1946.

Eggleston, George Cary. *The American Immortals: The Record of Men Who, by Their Achievements in Statecraft, War, Science, Literature, Art, Law and Commerce, Have Created the American Republic and Whose Names Are Inscribed in the Hall-of-Fame.* New York: Putnam, 1901.

Ely, James W., Jr. *The Chief Justiceship of Melville W. Fuller, 1888–1910.* Columbia: University of South Carolina Press, 1995.

————. *The Guardian of Every Other Right: A Constitutional History of Property Rights.* 2d ed. New York: Oxford University Press, 1998.

Emert, Phyllis Raybin. *Top Lawyers and Their Famous Cases.* Minneapolis: Oliver Press, 1996.

Evans, Eli N. *Judah P. Benjamin: The Jewish Confederate*. New York: Free Press, 1988.

Evarts, Sherman, ed. *Arguments and Speeches of William Maxwell Evarts*. 3 vols. New York: Macmillan, 1919.

Field, Henry M. *The Life of David Dudley Field*. New York: Scribner, 1898.

Formley, Ken. *Archibald Cox: Conscience of a Nation*. Boston: Addison-Wesley, 1997.

Fortas, Abe. "Thurman Arnold and the Theatre of the Law." *Yale Law Journal* 79 (May 1970), 988–1004.

Fowler, Gene. *The Great Mouthpiece: A Life Story of William J. Fallon*. New York: Collier, 1931.

Fox, Mary Virginia. *Lady for the Defense: A Biography of Belva Lockwood*. New York: Harcourt Brace Jovanovich, 1975.

Frank, John P. *Lincoln as a Lawyer*. Urbana: University of Illinois Press, 1961.

Franklin, John Hope. *From Slavery to Freedom: A History of African Americans*. 8th ed. Boston: McGraw-Hill, 2000.

Frantz, Douglas, and David McKean. *Friends in High Places: The Rise and Fall of Clark Clifford*. Boston: Little, Brown, 1995.

Fuess, Claude M. *Caleb Cushing*. 2 vols. New York: Harcourt, Brace, 1923.

_____. *Rufus Choate: The Wizard of the Law*. New York: Minton, Balch, 1928.

Gale, Robert L. *Richard Henry Dana, Jr.* New York: Twayne, 1969.

Galvin, John R. *Three Men of Boston*. New York: Thomas Y. Crowell, 1976.

Gardner, Warner W. "Robert H. Jackson: 1892–1954—Government Attorney." *Columbia Law Review* 55 (April 1955): 438–444.

Garraty, John A., ed. *Quarrels That Have Shaped the Constitution*. Rev. ed. New York: Harper & Row, 1987.

Garraty, John A., and Mark C. Carnes, eds. *American National Biography*. 24 vols. New York: Oxford University Press, 1999.

Gerhart, Eugene C. *Arthur T. Vanderbilt: The Compleat Counsellor*. Albany: Q Corporation, 1980.

_____. *Supreme Court Justice Jackson: Lawyer's Judge*. Albany: Q Corporation, 1961.

Giesler, Jerry, with Pete Martin. *The Jerry Giesler Story*. New York: Simon & Schuster, 1960.

Gilbert, Lynn, and Gaylen Moore. *Particular Passions: Talks with Women Who Have Shaped Our Times*. New York: Crown Books, 1981.

Gill, Ann. "The Oral Tradition of Gerry Spence in *Pring v. Penthouse*." *Southwestern University Law Review* 17 (1988): 693–706.

Ginger, Ann Fagan. *Carol Weiss King: Human Rights Lawyer, 1895–1952*. Niwot: University Press of Colorado, 1993.

_____, ed. *The Relevant Lawyers: Conversations out of Court on Their Clients, Their Practice, Their Politics, Their Life Style*. New York: Simon & Schuster, 1972.

Ginger, Ann Fagan, and Eugine M. Tobin, eds. *The National Lawyers Guild: From Roosevelt through Reagan*. Philadephia: Temple University Press, 1988.

Ginsburg, Ruth B. "Remarks on Women Becoming Part of the Constitution." *Journal of Law and Inequality* 6 (1988): 17.

Glad, Betty. *Charles Evans Hughes and the Illusions of Innocence: A Study in American Diplomacy*. Champaign: University of Illinois Press, 1966.

Glendon, Mary Ann. *A Nation under Lawyers*. New York: Farrar, Straus & Giroux, 1994.

Goebel, Julius, Jr., and Joseph H. Smith, eds. *The Law Practice of Alexander Hamilton*. 5 vols. New York: Columbia University Press, 1964–1981.

Goodhart, Arthur L. *Five Jewish Lawyers of the Common Law*. Freeport, NY: Books for Libraries Press, 1971.

Gould, Milton S. *The Witness Who Spoke with God and Other Tales from the Courthouse*. New York: Viking Press, 1979.

Goulden, Joseph C. *The Million Dollar Lawyers*. New York: Putnam, 1978.

Greenberg, Jack. "A Crusader in the Court: Comments on the Civil Rights Movement." *University of Missouri–Kansas City Law Review* 63 (1994): 207–227.

_____. *Crusaders in the Courts: How a Dedicated Band of Lawyers Fought for the Civil Rights Revolution*. New York: Basic Books, 1994.

Greenspan, Edward L., and George Jonas. *Greenspan: The Case for the Defence*. Toronto: Macmillan of Canada, 1987.

Gressley, Gene M., ed. *Voltaire and the Cowboy: The Letters of Thurman Arnold*. Boulder: Colorado Associated University Press, 1977.

Griffith, Robert. *The Politics of Fear: Joseph R. McCarthy and the Senate*. Amherst: University of Massachusetts Press, 1987.

Griswold, Erwin N. *The Fifth Amendment Today: Three Speeches by Erwin Griswold*. Cambridge: Harvard University Press, 1955.

_____. *Law and Lawyers in the United States: The Common Law under Stress*. Cambridge: Harvard University Press, 1964.

_____. *Ould Fields, New Corne: The Personal Memoirs of a Twentieth Century Lawyer*. St. Paul: West, 1992.

Guelzo, Allen C. *Abraham Lincoln: Redeemer President*. Grand Rapids, MI: Eerdmans, 1999.

Gurko, Miriam. *Clarence Darrow*. New York: Thomas Y. Crowell, 1965.

Guthrie, William D. *Lectures on the Fourteenth Amendment*. New York: Da Capo Press, 1898.

_____. *Magna Carta and Other Addresses*. New York: Columbia University Press, 1916.

Hagan, Horace H. *Eight Great American Lawyers*. Oklahoma City: Harlow, 1923.

Hall, Kermit L. *The Magic Mirror: Law in American History*. New York: Oxford University Press, 1989.

_____, ed. *The Oxford Companion to the Supreme Court of the United States*. New York: Oxford University Press, 1992.

Hamilton, Alexander. *The Papers of Alexander Hamilton*. Edited by Harold C. Syrett. New York: Columbia University Press, 1964–1981.

Harbaugh, William H. *Lawyer's Lawyer: The Life of John W. Davis*. New York: Oxford University Press, 1973.

Hare, Francis Hutcheson. *My Learned Friends: Memories of a Trial Lawyer*. Cincinnati: Anderson, 1976.

Harlan, John M. *The Evolution of a Judicial Philosophy: Selected Opinions and Papers of Justice John M. Harlan*. Edited by David L. Shapiro. Cambridge: Harvard University Press, 1969.

Harris, Mary Belle. *I Knew Them in Prison*. New York: Viking Press, 1936.

Hart, Albert Bushnell. *Salmon Portland Chase*. New York: Greenwood Press, 1969.

Hays, Arthur Garfield. *City Lawyer: The Autobiography of a Law Practice*. New York: Simon & Schuster, 1942.

Henry, William Wirt. *Patrick Henry: Life, Correspondence and Speeches*. 2 vols. New York: Burt Franklin, 1891. Reprint, 1969.

Herndon, William H. *Herndon's Lincoln: The True Story of a Great Life*. Edited by David F. Hawke. Indianapolis: Bobbs-Merrill, 1970.

Hockett, Jeffrey D. *New Deal Justice: The Constitutional Jurisprudence of Hugo L. Black, Felix Frankfurter and Robert H. Jackson*. Lanham, MD: Rowman & Littlefield, 1996.

Holcomb, David J. "The Nexus of Freedom of Religion and Separation of Church and State in the Thought of Leo Pfeffer." Ph.D. dissertation, Baylor University, 1997.

Horwitz, Morton J. *The Transformation of American Law: 1870–1960*. New York: Oxford University Press, 1992.

Hughes, Charles Evans. *The Autobiographical Notes of Charles Evan Hughes*. Edited by David J. Danelski and Joseph S. Tulchin. Cambridge: Harvard University Press, 1973.

Hyman, Harold M. *The Reconstruction Justice of Salmon P. Chase: In Re Turner and Texas v. White*. Lawrence: University Press of Kansas, 1997.

Hynd, Alan. *Defenders of the Damned*. New York: A. S. Barnes, 1960.

Ireland, Robert M. *The Legal Career of William Pinkney 1764–1822*. New York: Garland, 1986.

Irons, Peter. *The New Deal Lawyers*. Princeton, NJ: Princeton University Press, 1982. Reprint, 1993.

Jackson, Kenneth, Karen Markoe, and Arnold Markoe, eds. *The Scribner Encyclopedia of American Lives*. New York: Scribner, 1999.

James, Marlise. *The People's Lawyers*. New York: Holt, Rhinehart & Winston, 1973.

Jaworski, Leon. *The Right and the Power: The Prosecution of Watergate*. New York: Reader's Digest Press, 1976.

Jaworski, Leon, with Mickey Herskowitz. *Confession and Avoidance: A Memoir*. Garden City, NY: Anchor Press/Doubleday, 1979.

Jaworski, Leon, with Dick Schneider. *Crossroads*. Elgin, IL: David C. Cook, 1981.

Jessup, Philip. *Elihu Root*. New York: Archon Books, 1964.

Johannsen, Robert W. *Stephen A. Douglas*. Urbana: University of Illinois Press, 1997.

Johnson, John W. *Historic U.S. Court Cases 1690–1990: An Encyclopedia*. New York: Garland, 1972.

Kalman, Laura. *Abe Fortas: A Biography*. New Haven: Yale University Press, 1990.

Kearney, Edward N. *Thurman Arnold, Social Critic: The Satirical Challenge to Orthodoxy*. Albuquerque: University of New Mexico Press, 1970.

Kelly, Alfred H., Winfred A. Harbison, and Herman Belz. *The American Constitution: Its Origins and Developments*. 7th ed. 2 vols. New York: W. W. Norton, 1991.

Kennedy, John P. *Memoirs of the Life of William Wirt*. 2 vols. Philadelphia: Lea & Blanchard, 1840.

Kennedy, Randall. "The Moses of That Journey." *Constitution* 5 (Winter 1993): 29–35.

Kerber, Linda K. *No Constitutional Right to be Ladies: Women and the Obligations of Citizenship*. New York: Hill & Wang, 1998.

Kerr, Laura. *The Girl Who Ran for President*. New York: Thomas Nelson, 1947.

Kilbourn, Dwight C. *The Bench and Bar of Litchfield County, Connecticut 1709–1909*. Litchfield, CT: Privately printed, 1909.

Kirtland, Robert B. *George Wythe: Lawyer, Revolutionary, Judge*. New York: Garland, 1986.

Kluger, Richard. *Simple Justice: The History of Brown v. Board of Education and Black America's Struggle for Equality*. New York: Alfred A. Knopf, 1976.

Knappman, Edward W., ed. *Great American Trials: From Salem Witchcraft to Rodney King*. Detroit: Visible Ink Press, 1994.

Kogan, Herman. *The First Century: The Chicago Bar Association, 1874–1974*. Chicago: Rand McNally, 1974.

Konkle, Burton Alva. *Joseph Hopkinson, 1770–1842, Jurist: Scholar: Inspirer of the Arts*. Philadelphia: University of Pennsylvania Press, 1931.

_____. *The Life of Andrew Hamilton, 1676–1741, "The Day-Star of the American Revolution."* Freeport, NY: Books for Libraries Press, 1941.

Kornstein, Daniel J. *Thinking under Fire: Great Courtroom Lawyers and Their Impact on American History*. New York: Dodd, Mead, 1987.

Kunstler, William M. *Deep in My Heart*. New York: William Morrow, 1966.

Kunstler, William M., with Sheila Isenberg. *My Life as a Radical Lawyer*. New York: Birch Lane Press, 1994.

Kurland, Phillip B., Gerhard Casper, and Dennis J. Hutchinson. *The Supreme Court Review, 1988, 1990*. Chicago: University of Chicago Press, 1989, 1991.

Kutler, Stanley I. *The American Inquisition: Justice and Injustice in the Cold War*. New York: Hill & Wang, 1982.

_____. *The Wars of Watergate: The Last Crisis of Richard Nixon*. New York: Alfred A. Knopf, 1990.

Langford, Gerald. *The Murder of Stanford White*. Indianapolis: Bobbs-Merrill, 1962.

Langston, John Mercer. *Freedom and Citizenship*. Washington: Rufus H. Darby, 1883. Reprint, Miami: Mnemosyne, 1969.

_____. *From the Virginia Plantation to the National Capital*. Hartford, CT: American, 1894. Reprint, New York: Bergman, 1969.

Langum, David J. *William M. Kunstler: The Most Hated Lawyer in America*. New York: New York University Press, 1999.

Larson, Edward J. *Summer for the Gods: The Scopes Trial and America's Continuing Debate over Science and Religion*. New York: Basic Books, 1997.

Leach, Richard H. "Benjamin Robbins Curtis: Case Study of a Supreme Court Justice." Ph.D. dissertation, Princeton University, 1951.

Lee, Rex E. *A Lawyer Looks at the Constitution*. Provo, UT: Brigham Young University Press, 1981.

_____. *A Lawyer Looks at the Equal Rights Amendment*. Provo, UT: Brigham Young University Press, 1980.

Leibowitz, Robert. *The Defender: The Life and Career of Samuel S. Leibowitz, 1893–1933*. Englewood Cliffs, NJ: Prentice-Hall, 1981.

Leonard, Charles A. *A Search for a Judicial Philosophy: Mr. Justice Roberts and the Constitutional Revolution of 1937*. Port Washington, NY: Kennikat Press, 1971.

Leopold, Richard W. *Elihu Root: The Conservative Tradition*. Boston: Little, Brown, 1954.

Lewis, William Draper. *Great American Lawyers*. 8 vols. Philadelphia: John C. Winston, 1907.

Lief, Michael S., H. Mitchell Caldwell, and Benjamin Byucel. *Ladies and Gentlemen of the Jury: Greatest Closing Arguments in American Law*. New York: Scribner, 1998.

Lincoln, Abraham. *The Collected Works of Abraham Lincoln*. Edited by Rob P. Basler. 9 vols. New Brunswick, NJ: Rutgers University Press, 1953.

Linn, Edward. "F. Lee Bailey: Renegade in the Courtroom." *Saturday Evening Post*, 5 November 1966, 80–93.

Linowitz, Sol, with Martin Mayer. *The Betrayed Profession: Lawyering at the End of the Twentieth Century*. New York: Scribner, 1994.

Lisagor, Nancy, and Franki Lipsius. *A Law unto Itself: The Untold Story of the Law Firm Sullivan & Cromwell, 100 Years of Creating Power & Wealth*. New York: William Morrow, 1988.

Litwak, Lee, and August Meier, eds. *Black Leaders of the Nineteenth Century*. Urbana: University of Illinois Press, 1988.

Litwak, Mark. *Courtroom Crusaders: American Lawyers Who Refuse to Fit the Mold*. New York: William Morrow, 1989.

Long, John. *The Law of Illinois*. Vol. 1, *Lincoln's Cases before the Illinois Supreme Court from His Entry into the Practice of Law until His Entry into Congress*. Shiloh, IL: Illinois Company, 1993.

Lowery, Charles, and John Marszalek, eds. *Encyclopedia of African-American Civil Rights: From Emancipation to the Present*. New York: Greenwood Press, 1992.

Lucid, Robert F., ed. *The Journal of Richard Henry Dana, Jr.* 3 vols. Cambridge: Belknap Press of Harvard University Press, 1968.

Lukas, J. Anthony. *Nightmare: The Underside of the Nixon Years*. New York: Viking Press, 1976.

Magee, Nanneska Nall. "Playing It Dangerous: Justice Jackson's Passionate Style." *Scribes Journal of Legal Writing* (1991): 123–141.

Malone, Dumas, ed. *Dictionary of American Biography*. 10 vols., 10 supplements. New York: Scribner, 1943–1995.

Marcus, Robert D., and Anthony Marcus. *On Trial: American History through Court Proceedings and Hearings*. 2 vols. St. James, NY: Brandywine Press, 1998.

Martin, Edward S. *The Life of Joseph Hodges Choate*. New York: Scribner, 1927.

Mason, Alpheus T. *Brandeis, A Free Man's Life*. New York: Viking Press, 1946.

Mason, Jeremiah. *Memoir, Autoboigraphy and Correspondence of Jeremiah Mason*. Kansas City, MO: Lawyer's International, 1917.

Matthews, Elizabeth W. *Lincoln as a Lawyer: An Annotated Bibliography*. Carbondale: Southern Illinois University Press, 1991.

Matthews, Jean V. *Rufus Choate: The Law and Civic Virtue*. Philadelphia: Temple University Press, 1980.

Mayer, Martin. *The Lawyers*. New York: Harper & Row, 1967.

Mayo, Bernard. *Henry Clay: Spokesman for the New West*. Boston: Houghton Mifflin, 1937.

Mays, David John. *Edmund Pendleton, 1721–1803: A Biography*. 2 vols. Richmond: Virginia State Library, 1952.

McClellan, James Joseph. *Joseph Story and the American Constitution*. Norman: University of Oklahoma Press, 1971.

McCracken, Robert T. "Owen J. Roberts—Master Advocate." *University of Pennsylvania Law Review* 104 (1955): 322–331.

McDonald, Forrest. *Alexander Hamilton: A Biography*. New York: W. W. Norton, 1979.

McGraw, Thomas K. *Prophets of Regulation: Charles Francis Adams, Louis D. Brandeis, James M. Landis, Alfred E. Kahn*. Cambridge: Belknap Press of Harvard University Press, 1984.

McGuire, Phillip. *He, Too, Spoke for Democracy: Judge Hastie, World War II, and the Black Soldier*. Westport, CT: Greenwood Press, 1988.

McKenna, Marian C. *Tapping Reeve and the Litchfield Law School*. New York: Oceana, 1986.

McNeil, Gena Rae. *Groundwork: Charles Hamilton Houston and the Struggle for Civil Rights*. Philadelphia: University of Pennsylvania Press, 1983.

McWhirter, Darien A. *The Legal 100: A Ranking of the Individuals Who Have Most Influenced the Law*. Secaucus, NJ: Carol, 1998.

Meade, Robert D. *Judah P. Benjamin: Confederate Statesman*. New York: Oxford University Press, 1943.

_____. *Patrick Henry: Patriot in the Making*. Philadelphia: J. B. Lippincott, 1957.

_____. *Patrick Henry: Practical Revolutionary*. Philadelphia: J. B. Lippincott, 1969.

Mitford, Jessica. *The Trial of Dr. Spock: The Rev. William Sloane Coffin, Jr., Michael Ferber, Mitchell Goodman, and Marcus Raskin*. New York: Alfred A. Knopf, 1969.

Morello, Karen B. *The Invisible Bar: The Woman Lawyer in America: 1638 to the Present*. New York: Random House, 1986.

Motley, Constance Baker. *Equal Justice under Law*. New York: Farrar, Straus & Giroux, 1998.

"Mr. Justice Harlan: A Symposium." *Harvard Law Review* 85 (1971): 369–391.

Mullen, Arthur F. *Western Democrat*. New York: Wilfred Funk, 1940.

Murphy, Bruce A. *The Brandeis-Frankfurter Connection*. New York: Oxford University Press, 1982.

_____. *Fortas: The Rise and Ruin of a Supreme Court Justice*. New York: William Morrow, 1988.

Mushkat, Jerome, and Joseph G. Rayback. *Martin Van Buren: Law, Politics, and the Shaping of Republican Ideology*. DeKalb: Northern Illinois University Press, 1997.

Nagel, Paul C. *John Quincy Adams: A Public Life, A Private Life*. Cambridge: Harvard University Press, 1997.

Naifeh, Steven, and Gregory W. Smith. *The Best Lawyers in America*. Aiken, SC: Woodward & White, 1991.

_____. *Final Justice: The True Story of the Richest Man Ever Tried for Murder*. New York: Onyx, 1994.

Neely, Mark E., Jr. *The Fate of Liberty: Abraham Lincoln and Civil Liberties*. New York: Oxford University Press, 1991.

Neiman, S. I. *Judah Benjamin*. Indianapolis: Bobbs-Merrill, 1963.

Newmyer, R. Kent. *Supreme Court Justice Joseph Story: Statesman of the Old Republic*. Chapel Hill: University of North Carolina Press, 1985.

Newton, Merlin Owen. *Armed with the Constitution: Jehovah's Witnesses in Alabama and the U.S. Supreme Court, 1939–1946*. Tuscaloosa: University of Alabama Press, 1995.

Nieman, Donald G. *Promises to Keep: African-Americans and the Constitutional Order, 1776 to the Present*. New York: Oxford University Press, 1991.

Niven, John. *Martin Van Buren: The Romantic Age of American Politics*. New York: Oxford University Press, 1983.

_____. *Salmon P. Chase: A Biography*. New York: Oxford University Press, 1995.

Nix, Foster C. "Andrew Hamilton's Early Years in the American Colonies." *William and Mary Quarterly*, 3d ser., 21 (1964): 390–407.

Nizer, Louis. *Catspaw: The Famed Trial Attorney's Heroic Defense of a Man Unjustly Accused*. New York: D. I. Fine, 1992.

_____. *The Implosion Conspiracy*. New York: Doubleday, 1973.

_____. *The Jury Returns*. Garden City, NY: Doubleday, 1967.

_____. *My Life in Court*. Garden City, NY: Doubleday, 1961.

_____. *Reflections without Mirrors: An Autobiography of the Mind*. New York: Doubleday, 1978.

Noble, John Wesley, and Bernard Averbuch. *Never Plead Guilty: The Story of Jake Ehrlich the Brilliant Criminal Lawyer*. New York: Farrar, Straus & Cudahy, 1955.

Noonan, John T., Jr. *Persons and Masks of the Law: Cardozo, Holmes, Jefferson, and Wythe as Makers of the Masks*. New York: Farrar, Straus & Giroux, 1976.

Ogletree, Charles J., Jr. "Personal and Professional Integrity in the Legal Profession: Lessons from President Clinton and Kenneth Starr." *Washington & Lee Law Review* 56 (1999): 851.

Pack, Robert. *Edward Bennett Williams for the Defense*. New York: Harper & Row, 1983.

Paddock, Lisa. *Facts about the Supreme Court of the United States*. New York: H. W. Wilson, 1920.

Parker, Edward G. *Reminiscences of Rufus Choate, the Great American Advocate*. New York: Mason Brothers, 1860.

Parsons, Lynn Hudson. *John Quincy Adams*. Madison, WI: Madison House, 1988.

Parsons, Theophilus. *Memoir of Theophilus Parsons*. Boston: Ticknor & Fields, 1859.

Partridge, Bellamy. *Country Lawyer*. New York: Grosset & Dunlap, 1939.

Pasley, Fred D. *Not Guilty! The Story of Samuel S. Leibowitz*. New York: G. P. Putnam, 1933.

Pepper, George Wharton. *Philadelphia Lawyer: An Autobiography*. Philadelphia: J. B. Lippincott, 1944.

Peters, Shawn Francis. *Judging Jehovah's Witnesses: Religious Persecution and the Dawn of the Rights Revolution*. Lawrence: University Press of Kansas, 2000.

Peterson, Merrill D. *The Great Triumvirate: Webster, Clay, and Calhoun*. New York: Oxford University Press, 1987.

Peterson, Norma Lois. *Littleton Waller Tazewell*. Charlottesville: University Press of Virginia, 1983.

Pfeffer, Leo. *Church, State and Freedom*. Boston: Beacon Press, 1953. Revised, 1967.

_____. *God, Caesar, and the Constitution: The Court as Referee of Church-State Confrontation*. Boston: Beacon Press, 1974.

_____. *Leo Pfeffer's Papers and Publications*. 22 vols. Compiled by the J. M. Dawson Institute of Church-State Studies, Baylor University, 1985.

_____. *Religion, State, and the Burger Court*. Buffalo, NY: Prometheus, 1985.

_____. *This Honorable Court: A History of the United States Supreme Court*. Boston: Beacon Press, 1965.

Phillips, David A. *The Great Texas Murder Trials: A Compelling Account of the Sensational T. Cullen Davis Case*. New York: Macmillan, 1979.

Pinkney, William. *The Life of William Pinkney*. New York: D. Appleton, 1853. Reprint, New York: Da Capo Press, 1969.

Ploski, Harry, and James Williams, eds. *The Negro Almanac: A Reference Work on the African American*. Detroit: Gale Research, 1989.

Presser, Steven B., and Jamil Azinaldin. *Law and American History*. St. Paul: West, 1987.

Pruiett, Moman. *Moman Pruiett: Criminal Lawyer*. Oklahoma City: Harlow, 1945.

Pusey, Merlo J. *Charles Evans Hughes*. 2 vols. New York: Columbia University Press, 1963.

Quade, Vicki. "Women in the Law: Twelve Success Stories." *American Bar Association Journal* 69 (October 1983).

Quarles, Benjamin. *Black Abolitionists*. New York: Oxford University Press, 1969.

Raby, R. Cornelius. *Fifty Famous Trials*. Washington: Washington Law Book, 1937.

Randall, James G. *Constitutional Problems under Lincoln*. Urbana: University of Illinois Press, 1951.

Randolph, Edmund. *History of Virginia*. Edited by Arthur H. Shaffer. Charlottesville: University Press of Virginia, 1970.

Reardon, John J. *Edmund Randolph: A Biography*. New York: Macmillan, 1974.

Rehnquist, William H. "Robert H. Jackson: A Perspective Twenty-Five Years Later." *Albany Law Review* 44 (April 1980): 533–541.

Reid, John Phillips. "A Lawyer Acquitted: John Adams and the Boston Massacre Trials." *American Journal of Legal History* 18 (1974): 189–207.

Remini, Robert V. *Daniel Webster: The Man and His Time*. New York: W. W. Norton, 1997.

―――. *Henry Clay: Statesman for the Union*. New York: W. W. Norton, 1991.

Reppy, Alison, ed. *David Dudley Field: Centenary Essays Celebrating One Hundred Years of Legal Reform*. New York: New York University School of Law, 1949.

Reynolds, Quentin. *Courtroom: The Story of Samuel S. Leibowitz*. New York: Farrar, Straus, 1950.

Richards, Leonard L. *The Life and Times of Congressman John Quincy Adams*. New York: Oxford University Press, 1986.

Robert, Joseph C. "William Wirt, Virginian." *Virginia Magazine of History and Biography* 80 (1972): 387–441.

Roberts, Owen J. *The Court and the Constitution: The Oliver Wendell Holmes Lectures 1951*. Port Washington, NY: Kennikat Press, 1969.

Robinson, Thomas P. "The Life of Thomas Addis Emmet." Ph.D. dissertation, New York University, April 1955.

Robinson, W. W. *Lawyers of Los Angeles*. Los Angeles: Los Angeles Bar Association, 1959.

Roscoe, Henry. *Lives of Eminent British Lawyers*. London: Longman, 1830.

Ross, William G. *Forging New Freedoms: Nativism, Education, and the Constitution, 1917–1927*. Lincoln: University of Nebraska Press, 1994.

―――. "The Legal Career of John Quincy Adams." *Akron Law Review* 23 (Spring 1990): 415–453.

Rovere, Richard H. *Howe & Hummel: Their True and Scandalous History*. New York: Farrar, Straus & Giroux, 1947.

Rowan, Carl T. *Dream Makers, Dream Breakers: The World of Justice Thurgood Marshall*. Boston: Little, Brown, 1993.

Rubin, Ellis, and Dary Matera. *"Get Me Ellis Rubin!": The Life, Times, and Cases of a Maverick Lawyer*. New York: St. Martin's Press, 1989.

Rudenstine, David. *The Day the Presses Stopped: A History of the Pentagon Papers Case*. Berkeley: University of California Press, 1996.

Rusch, Jonathan J. "William H. Hastie and the Vindication of Civil Rights." *Howard Law Journal* 21 (1978): 749–820.

Salmond, John A. *The Conscience of a Lawyer: Clifford J. Durr and American Civil Liberties, 1899–1975*. Tuscaloosa: University of Alabama Press, 1990.

Salokar, Rebecca Mae. *The Solicitor General: The Politics of Law*. Philadelphia: Temple University Press, 1992.

Scheck, Barry, Peter Neufeld, and Jim Dwyer. *Actual Innocence: Five Days to Execution and Other Dispatches from the Wrongly Convicted*. New York: Doubleday, 2000.

Schmidt, Susan, and Michael Weisskopf. *Truth at any Cost: Ken Starr and the Unmaking of Bill Clinton*. New York: HarperCollins, 2000.

Schrager, Sam. *The Trial Lawyer's Art*. Philadelphia: Temple University Press, 1999.

Schwartz, Bernard. *A Book of Legal Lists*. New York: Oxford University Press, 1997.

———. *Main Currents in American Legal Thought*. Durham, NC: Carolina Academic Press, 1993.

Schwartz, Bernard, with Barbara W. Kern and R. B. Bernstein. *Thomas Jefferson and Bolling v. Bolling*. San Marino, Calif.: Huntington Library, 1997.

Scott, Henry W. *Distinguished American Lawyers with Their Struggles and Triumphs in the Forum*. New York: Charles L. Webster, 1891.

Segal, Geraldine R. *Blacks in the Law: Philadelphia and the Nation*. Philadelphia: University of Pennsylvania Press, 1983.

Sevareid, Paul A. *The People's Lawyer: The Life of Eugene A. Rerat*. Minneapolis: Ross & Haines, 1963.

Shapiro, Samuel. *Richard Henry Dana Jr.: 1815–1882*. East Lansing: Michigan State University Press, 1961.

Sheresky, Norman. *On Trial: Masters of the Courtroom*. New York: Viking Press, 1977.

Silver, David M. *Lincoln's Supreme Court*. Urbana: University of Illinois Press, 1998.

Silverman, Ira, and Fredric Dannen. "A Complicated Life." *New Yorker*, 22 March 1996, 44–53.

Smith, J. Clay, Jr. *Emancipation: The Making of the Black Lawyer, 1844–1944*. Philadelphia: University of Pennsylvania Press, 1993.

———. "Forgotten Hero." *Harvard Law Review* 98 (1984): 482–491.

———. *Rebels in Law: Voices in History of Black Women Lawyers*. Ann Arbor: University of Michigan Press, 2000.

Smith, Jean Edward. *John Marshall: Definer of a Nation*. New York: Henry Holt, 1996.

Smith, Richard Norton. *Thomas E. Dewey and His Times*. New York: Simon & Schuster, 1982.

Snow, Richard F. "Counsel for the Indefensible." *American Heritage*, February/March 1987, 96–97.

Snyder, William L. *Great Speeches of Great Lawyers*. New York: Baker, Voorhis, 1892.

Spence, Gerry. *The Making of a Country Lawyer*. New York: St. Martin's Press, 1996.

Spence, Gerry, and Anthony Polk. *Gunning for Justice*. New York: Doubleday, 1982.

St. Johns, Adela Rogers. *Final Verdict*. Garden City, NY: Doubleday, 1962.

Stein, Leon. *The Triangle Fire*. New York: Carroll & Graf/Quicksilver Books, 1985.

Steiner, Bernard C. *Life of Reverdy Johnson*. Baltimore: Norman, Remington, 1914.

Stephenson, D. Grier, Jr., ed. *An Essential Safeguard: Essays on the United States Supreme Court and Its Justices*. New York: Greenwood Press, 1991.

Steuer, Aaron. *Max D. Steuer, Trial Lawyer*. New York: Random House, 1950.

Stites, Francis N. *Private Interest & Public Gain: The Dartmouth College Case, 1819*. Amherst: University of Massachusetts Press, 1972.

Stolberg, Mary. *Fighting Organized Crime: Politics, Justice, and the Legacy of Thomas E. Dewey*. Boston: Northeastern University Press, 1995.

Stone, Irving. *Clarence Darrow for the Defense*. New York: Doubleday, 1941.

Stories of Great Crimes & Trials from American Heritage Magazine. New York: McGraw-Hill, 1973.

Story, William W., ed. *Life and Letters of Joseph Story*. 1851. Reprint, Freeport, NY: Books for Libraries Press, 1971.

Strong, Theron G. *Joseph H. Choate*. New York: Dodd, Mead, 1917.

Strum, Phillipa. *Louis D. Brandeis: Justice for the People*. Cambridge: Harvard University Press, 1984.

Summerville, James. *Colleagues on the Cumberland: A History of the Nashville Legal Profession*. Dallas: Taylor Publishing Company, 1996.

Sumner, Charles. *The Scholar, the Jurist, the Artist, the Philanthropist*. Boston: William B. Ticknor, 1846.

Tatolovich, Raymond. *Nativism Reborn?: The Official English Language Movement and the American States*. Lexington: University Press of Kentucky, 1995.

Thomas, Evan. *The Man to See: Edward Bennett Williams: Ultimate Insider, Legendary Trial Lawyer*. New York: Simon & Schuster, 1991.

Thomas, F. W. *John Randolph of Roanoke and Other Sketches of Character, including William Wirt*. Philadelphia: Hart, 1853.

Thompson, Thomas. *Blood and Money*. Garden City, NY: Doubleday, 1976.

Thorpe, Francis Newton. "Jeremiah S. Black." *Pennsylvania Magazine of History and Biography* 50 (1926): 117–133, 273–286.

Tidyman, Ernest. *Dummy*. Boston: Little, Brown, 1974.

Tierney, John. *Darrow: A Biography*. New York: Thomas Y. Crowell, 1979.

Tigar, Michael E. *Examining Witnesses*. Chicago: Section of Litigation, American Bar Association, 1993.

———. *Law and the Rise of Capitalism*. New York: Monthly Review Press, 1977.

———. *Persuasion: The Litigator's Art*. Chicago: Section of Litigation, American Bar Association, 1999.

Tigar, Michael E., and Jane B. Tigar. *Federal Appeals: Jurisdiction and Practice*. 3d ed. St. Paul: West, 1999.

Tocqueville, Alexis de. *Democracy in America*. Translated by George Lawrence. Edited by J. P. Mayer. Garden City, NY: Anchor Books, 1969.

Toobin, Jefrey. "The Man with Timothy McVeigh." *New Yorker*, 30 September 1996, 48–54.

Train, Arthur. *The Adventures of Ephraim Tutt: Attorney and Counsellor-at-Law*. New York: Scribner, 1940.

Trefousse, Hans L. *Impeachment of a President: Andrew Johnson, the Blacks, and Reconstruction*. Knoxville: University of Tennessee Press, 1975.

Tribe, Laurence. *Abortion: The Clash of Absolutes*. New York: W. W. Norton, 1990.
_____. *American Constitutional Law*. 2d ed. Mineola, NY: Foundation Press, 1988.
_____. *Constitutional Choices*. Cambridge: Harvard University Press, 1985.
_____. *God Save This Honorable Court: How the Choice of Supreme Court Justices Shapes Our History*. New York: Random House, 1985.

Tudor, William. *The Life of James Otis of Massachusetts*. New York: Da Capo Press, 1970.

Turley, Jonathan. "The Trial Lawyers of the Century." *Recorder*, 25 December 1999, 4.

Tushnet, Mark. *Making Civil Rights Law: Thurgood Marshall and the Supreme Court, 1936–1961*. New York: Oxford University Press, 1994.
_____. *The NAACP's Legal Strategy against Segregated Education, 1925–1950*. Chapel Hill: University of North Carolina Press, 1988.

Tutt, Ephraim. *Yankee Lawyer: The Autobiography of Ephraim Tutt*. New York: Scribner, 1944.

Twiss, Benjamin R. *Lawyers and the Constitution: How Laissez Faire Came to the Supreme Court*. New York: Russell & Russell, 1962.

Tyler, Moses C. *Patrick Henry*. Boston: Houghton Mifflin, 1898. Reprint, Ithaca: Great Seal Books, 1962.

Uelmen, Gerald F. "Legends and Landmarks: Moman Pruiett, Criminal Lawyer." *Criminal Defense*, May/June 1982.
_____. "The Trial of the Century?" *Criminal Defense*, November/December 1982, 49–50.
_____. "Who Is the Lawyer of the Century?" *Loyola of Los Angeles Law Review* 33 (January 2000): 613–653.

Urofsky, Melvin I. *A March of Liberty: A Constitutional History of the United States*. New York: Alfred A. Knopf, 1988.

Van Buren, Martin. *The Autobiography of Martin Van Buren*. Edited by John C. Fitzpatrick. Washington: U.S. Government Printing Office, 1920.

Vanderbilt, Arthur T., II. *Changing Law: A Biography of Arthur T. Vanderbilt*. New Brunswick, NJ: Rutgers University Press, 1976.

Van Deusen, Glyndon G. *The Life of Henry Clay*. Boston: Little, Brown, 1937.

Veeder, Van Vechten, ed. *Legal Masterpieces: Specimens of Argumentation and Exposition by Eminent Lawyers*. 2 vols. St. Paul: Keefe-Davidson, 1902.

Vile, John R. *A Companion to the United States Constitution and Its Amendments*. 3d ed. Westport, CT: Praeger, 2001.
_____. *Encyclopedia of Constitutional Amendments, Proposed Amendments, and Amending Issues, 1789–1995*. Santa Barbara: ABC-CLIO, 1996.
_____. *History of American Legal System: An Interactive Encyclopedia*. Santa Barbara: ABC-CLIO, 1999. CD-ROM.

von Hoffman, Nicholas. *Citizen Cohn: The Life and Times of Roy Cohn*. New York: Doubleday, 1988.

Walker, Samuel. *In Defense of American Liberties: A History of the ACLU*. 2d ed. Carbondale: Southern Illinois University Press, 1990.

Walker, Stanley. *Dewey: An American of This Century*. New York: McGraw-Hill, 1944.

Warden, Robert B. *An Account of the Life and Public Services of Salmon Portland Chase*. Cincinnati: Wilstach, Baldwin, 1874.

Ware, Gilbert. *William Hastie: Grace under Pressure*. New York: Oxford University Press, 1984.

Warren, Charles. *A History of the American Bar*. New York: Howard Fertig, 1966.

———. *The Supreme Court In American History*. 2 vols. Boston: Little, Brown, 1926.

Warshaw, Bertram G., ed. *The Trial Masters: A Handbook of Strategies and Techniques That Win Cases*. Englewood Cliffs, NJ: Prentice-Hall, 1984.

Waters, John J., Jr. *The Otis Family: In Provincial and Revolutionary Massachusetts*. Chapel Hill: University of North Carolina Press, 1968.

Waterston, R. C. *A Discourse upon the Life and Character of the Hon. Joseph Story, LL.D*. Boston: William Crosby & H. P. Nichols, 1845.

Webster, Daniel. *The Papers of Daniel Webster*. Edited by Alfred S. Konefsky and Andrew J. King. Hanover, NH: University Press of New England, 1983.

Weddington, Sarah. *A Question of Choice*. New York: Putnam, 1992.

Weik, Jesse W. *The Real Lincoln: A Portrait*. Boston: Houghton Mifflin, 1922.

Weinberg, Arthur, and Lila Weinberg. *Clarence Darrow: Sentimental Rebel*. New York: Putnam, 1980.

Weisbrot, Robert. *Freedom Bound: A History of America's Civil Rights Movement*. New York: W. W. Norton, 1990.

Wellman, Francis L. *The Art of Cross-Examination*. Collier, 1962.

———. *Success in Court*. New York: Macmillan, 1941.

Werner, M. R., and John Starr. *Teapot Dome*. New York: Viking Press, 1959.

Wesser, R. F. *Charles Evans Hughes: Politics and Reform in New York, 1905–1910*. Ithaca: Cornell University Press, 1967.

Wexler, Sanford. *The Civil Rights Movement: An Eyewitness History*. New York: Facts on File, 1993.

White, G. Edward. *The American Judicial Tradition: Profiles of Leading American Judges*. New York: Oxford University Press, 1976.

———. *The Marshall Court and Cultural Change, 1814–1835*. New York: Oxford University Press, 1991.

Whitney, Henry C. *Life on the Circuit with Lincoln*. Caldwell, Idaho: Caxton Printers, 1940.

Willebrandt, Mabel Walker. *The Inside of Prohibition*. Indianapolis: Bobbs-Merrill, 1929.

Williams, Edward Bennett. *One Man's Freedom*. New York: Atheneum, 1982.

Williams, John H. *Sam Houston: A Biography of the Father of Texas*. New York: Simon & Schuster, 1993.

Williams, Juan. *Eyes on the Prize*. New York: Penguin Books, 1987.

———. *Thurgood Marshall: American Revolutionary*. New York: Random House, 1998.

Winkleman, Barnie F. *John G. Johnson, Lawyer and Art Collector*. Philadelphia: University of Pennsylvania Press, 1942.

Winner, Julia Hull. "Belva A. Lockwood: That Extraordinary Woman." *New York History* 39 (1958): 321.

Wirt, William. *Sketches of the Life and Character of Patrick Henry*. New York: Melrath & Bands, 1832.

Wood, James E., Jr. "A Tribute to Leo Pfeffer." *Journal of Church and State* 35 (1993): 605–606.

_____, ed. *Religion and the State: Essays in Honor of Leo Pfeffer*. Waco, TX: Baylor University Press, 1985.

Woodward, Bob, and Carl Bernstein. *The Final Days*. New York: Simon & Schuster, 1976.

Woychuk, Denis. *Attorney for the Damned: A Lawyer's Life with the Criminally Insane*. New York: Free Press, 1996.

Wythe, George. *Decisions of Cases in Virginia by the High Court of Chancery with Remarks upon Decrees by the Court of Appeals Reversing Some of These Decisions*. 2d ed. Edited by B. B. Minor. Richmond: J.W. Randolph, 1852.

Wyzanski, Charles E., Jr. *Whereas—A Judge's Premises*. Boston: Little, Brown, 1965.

Yarbrough, Tinsley E. *John Marshall Harlan: Great Dissenter of the Warren Court*. New York: Oxford University Press, 1992.

Younger, Irving, ed. *Classics of the Courtroom*. 8 vols. Minnetonka, MN: Professional Education, 1987–1988.

Zobel, Hiller B. *The Boston Massacre*. New York: W. W. Norton, 1970.

About the Editor & Contributors

Lee Allen (Ph.D., University of Utah; J.D., University of Houston) is an associate professor of political science who teaches in the Public Administration Program at Valdosta State University in Valdosta, Georgia.

Sarah Bartholomew (LL.M., University of Georgia; J.D., Mercer University) teaches in the Department of Political Science at Valdosta State University in Valdosta, Georgia.

Christian Biswell (M.A., Southern Illinois University) is a law student at Southern Illinois University in Carbondale.

Brandi Snow Bozarth is a recent graduate of Middle Tennessee State University and is attending law school at the University of Dayton in Dayton, Ohio.

Mark Byrnes (Ph.D., Vanderbilt University) is a professor of political science at Middle Tennessee State University. The author and editor of two previous books, he is now at work on *James K. Polk: A Biographical Companion*.

Cornell W. Clayton (D. Phil., Oxford University) is an associate professor of political science at Washington State University. He is the author of *The Politics of Justice: The Attorney General and the Making of Legal Policy* (1992), editor of *Government Lawyers: The Federal Legal Bureaucracy and Presidential Politics* (1995), and coeditor of *Supreme Court Decision-Making: New Institutionalist Interpretations* (1998).

Douglas Clouatre (Ph.D., University of Tennessee) teaches political science at Kennesaw State University in Kennesaw, Georgia.

Susan Coleman (J.D., Texas Tech University) is an instructor of political science at West Texas A & M University in Canyon, Texas.

Derek H. Davis (J.D., Baylor University; Ph.D., University of Texas at Dallas) is director of the J. M. Dawson Institute of Church-State Studies, Baylor University, and editor of *Journal of Church and State*. He is the author of *Original Intent: Chief Justice Rehnquist & the Court of American Church-State Relations* (1991) and *Religion* *and the Continental Congress, 1774–1789: Contributions to Original Intent* (2000) and is the editor or coeditor of eight other books.

Brannon P. Denning (J.D., University of Tennessee; LL.M., Yale University) is an assistant professor of law at Southern Illinois University in Carbondale.

Stephen Louis A. Dillard (J.D., Mississippi College) works with Stone & Baxter and is president of the Federalist Society of Georgia.

James W. Ely Jr. (LL.B., Harvard University; Ph.D., University of Virginia) is the Milton R. Underwood Professor of Law and professor of history at Vanderbilt University. His publications include *The Guardian of Every Other Right: A Constitutional History of Property Rights* (1992) and *The Chief Justiceship of Melville Fuller, 1888–1910* (1995). He has served as an editor of the *American Journal of Legal History*, and he is currently editing a book on the history of the Tennessee Supreme Court.

Jane Elza (Ph.D., University of Tennessee) is a professor of political science at Valdosta State University in Valdosta, Georgia.

Norman B. Ferris (LL.B., Blackstone School of Law; Ph.D., Emory University) is a professor emeritus of history at Middle Tennessee State University. His writings include *The Trent Affair* (1977).

Peter G. Fish (Ph.D., Johns Hopkins University) teaches political science at Duke University. He is the author of *The Politics of Federal Judicial Administration* (1973), *The Office of Chief Justice* (1984), *Federal Justice in the Mid-Atlantic South: United States Courts from Maryland to the Carolinas: 1789–1835* (forthcoming), and numerous articles on federal courts and judges.

Michael S. Foley (Ph.D., University of New Hampshire) is a visiting faculty member of the Department of History at the University of New Hampshire.

Lorien Foote (Ph.D., University of Oklahoma) wrote her dissertation on Francis George Shaw and is now an assistant professor of history at the University of Central Arkansas in Conway.

Richard A. Glenn (Ph.D., University of Tennessee) is an assistant professor of political science at Millersville University in Millersville, Pennsylvania.

Ken Gormley (J.D., Harvard University) teaches at the Duquesne University School of Law in Pittsburgh, Pennsylvania, and is the author of *Archibald Cox: Conscience of a Nation* (1997), which was nominated for a Pulitzer Prize and received the 1999 Bruce K. Gould Book Award for best book relating to the law. He is the mayor of Forest Hills, Pennsylvania, where he lives with his wife and four children.

Frank Guliuzza III (Ph.D., University of Notre Dame) is an associate professor of political science at Weber State University in Ogden, Utah, and is the author of *Over the Wall: Protecting Religious Expression in the Public Square* (2000).

Kermit L. Hall (Ph.D., University of Minnesota; M.S.L., Yale University) is president of Utah State University in Logan, Utah. He is the author and editor of numerous books, including *The Magic Mirror: Law in American History* (1989), the award-winning *Oxford Companion to the Supreme Court of the United States* (1992), and *The Oxford Guide to United States Supreme Court Decisions* (1999).

Jennifer Harrison teaches English composition and coordinates the disability and advising programs at North Carolina Wesleyan College, Rocky Mount, North Carolina.

Judith Haydel (Ph.D., University of New Orleans) is a professor of political science at McNeese State University in Lake Charles, Louisiana. She is coauthor of *Judicial Reform in the States* (1993).

Kenneth M. Holland (Ph.D., University of Chicago) is a professor of political science at the University of Memphis and the author and editor of numerous books.

Robert D. Howell is a lawyer with Lord, Bissell & Brook in Atlanta, Georgia.

Tim Hurley (Ph.D., University of Notre Dame) teaches philosophy at Furman University in Greensboro, South Carolina.

Margaret Jessup (M.L.S., Simmons College) is assistant curator for the Sophia Smith Collection at Smith College in Northampton, Massachusetts, where she processes manuscript collections, including the Mary Kaufman papers.

Ronald Kahn (Ph.D., University of Chicago) is James Monroe Professor of Politics and Law at Oberlin College, where he heads the Law and Society Program. He is also the author of *The Supreme Court and Constitutional Theory, 1953–1993* (1994) and numerous contributions to edited volumes, law reviews, and political science journals.

James A. Keim (Ph.D., University of Virginia) is a labor specialist doing legal research and writing related to labor and employment law for Husch & Eppenberger, a regional law firm with offices in St. Louis, Kansas City, Peoria, Jefferson City, Springfield, and Wichita.

Tyson King-Meadows (Ph.D., University of North Carolina) is an assistant professor of political science at Middle Tennessee State University.

David J. Langum (LL.M., S.J.D., University of Michigan) practiced law for twelve years and is now a professor of law at the Cumberland School of Law at Samford University in Birmingham, Alabama. He is the author of *Crossing the Line: Legislating Morality and the Mann Act* (1994), *From Maverick to Mainstream: Cumberland School of Law, 1847–1997* (1997), and *William M. Kunstler: The Most Hated Lawyer in America* (1999).

Paul Lawrence has taken graduate courses at the University of Tennessee, Knoxville, and is now a graduate student in political science at the University of Virginia in Charlottesville.

Emery G. Lee III (Ph.D., Vanderbilt University) teaches political science at Case Western Reserve University in Cleveland, Ohio, and is training to be a trial lawyer at the Case Western Reserve University School of Law, where he is a law review associate and winner of the 1999 Federal Bar Association Constitutional Law Award.

Janice M. Leone (Ph.D., Ohio State University) is an associate professor of history at Middle Tennessee State University, where she focuses on American women's history and the history of higher education.

Connie Mauney (Ph.D., University of Tennessee) is a professor of political science at Emporia State University, Emporia, Kansas.

Elizabeth Mazzara is a doctoral candidate in political science at Washington State University, Pullman, Washington, where she studies lawyering and the judiciary, with special emphasis on litigation strategies and social movements.

Robb A. McDaniel (Ph.D., Vanderbilt University) is an assistant professor of political science at Middle Tennessee State University.

Elizabeth Brand Monroe (Ph.D., University of Florida) is an associate professor and director of the graduate program in public history at Indiana University in Indianapolis. She is the author of *The Wheeling Bridge Case* (1992), which, like other articles she has written, addresses the interaction of law and technology. Monroe is currently working on a biography of William Wirt.

Bruce Murphy (Ph.D., University of Virginia) is the Fred Morgan Kirby Professor of Civil Rights at Lafayette College, Easton, Pennsylvania. His books include *The Brandeis/Frankfurter Connection* (1982), *Fortas: The Rise and Ruin of a Supreme Court Justice* (1988), *Portraits of American Politics* (1994), and (with Larry Berman) *Approaching Democracy* (1998). Murphy was assisted in the writing of his essays by Scott Featherman, a student at Lafayette College.

Marcus Pohlmann (Ph.D., Columbia University) teaches political science at Rhodes College, Memphis, Tennessee. His publications include *Black Politics in Conservative America* (1990), *Racial Politics at the Crossroads: Memphis Elects Dr. W. W. Herenton* (1996), and *Governing the Postindustrial City* (1993).

Lisa Pruitt (Ph.D., Vanderbilt University) is an assistant professor of history and director of the Al Gore, Sr., Center at Middle Tennessee State University.

John David Rausch Jr. (Ph.D., The Carl Albert Congressional Research and Studies Center and the University of Oklahoma) is a member of the Department of History and Political Science at West Texas A & M University in Canyon, Texas.

Peter G. Renstrom (Ph.D., Michigan State University) is a professor of political science at Western Michigan University, Kalamazoo, Michigan, and author of such books as *Constitutional Law and Young Adults* (2d ed., 1996), *The American Law Dictionary* (1991), and the *Constitutional Law Dictionary* (1985). He has served two terms on the Kalamazoo County Board of Commissioners and has successfully managed a number of political campaigns.

Steve Robertson (A.B.D., Vanderbilt University) is an adjunct professor of political science at Middle Tennessee State University and a contributor to Congressional Quarterly's *Guide to the Presidency* (1996) and other works.

William G. Ross (J.D., Harvard University) is a professor of law at the Cumberland School of Law at Samford University in Birmingham, Alabama. He practiced law for nine years in New York and is the author *of Forging New Freedoms: Nativism, Education, and the Constitution, 1917–1927* (1994), *A Muted Fury: Populists, Progressives, and Labor Unions Confront the Courts, 1890–1937* (1994), and *The Honest Hour: The Ethics of Time-Based Billing of Attorneys* (1996).

John M. Scheb II (Ph.D., University of Florida) is a professor of political science at the University of Tennessee, Knoxville, and is the coauthor of a number of books, including *Criminal Law and Procedure* (4th ed., 2001), *American Constitutional Law* (2d ed., 1998), and *American Government: Politics and Political Culture* (1995).

William Shulman (J.D., University of Tennessee) is an associate professor of criminal justice administration at Middle Tennessee State University.

Henry B. Sirgo (Ph.D., University of New Orleans) is a professor of government at McNeese State University, Lake Charles, Louisiana.

M. Keith Siskin (J.D., University of Georgia) is in private practice with Burger, Siskin, Whatley, Scott & Goad in Murfreesboro, Tennessee.

Thaddeus M. Smith (Ph.D., Brown University) is a professor and chair of the Department of History at Middle Tennessee State University. He has served as a consultant for the Southern Humanities Council; has published reviews in the *Journal of Mississippi History*, *Tennessee Historical Quarterly*, and the *Filson Club Quarterly*; and has contributed to the *Encyclopedia of African American Civil Rights*.

Donald Grier Stephenson Jr. (Ph.D., Princeton University) is Charles A. Dana Professor and chair of the Department of Government at Franklin and Marshall College in Lancaster, Pennsylvania. He is author and coauthor of numerous books, including *American Constitutional Law: Introductory Essays and Selected Cases* (1998) and *An Essential Safeguard: Essays on the United States Supreme Court and Its Justices* (1998).

Ruth Anne Thompson (J.D., University of Tennessee; Ph.D., Vanderbilt University) is an assistant professor of history at Georgia Southern University in Statesboro, Georgia.

John R. Vile (B.A., The College of William and Mary; Ph.D., University of Virginia) is professor and chair of the Department of Political Science at Middle Tennessee State University. In addition to writing numerous articles, essays, and reviews, he is the author and editor of ten previous books, including *Constitutional Amendments, Proposed Amendments, and Amending Issues, 1789–1995* (1996), *A Companion to the U.S. Constitution and Its Amendments* (2001), and a CD-ROM entitled *History of the American Legal System* (1999). He is also a coach of MTSU's mock trial teams.

Matthew Vile is a graduate student in the Department of Political Science at the University of New Orleans, where he serves as a graduate assistant in the University of New Orleans Survey Research Center.

James Wagoner (J.D., University of Louisville) is a solo practitioner in Louisville, Kentucky, and has contributed to a number of legal manuals. He is one of the coaches of the Bellarmine University, Lousiville, Kentucky, mock trial teams.

Chris Whaley (J.D., University of Tennessee) is an assistant professor of law and director of the Pre-Law, Paralegal, and Child Support Enforcement programs at Roane State Community College in Harriman, Tennessee. He is also associated with the firm of Cantrell, Pratt & Versalona in Clinton, Tennessee.

Frank J. Williams (J.D., Boston University), founding chairman of the Lincoln Forum, is chief justice of the Supreme Court of Rhode Island. He has been a leader in the Lincoln community for thirty years, first as president of both the Lincoln Group of Boston and the Abraham Lincoln Association. He is a member of the U.S. Lincoln Bicentennial Commission. In addition, he is a major collector of Lincolniana, a peripatetic lecturer before Lincoln and Civil War groups, and a scholar who serves as literary editor of the *Lincoln Herald*. His works include *Abraham Lincoln: Sources and Styles of Leadership* (1994) and *Abraham Lincoln Contemporary* (1995). His next book, due in 2001, is a collection of his articles entitled *Judging Mr. Lincoln*. He resides in Hope Valley, Rhode Island.

Clyde Willis (J.D., Ph.D., University of Tennessee) is an associate professor of political science at Middle Tennessee State University. He is working on a book on landmark congressional legislation involving the First Amendment.

Tinsley Yarbrough (Ph.D., University of Alabama) is a professor of political science at East Carolina State University. His books include *A Passion for Justice: J. Waties Waring and Civil Rights* (1987), *Mr. Justice Black and His Critics* (1988), *Judge Frank Johnson and Human Rights in Alabama* (1981), *John Marshall Harlan: Great Dissenter of the Warren Court* (1992), and *The Rehnquist Court and the Constitution* (2000).

Index

Alcoholism
    "alcoholic insanity
        defense," 605
    Luther Martin, 501–502,
        504
    Earl Rogers, 606–607
Algonquin Hotel Round
    Table, 535
Ali, Muhammad, 134(fig.),
    135
Aliens, 109
    denial of pensions, 143
    Emmet as, 247
    *Fong Yue Ting v. United
        States*, 104
    foreign language instruc-
        tion and information,
        519–522
    Japanese-American intern-
        ment, 55–56
    registration during WWII,
        54–55
Allen, Woody, 201
Allen charges, 227
Alterman, Kate, 651–652
Altman, Richard, 633
Ambassadors
    to England, 188, 570
    to Great Britain, 101, 399,
        413
    to Russia, 13
    to Spain, 169
*Amchem Products, Inc. v.
    Windsor*, 675–676
American Bar Association,
    101
    accreditation of Howard
        University, 375
    presidents of, 270, 414
    Taxation Committee, 305,
        713
    Arthur Vanderbilt, 696
American Civil Liberties
    Union (ACLU), 21, 181
    Freedom Riders case, 224,
        440, 513
    general counsel, 295
    Planned parenthood case,
        631–634

Tennessee v. Scopes,
    182–184
Women's Rights Project,
    296
See also Legal Defense
    Fund
American Colonization
    Society, 422
American Constitutional Law
    (Tribe), 682
American Federation of
    Labor, 180–181
American Indian Movement,
    442–443
American Inns of Court, 458
American Jewish Congress,
    562–567
American Law Institute, 305
The American Law Register,
    589
American Legal Realism, 17
American Museum of Natural
    History, 101
American Revolution. *See*
    Revolutionary War
American Sugar Refining
    Company, 406–407, 616
Amish children, 454
Amistad (ship), 13–14, 306
Animal rights cases, 152, 281
Anthony, Susan B., 476
Anti-Communist activities,
    18–21
Anti-Defamation League, 205
Anti-Federalist lawyers,
    246–251, 498
Anti-slavery laws, 91–92
Anti-trust disputes
    Thurman Arnold, 16–21
    David Boies and, 67–68
    cities as economic partici-
        pants, 680
    Clayton Antitrust Act, 187
    Homer Cummings, 152
    Du Pont conspiracy, 339
    Goodyear v. Providence, 169
    IBM Corporation, 66
    Microsoft Corporation, 67
    railroad mergers, 75–76

Sherman Anti-Trust Act,
    218, 616
sugar monopolies, 616
trade restraint, 405–406
See also Monopolies
Anti-war protestors, 663–670
Appellate Court judges. *See*
    Courts of Appeals judges
Appellate judges, federal,
    50–57
Appellate lawyers
    Alan Dershowitz, 198–207
    Jack Greenberg, 292–299
    Constance Baker Motley,
        511–516
    Louis Nizer, 530–537
    Kenneth Starr, 628–636
    Joseph Story, 654–661
    Daniel Webster, 701–708
    William Wirt, 726–729
Apportionment scheme, 147
Arabs, 445
Arms, right to bear, 682
Army-McCarthy hearings,
    376, 638–639, 719
Arnold, Isaac N., 470
Arnold, Thurman Wesley,
    16–21, 16(fig.), 280–281
Arnstein, Jules, 263
Arson, 262
Art collectors, 408
The Art of Advocacy (Stryker),
    24
The Art of Cross Examination
    (Wellman), 52
Arthur, Chester A., 615
Artists, lawyers as, 535,
    622–623
Asbestos industry, 673,
    675–676
Assassinations and assassina-
    tion attempts
    conspiracy to assassinate,
        179–180
    Kennedy assassination,
        40–41
    Lincoln assassination, 255,
        412
    Reagan attempt, 722

state taxes, 495
See also Voting rights
Eleventh Amendment, 486, 500
Ellery Street, 531–532
Ellsberg, Daniel, 307
Ellsworth, E. E., 34
Emancipation Proclamation, 33
Embezzlement, 107–108, 261, 581, 617
Emmet, Thomas Addis, **246–251,** 246(fig.), 574, 726, 728–729
Endangered Species Act, 69
Enforcement Act (1870), 269
Engel v. Vitale, 566
England, Benjamin's practice in, 47–49
English law, 655–656
Entertainment industry, 41, 530–537
Environmental issues, 124–125
Equal protection clause, 288
  housing discrimination, 494, 681
  physician-assisted suicide, 680
  University of California Regents v. Bakke, 241
Equal Rights Amendment, 453, 681
Equal Rights Association, 477
Equal rights for women and slaves, 540–541
Equal Rights Party, 480
Equality, sexual, 584
Erie Railroad Co. v. Tompkins, 77–78
Erie Wars, 266
Ervin, Sam, 442–443
Escola v. Coca-Cola, 40
Espionage, 18–21, 54–55, 136, 201, 590–591, 717
Esquire magazine, 17–18, 295
Establishment clause cases, 561
Estates. *See* Wills and estates

Ethics, legal, 30, 73–74, 263
  defending guilty clients, 607
  Dershowitz on, 206
  disallowing perjury, 564
  enforcing *Canons of Judicial Ethics,* 698
  fabrication of facts, 132
  Abe Fortas, 282–283
  lawyers as scoundrels, 545
Evarts, William M., **252–257,** 252(fig.)
  Joseph Choate and, 100, 102
  colleagues and partners of, 176
  influence on Archibald Cox, 142
  Johnson impeachment, 161
Evers, Medgar, 224
Evidence
  blood spatter arrays, 25
  circumstantial, 82
  demonstrative, 42
  DNA evidence, 123
  hearsay, 608–609
  manipulation of and tampering with, 606, 624–625
  medical evidence against segregation, 294
  polygraph tests, 24–25, 28
  pretrial examination of witnesses, 527–528
  scientific, 23, 287
  social scientific evidence, 75
Evolutionary theory, 178, 182–184
Ex parte McCardle, 62, 268–269
Ex parte Merryman, 33, 411, 473
Ex parte Milligan, 61, 267–268, 412, 473
Executive legislation, publication of, 304
Executive privilege claim, 642–643

Expansionism, 234
Expression, freedom of, 533–534
Extremist organizations. *See* Ku Klux Klan; White supremacists
Exxon Corporation, 525, 527
Exxon Valdez case, 527
Eyewitness testimony. *See* Witnesses

Fairfax, Denny Martin, 486
Fairfax, Lord, 485–486
Fairstein, Linda, 242
Fall, Albert B., 592–594
Fallon, William J., **259–264,** 259(fig.)
Falwell, Jerry, 204
Farrakhan, Louis, 446
Farrow, Mia, 201
Father-son adversaries, 539
Faulk, John Henry, 532–533
FBI. *See* Federal Bureau of Investigation
FCC. *See* Federal Communications Commission
The Fear of Freedom (Biddle), 56
Federal Bureau of Investigation (FBI), 153, 434, 443, 643
Federal Communications Commission (FCC), 599, 677
Federal courts. *See* Courts of Appeals judges
Federal Election Reform Act, 148
Federal judges, 365–371
Federal judiciary, expansion of, 166–167
Federal Justice (Cummings and McFarland), 155
Federal prosecutors
  James F. Neal, 523–528
  Owen Roberts, 589–595
Federal Radio Commission v. Nelson Brothers Bond & Mortgage, 714

MacDonald, Jeffrey, 82
Madison, James, 13, 551, 660, 689–690
Maher v. Roe, 522
Mail fraud, 28
Mansfield, Belle Babb, 11
Manslaughter, 7
Manson, Charles, 79–81
Marcos, Imelda, 620
Margarine. *See* Oleomargarine
Margold, Nathan R., 345
Marine insurance, 320
Marine national Bank, 617
Maritime law
    John Adams, 7–8
    blockades, 174–175, 255
    British jurisdiction, 48
    Benjamin Curtis, 159
    Richard Henry Dana, 171–173
    Thomas Addis Emmet, 248–250
    Joseph Hopkinson, 365–371
    liquor smuggling, 713
    Daniel Webster, 702
Marshall, John, 362, **482–488,** 482(fig.)
    Burr trial, 724–725
    Dartmouth College Case, 704
    Hite v. Fairfax, 578
    judicial experience, 493
    on William Pinkney, 571
    Wythe and, 735
Marshall, Thurgood, **489–496,** 489(fig.)
    Brown v. Board of Education, 189–190
    Jack Greenberg and, 294, 296
    William Henry Hastie and, 345
    Constance Baker Motley and, 512
    racial discrimination cases, 347
    Spottswood Robinson and, 601

segregation in professional schools, 308
Marshall Islands, 674
Martin, Luther, 418, 420, **498–504,** 498(fig.), 571, 726
Martin v. Hunter's Lessee, 486
Martinsville Seven, 602
Mason, George, 551
Mason, Jeremiah, **505–509,** 505(fig.)
Mason, Perry, 144, 666–667
Mass Defense Office (MDO), 429–430
Massachusetts Dispute, 321
Masters, Edgar Lee, 472
Mather, Cotton, 329
Maverick, Samuel, 352
May, William L., 232
Mayor of the City of New York v. Miln, 421
Mayors
    Annapolis, 570
    Homer Cummings, 152
    Williamsburg, 578
McCardle, William, 62–63
McCarran, Pat, 19
McCarran Committee, 19
McCarthy, Joseph
    Army-McCarthy hearings, 376, 638–639, 719
    Francis Biddle on, 56
    defense attorneys for, 716, 719
    Fortas's pro bono defense against, 281
    Lattimore case, 18–21
McCarthy, Nancy, 123–124
McCarthy hearings
    Army-McCarthy hearings, 638–639
    Erwin Griswold and, 305–307
McClellan, George, 412
McClellan, James, 455
McCollum v. Board of Education, 565
McComb, H. S., 63–64
McCord, James, 28

McCray v. United States, 315–316
McCready v. Hunt, 558
McCulloch v. Maryland, 370, 420, 498, 500, 705, 723
    Pinkney's arguments, 571–572
    William Wirt and, 727
McDonald's Corporation, 620
McGuire v. Massachusetts, 167
McKinley, William, 617
McLaurin v. Oklahoma State Regents for Higher Education, 308
McLean, John, 96
McNamara, James, 180–181, 609
McNamara, John, 180–181, 609
McNamara, Robert S., 307
McNary-Watres Act, 714
McNaughten Rule, 26
McReynold, James, 521
McVeigh, Timothy, 668–669
MDO. *See* Mass Defense Office
Means, Russell, 443
Media, 119
    California v. Simpson, 122–124
    on Alan Dershowitz, 199
    Ford Pinto case, 526
    labor cases, 742
    Manson trial coverage, 81
    as tool for criminal defense, 21, 25, 28–29, 198, 202
Mediation, advocates of, 555–556
Medical evidence, against segregation, 294
Medical malpractice cases, 39–40
Medina, Ernest, 28
Meeks, Debra, 669
Mellon, Andrew, 391
Melvin v. Reid, 607
Menendez, Eric, 287
Menendez, Lyle, 287
Mental illness, 26